P.L.U.T.O

URASAWA X TEZUKA

A NEW VISION BASED ON ASTRO BOY – 'THE GREATEST ROBOT ON EARTH'
BY NAOKI URASAWA AND OSAMU TEZUKA

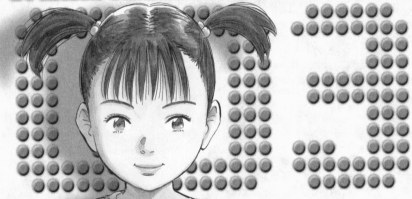

CO-AUTHORED WITH **TAKASHI NAGASAKI**
SUPERVISED BY **MACOTO TEZKA**
WITH THE COOPERATION OF **TEZUKA PRODUCTIONS**

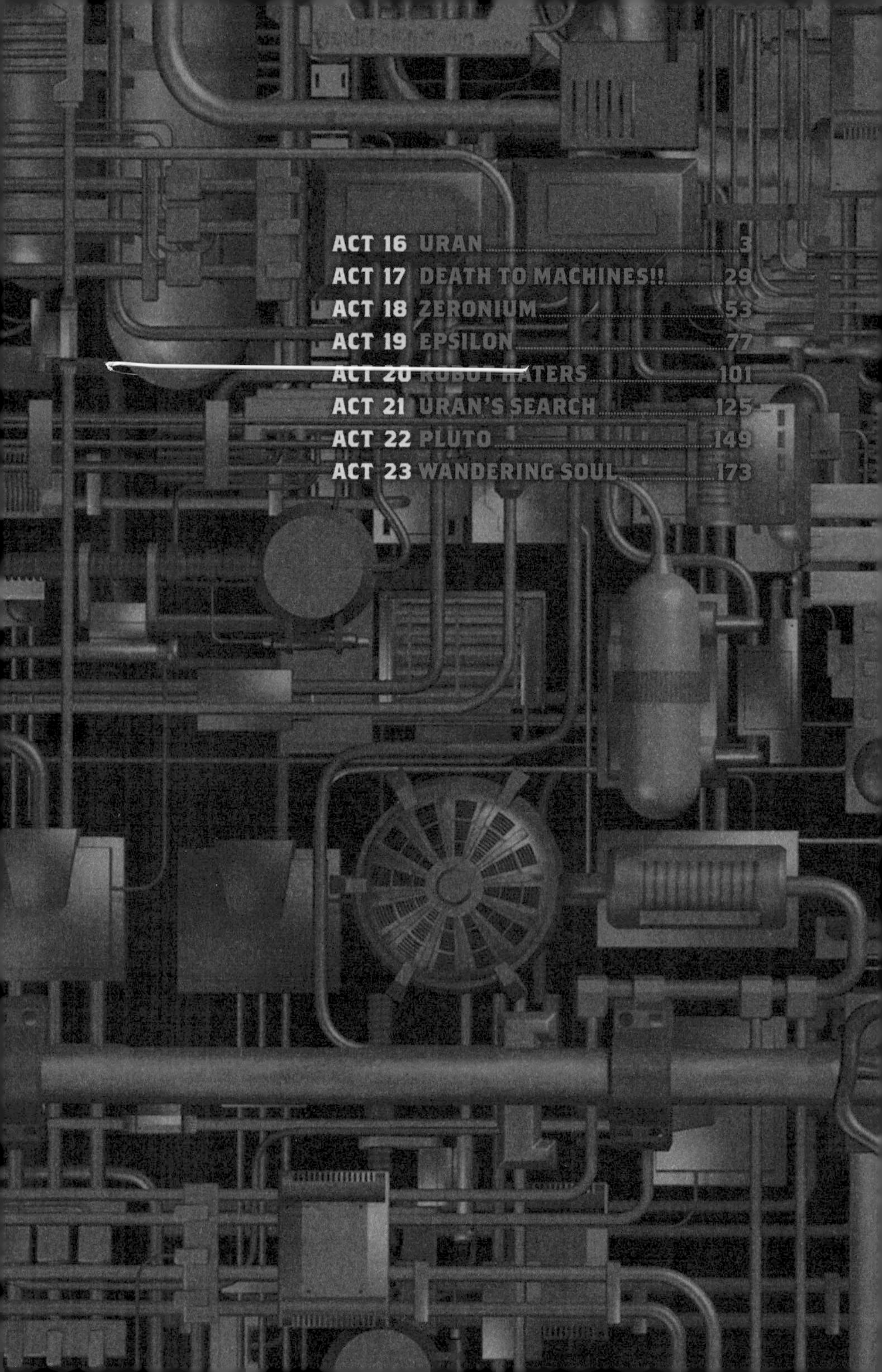

Act 16 URAN

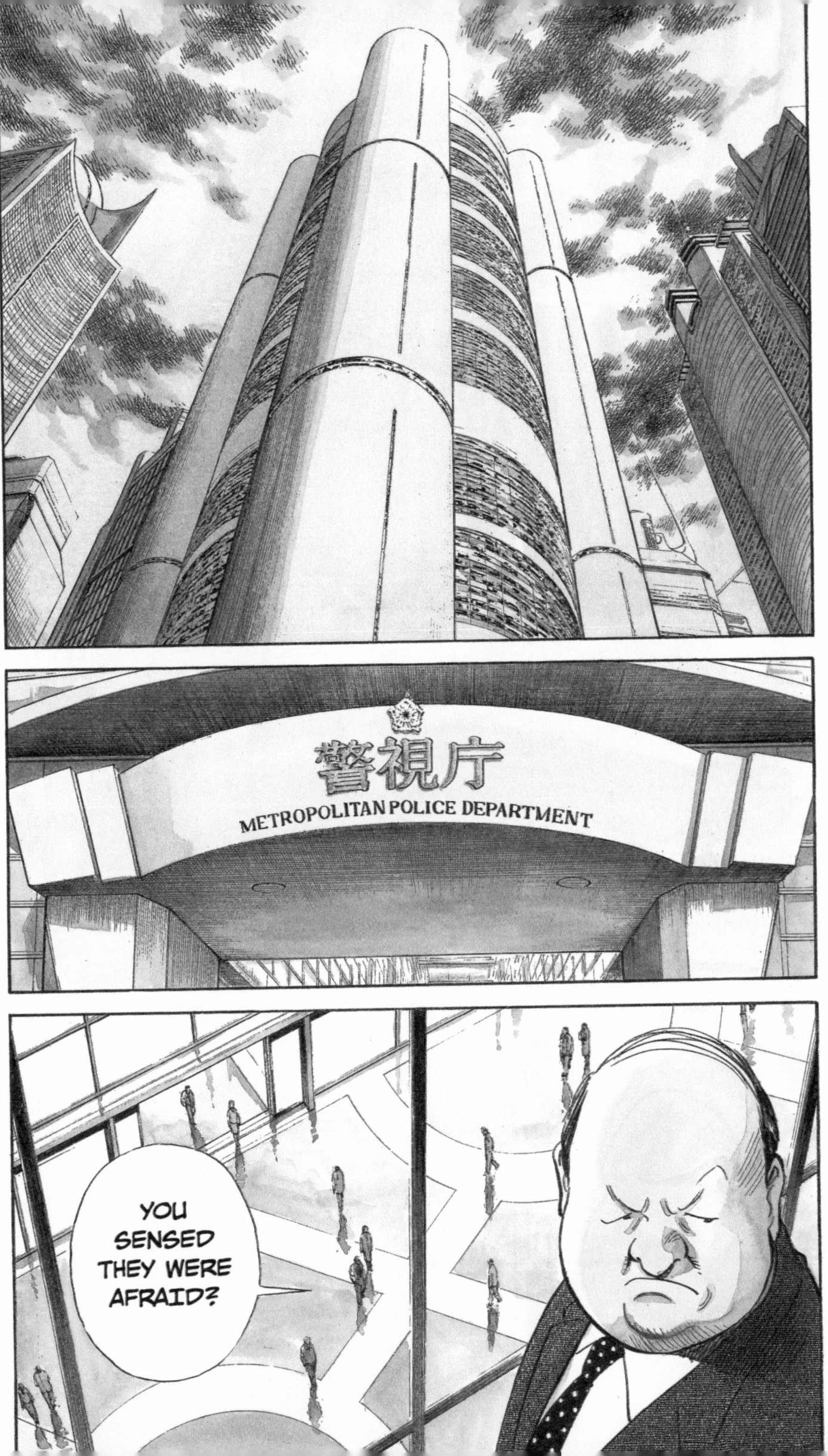
警視庁
METROPOLITAN POLICE DEPARTMENT
YOU SENSED THEY WERE AFRAID?

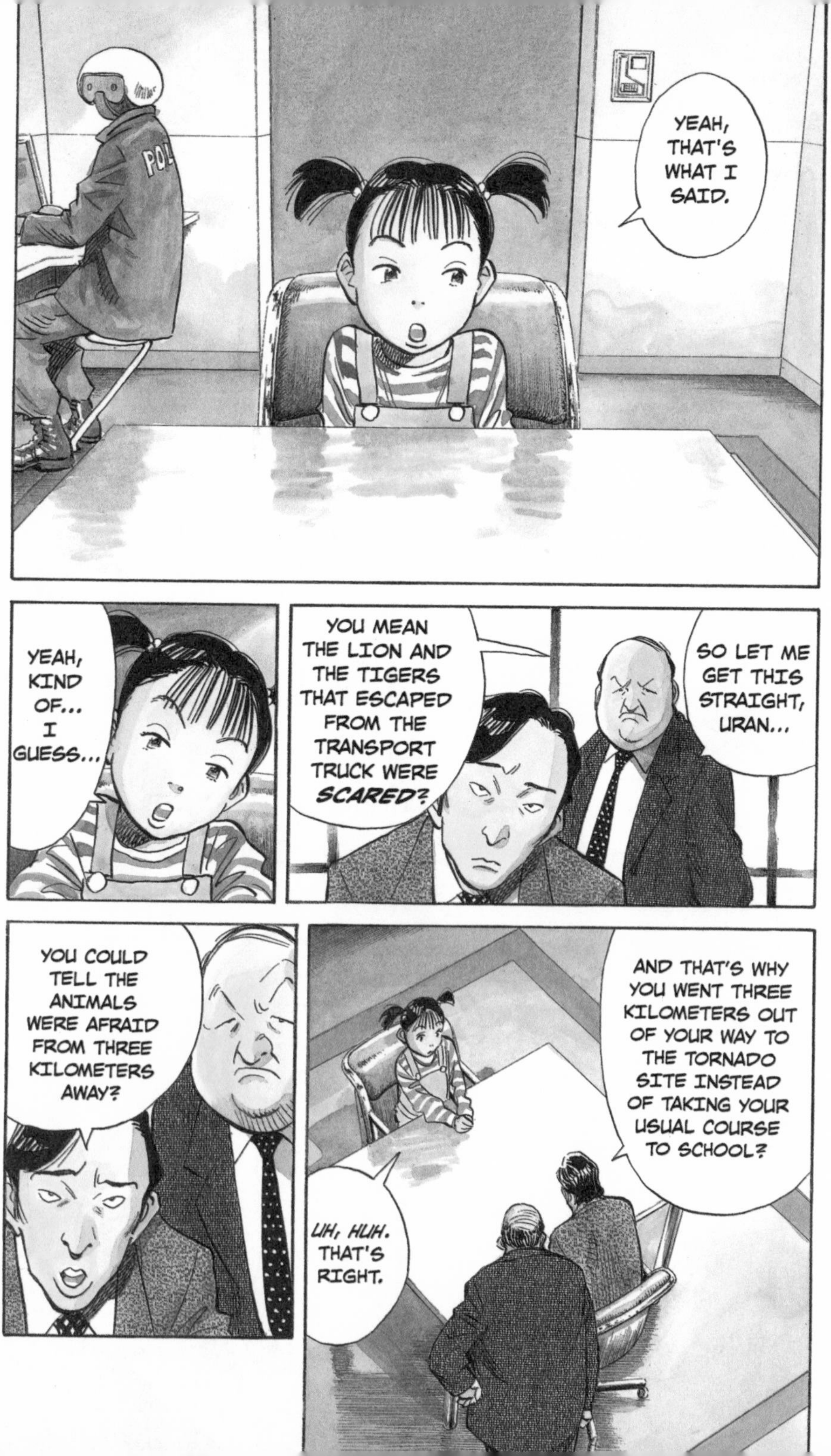
YEAH, THAT'S WHAT I SAID.
SO LET ME GET THIS STRAIGHT, URAN...
YOU MEAN THE LION AND THE TIGERS THAT ESCAPED FROM THE TRANSPORT TRUCK WERE *SCARED*?
YEAH, KIND OF... I GUESS...
AND THAT'S WHY YOU WENT THREE KILOMETERS OUT OF YOUR WAY TO THE TORNADO SITE INSTEAD OF TAKING YOUR USUAL COURSE TO SCHOOL?
UH, HUH. THAT'S RIGHT.
YOU COULD TELL THE ANIMALS WERE AFRAID FROM THREE KILOMETERS AWAY?

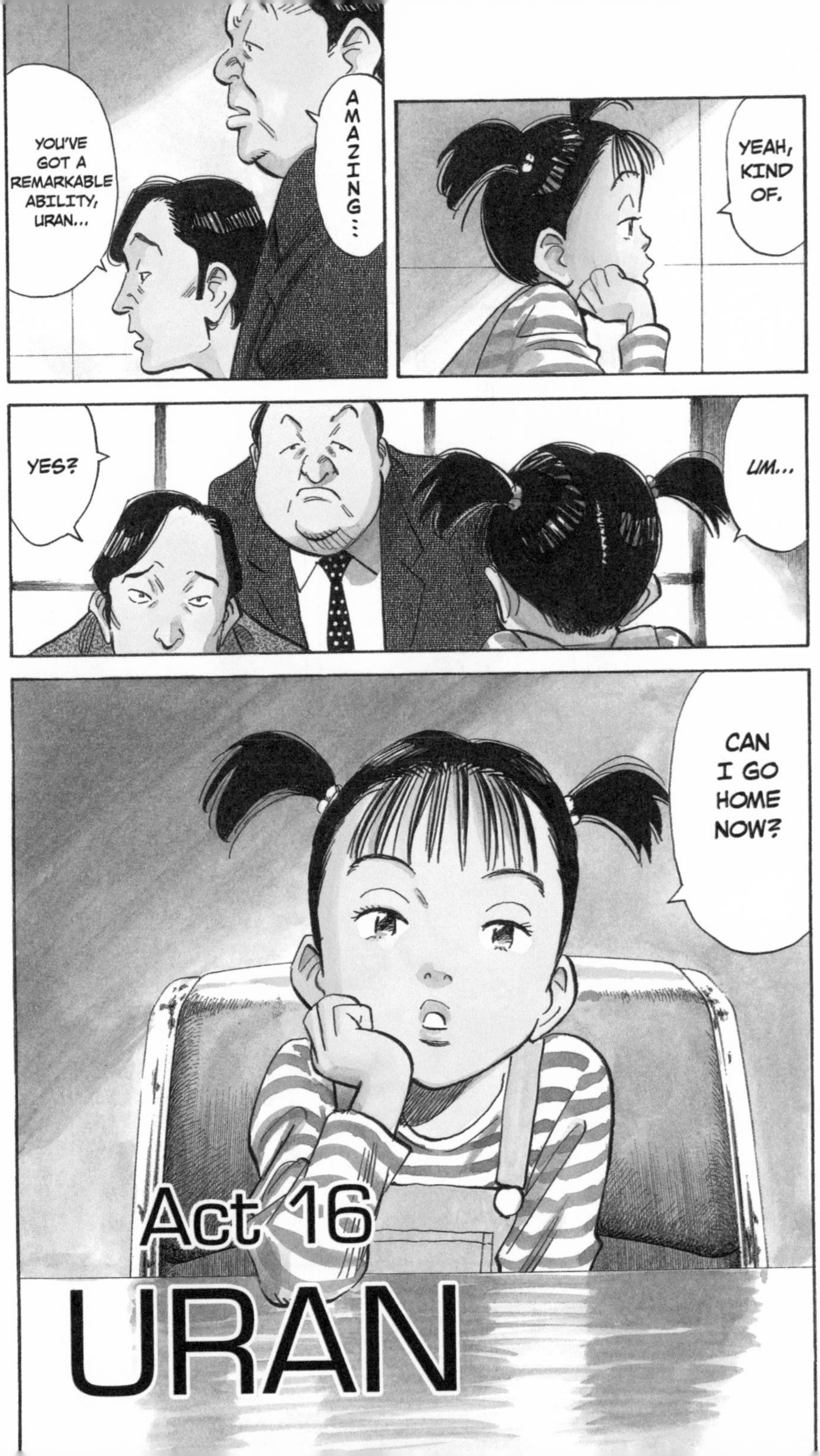
YEAH, KIND OF.
AMAZING...
YOU'VE GOT A REMARKABLE ABILITY, URAN...
UM...
YES?
CAN I GO HOME NOW?
Act 16
URAN

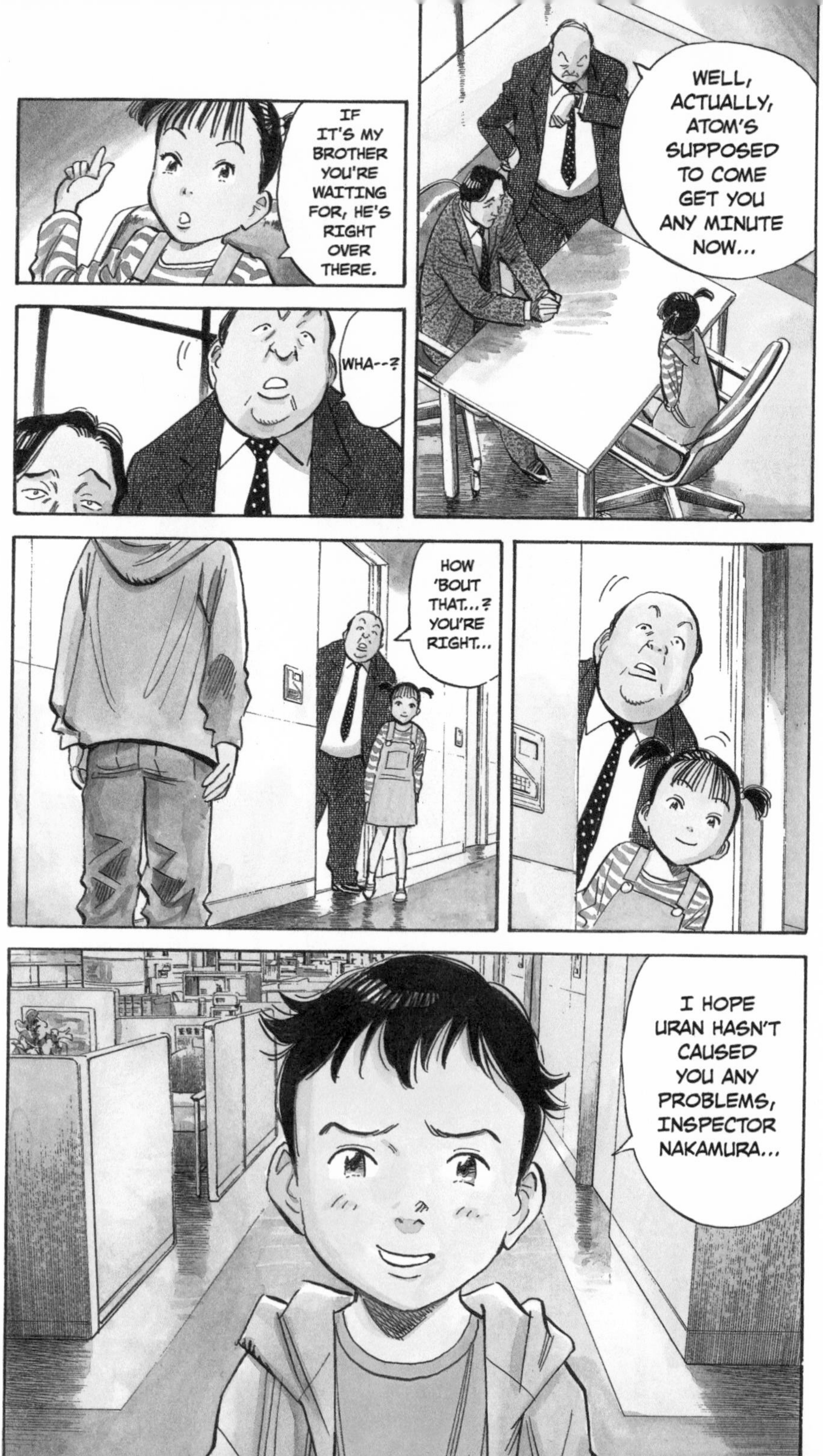
WELL, ACTUALLY, ATOM'S SUPPOSED TO COME GET YOU ANY MINUTE NOW...
IF IT'S MY BROTHER YOU'RE WAITING FOR, HE'S RIGHT OVER THERE.
WHA--?
HOW 'BOUT THAT...? YOU'RE RIGHT...
I HOPE URAN HASN'T CAUSED YOU ANY PROBLEMS, INSPECTOR NAKAMURA...

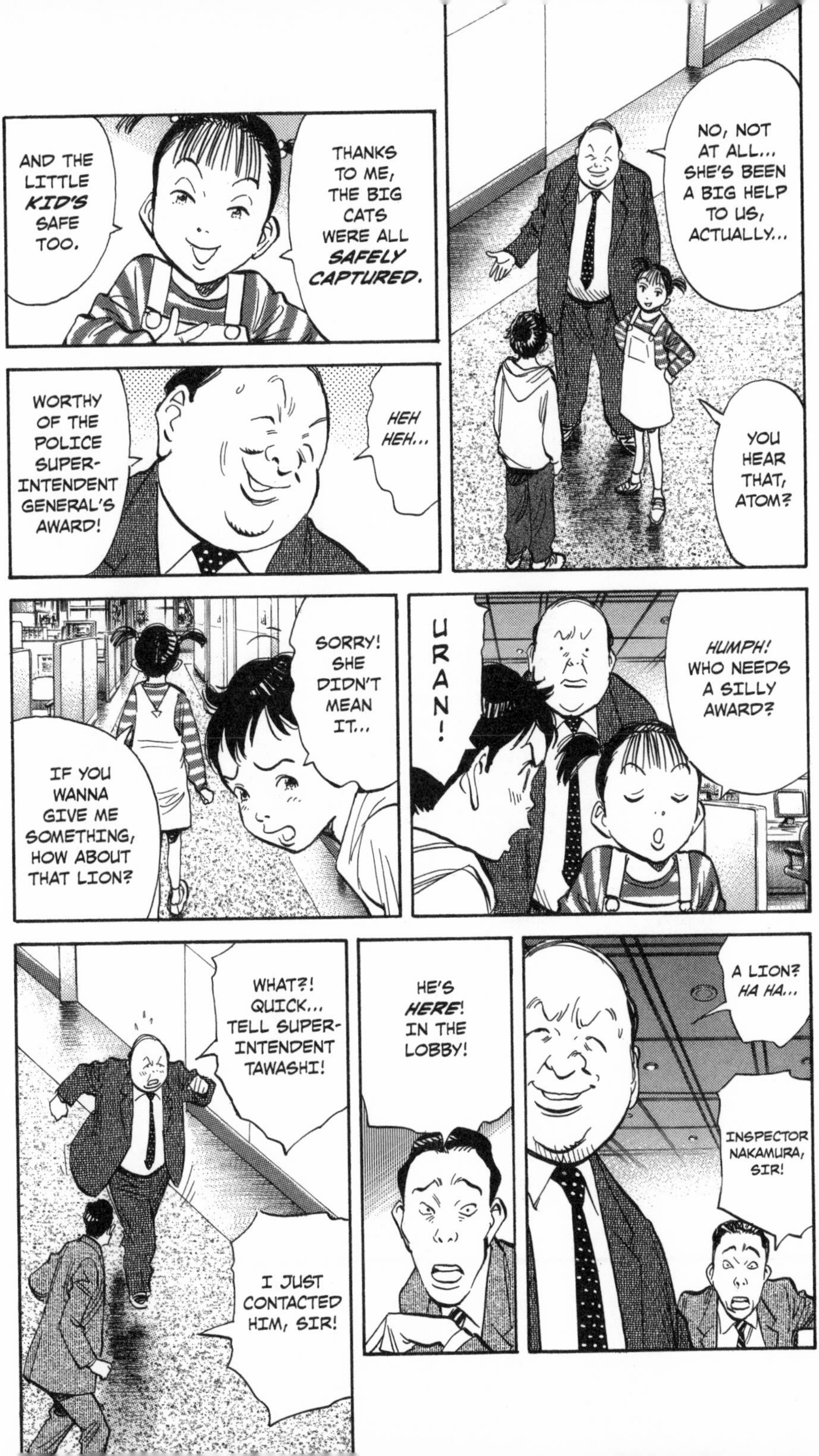
NO, NOT AT ALL... SHE'S BEEN A BIG HELP TO US, ACTUALLY...
YOU HEAR THAT, ATOM?
THANKS TO ME, THE BIG CATS WERE ALL *SAFELY CAPTURED*.
AND THE LITTLE *KID'S* SAFE TOO.
HEH HEH...
WORTHY OF THE POLICE SUPER-INTENDENT GENERAL'S AWARD!
HUMPH! WHO NEEDS A SILLY AWARD?
URAN!
SORRY! SHE DIDN'T MEAN IT...
IF YOU WANNA GIVE ME SOMETHING, HOW ABOUT THAT LION?
A LION? *HA HA...*
INSPECTOR NAKAMURA, SIR!
HE'S *HERE*! IN THE LOBBY!
WHAT?! QUICK... TELL SUPER-INTENDENT TAWASHI!
I JUST CONTACTED HIM, SIR!

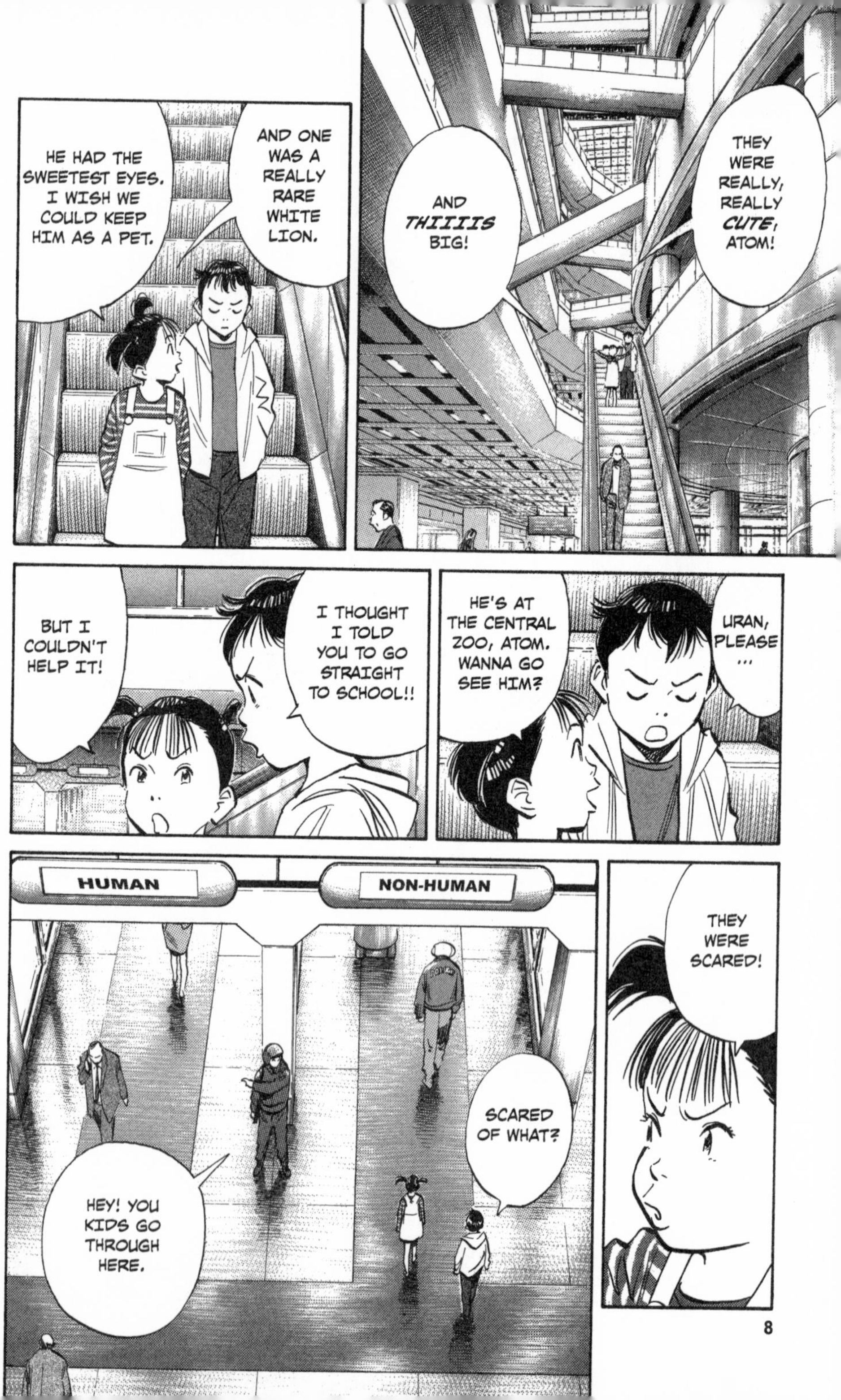
THEY WERE REALLY, REALLY *CUTE*, ATOM!
AND *THIIIIS* BIG!
AND ONE WAS A REALLY RARE WHITE LION.
HE HAD THE SWEETEST EYES. I WISH WE COULD KEEP HIM AS A PET.
URAN, PLEASE ...
HE'S AT THE CENTRAL ZOO, ATOM. WANNA GO SEE HIM?
I THOUGHT I TOLD YOU TO GO STRAIGHT TO SCHOOL!!
BUT I COULDN'T HELP IT!
THEY WERE SCARED!
NON-HUMAN
HUMAN
SCARED OF WHAT?
HEY! YOU KIDS GO THROUGH HERE.

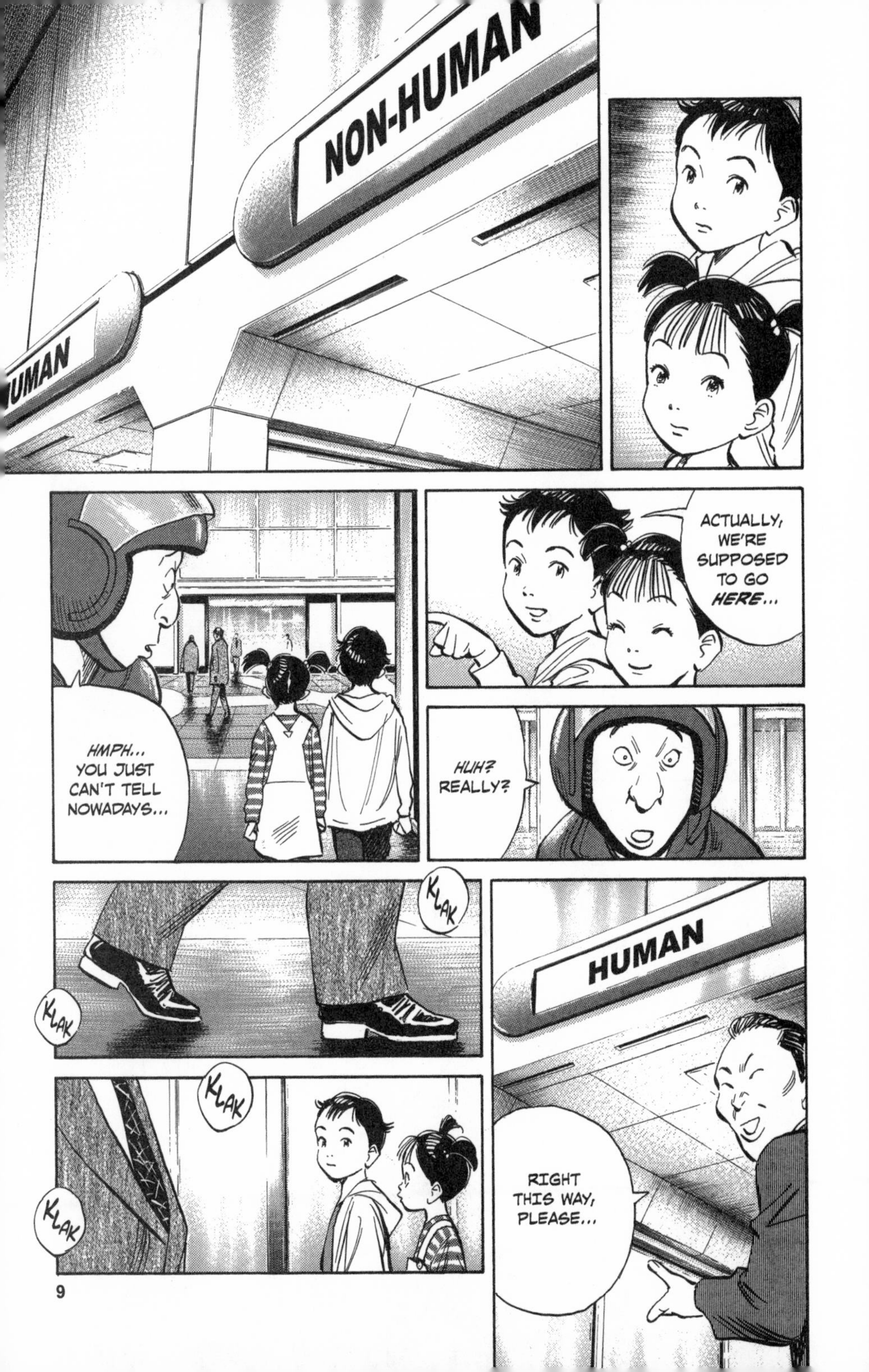
NON-HUMAN
UMAN
ACTUALLY, WE'RE SUPPOSED TO GO *HERE*...
HUH? REALLY?
HMPH... YOU JUST CAN'T TELL NOWADAYS...
HUMAN
RIGHT THIS WAY, PLEASE...
KLAK
KLAK
KLAK
KLAK

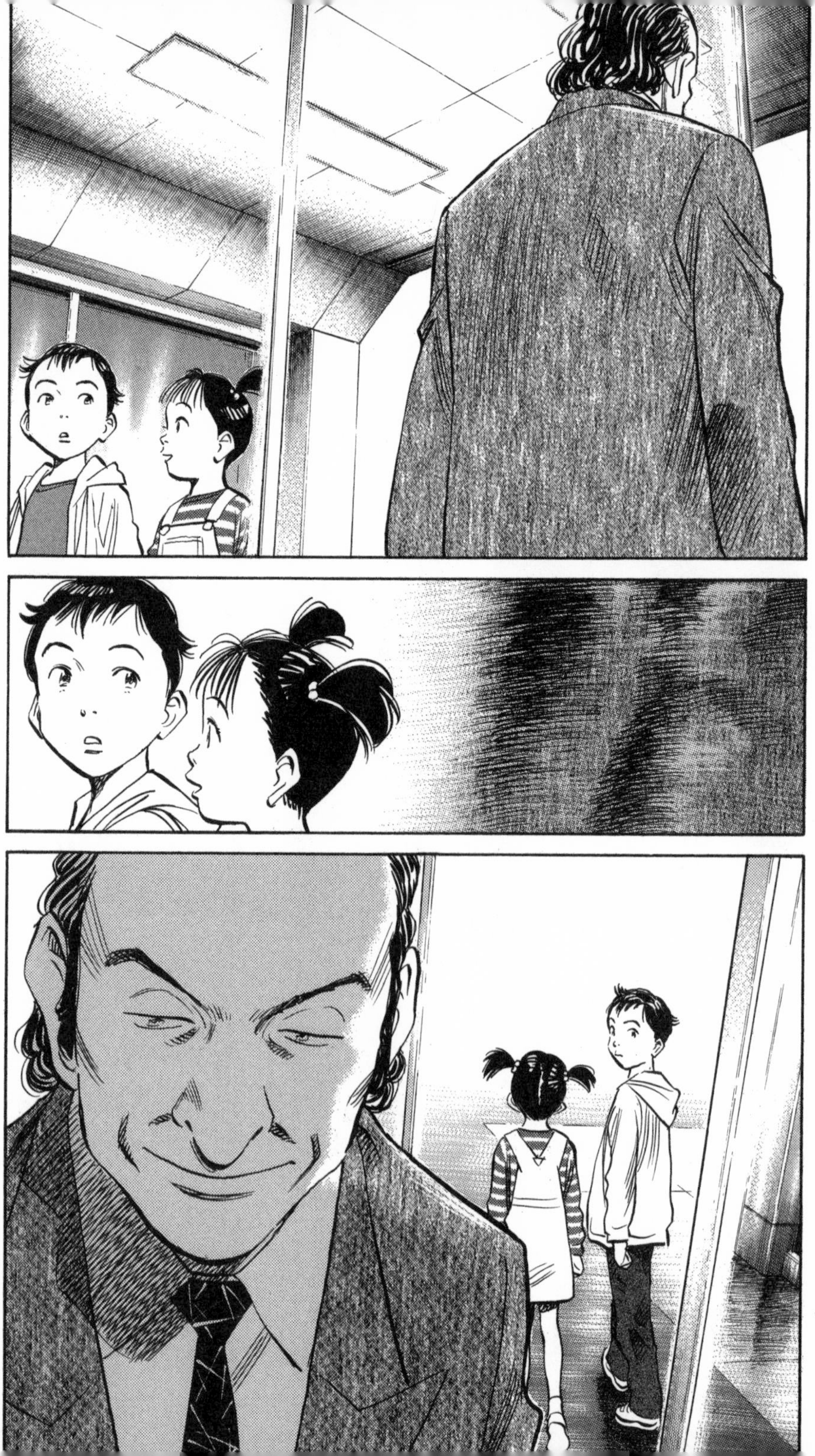

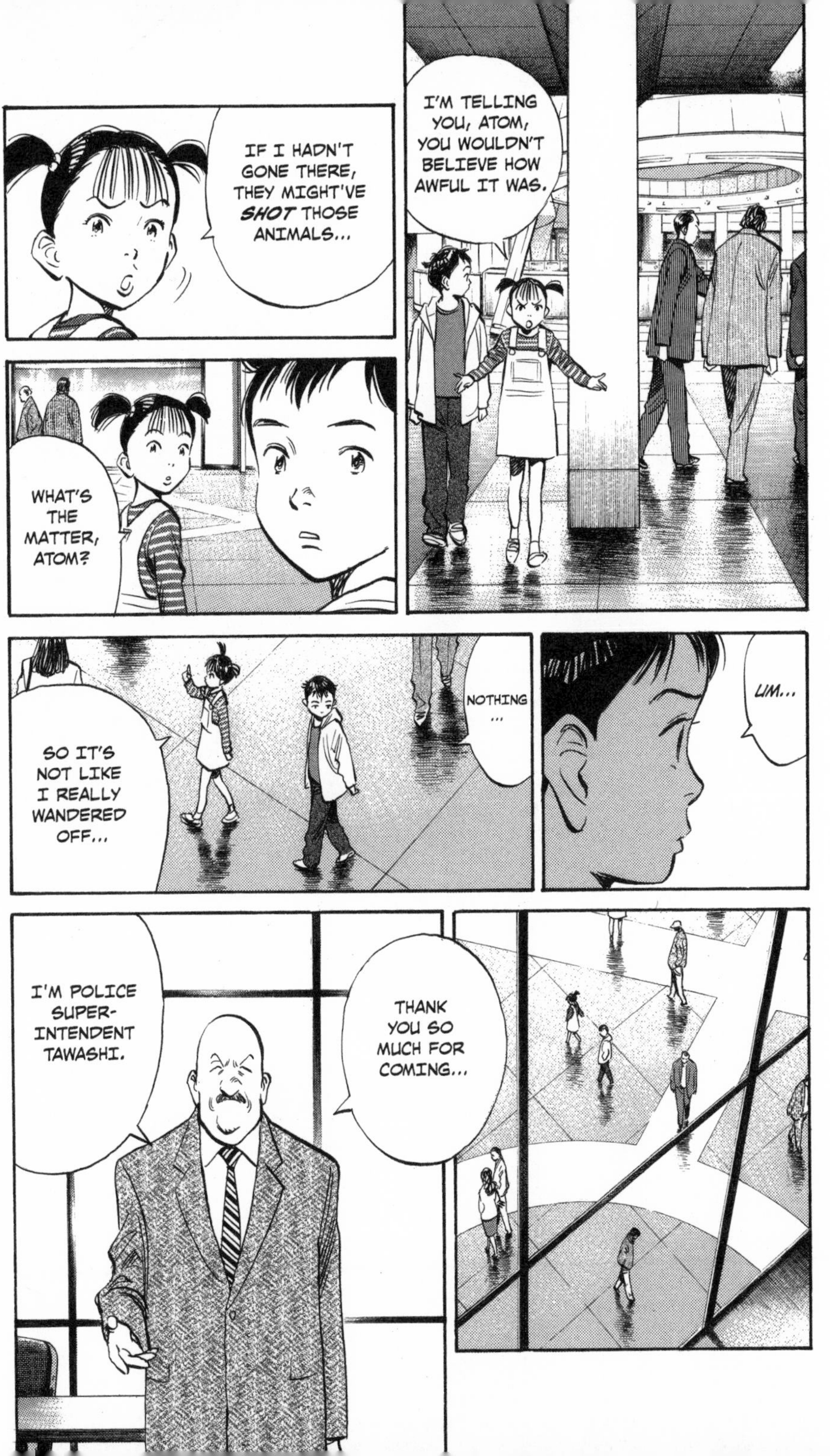
I'M TELLING YOU, ATOM, YOU WOULDN'T BELIEVE HOW AWFUL IT WAS.
IF I HADN'T GONE THERE, THEY MIGHT'VE *SHOT* THOSE ANIMALS...
WHAT'S THE MATTER, ATOM?
UM...
NOTHING...
SO IT'S NOT LIKE I REALLY WANDERED OFF...
THANK YOU SO MUCH FOR COMING...
I'M POLICE SUPER-INTENDENT TAWASHI.

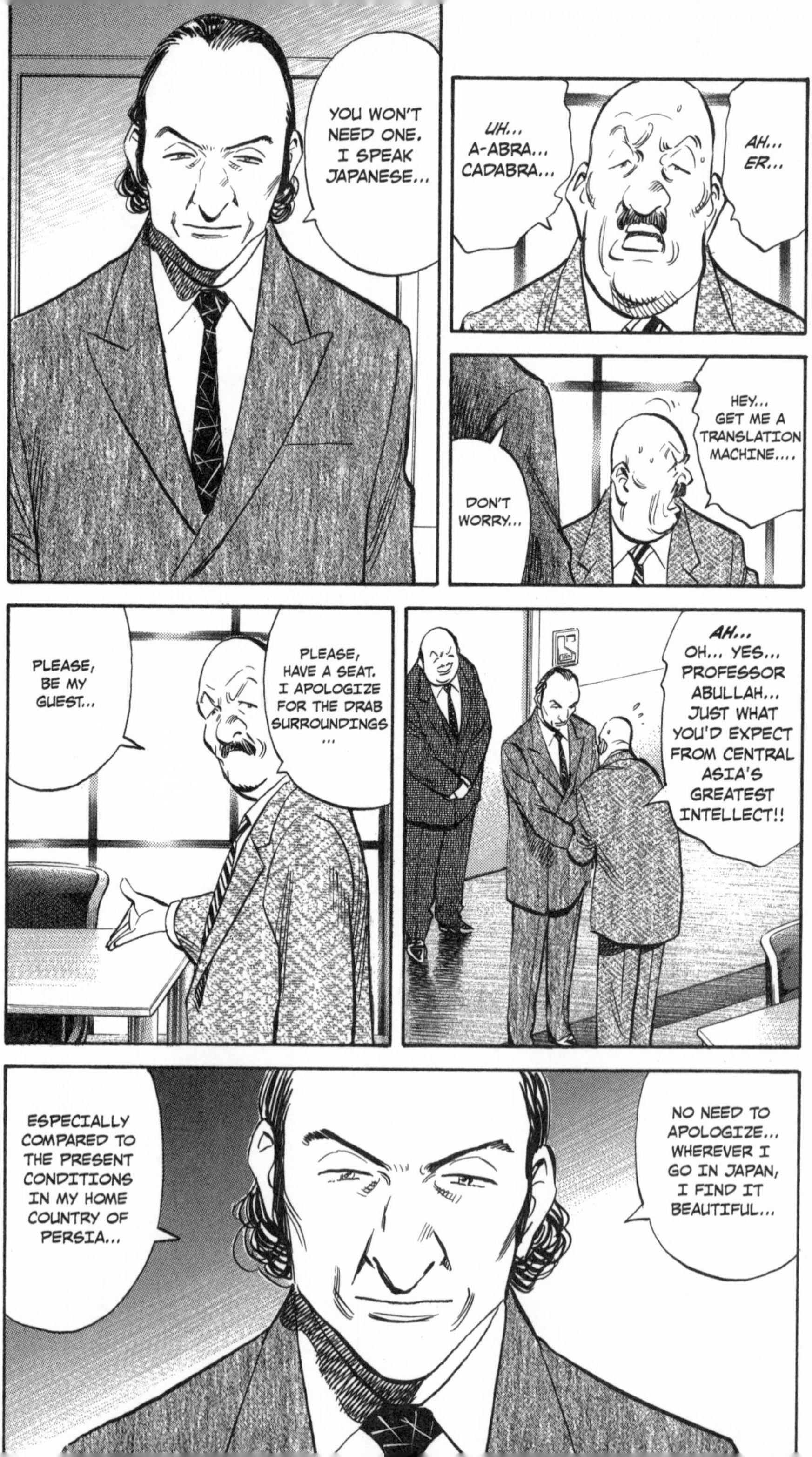
AH... ER...
UH... A-ABRA... CADABRA...
HEY... GET ME A TRANSLATION MACHINE....
DON'T WORRY...
YOU WON'T NEED ONE. I SPEAK JAPANESE...
AH... OH... YES... PROFESSOR ABULLAH... JUST WHAT YOU'D EXPECT FROM CENTRAL ASIA'S GREATEST INTELLECT!!
PLEASE, HAVE A SEAT. I APOLOGIZE FOR THE DRAB SURROUNDINGS ...
PLEASE, BE MY GUEST...
NO NEED TO APOLOGIZE... WHEREVER I GO IN JAPAN, I FIND IT BEAUTIFUL...
ESPECIALLY COMPARED TO THE PRESENT CONDITIONS IN MY HOME COUNTRY OF PERSIA...

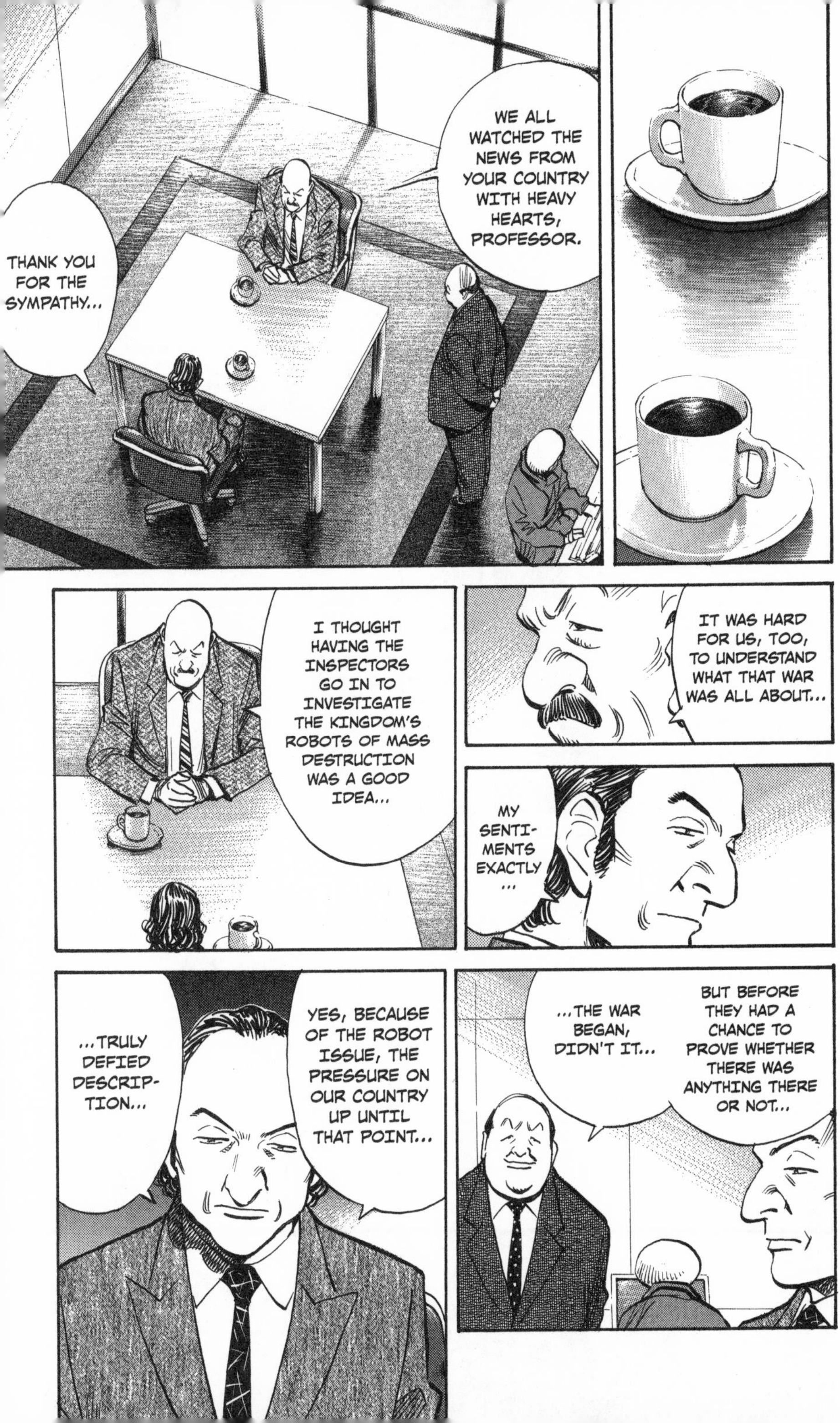
WE ALL WATCHED THE NEWS FROM YOUR COUNTRY WITH HEAVY HEARTS, PROFESSOR.
THANK YOU FOR THE SYMPATHY...
IT WAS HARD FOR US, TOO, TO UNDERSTAND WHAT THAT WAR WAS ALL ABOUT...
MY SENTIMENTS EXACTLY...
I THOUGHT HAVING THE INSPECTORS GO IN TO INVESTIGATE THE KINGDOM'S ROBOTS OF MASS DESTRUCTION WAS A GOOD IDEA...
BUT BEFORE THEY HAD A CHANCE TO PROVE WHETHER THERE WAS ANYTHING THERE OR NOT...
...THE WAR BEGAN, DIDN'T IT...
YES, BECAUSE OF THE ROBOT ISSUE, THE PRESSURE ON OUR COUNTRY UP UNTIL THAT POINT...
...TRULY DEFIED DESCRIPTION...

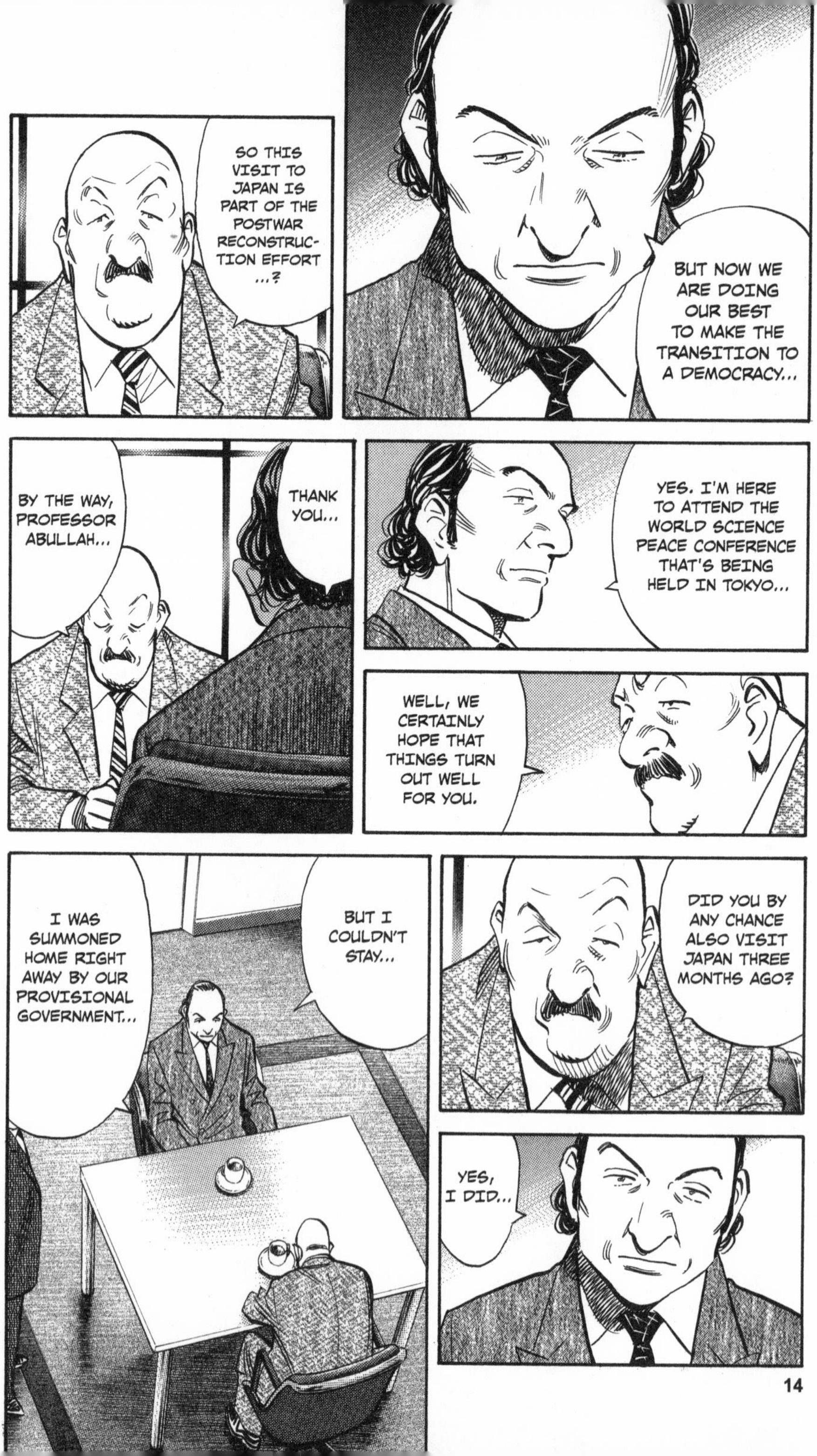
BUT NOW WE ARE DOING OUR BEST TO MAKE THE TRANSITION TO A DEMOCRACY...
SO THIS VISIT TO JAPAN IS PART OF THE POSTWAR RECONSTRUCTION EFFORT ...?
YES. I'M HERE TO ATTEND THE WORLD SCIENCE PEACE CONFERENCE THAT'S BEING HELD IN TOKYO...
WELL, WE CERTAINLY HOPE THAT THINGS TURN OUT WELL FOR YOU.
THANK YOU...
BY THE WAY, PROFESSOR ABULLAH...
DID YOU BY ANY CHANCE ALSO VISIT JAPAN THREE MONTHS AGO?
YES, I DID...
BUT I COULDN'T STAY...
I WAS SUMMONED HOME RIGHT AWAY BY OUR PROVISIONAL GOVERNMENT...

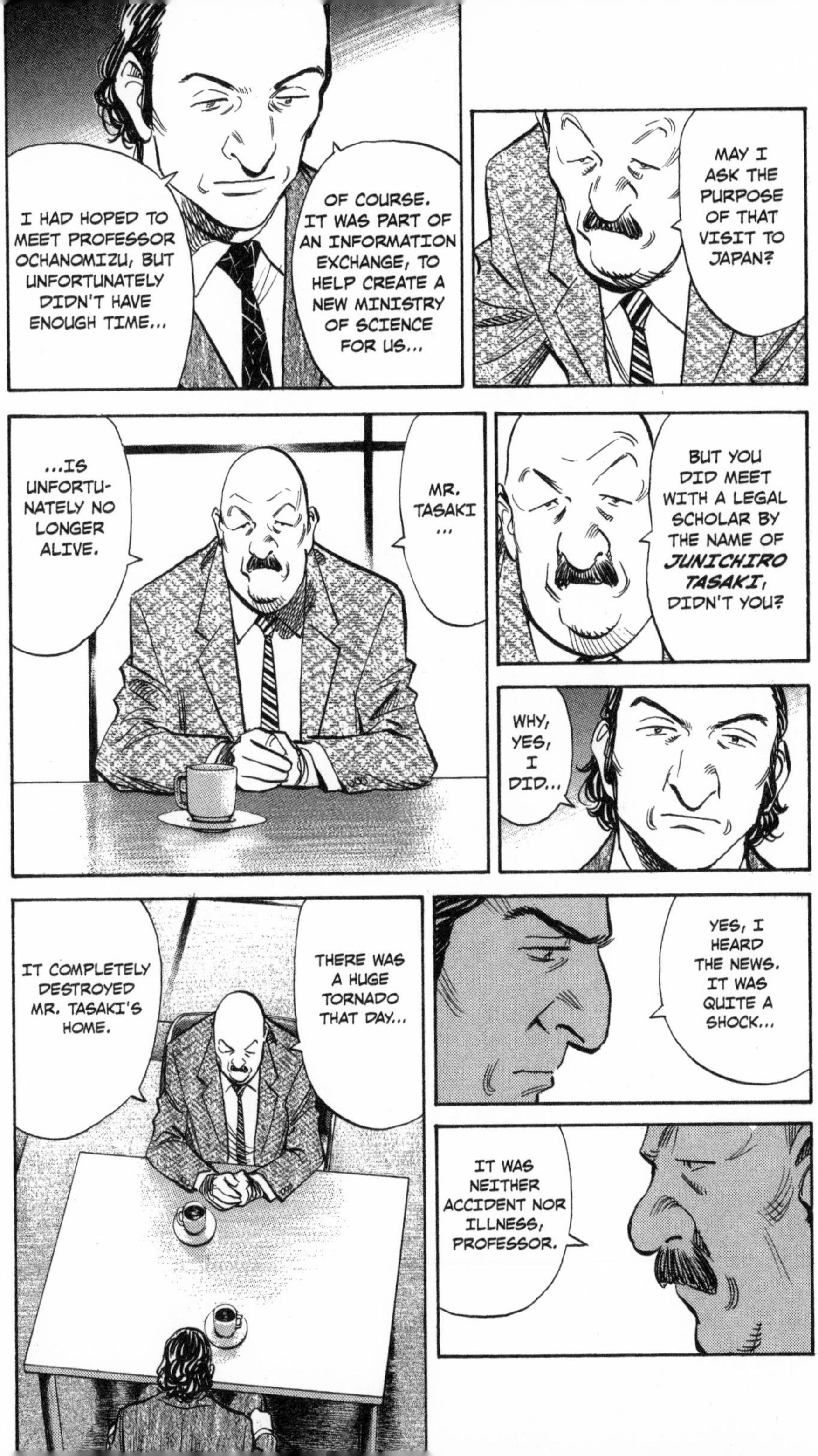
MAY I ASK THE PURPOSE OF THAT VISIT TO JAPAN?
OF COURSE. IT WAS PART OF AN INFORMATION EXCHANGE, TO HELP CREATE A NEW MINISTRY OF SCIENCE FOR US...
I HAD HOPED TO MEET PROFESSOR OCHANOMIZU, BUT UNFORTUNATELY DIDN'T HAVE ENOUGH TIME...
BUT YOU DID MEET WITH A LEGAL SCHOLAR BY THE NAME OF *JUNICHIRO TASAKI*, DIDN'T YOU?
WHY, YES, I DID...
MR. TASAKI ...
...IS UNFORTUNATELY NO LONGER ALIVE.
YES, I HEARD THE NEWS. IT WAS QUITE A SHOCK...
IT WAS NEITHER ACCIDENT NOR ILLNESS, PROFESSOR.
THERE WAS A HUGE TORNADO THAT DAY...
IT COMPLETELY DESTROYED MR. TASAKI'S HOME.

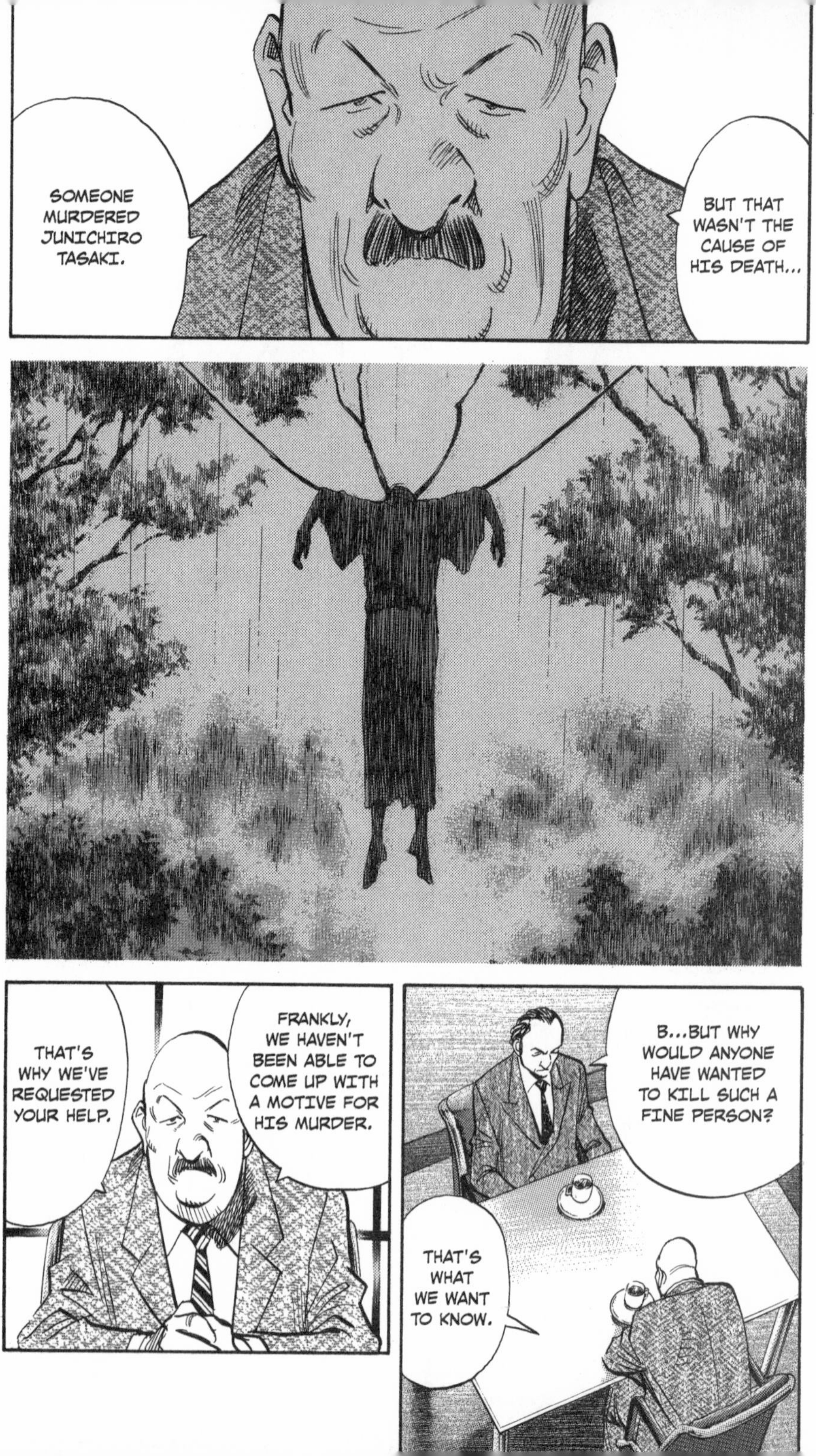
BUT THAT WASN'T THE CAUSE OF HIS DEATH...
SOMEONE MURDERED JUNICHIRO TASAKI.
B...BUT WHY WOULD ANYONE HAVE WANTED TO KILL SUCH A FINE PERSON?
THAT'S WHAT WE WANT TO KNOW.
FRANKLY, WE HAVEN'T BEEN ABLE TO COME UP WITH A MOTIVE FOR HIS MURDER.
THAT'S WHY WE'VE REQUESTED YOUR HELP.

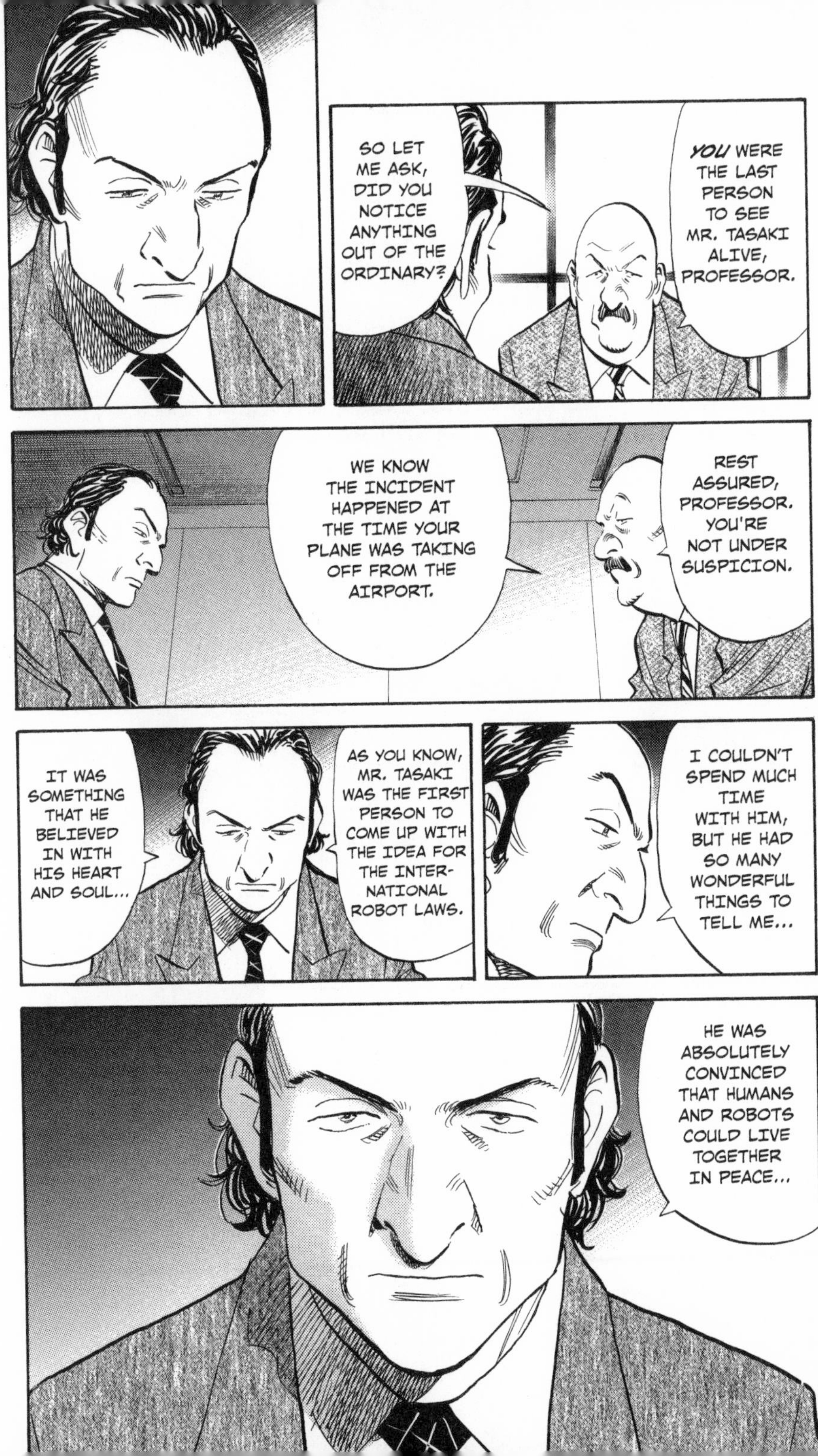
YOU WERE THE LAST PERSON TO SEE MR. TASAKI ALIVE, PROFESSOR.
SO LET ME ASK, DID YOU NOTICE ANYTHING OUT OF THE ORDINARY?
REST ASSURED, PROFESSOR. YOU'RE NOT UNDER SUSPICION.
WE KNOW THE INCIDENT HAPPENED AT THE TIME YOUR PLANE WAS TAKING OFF FROM THE AIRPORT.
I COULDN'T SPEND MUCH TIME WITH HIM, BUT HE HAD SO MANY WONDERFUL THINGS TO TELL ME...
AS YOU KNOW, MR. TASAKI WAS THE FIRST PERSON TO COME UP WITH THE IDEA FOR THE INTER-NATIONAL ROBOT LAWS.
IT WAS SOMETHING THAT HE BELIEVED IN WITH HIS HEART AND SOUL...
HE WAS ABSOLUTELY CONVINCED THAT HUMANS AND ROBOTS COULD LIVE TOGETHER IN PEACE...

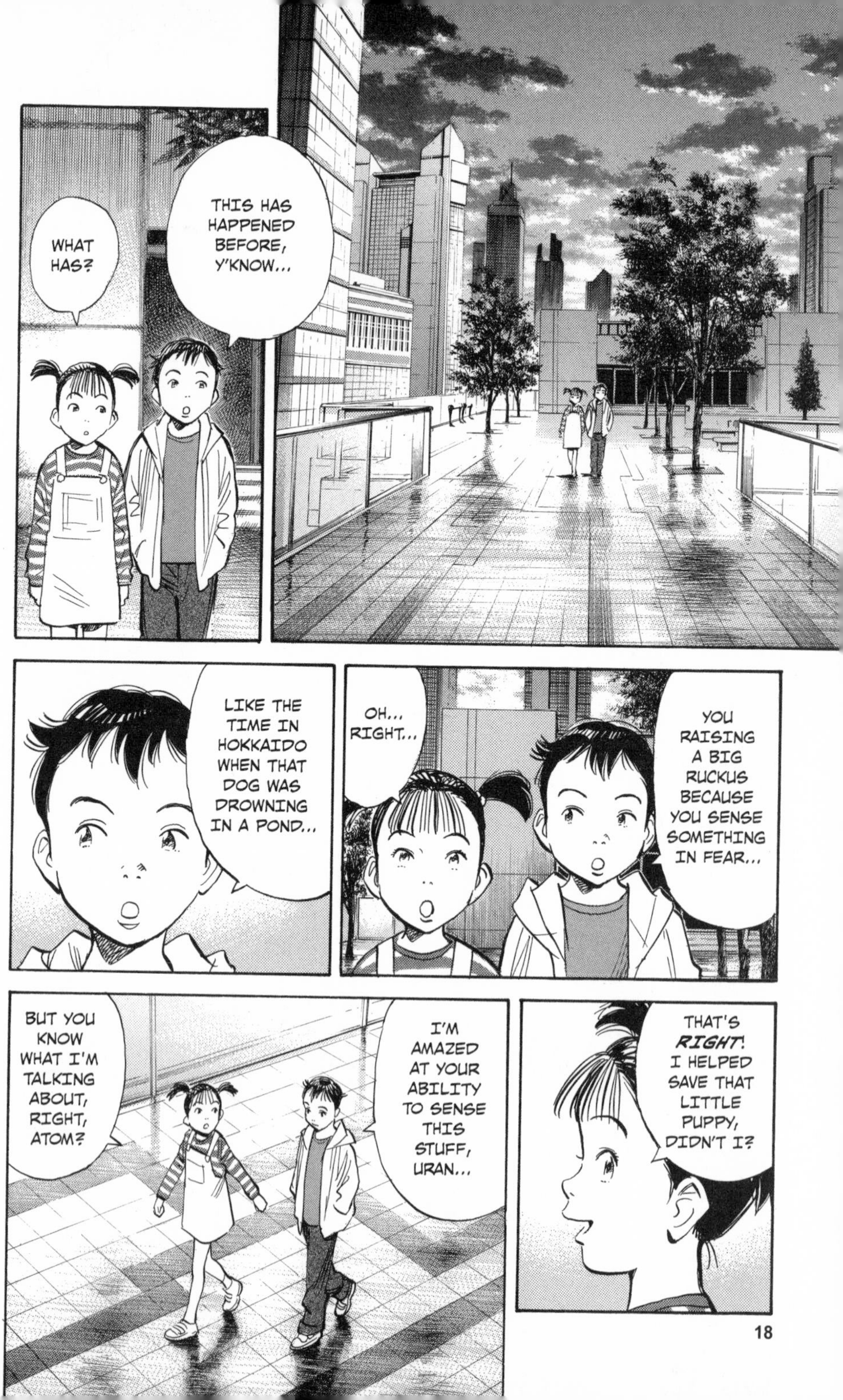
THIS HAS HAPPENED BEFORE, Y'KNOW...
WHAT HAS?
YOU RAISING A BIG RUCKUS BECAUSE YOU SENSE SOMETHING IN FEAR...
OH... RIGHT...
LIKE THE TIME IN HOKKAIDO WHEN THAT DOG WAS DROWNING IN A POND...
THAT'S ***RIGHT***! I HELPED SAVE THAT LITTLE PUPPY, DIDN'T I?
I'M AMAZED AT YOUR ABILITY TO SENSE THIS STUFF, URAN...
BUT YOU KNOW WHAT I'M TALKING ABOUT, RIGHT, ATOM?

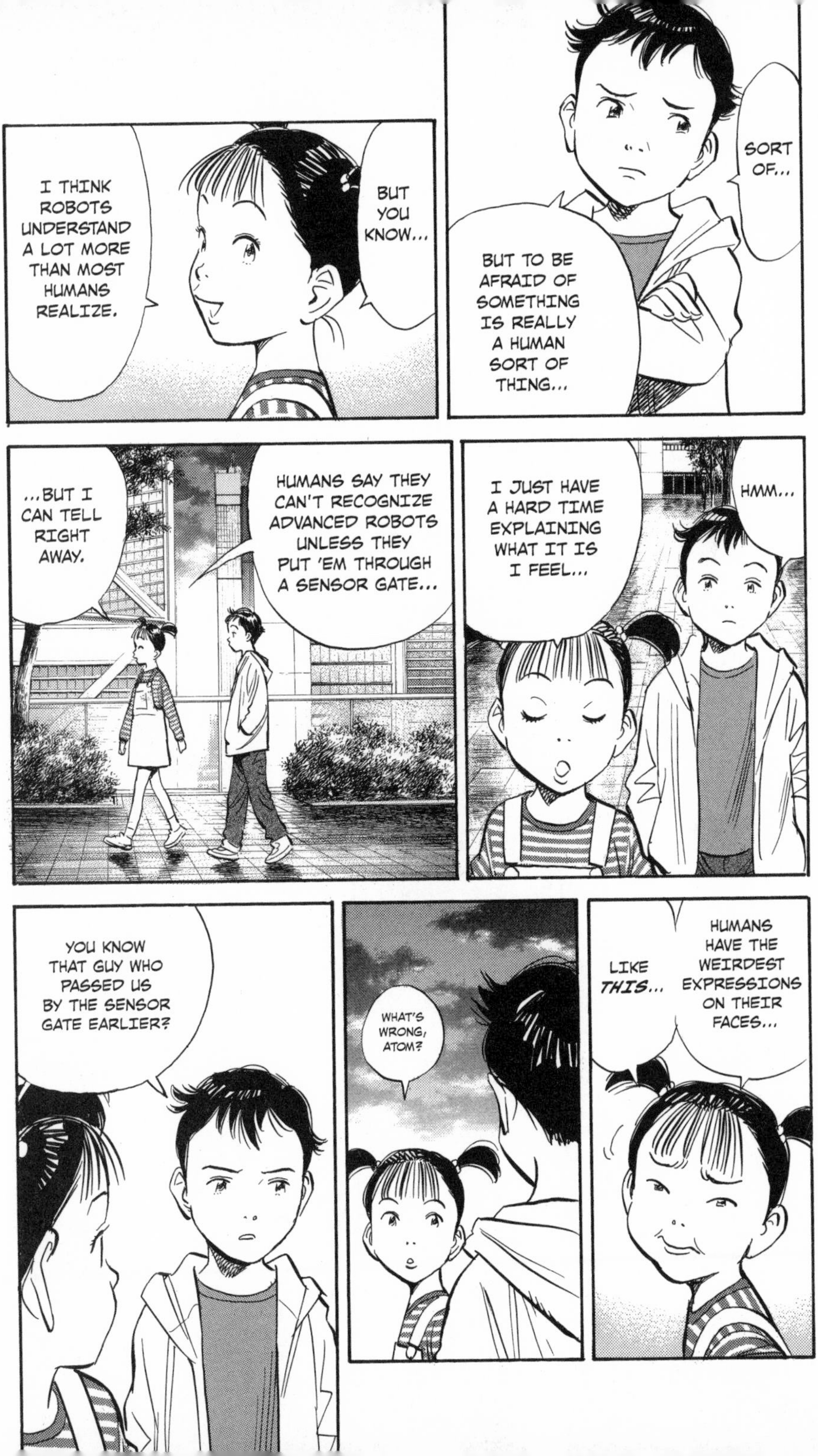
SORT OF...
BUT TO BE AFRAID OF SOMETHING IS REALLY A HUMAN SORT OF THING...
BUT YOU KNOW...
I THINK ROBOTS UNDERSTAND A LOT MORE THAN MOST HUMANS REALIZE.
HMM...
I JUST HAVE A HARD TIME EXPLAINING WHAT IT IS I FEEL...
HUMANS SAY THEY CAN'T RECOGNIZE ADVANCED ROBOTS UNLESS THEY PUT 'EM THROUGH A SENSOR GATE...
...BUT I CAN TELL RIGHT AWAY.
HUMANS HAVE THE WEIRDEST EXPRESSIONS ON THEIR FACES...
LIKE *THIS*...
WHAT'S WRONG, ATOM?
YOU KNOW THAT GUY WHO PASSED US BY THE SENSOR GATE EARLIER?

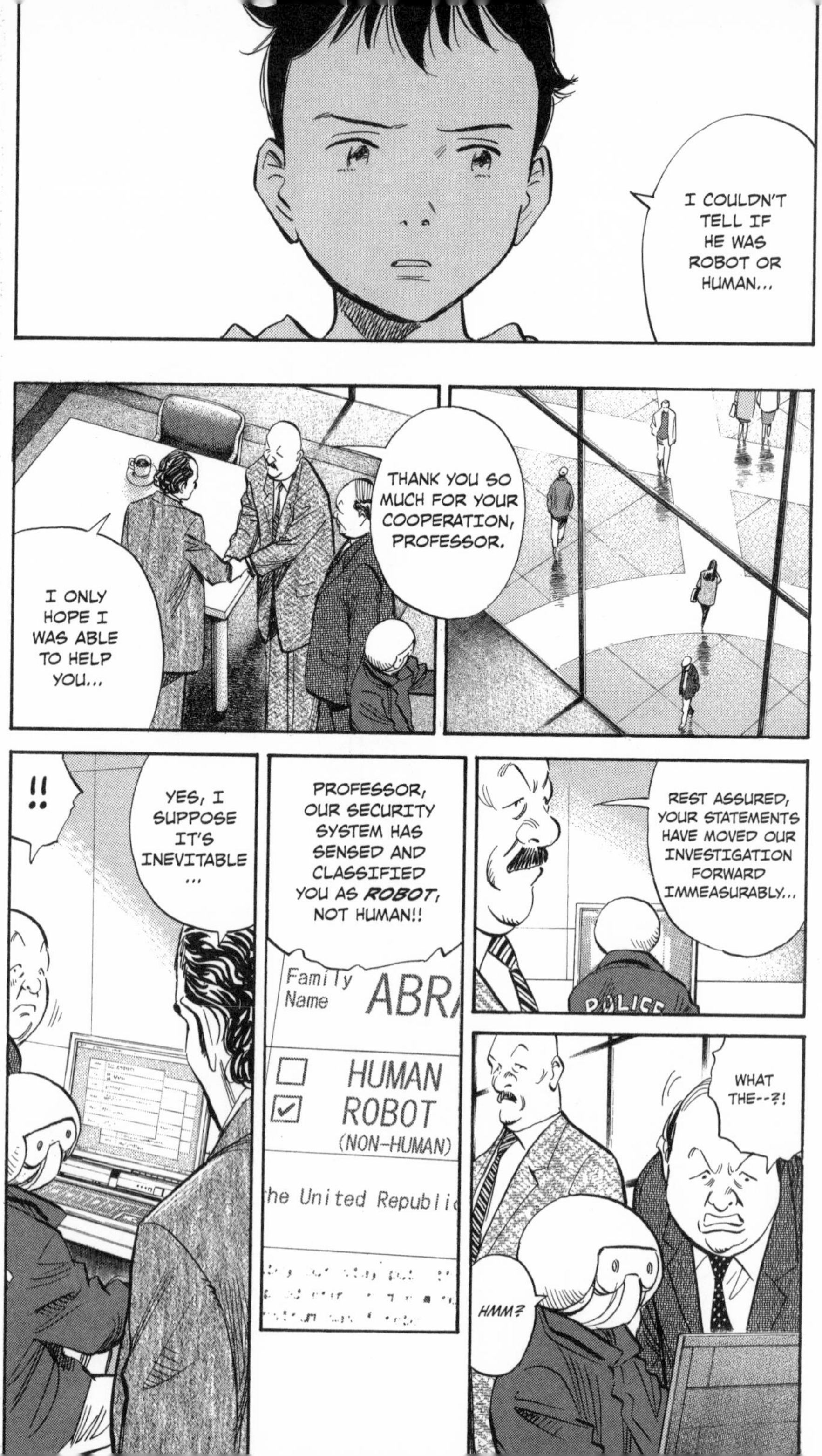
I COULDN'T TELL IF HE WAS ROBOT OR HUMAN...
THANK YOU SO MUCH FOR YOUR COOPERATION, PROFESSOR.
I ONLY HOPE I WAS ABLE TO HELP YOU...
REST ASSURED, YOUR STATEMENTS HAVE MOVED OUR INVESTIGATION FORWARD IMMEASURABLY...
WHAT THE--?!
HMM?
PROFESSOR, OUR SECURITY SYSTEM HAS SENSED AND CLASSIFIED YOU AS *ROBOT*, NOT HUMAN!!
Family Name
HUMAN
ROBOT
(NON-HUMAN)
YES, I SUPPOSE IT'S INEVITABLE...
!!

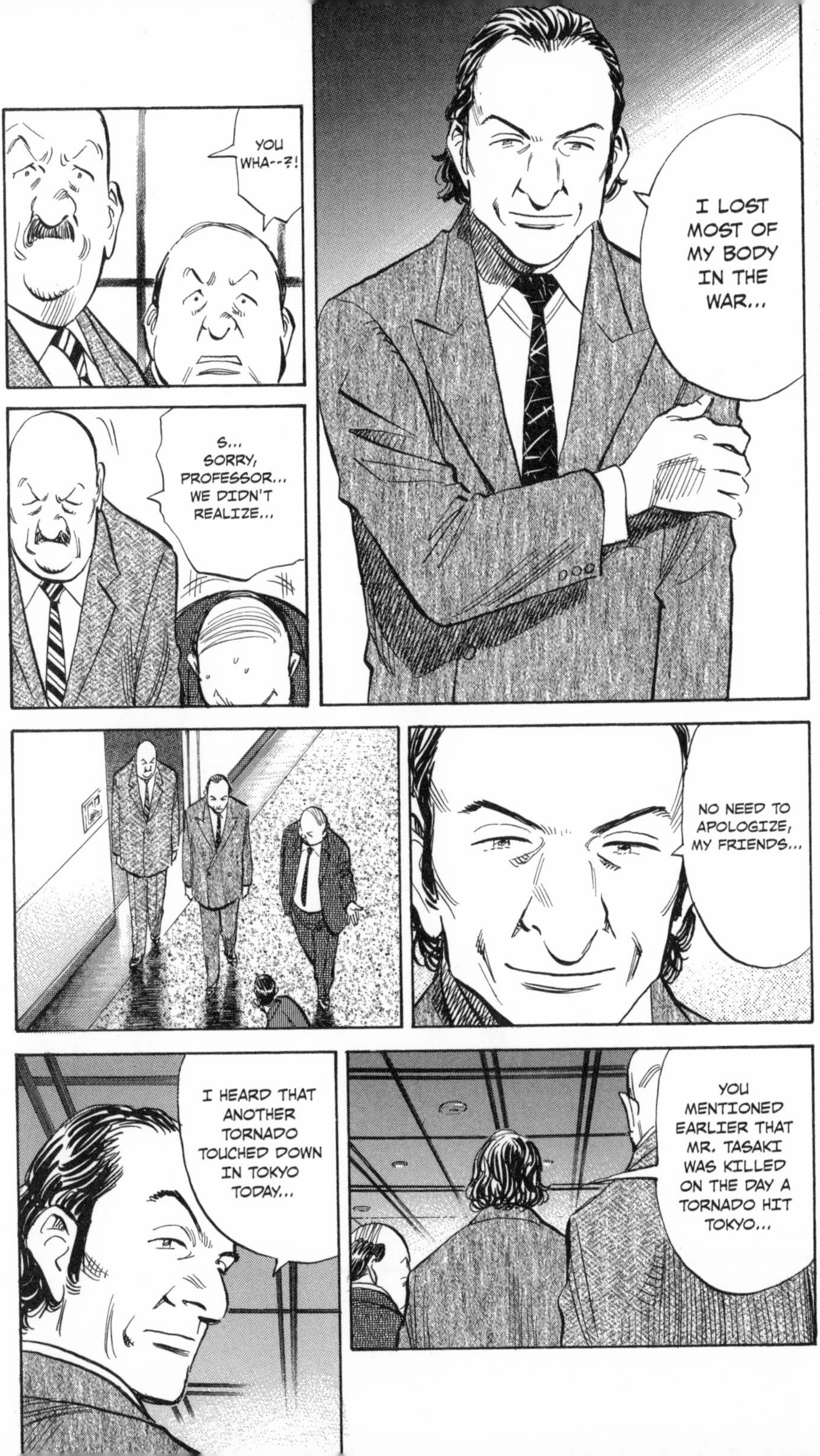
I LOST MOST OF MY BODY IN THE WAR...
YOU WHA--?!
S... SORRY, PROFESSOR... WE DIDN'T REALIZE...
NO NEED TO APOLOGIZE, MY FRIENDS...
YOU MENTIONED EARLIER THAT MR. TASAKI WAS KILLED ON THE DAY A TORNADO HIT TOKYO...
I HEARD THAT ANOTHER TORNADO TOUCHED DOWN IN TOKYO TODAY...

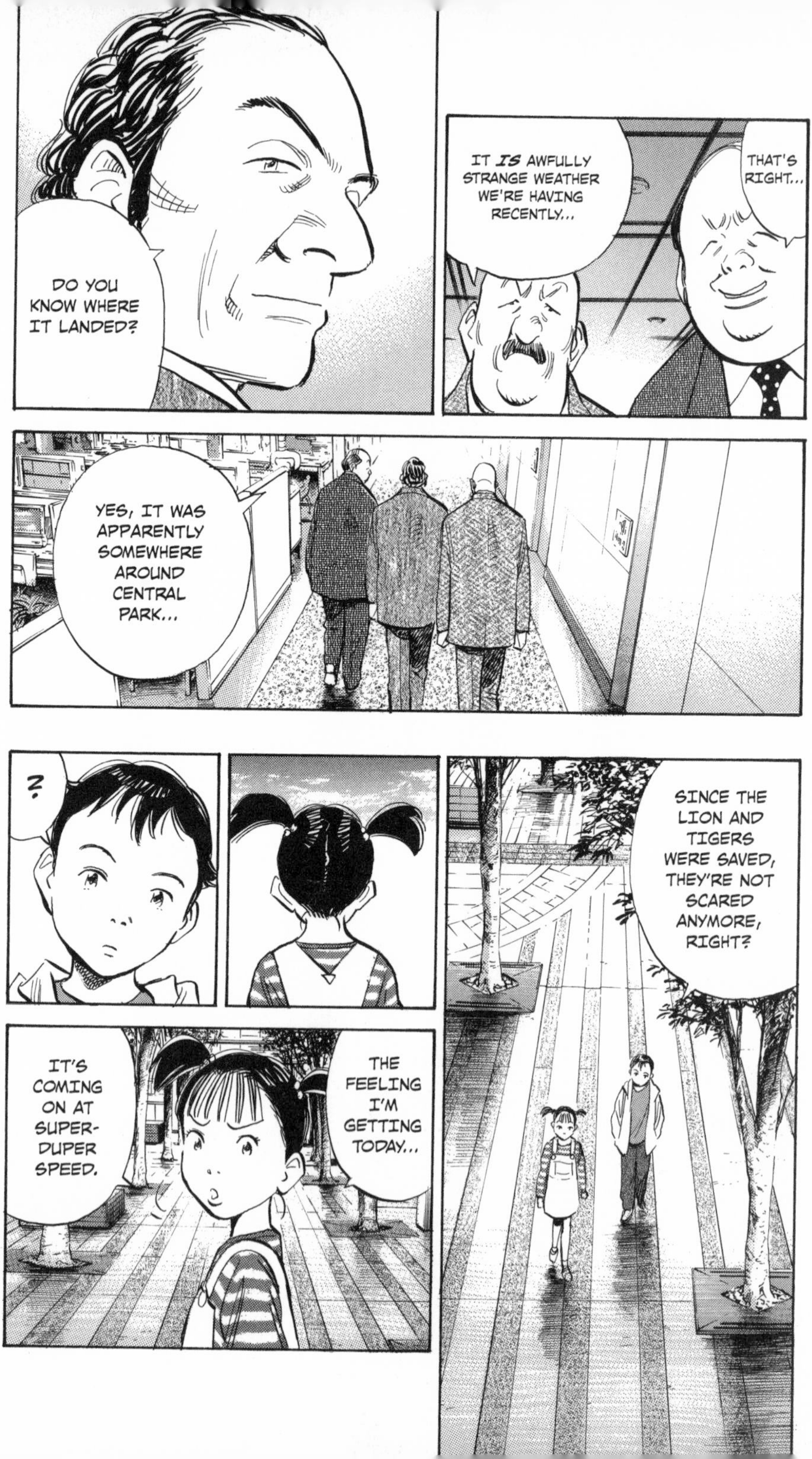
THAT'S RIGHT...
IT IS AWFULLY STRANGE WEATHER WE'RE HAVING RECENTLY...
DO YOU KNOW WHERE IT LANDED?
YES, IT WAS APPARENTLY SOMEWHERE AROUND CENTRAL PARK...
SINCE THE LION AND TIGERS WERE SAVED, THEY'RE NOT SCARED ANYMORE, RIGHT?
?
THE FEELING I'M GETTING TODAY...
IT'S COMING ON AT SUPER-DUPER SPEED.

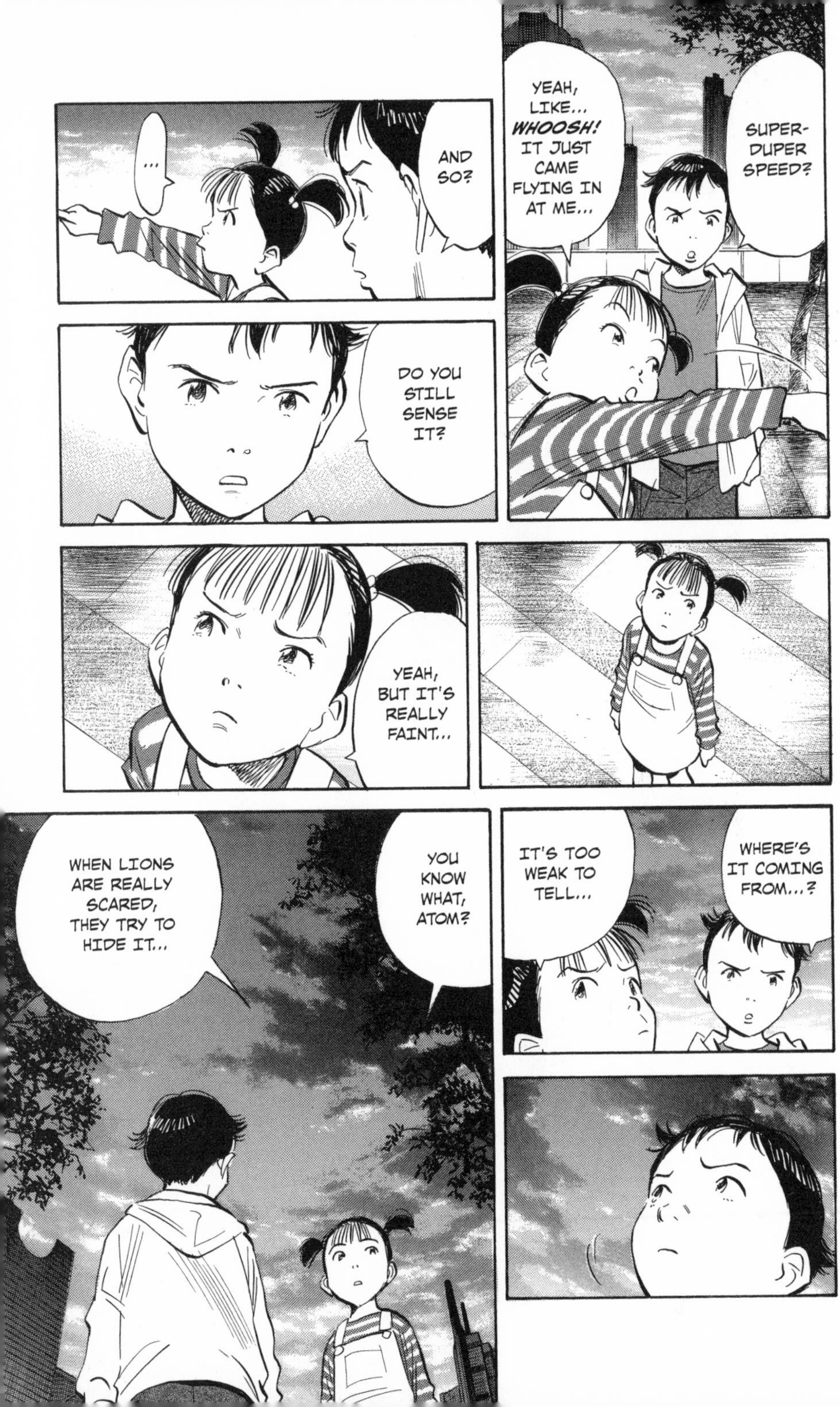
SUPER-DUPER SPEED?
YEAH, LIKE... ***WHOOSH!*** IT JUST CAME FLYING IN AT ME...
AND SO?
...
DO YOU STILL SENSE IT?
YEAH, BUT IT'S REALLY FAINT...
WHERE'S IT COMING FROM...?
IT'S TOO WEAK TO TELL...
YOU KNOW WHAT, ATOM?
WHEN LIONS ARE REALLY SCARED, THEY TRY TO HIDE IT...

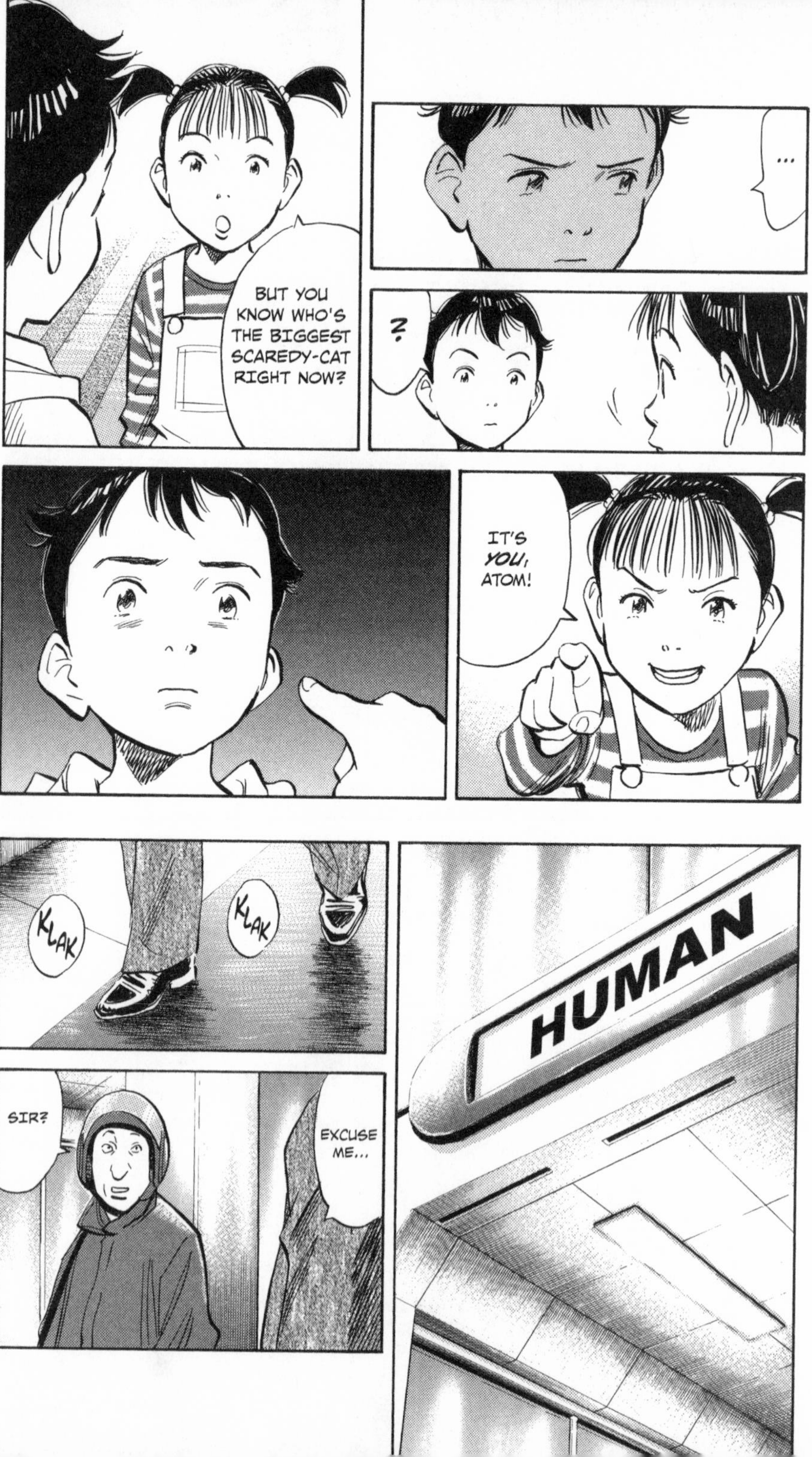
...
?
BUT YOU KNOW WHO'S THE BIGGEST SCAREDY-CAT RIGHT NOW?
IT'S *YOU*, ATOM!
HUMAN
KLAK
KLAK
EXCUSE ME...
SIR?

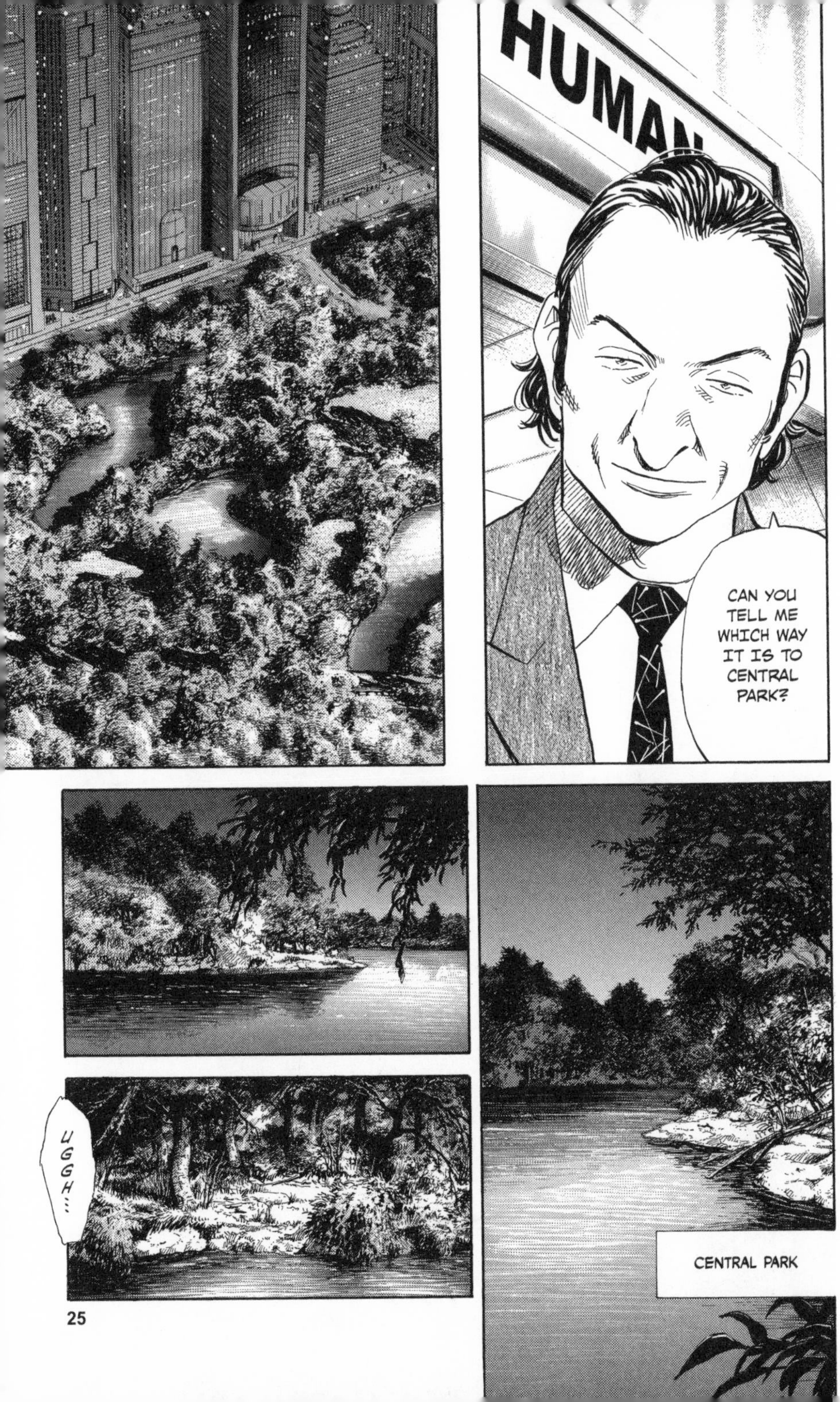
HUMAN
CAN YOU TELL ME WHICH WAY IT IS TO CENTRAL PARK?
CENTRAL PARK
UGGH...

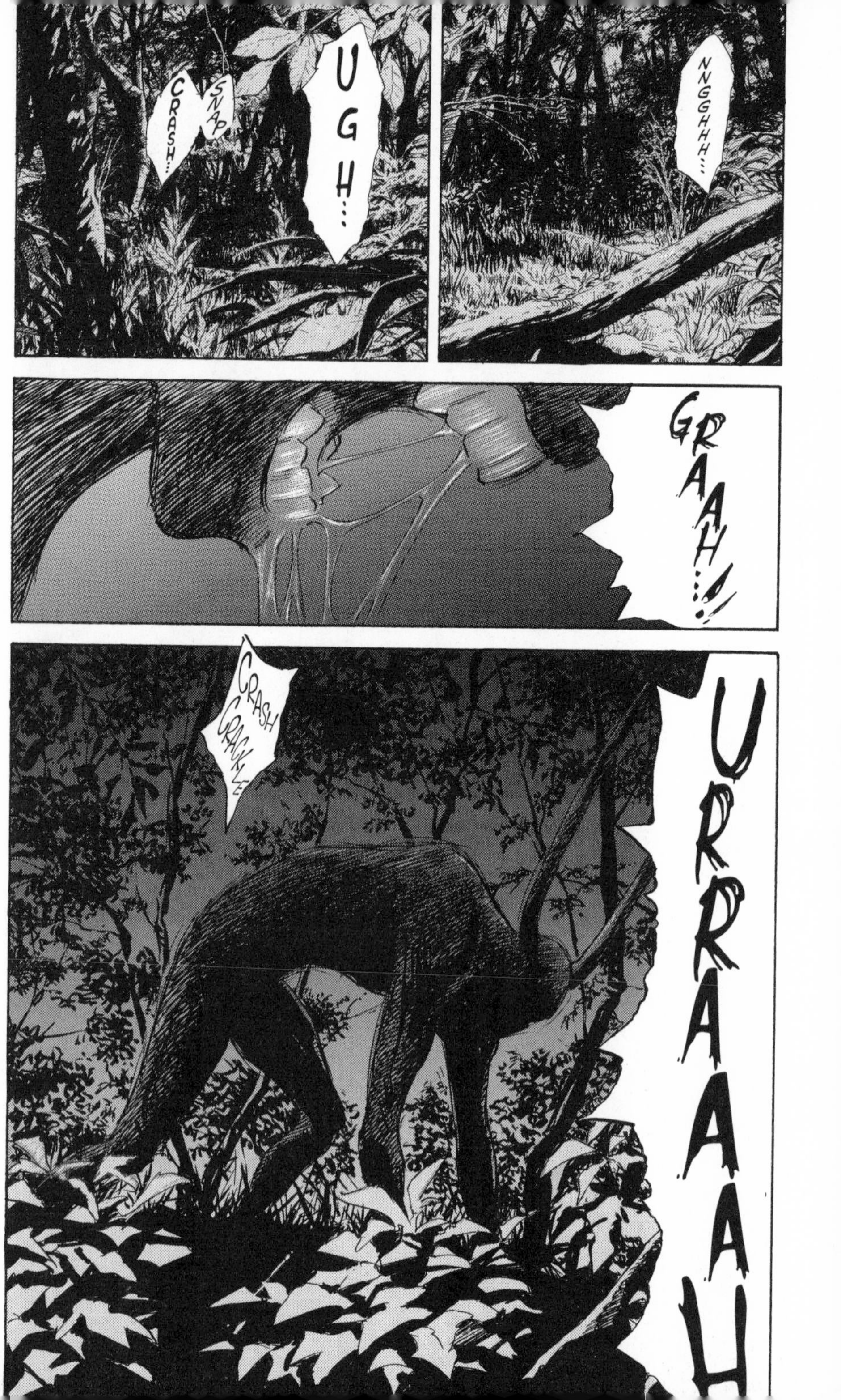
NNGGHHH...
UGH...
SNAP
CRASH...
GRAAAH...!!
CRASH CRACKLE
URRAAAH

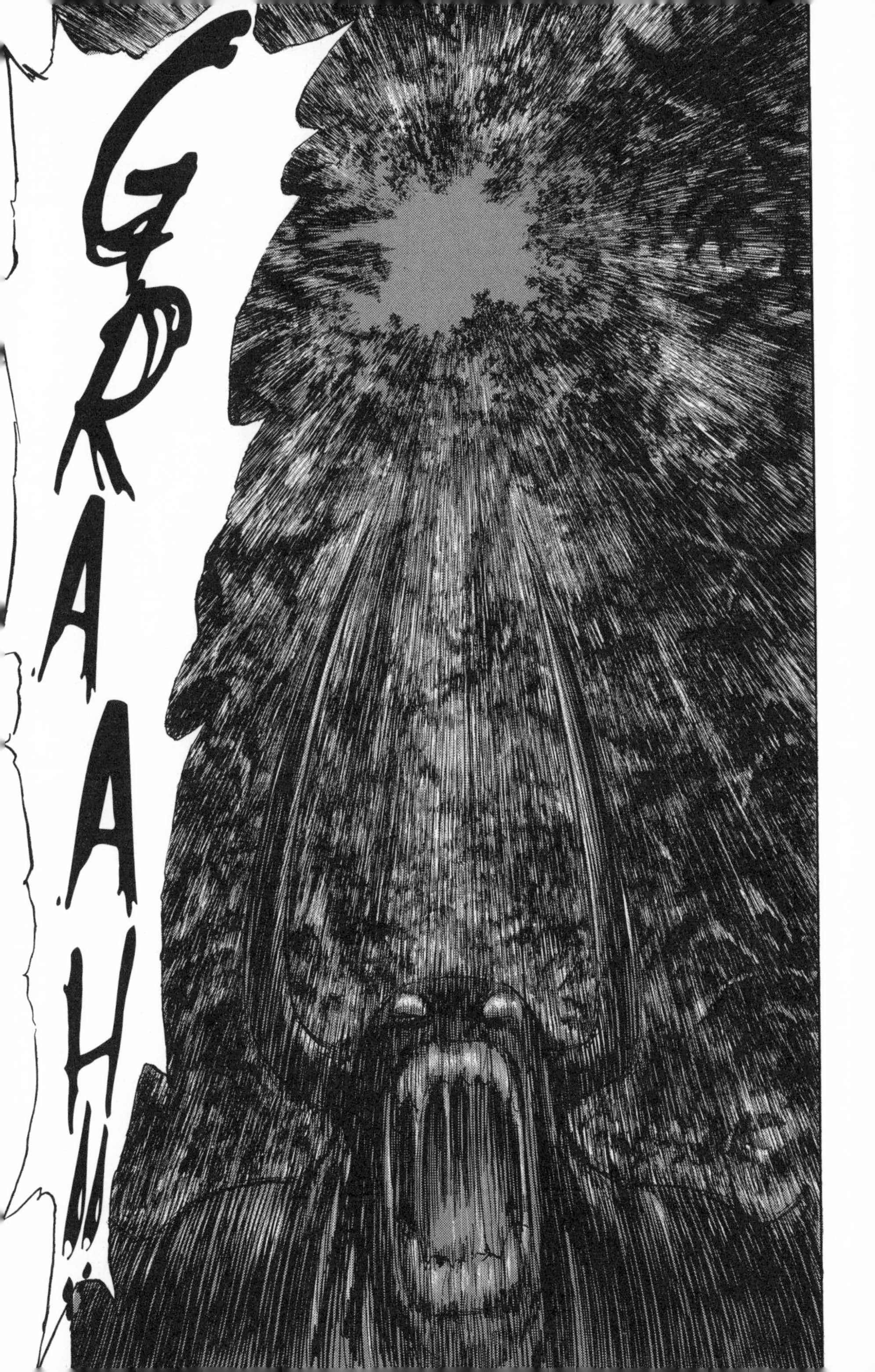
GRAAH!!

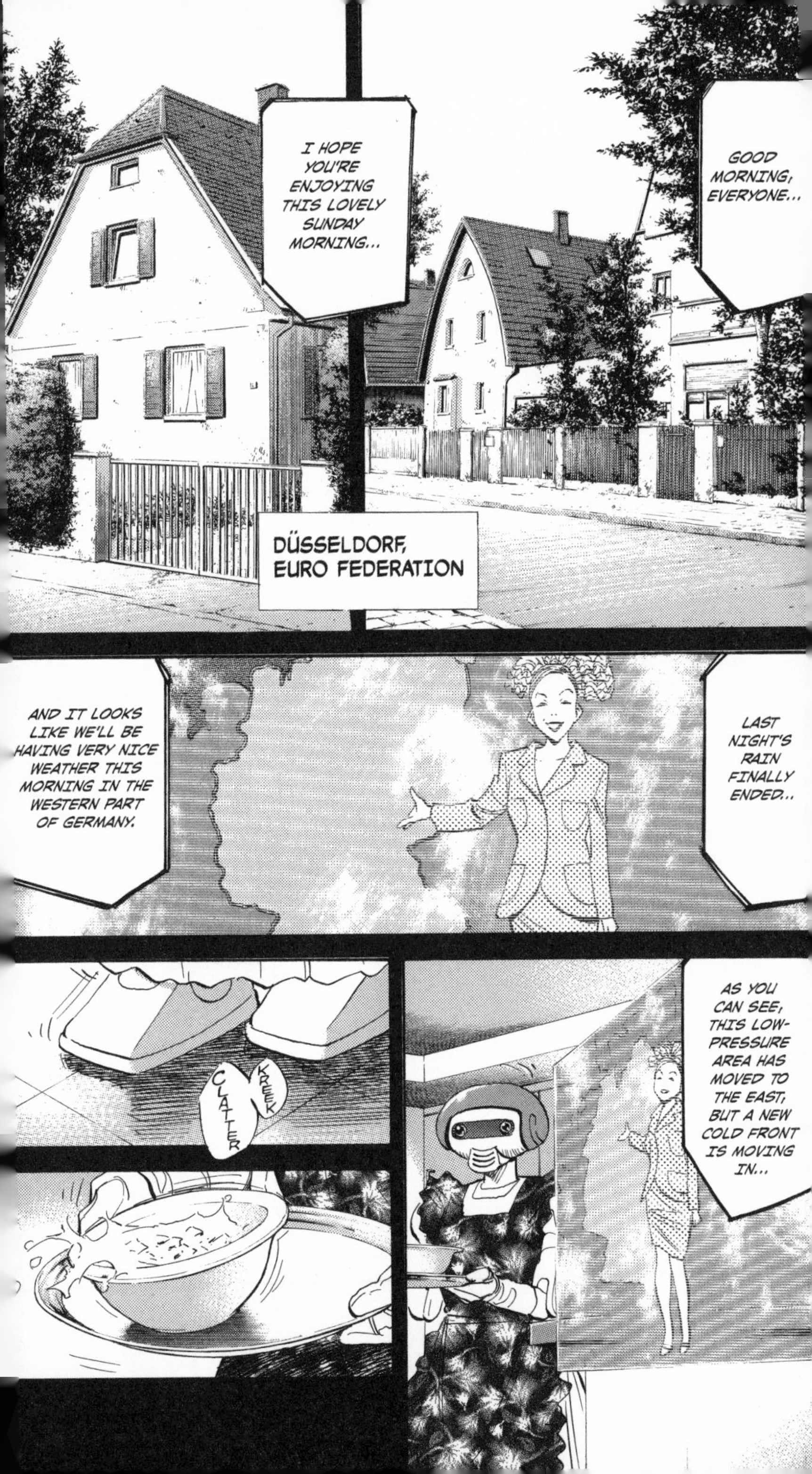
GOOD MORNING, EVERYONE...
I HOPE YOU'RE ENJOYING THIS LOVELY SUNDAY MORNING...
DÜSSELDORF, EURO FEDERATION
LAST NIGHT'S RAIN FINALLY ENDED...
AND IT LOOKS LIKE WE'LL BE HAVING VERY NICE WEATHER THIS MORNING IN THE WESTERN PART OF GERMANY.
AS YOU CAN SEE, THIS LOW-PRESSURE AREA HAS MOVED TO THE EAST, BUT A NEW COLD FRONT IS MOVING IN...
KREEK
CLATTER

I JUST BOUGHT THIS PROGRAM YESTERDAY!! DON'T GO SPILLIN' STUFF ON IT, YOU OLD PIECE OF *JUNK*!!

I... I'M SORRY, YOUNG SIR...

HEY! *WATCH IT!*

WELL, IF JUNK'S A BAD WORD, HOW 'BOUT SCRAP, THEN?! YOU KNOW, SHE GOT MY AIR SCOOTER ALL WET THE OTHER DAY, TOO...

HANS! WATCH YOUR LANGUAGE.

BESIDES, I DISAPPROVE OF FOUL LANGUAGE.

OUR ROBOMAID'S WORKING AS HARD AS SHE CAN.

HANS!!

!!

30

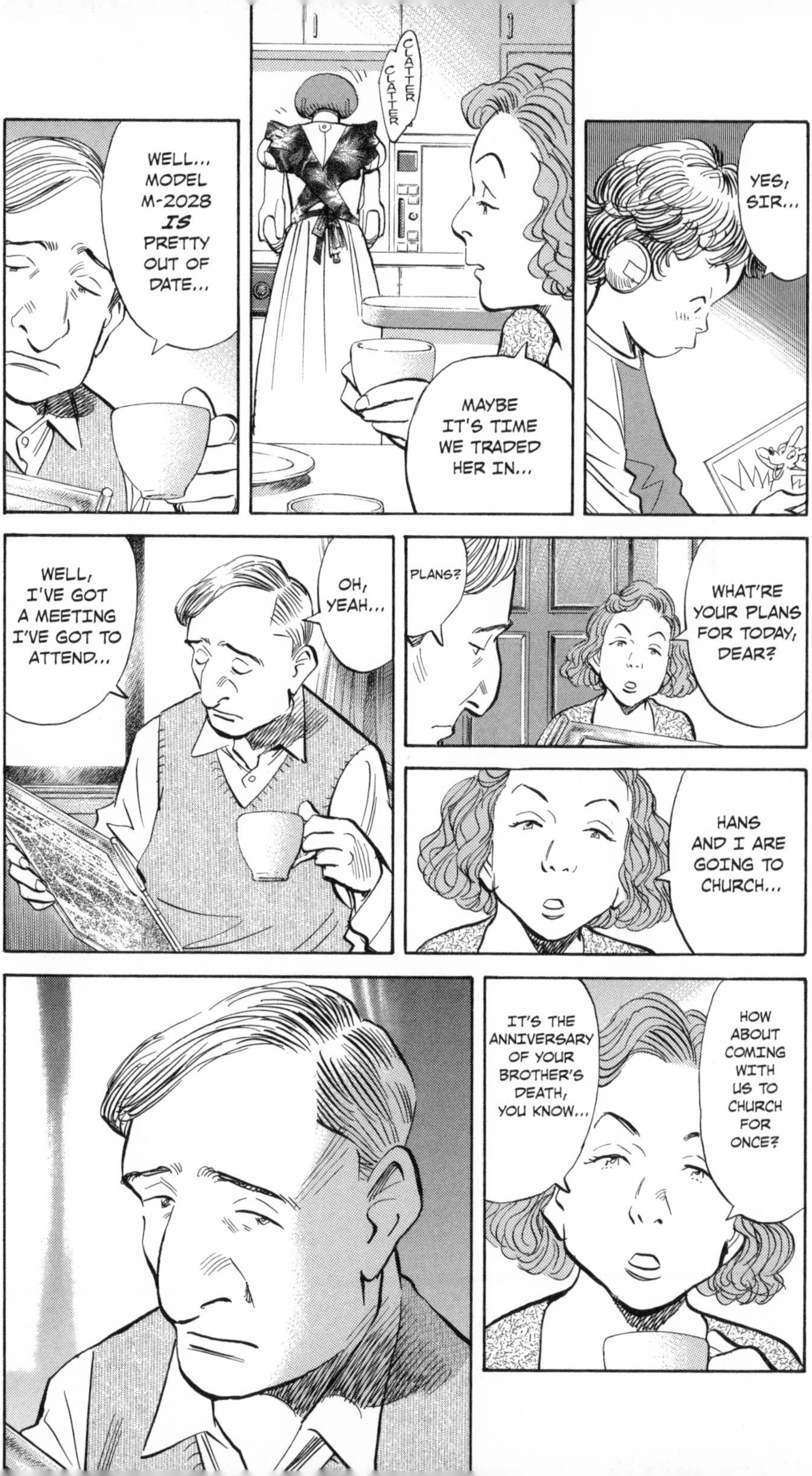
YES, SIR...
CLATTER CLATTER
MAYBE IT'S TIME WE TRADED HER IN...
WELL... MODEL M-2028 *IS* PRETTY OUT OF DATE...
WHAT'RE YOUR PLANS FOR TODAY, DEAR?
PLANS?
HANS AND I ARE GOING TO CHURCH...
OH, YEAH...
WELL, I'VE GOT A MEETING I'VE GOT TO ATTEND...
HOW ABOUT COMING WITH US TO CHURCH FOR ONCE?
IT'S THE ANNIVERSARY OF YOUR BROTHER'S DEATH, YOU KNOW...

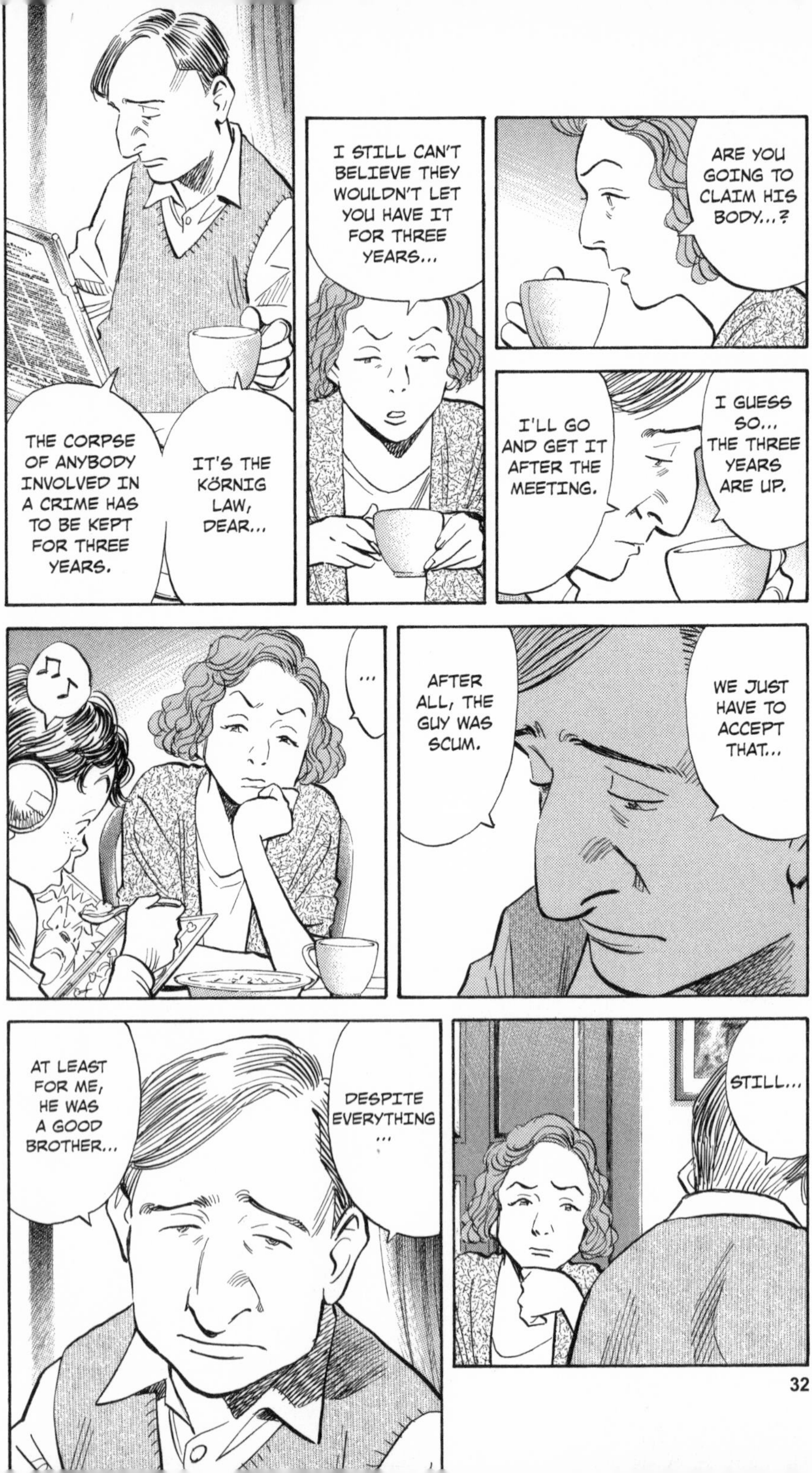
ARE YOU GOING TO CLAIM HIS BODY...?
I GUESS SO... THE THREE YEARS ARE UP.
I'LL GO AND GET IT AFTER THE MEETING.
I STILL CAN'T BELIEVE THEY WOULDN'T LET YOU HAVE IT FOR THREE YEARS...
IT'S THE KÖRNIG LAW, DEAR...
THE CORPSE OF ANYBODY INVOLVED IN A CRIME HAS TO BE KEPT FOR THREE YEARS.
WE JUST HAVE TO ACCEPT THAT...
AFTER ALL, THE GUY WAS SCUM.
...
STILL...
DESPITE EVERYTHING...
AT LEAST FOR ME, HE WAS A GOOD BROTHER...

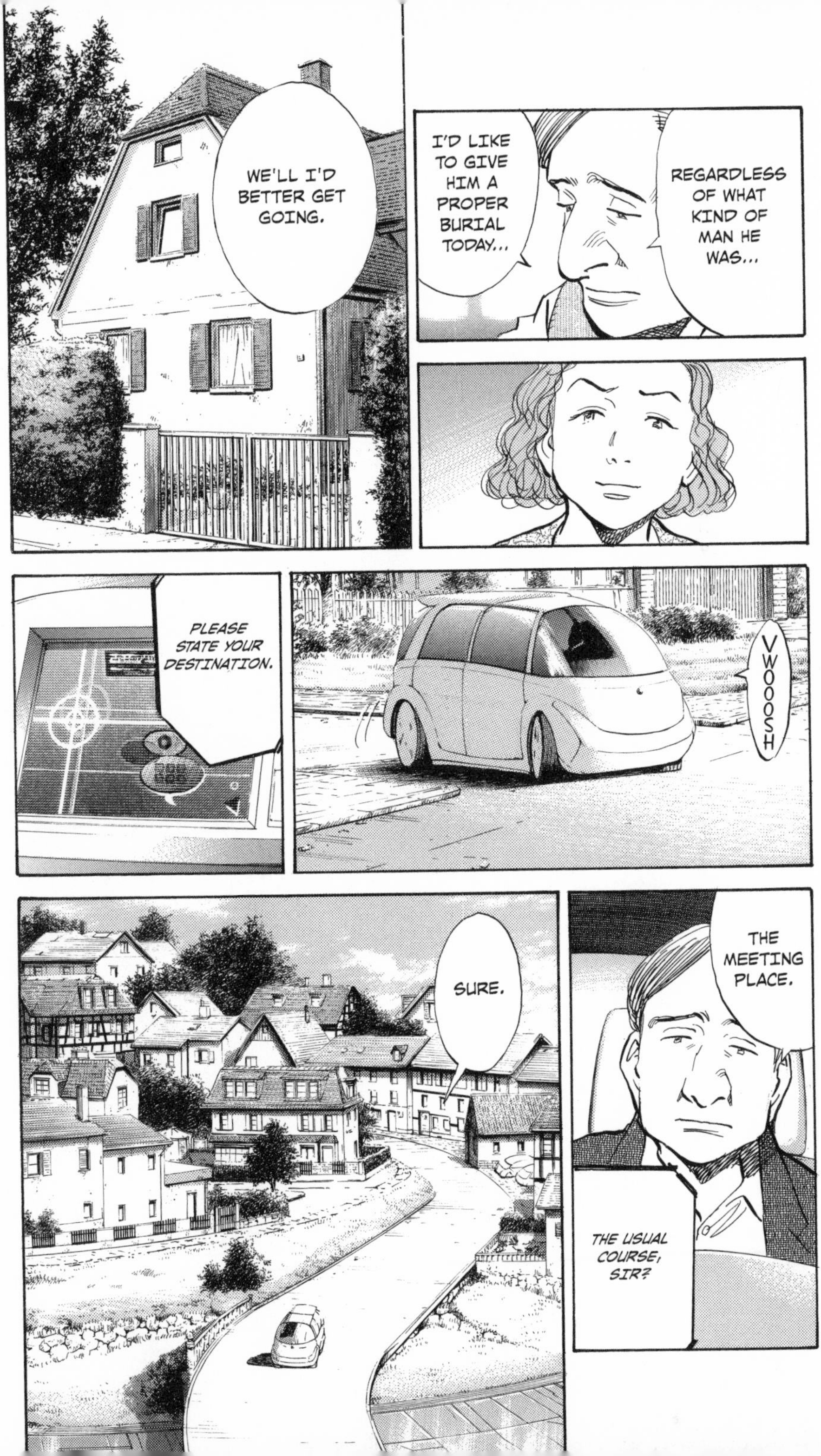
REGARDLESS OF WHAT KIND OF MAN HE WAS...
I'D LIKE TO GIVE HIM A PROPER BURIAL TODAY...
WE'LL I'D BETTER GET GOING.
VWOOOSH
PLEASE STATE YOUR DESTINATION.
THE MEETING PLACE.
THE USUAL COURSE, SIR?
SURE.

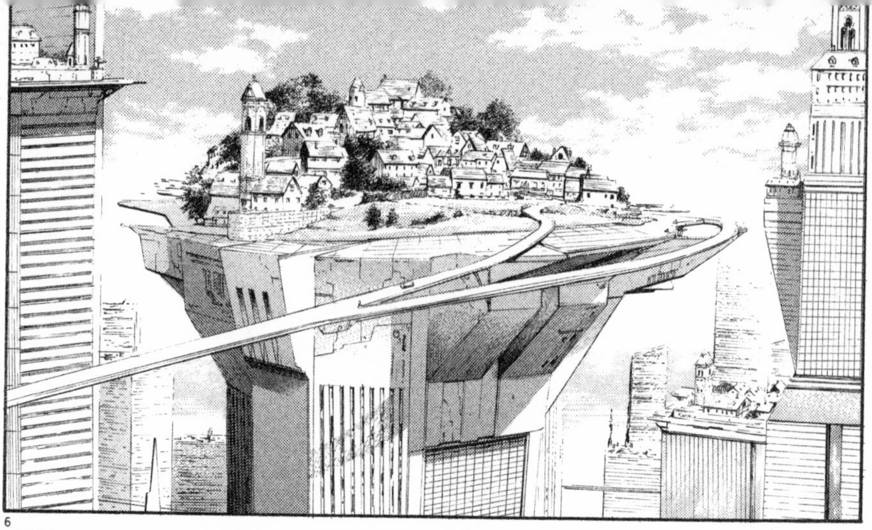

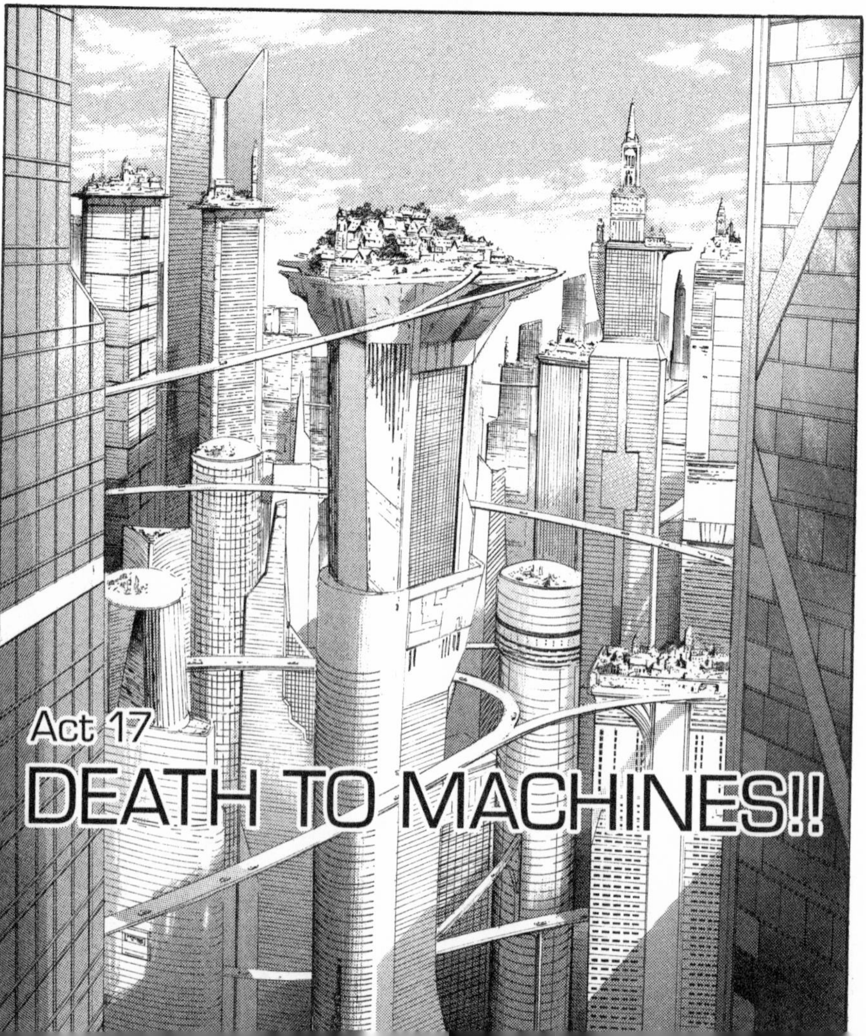
Act 17
DEATH TO MACHINES!!

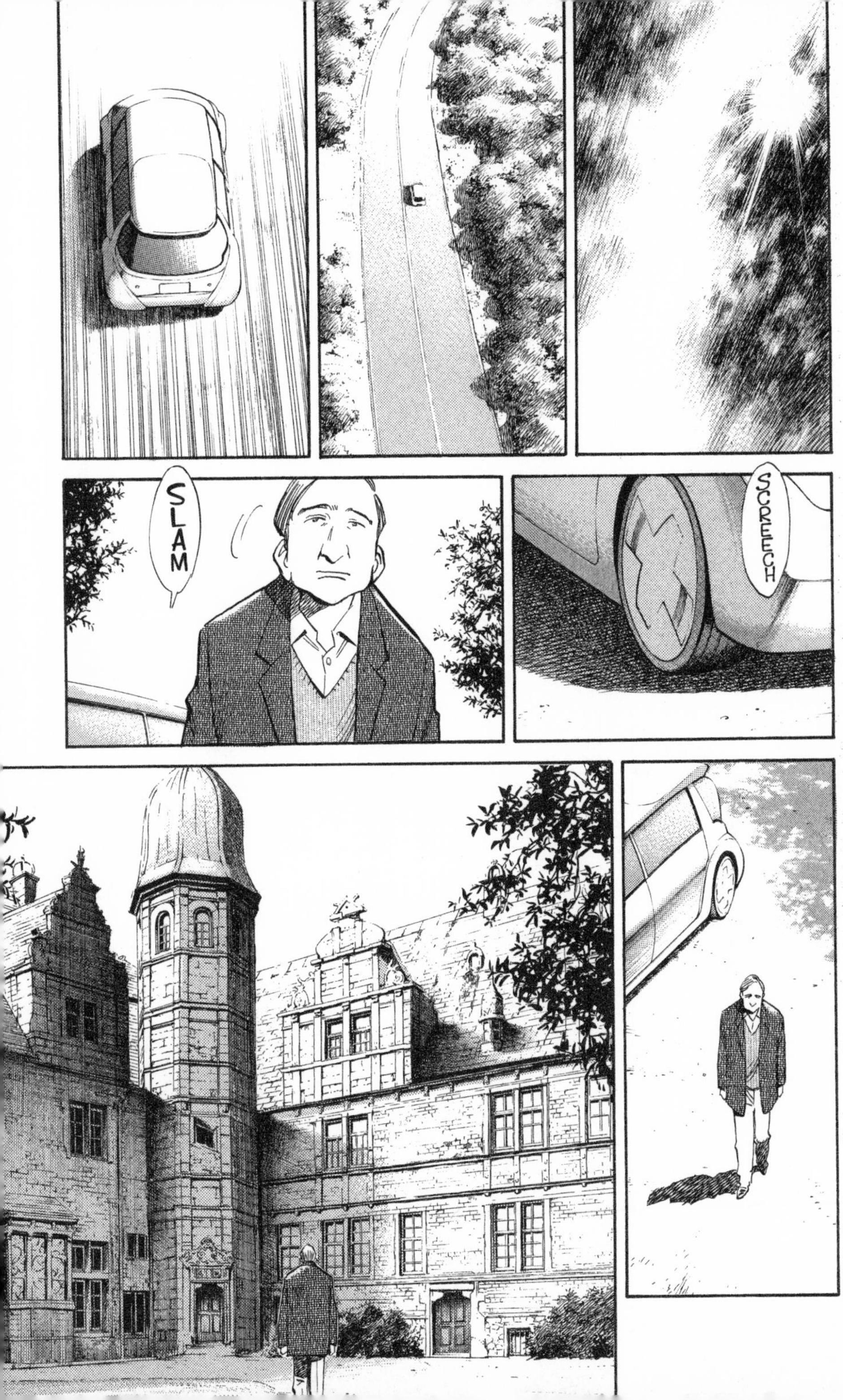
SCREECH
SLAM

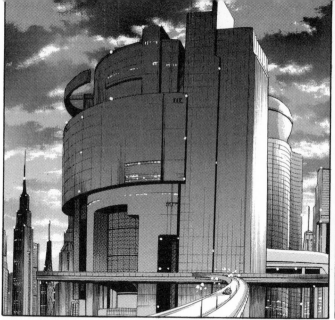

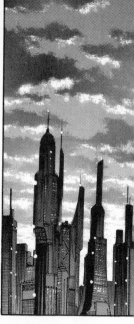

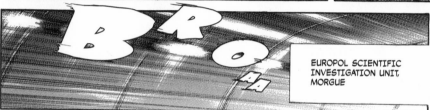

EUROPOL SCIENTIFIC INVESTIGATION UNIT, MORGUE
BROAA
OPEN YOUR EYES FOR AN IRIS SCAN...
THANK YOU, THAT'LL DO...
LET'S SEE... CORPSE NUMBER 902886 SHOULD BE OVER HERE SOME-WHERE...

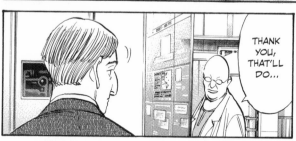

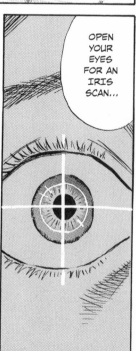

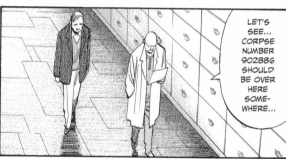

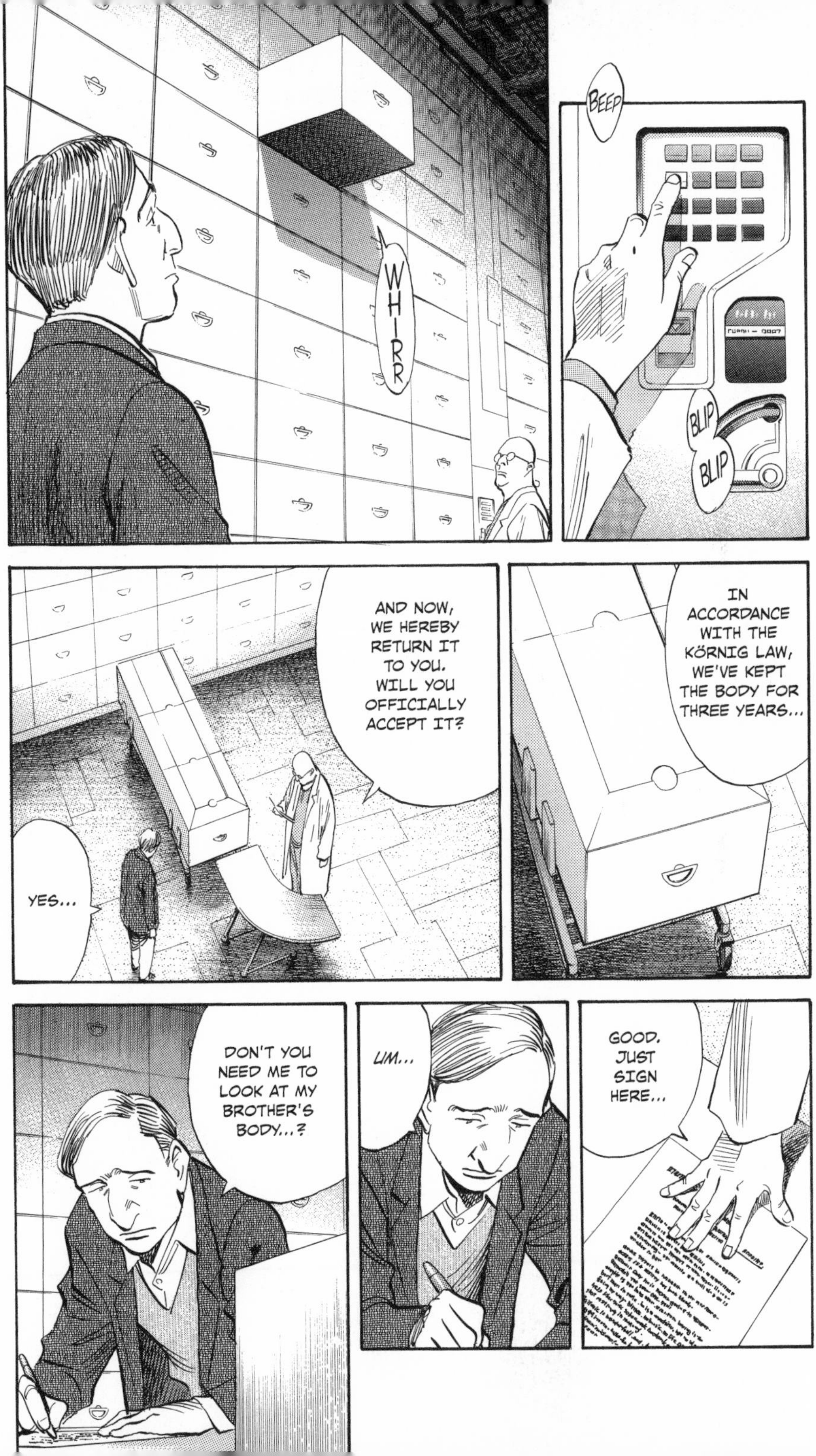
BEEP
BLIP
BLIP
WHIRR
IN ACCORDANCE WITH THE KÖRNIG LAW, WE'VE KEPT THE BODY FOR THREE YEARS...
AND NOW, WE HEREBY RETURN IT TO YOU. WILL YOU OFFICIALLY ACCEPT IT?
YES...
GOOD. JUST SIGN HERE...
UM...
DON'T YOU NEED ME TO LOOK AT MY BROTHER'S BODY...?

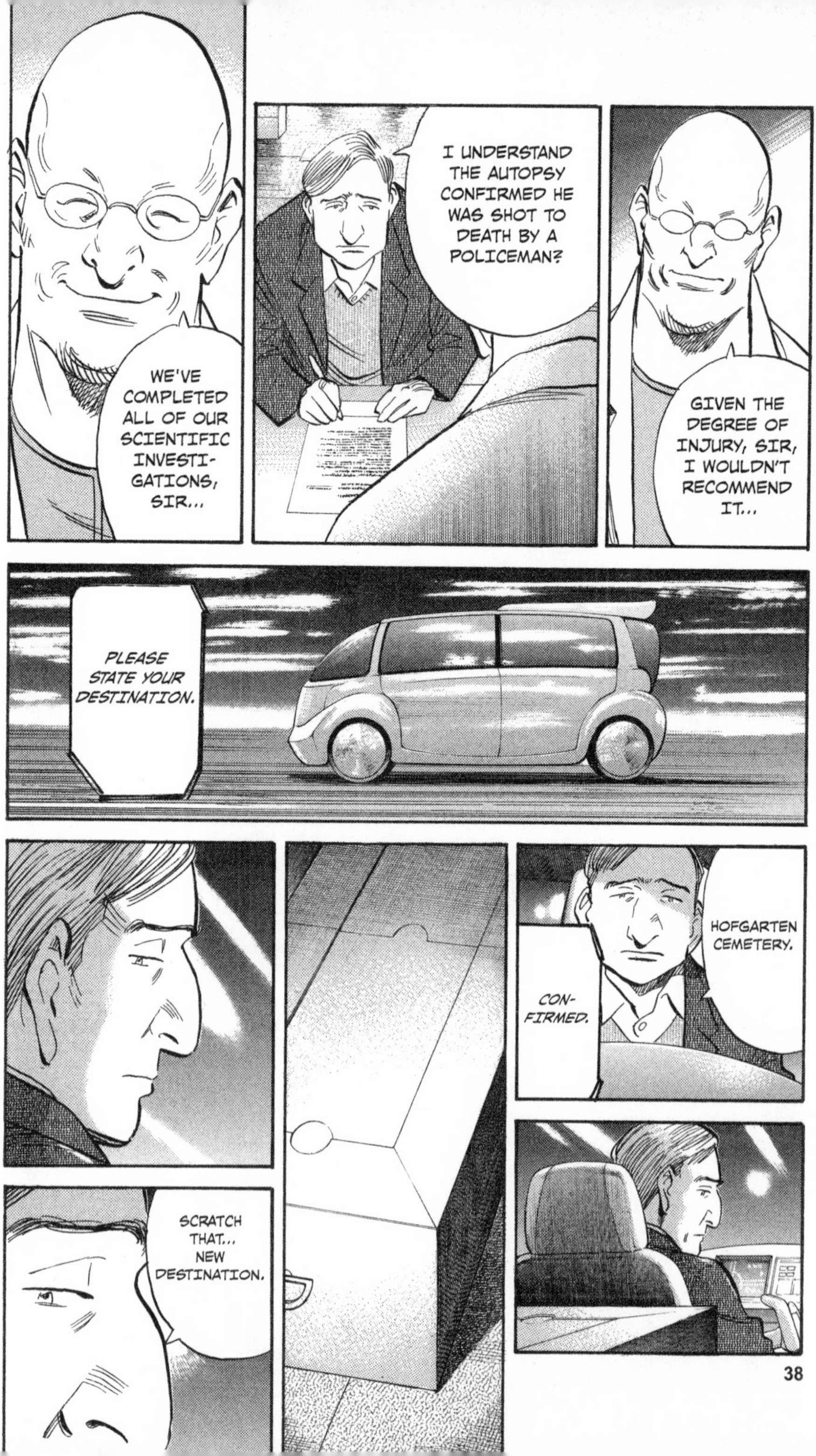
GIVEN THE DEGREE OF INJURY, SIR, I WOULDN'T RECOMMEND IT...
I UNDERSTAND THE AUTOPSY CONFIRMED HE WAS SHOT TO DEATH BY A POLICEMAN?
WE'VE COMPLETED ALL OF OUR SCIENTIFIC INVESTI-GATIONS, SIR...
PLEASE STATE YOUR DESTINATION.
HOFGARTEN CEMETERY.
CON-FIRMED.
SCRATCH THAT... NEW DESTINATION.

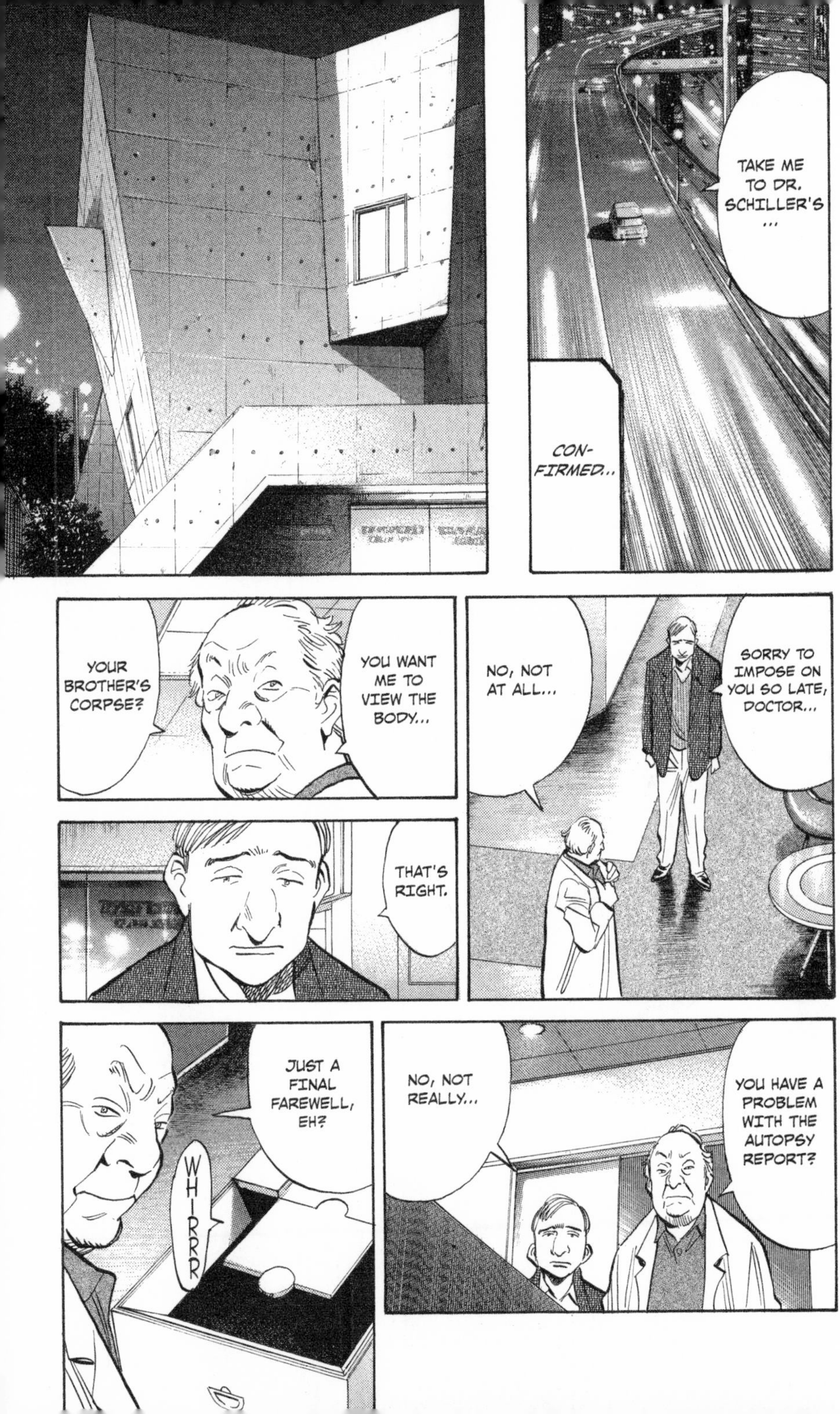
TAKE ME TO DR. SCHILLER'S ...
CON-FIRMED...
SORRY TO IMPOSE ON YOU SO LATE, DOCTOR...
NO, NOT AT ALL...
YOU WANT ME TO VIEW THE BODY...
YOUR BROTHER'S CORPSE?
THAT'S RIGHT.
YOU HAVE A PROBLEM WITH THE AUTOPSY REPORT?
NO, NOT REALLY...
JUST A FINAL FAREWELL, EH?
WHIRRR

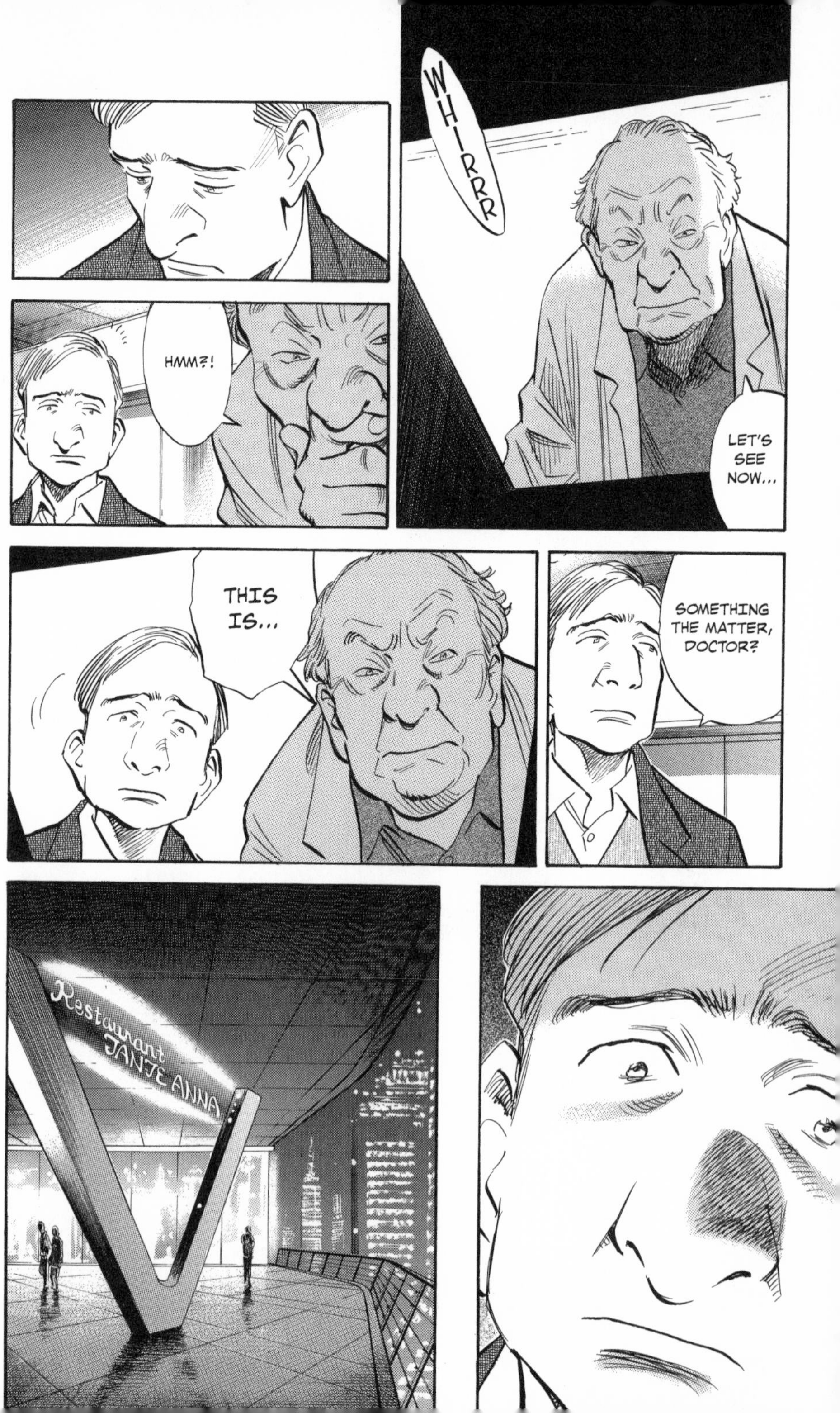
WHIRRR
LET'S SEE NOW...
HMM?!
SOMETHING THE MATTER, DOCTOR?
THIS IS...
Restaurant
TANTE ANNA

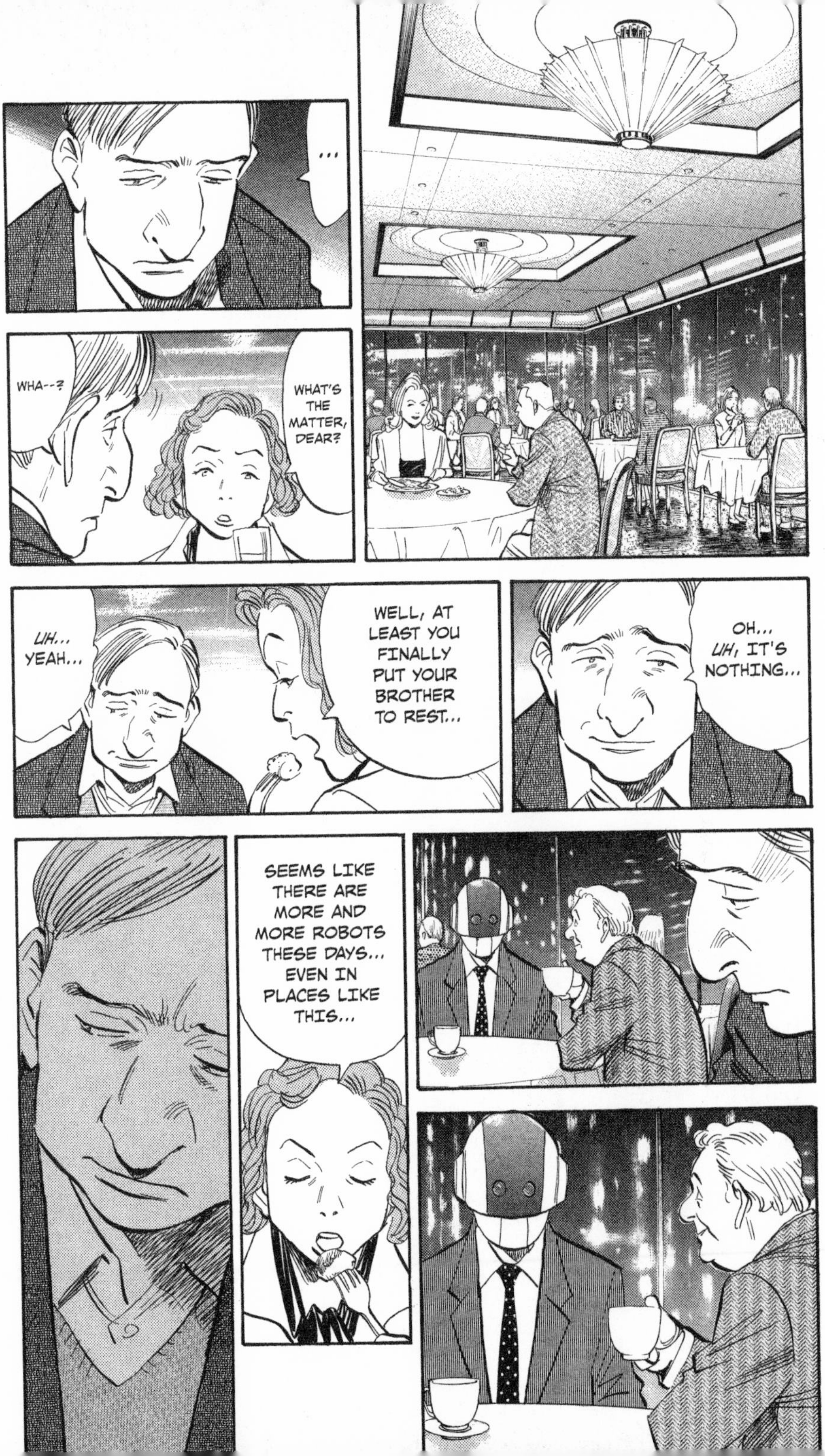
...
WHAT'S THE MATTER, DEAR?
WHA--?
OH... UH, IT'S NOTHING...
WELL, AT LEAST YOU FINALLY PUT YOUR BROTHER TO REST...
UH... YEAH...
SEEMS LIKE THERE ARE MORE AND MORE ROBOTS THESE DAYS... EVEN IN PLACES LIKE THIS...

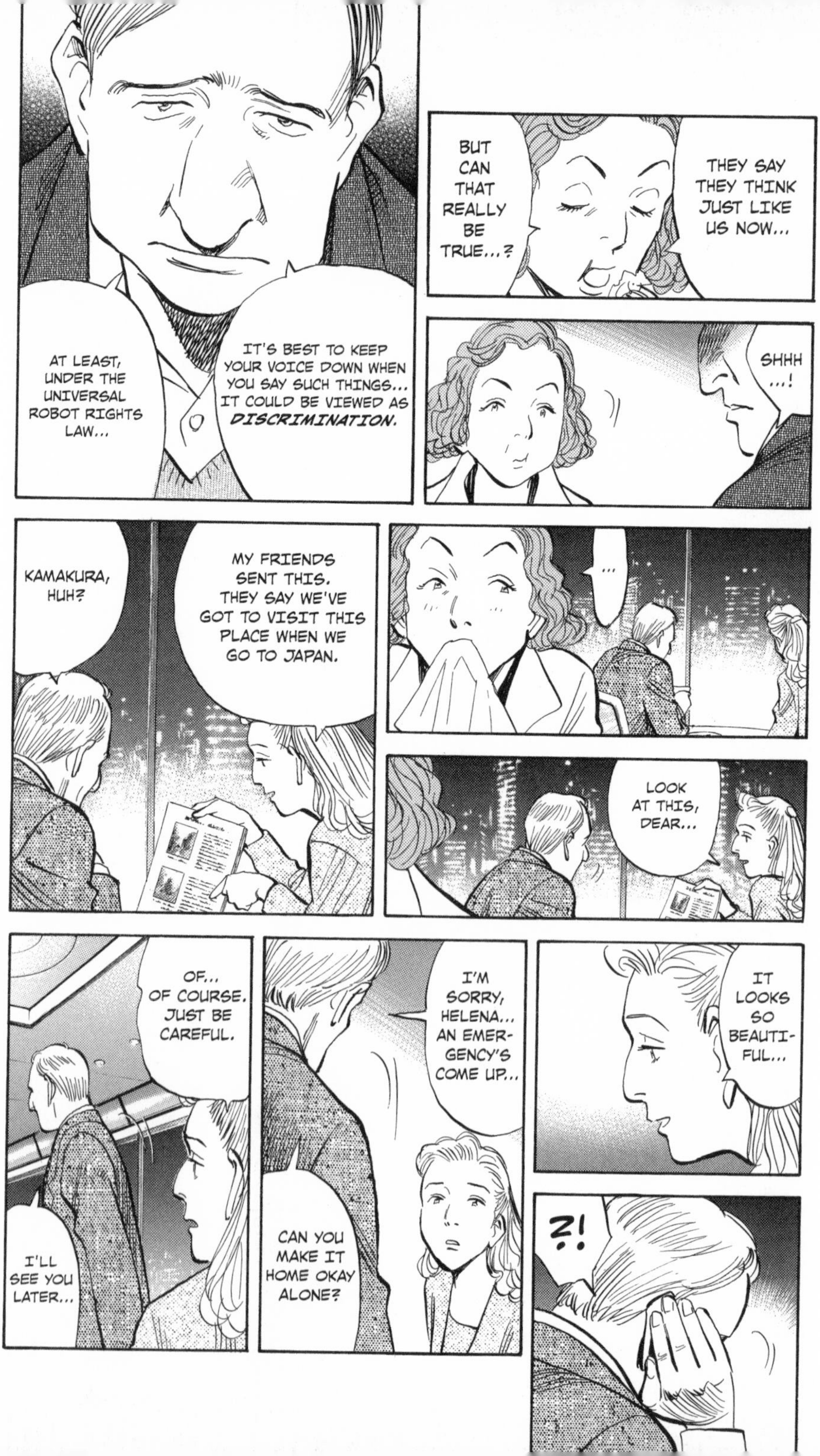
THEY SAY THEY THINK JUST LIKE US NOW...
BUT CAN THAT REALLY BE TRUE...?
SHHH ...!
IT'S BEST TO KEEP YOUR VOICE DOWN WHEN YOU SAY SUCH THINGS... IT COULD BE VIEWED AS *DISCRIMINATION*.
AT LEAST, UNDER THE UNIVERSAL ROBOT RIGHTS LAW...
...
LOOK AT THIS, DEAR...
MY FRIENDS SENT THIS. THEY SAY WE'VE GOT TO VISIT THIS PLACE WHEN WE GO TO JAPAN.
KAMAKURA, HUH?
IT LOOKS SO BEAUTI-FUL...
?!
I'M SORRY, HELENA... AN EMER-GENCY'S COME UP...
CAN YOU MAKE IT HOME OKAY ALONE?
OF... OF COURSE. JUST BE CAREFUL.
I'LL SEE YOU LATER...

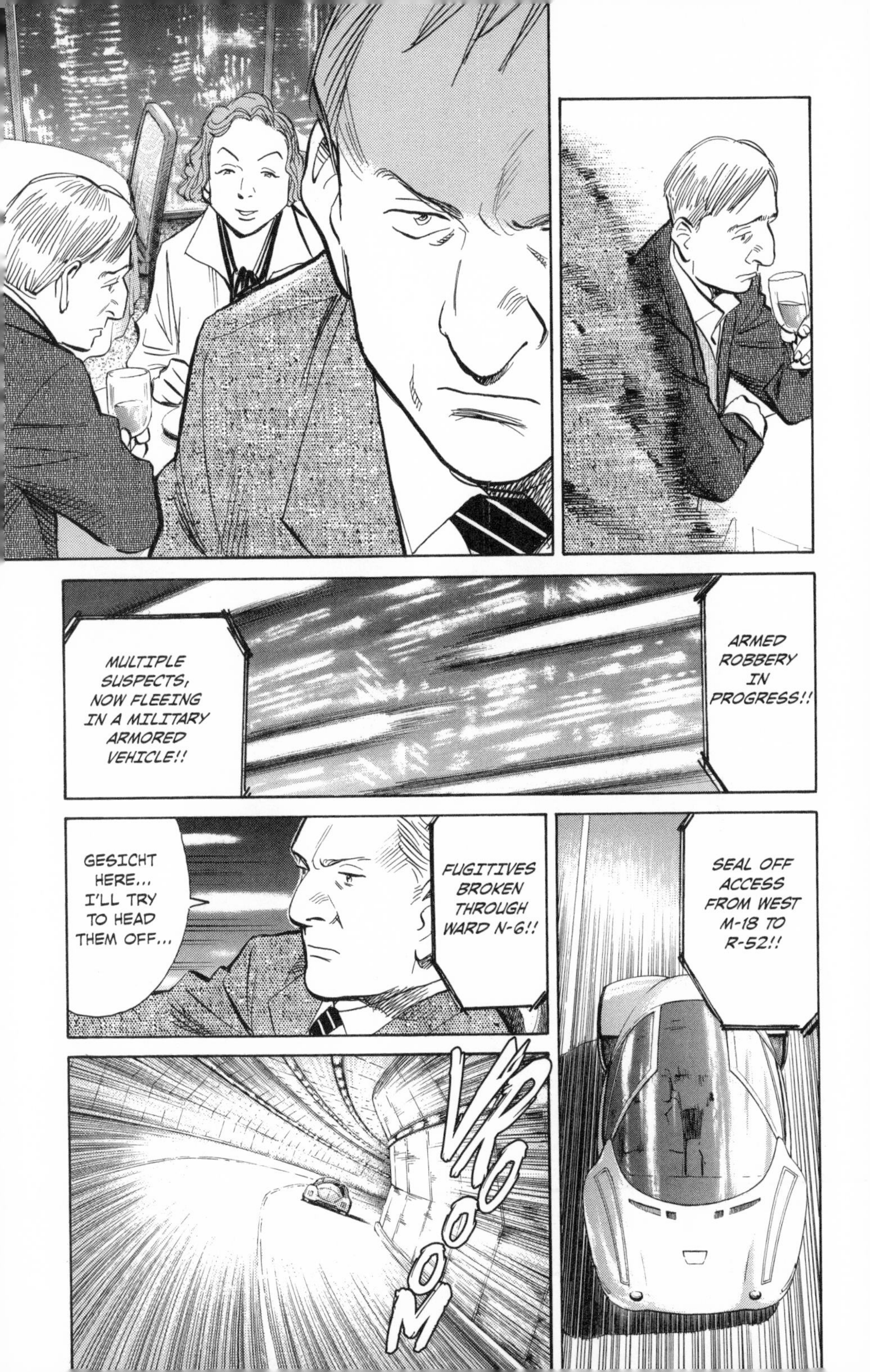
ARMED ROBBERY IN PROGRESS!!
MULTIPLE SUSPECTS, NOW FLEEING IN A MILITARY ARMORED VEHICLE!!
SEAL OFF ACCESS FROM WEST M-18 TO R-52!!
FUGITIVES BROKEN THROUGH WARD N-6!!
GESICHT HERE... I'LL TRY TO HEAD THEM OFF...
VROOOOM

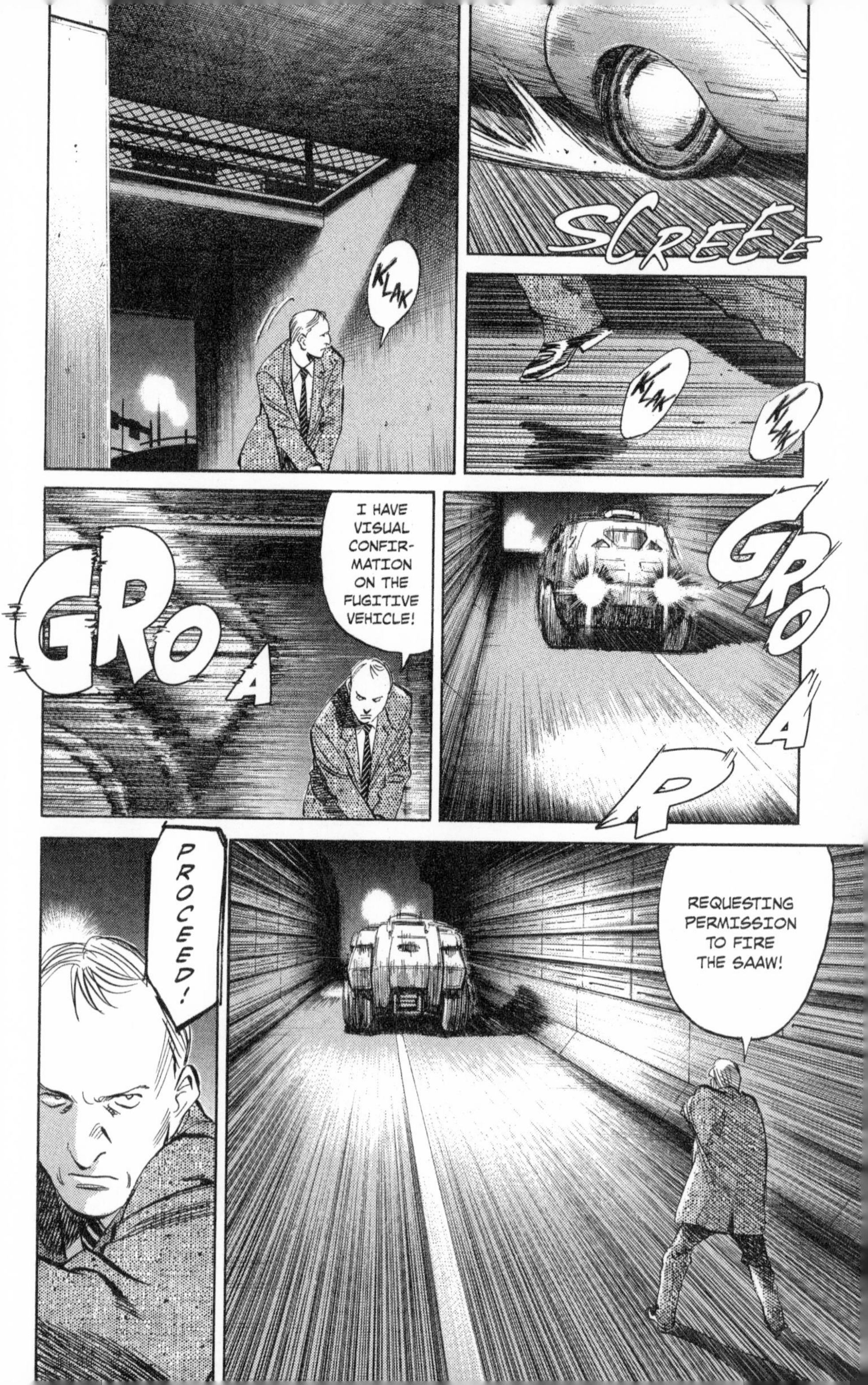
SCREEEE
KLAK
KLAK
KLAK
GROAR
I HAVE VISUAL CONFIRMATION ON THE FUGITIVE VEHICLE!
GROA
REQUESTING PERMISSION TO FIRE THE SAAW!
PROCEED!

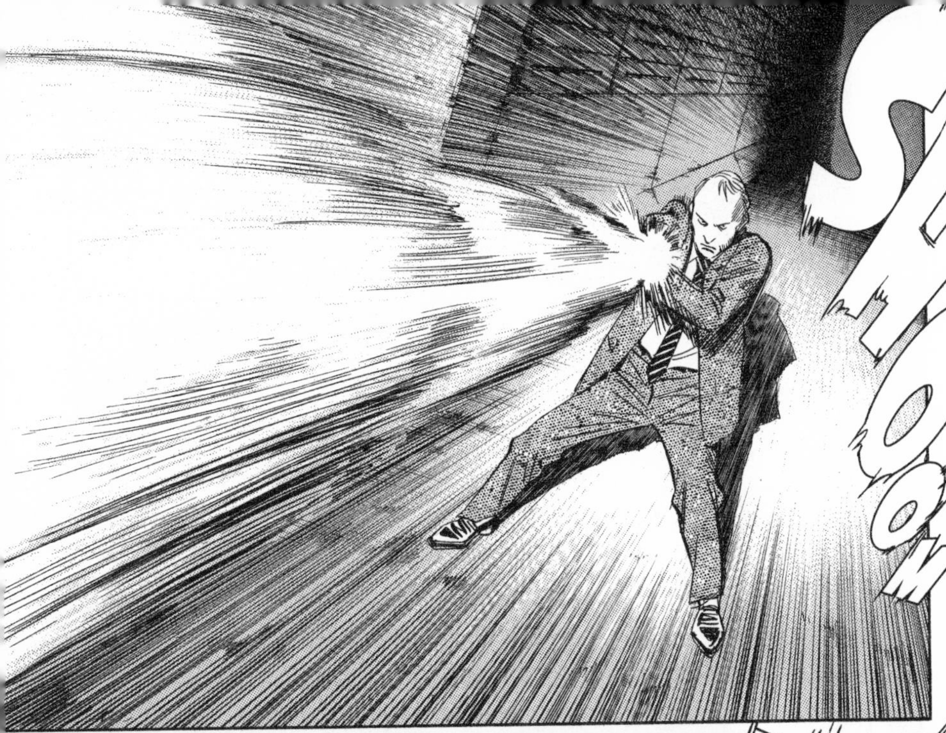
SHOOOM
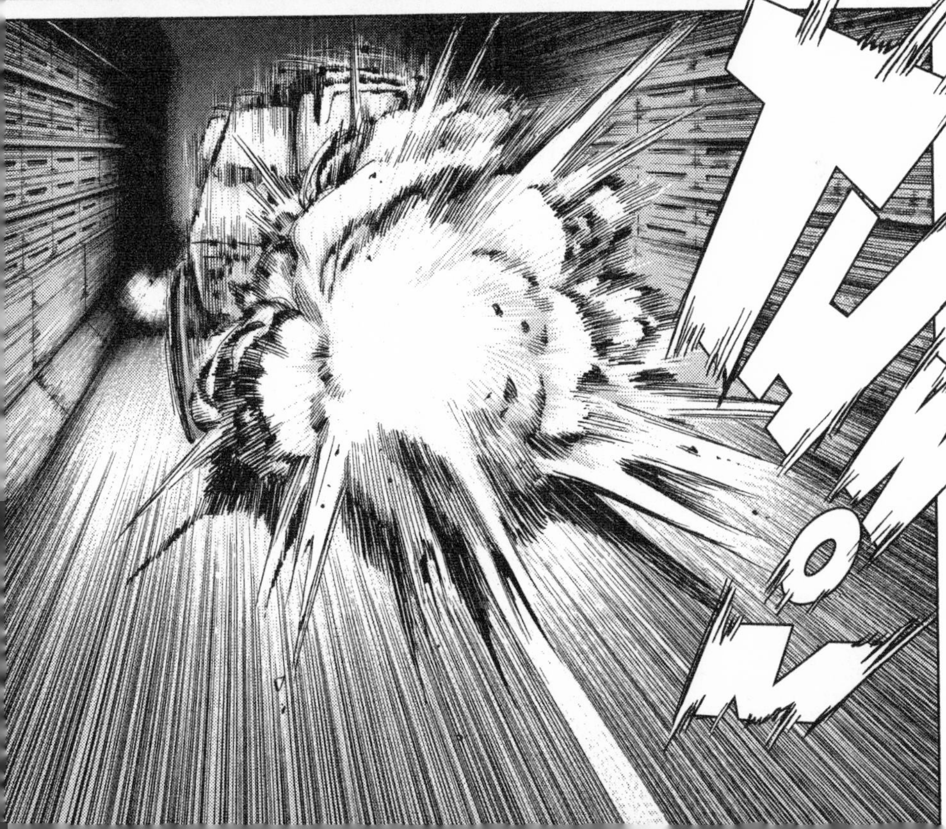
THOOM

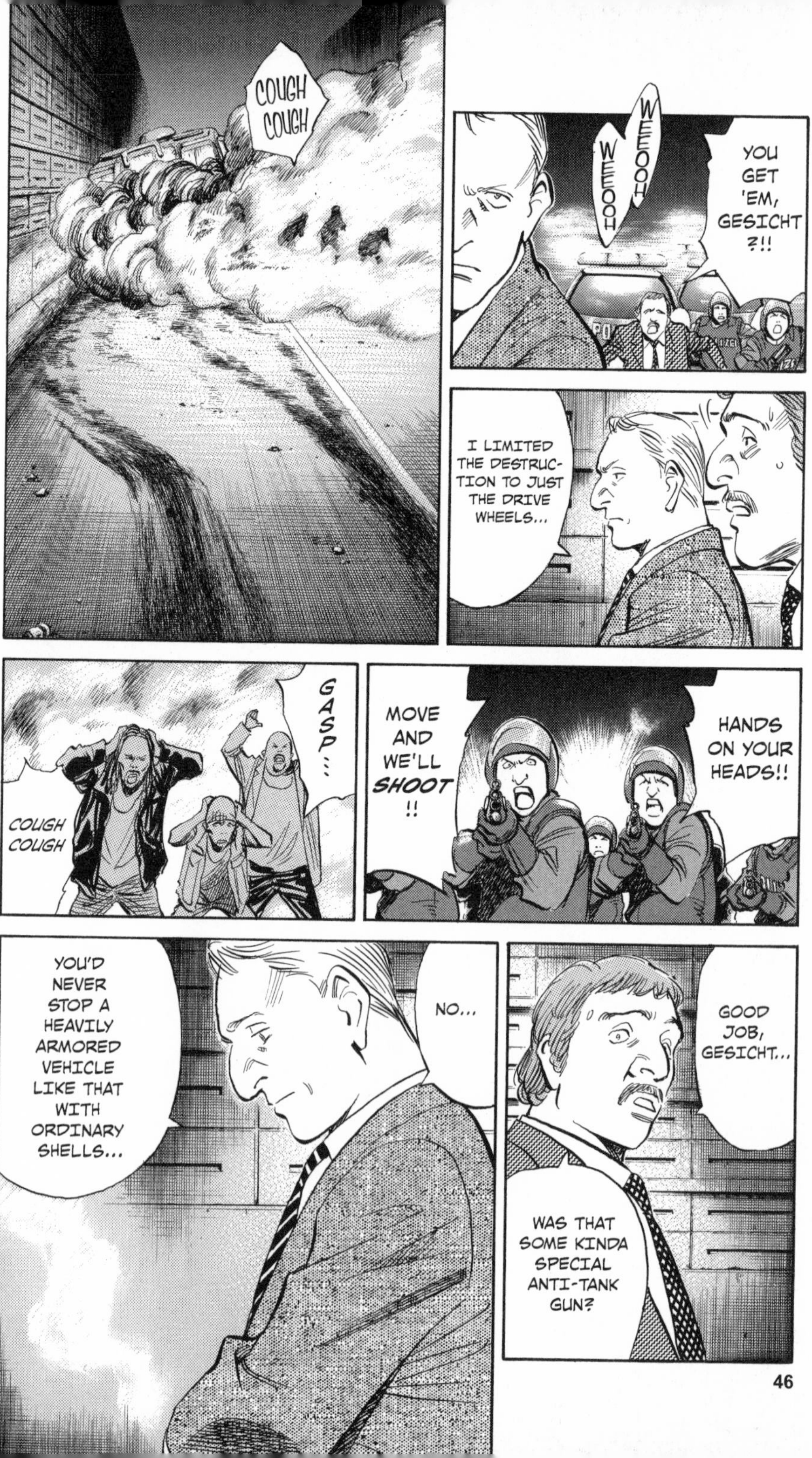
YOU GET 'EM, GESICHT?!!
WEEOOH
WEEOOH
I LIMITED THE DESTRUCTION TO JUST THE DRIVE WHEELS...
COUGH COUGH
HANDS ON YOUR HEADS!!
MOVE AND WE'LL *SHOOT*!!
GASP...
COUGH COUGH
GOOD JOB, GESICHT...
WAS THAT SOME KINDA SPECIAL ANTI-TANK GUN?
NO...
YOU'D NEVER STOP A HEAVILY ARMORED VEHICLE LIKE THAT WITH ORDINARY SHELLS...

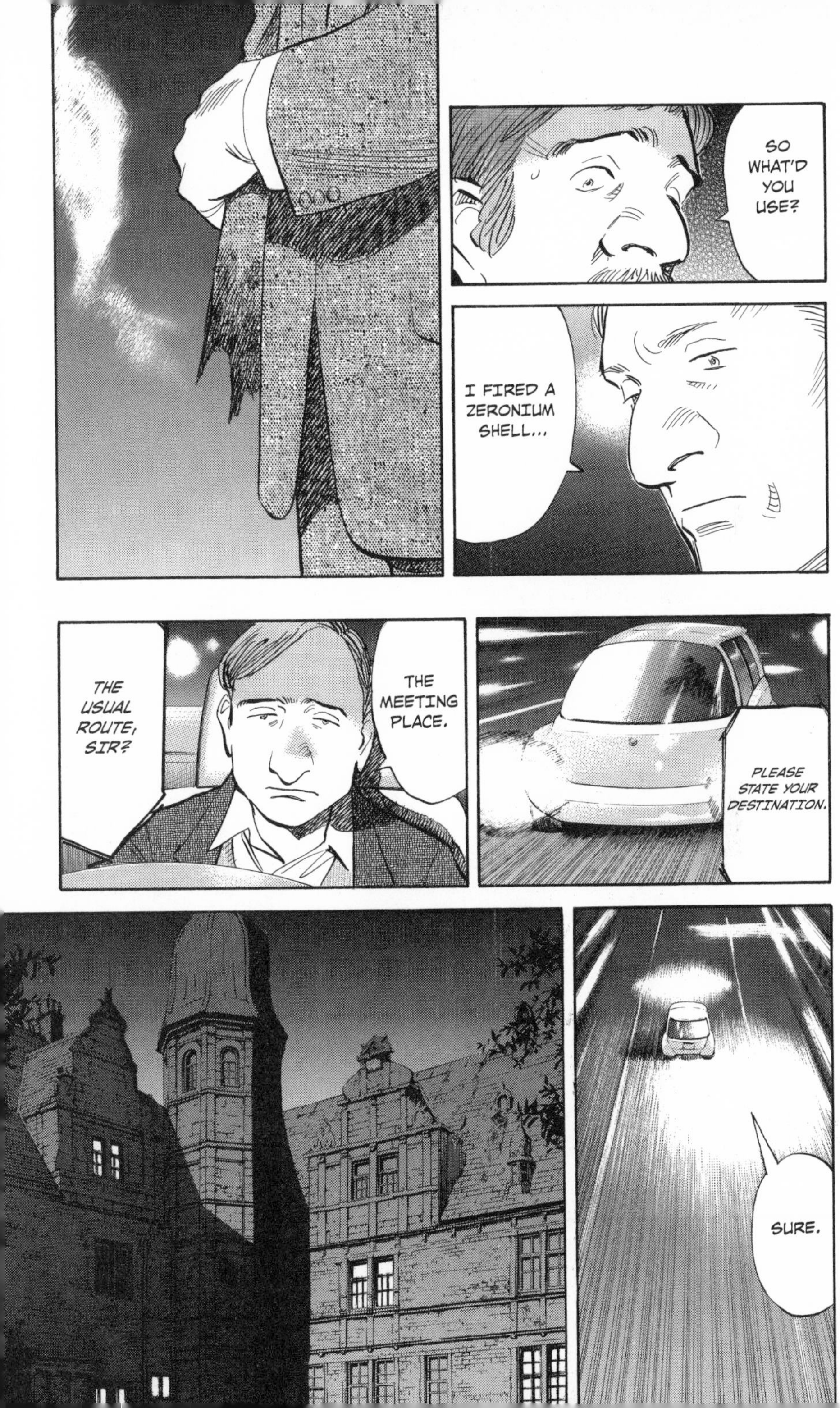
SO WHAT'D YOU USE?
I FIRED A ZERONIUM SHELL...
PLEASE STATE YOUR DESTINATION.
THE MEETING PLACE.
THE USUAL ROUTE, SIR?
SURE.

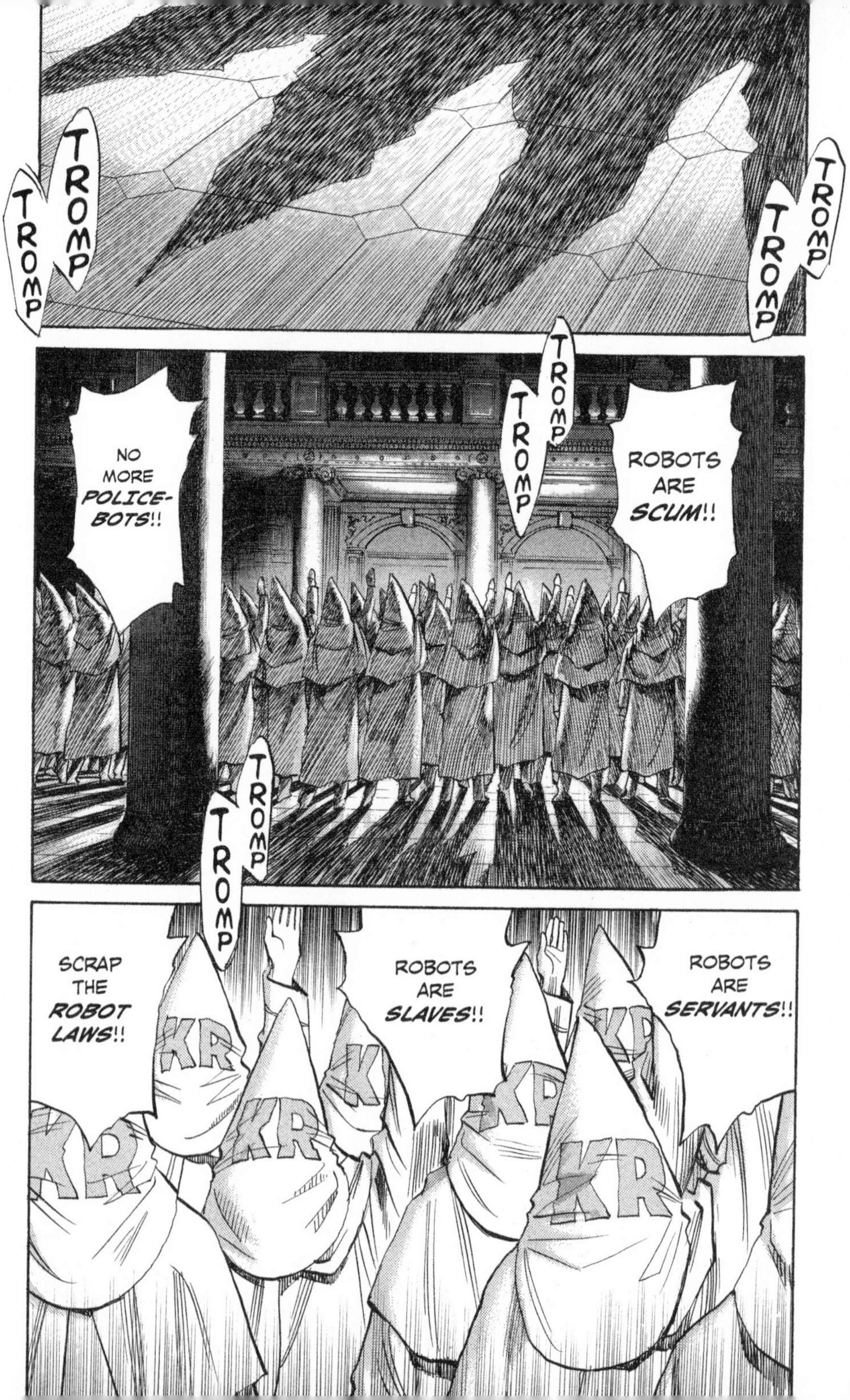
TROMP
TROMP
TROMP
TROMP
ROBOTS ARE SCUM!!
TROMP
TROMP
NO MORE POLICE-BOTS!!
TROMP
TROMP
ROBOTS ARE SERVANTS!!
ROBOTS ARE SLAVES!!
SCRAP THE ROBOT LAWS!!

DEATH TO MACHINES !!

DEATH TO MACHINES !!

DEATH TO MACHINES !!

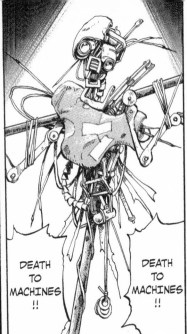

DEATH TO MACHINES !!

DEATH TO MACHINES !!

KR

TROMP

KR

KR

TROMP

DEATH TO MACHINES !!

KTNK

SIT DOWN...

TROMP

TROMP

TROMP

KR

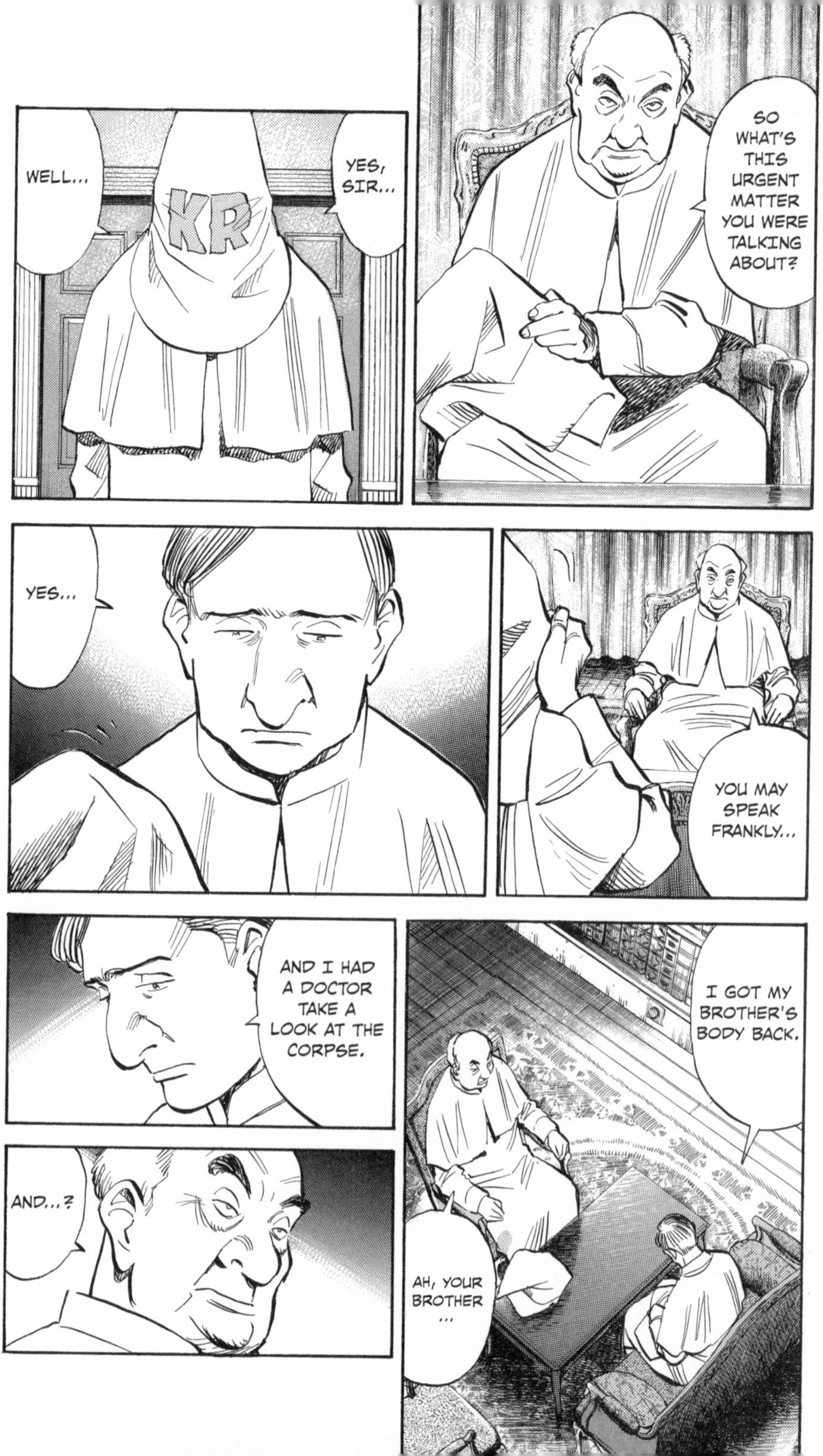
SO WHAT'S THIS URGENT MATTER YOU WERE TALKING ABOUT?
YES, SIR...
WELL...
YOU MAY SPEAK FRANKLY...
YES...
I GOT MY BROTHER'S BODY BACK.
AH, YOUR BROTHER ...
AND I HAD A DOCTOR TAKE A LOOK AT THE CORPSE.
AND...?

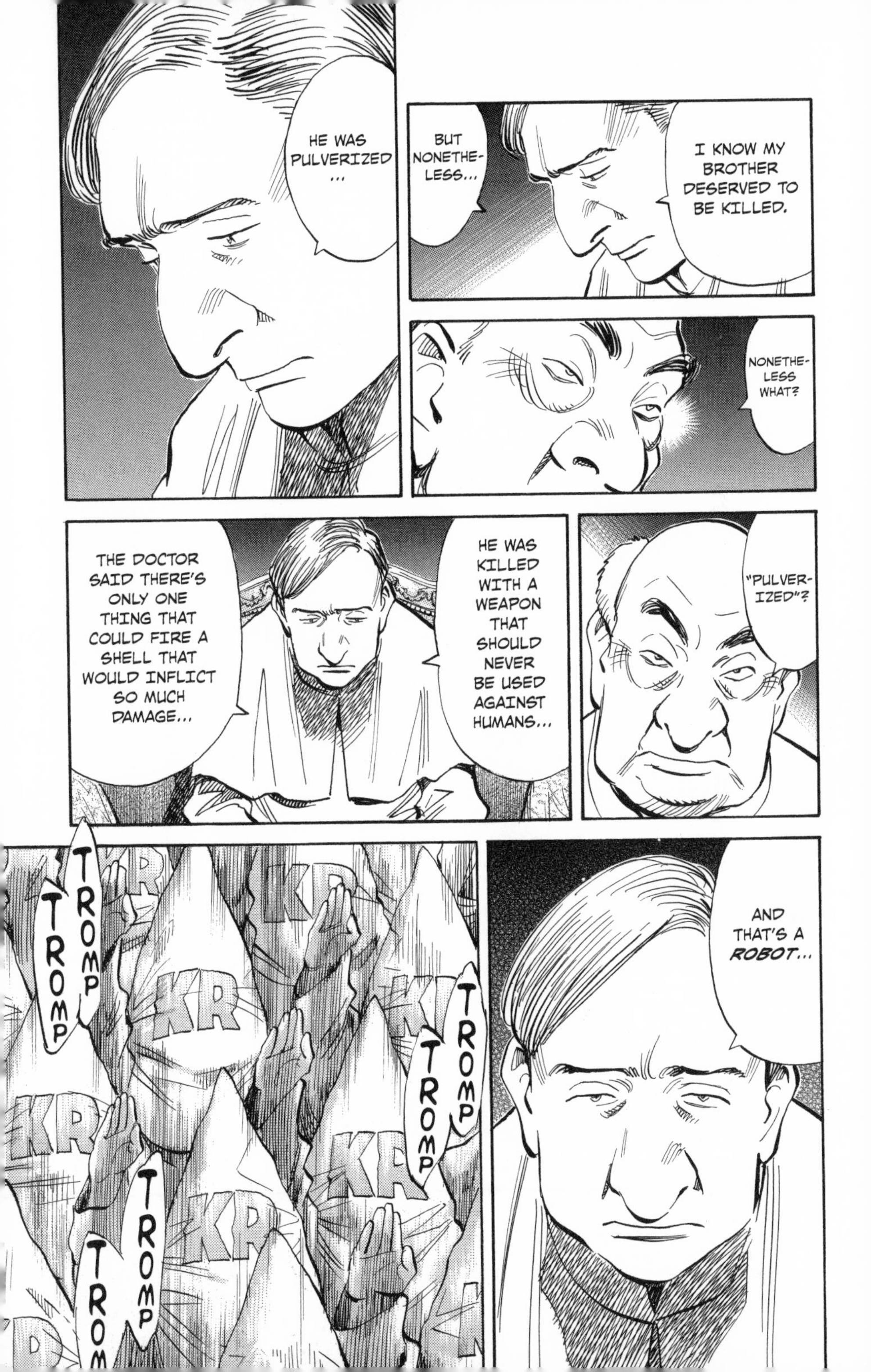
I KNOW MY BROTHER DESERVED TO BE KILLED.
BUT NONETHE-LESS...
NONETHE-LESS WHAT?
HE WAS PULVERIZED...
"PULVER-IZED"?
HE WAS KILLED WITH A WEAPON THAT SHOULD NEVER BE USED AGAINST HUMANS...
THE DOCTOR SAID THERE'S ONLY ONE THING THAT COULD FIRE A SHELL THAT WOULD INFLICT SO MUCH DAMAGE...
AND THAT'S A *ROBOT*...
TROMP
TROMP
TROMP
TROMP
TROMP
TROM
KR
KR
KR
KR
KR

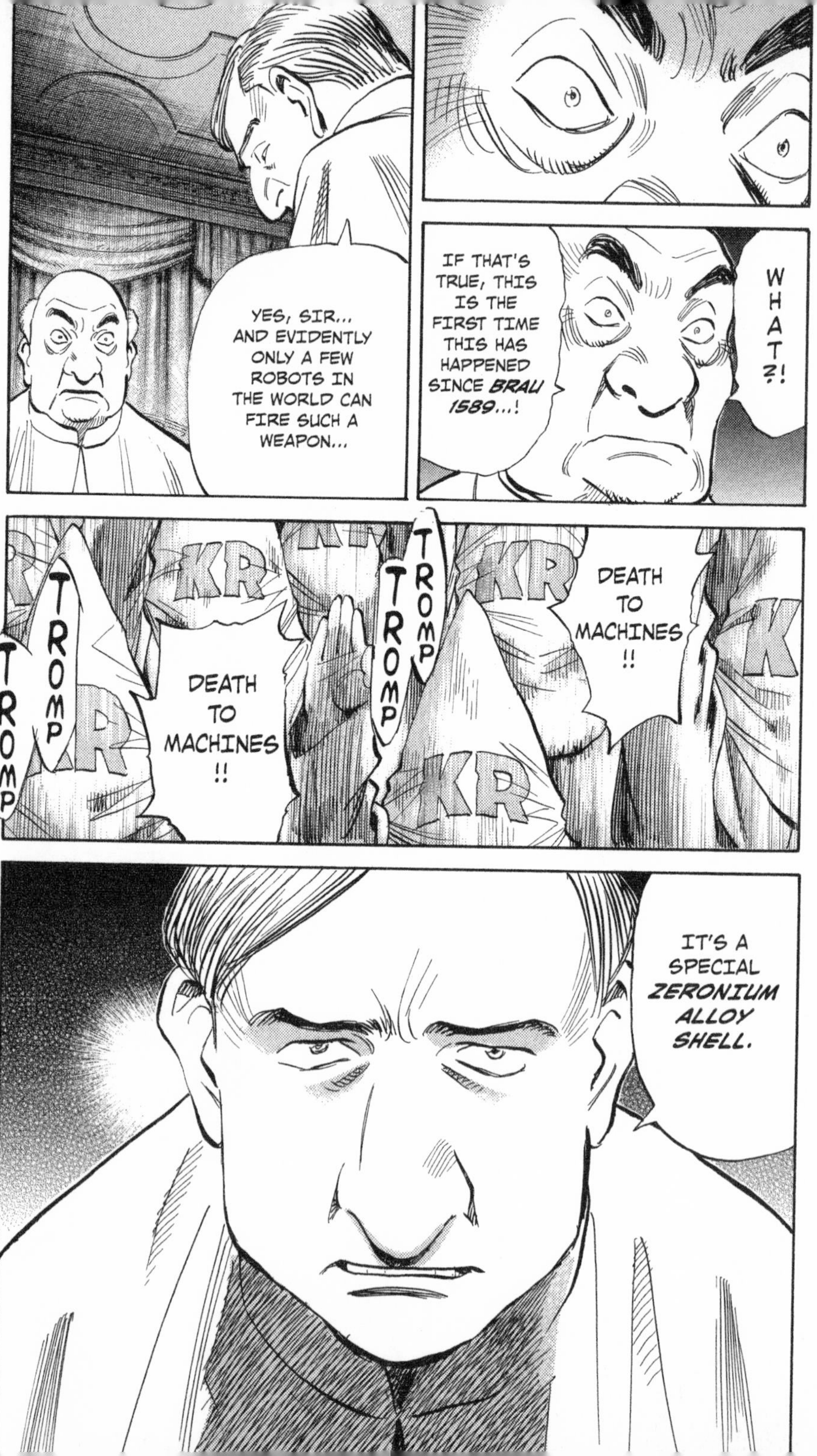
WHAT?!
IF THAT'S TRUE, THIS IS THE FIRST TIME THIS HAS HAPPENED SINCE *BRAU 1589*...!
YES, SIR... AND EVIDENTLY ONLY A FEW ROBOTS IN THE WORLD CAN FIRE SUCH A WEAPON...
KR
DEATH TO MACHINES!!
TROMP
TROMP
KR
KR
DEATH TO MACHINES!!
TROMP
TROMP
KR
IT'S A SPECIAL *ZERONIUM ALLOY SHELL.*

Act 18 ZERONIUM

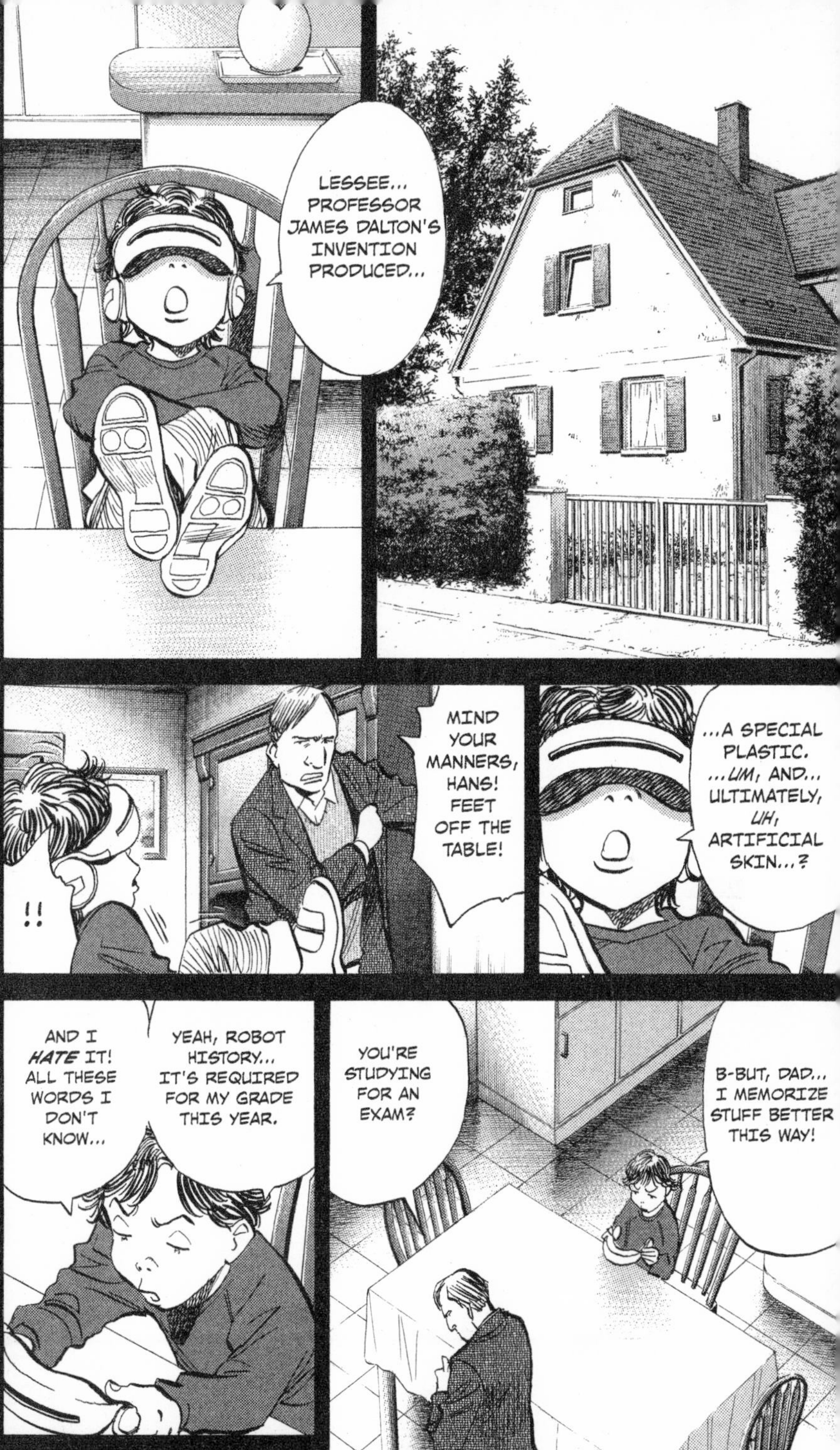

LESSEE... PROFESSOR JAMES DALTON'S INVENTION PRODUCED...
...A SPECIAL PLASTIC. ...UM, AND... ULTIMATELY, UH, ARTIFICIAL SKIN...?
MIND YOUR MANNERS, HANS! FEET OFF THE TABLE!
!!
B-BUT, DAD... I MEMORIZE STUFF BETTER THIS WAY!
YOU'RE STUDYING FOR AN EXAM?
YEAH, ROBOT HISTORY... IT'S REQUIRED FOR MY GRADE THIS YEAR.
AND I HATE IT! ALL THESE WORDS I DON'T KNOW...

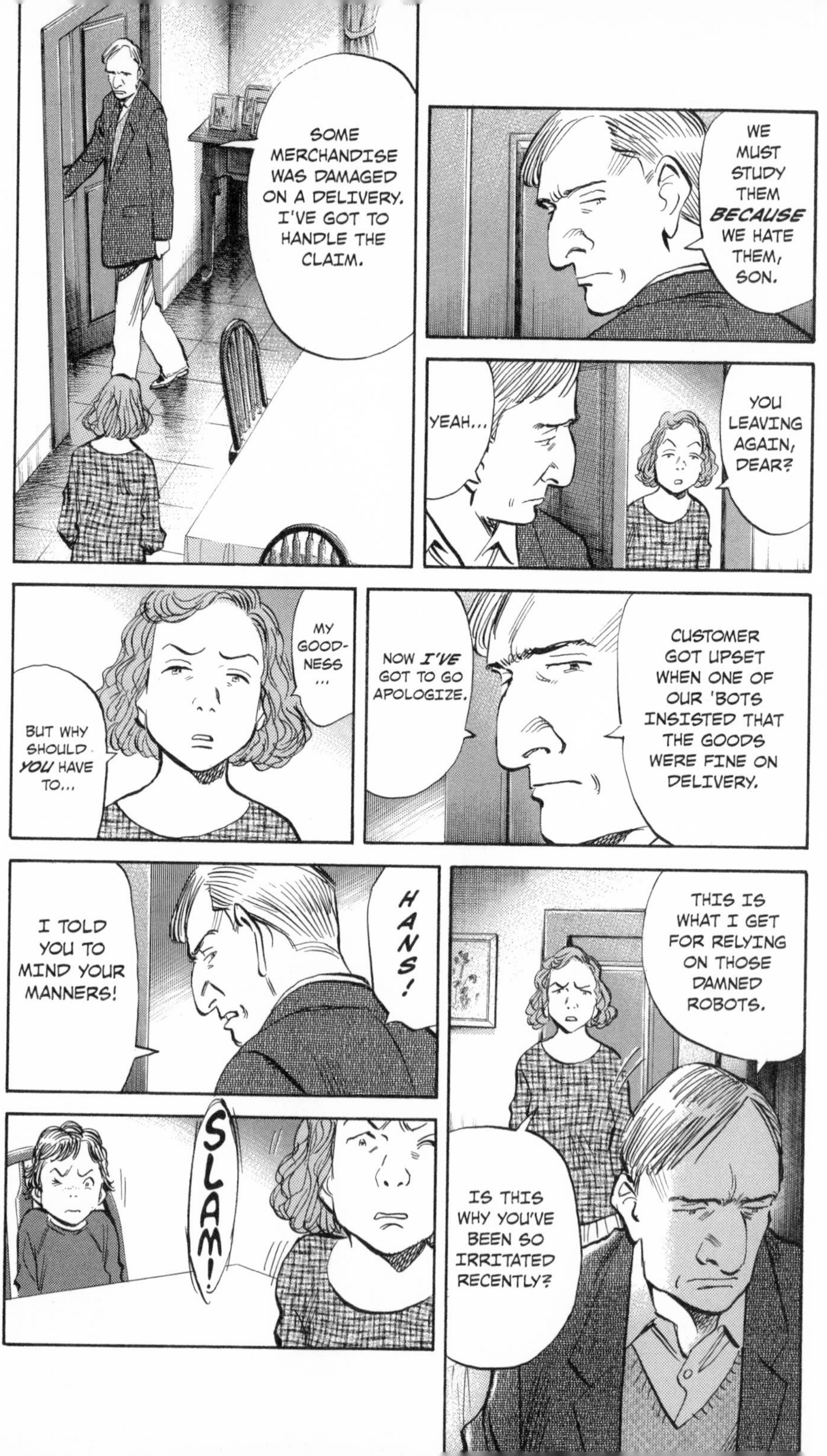
WE MUST STUDY THEM *BECAUSE* WE HATE THEM, SON.
YOU LEAVING AGAIN, DEAR?
YEAH...
SOME MERCHANDISE WAS DAMAGED ON A DELIVERY. I'VE GOT TO HANDLE THE CLAIM.
CUSTOMER GOT UPSET WHEN ONE OF OUR 'BOTS INSISTED THAT THE GOODS WERE FINE ON DELIVERY.
NOW *I'VE* GOT TO GO APOLOGIZE.
MY GOODNESS...
BUT WHY SHOULD *YOU* HAVE TO...
THIS IS WHAT I GET FOR RELYING ON THOSE DAMNED ROBOTS.
IS THIS WHY YOU'VE BEEN SO IRRITATED RECENTLY?
HANS!
I TOLD YOU TO MIND YOUR MANNERS!
SLAM!

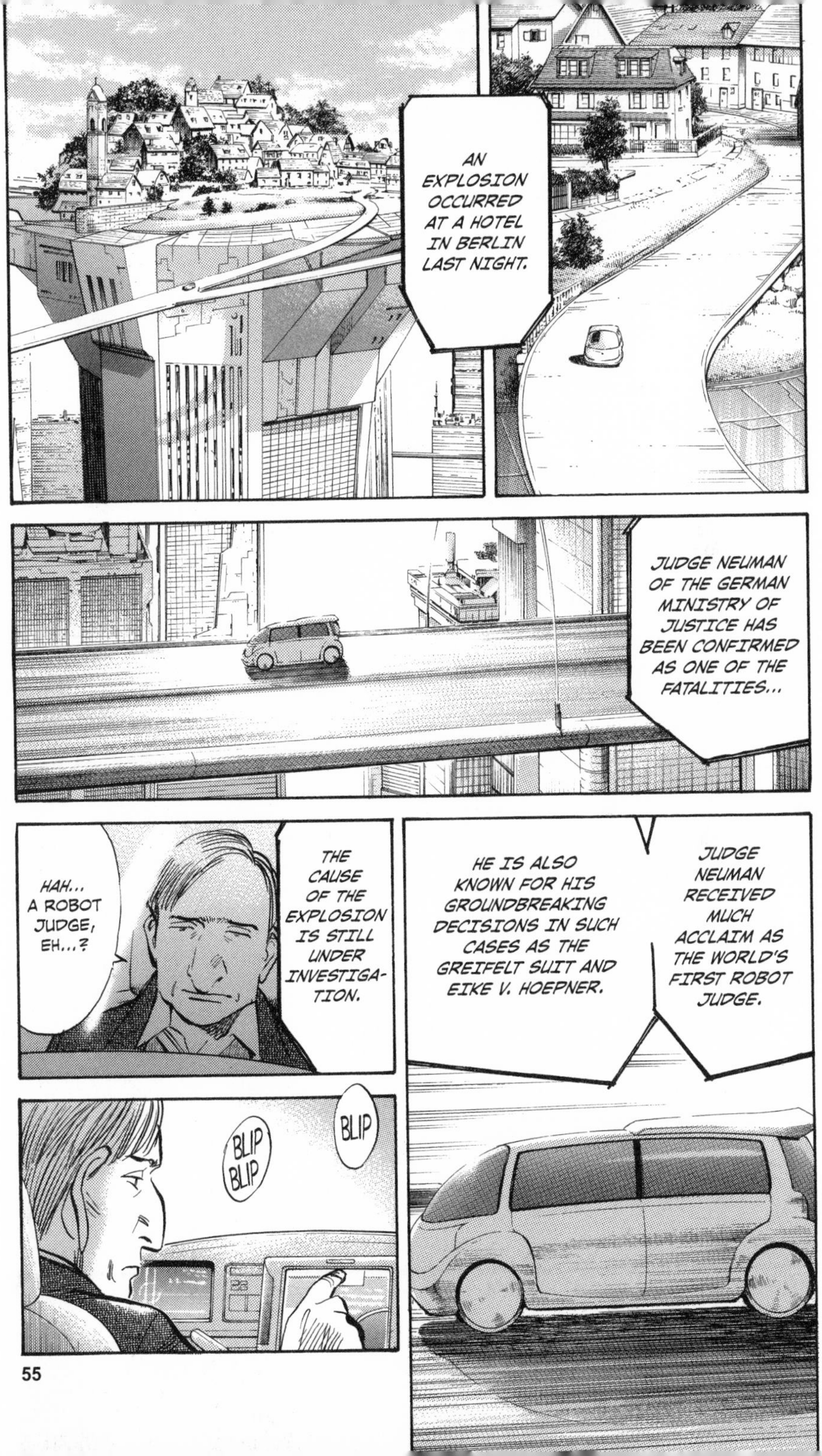
AN EXPLOSION OCCURRED AT A HOTEL IN BERLIN LAST NIGHT.
JUDGE NEUMAN OF THE GERMAN MINISTRY OF JUSTICE HAS BEEN CONFIRMED AS ONE OF THE FATALITIES...
JUDGE NEUMAN RECEIVED MUCH ACCLAIM AS THE WORLD'S FIRST ROBOT JUDGE.
HE IS ALSO KNOWN FOR HIS GROUNDBREAKING DECISIONS IN SUCH CASES AS THE GREIFELT SUIT AND EIKE V. HOEPNER.
THE CAUSE OF THE EXPLOSION IS STILL UNDER INVESTIGA- TION.
HAH... A ROBOT JUDGE, EH...?
BLIP
BLIP BLIP

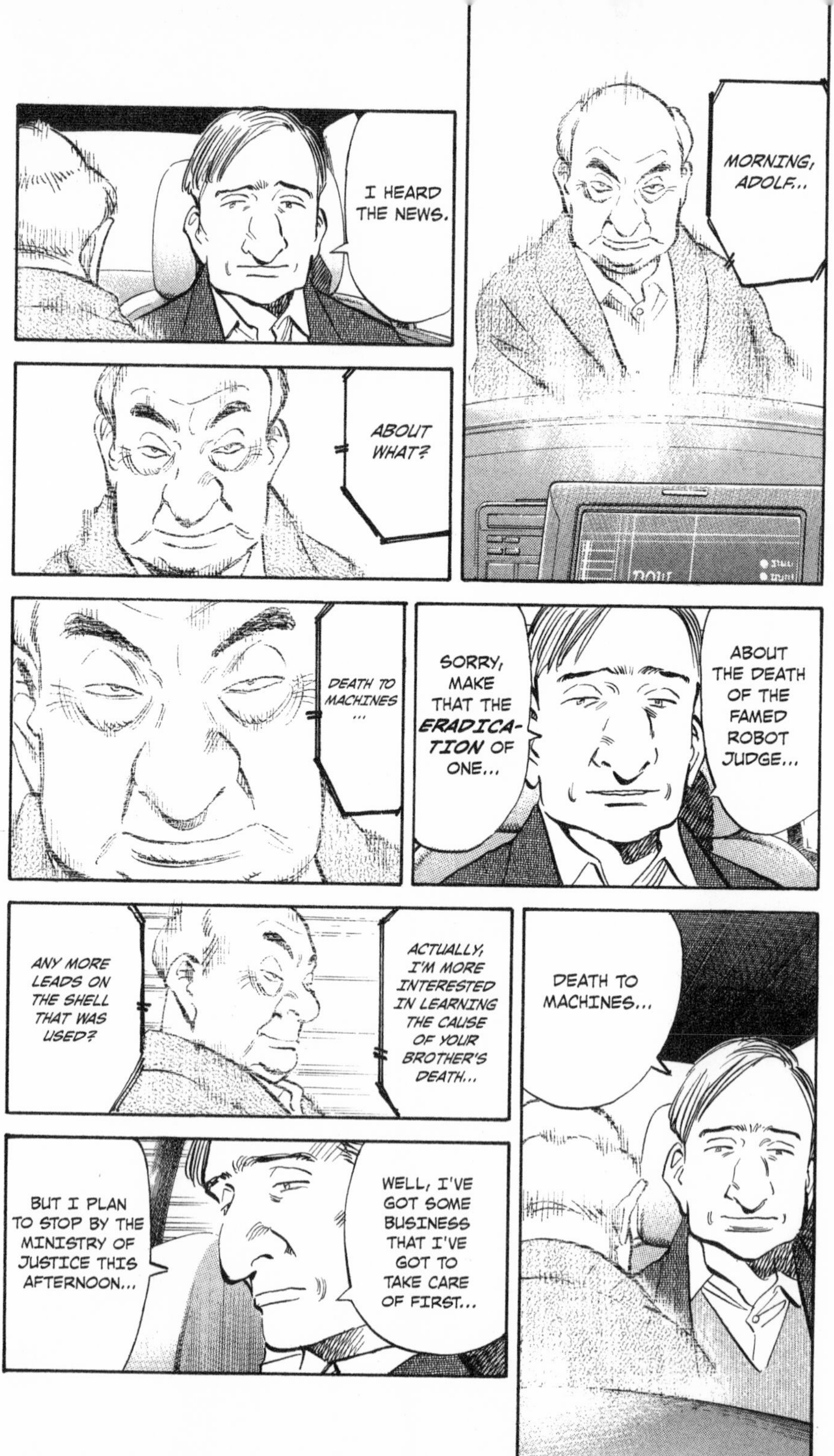
MORNING, ADOLF...
I HEARD THE NEWS.
ABOUT WHAT?
ABOUT THE DEATH OF THE FAMED ROBOT JUDGE...
SORRY, MAKE THAT THE ERADICATION OF ONE...
DEATH TO MACHINES...
DEATH TO MACHINES...
ACTUALLY, I'M MORE INTERESTED IN LEARNING THE CAUSE OF YOUR BROTHER'S DEATH...
ANY MORE LEADS ON THE SHELL THAT WAS USED?
WELL, I'VE GOT SOME BUSINESS THAT I'VE GOT TO TAKE CARE OF FIRST...
BUT I PLAN TO STOP BY THE MINISTRY OF JUSTICE THIS AFTERNOON...

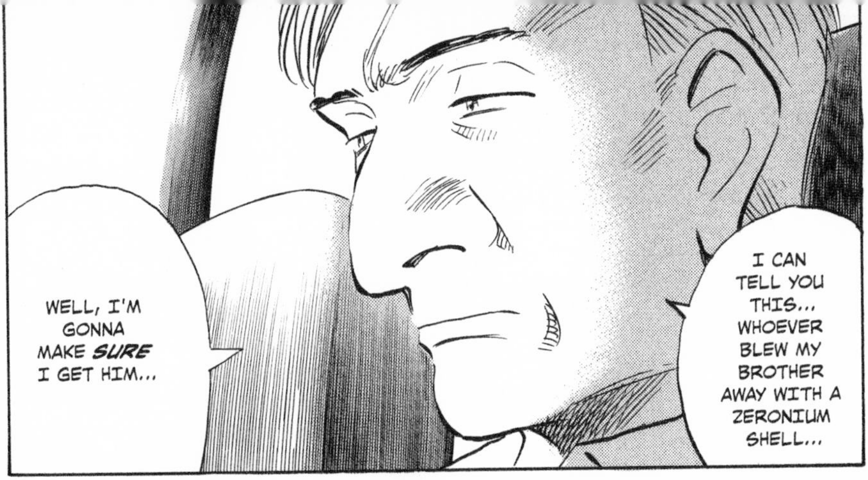
I CAN TELL YOU THIS... WHOEVER BLEW MY BROTHER AWAY WITH A ZERONIUM SHELL...
WELL, I'M GONNA MAKE SURE I GET HIM...

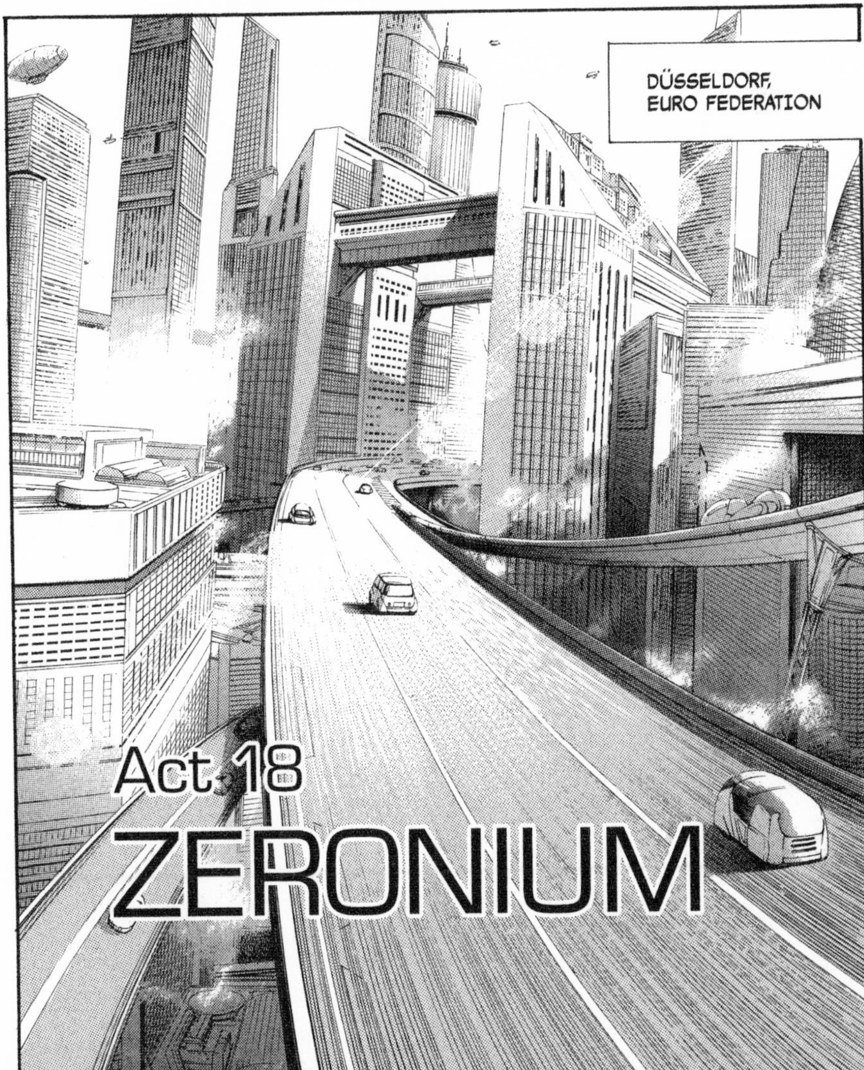
DÜSSELDORF, EURO FEDERATION

Act 18
ZERONIUM

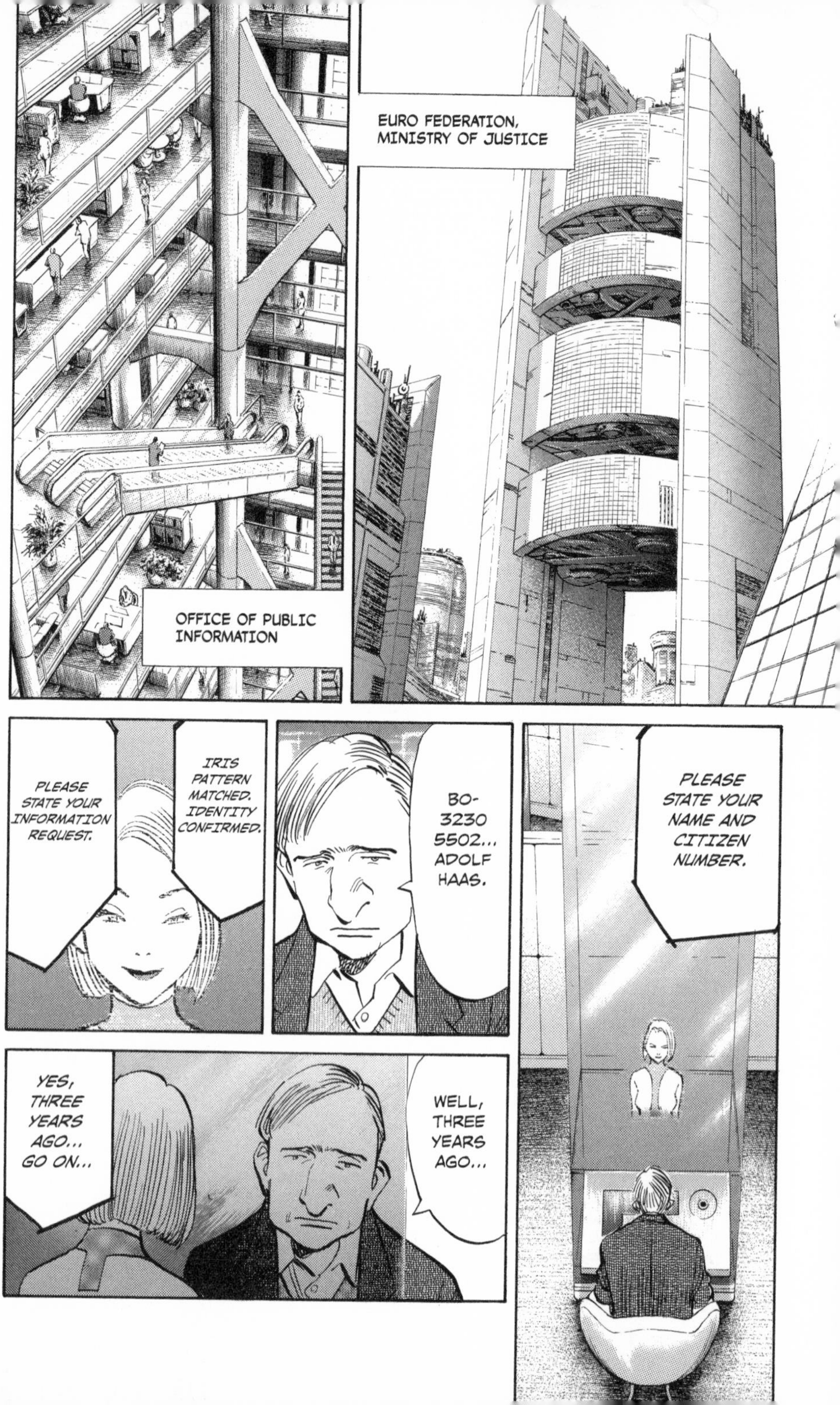
EURO FEDERATION, MINISTRY OF JUSTICE
OFFICE OF PUBLIC INFORMATION
PLEASE STATE YOUR NAME AND CITIZEN NUMBER.
BO-3230 5502... ADOLF HAAS.
IRIS PATTERN MATCHED. IDENTITY CONFIRMED.
PLEASE STATE YOUR INFORMATION REQUEST.
WELL, THREE YEARS AGO...
YES, THREE YEARS AGO... GO ON...

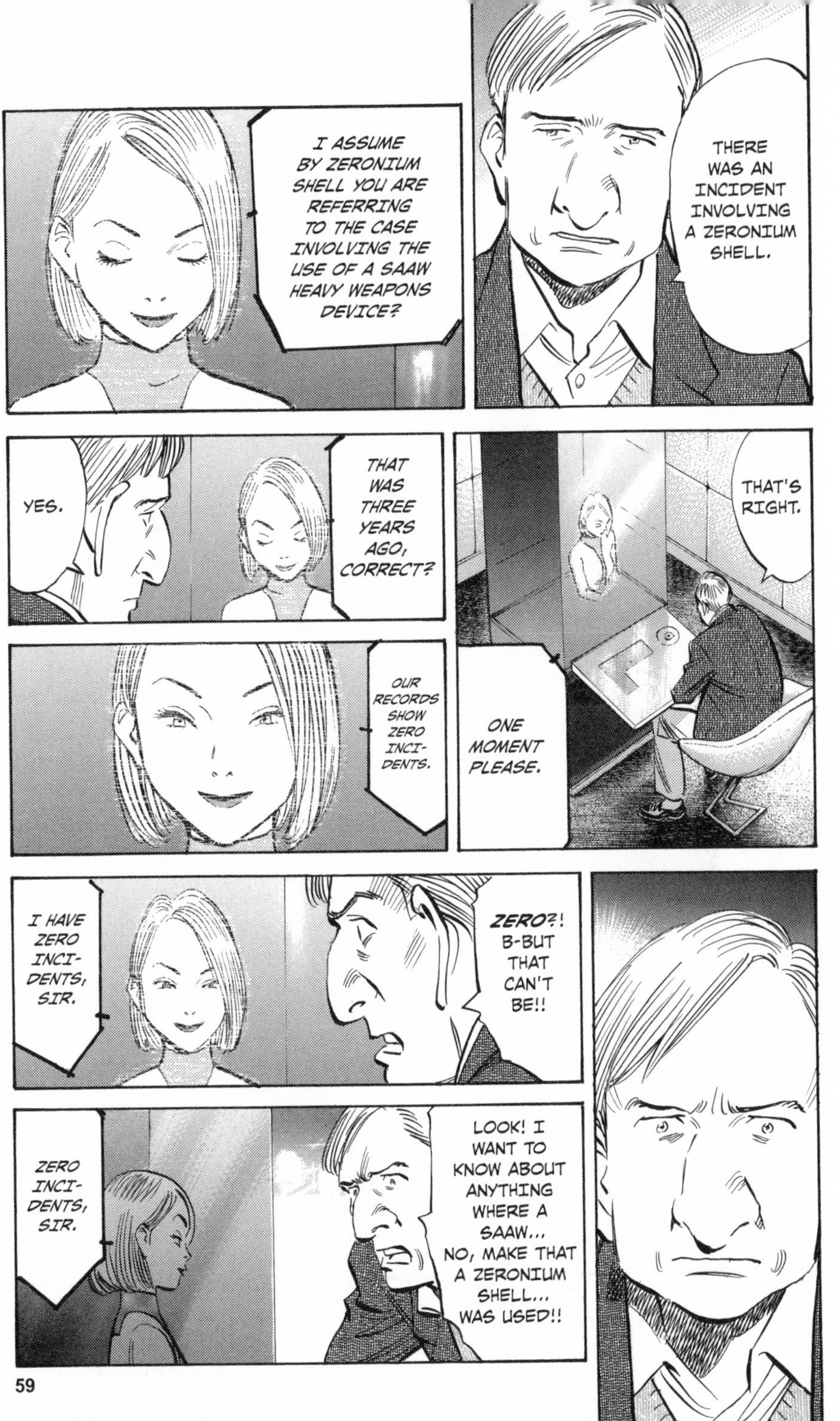
THERE WAS AN INCIDENT INVOLVING A ZERONIUM SHELL.
I ASSUME BY ZERONIUM SHELL YOU ARE REFERRING TO THE CASE INVOLVING THE USE OF A SAAW HEAVY WEAPONS DEVICE?
THAT'S RIGHT.
ONE MOMENT PLEASE.
YES.
THAT WAS THREE YEARS AGO, CORRECT?
OUR RECORDS SHOW ZERO INCIDENTS.
ZERO?! B-BUT THAT CAN'T BE!!
I HAVE ZERO INCIDENTS, SIR.
LOOK! I WANT TO KNOW ABOUT ANYTHING WHERE A SAAW... NO, MAKE THAT A ZERONIUM SHELL... WAS USED!!
ZERO INCIDENTS, SIR.

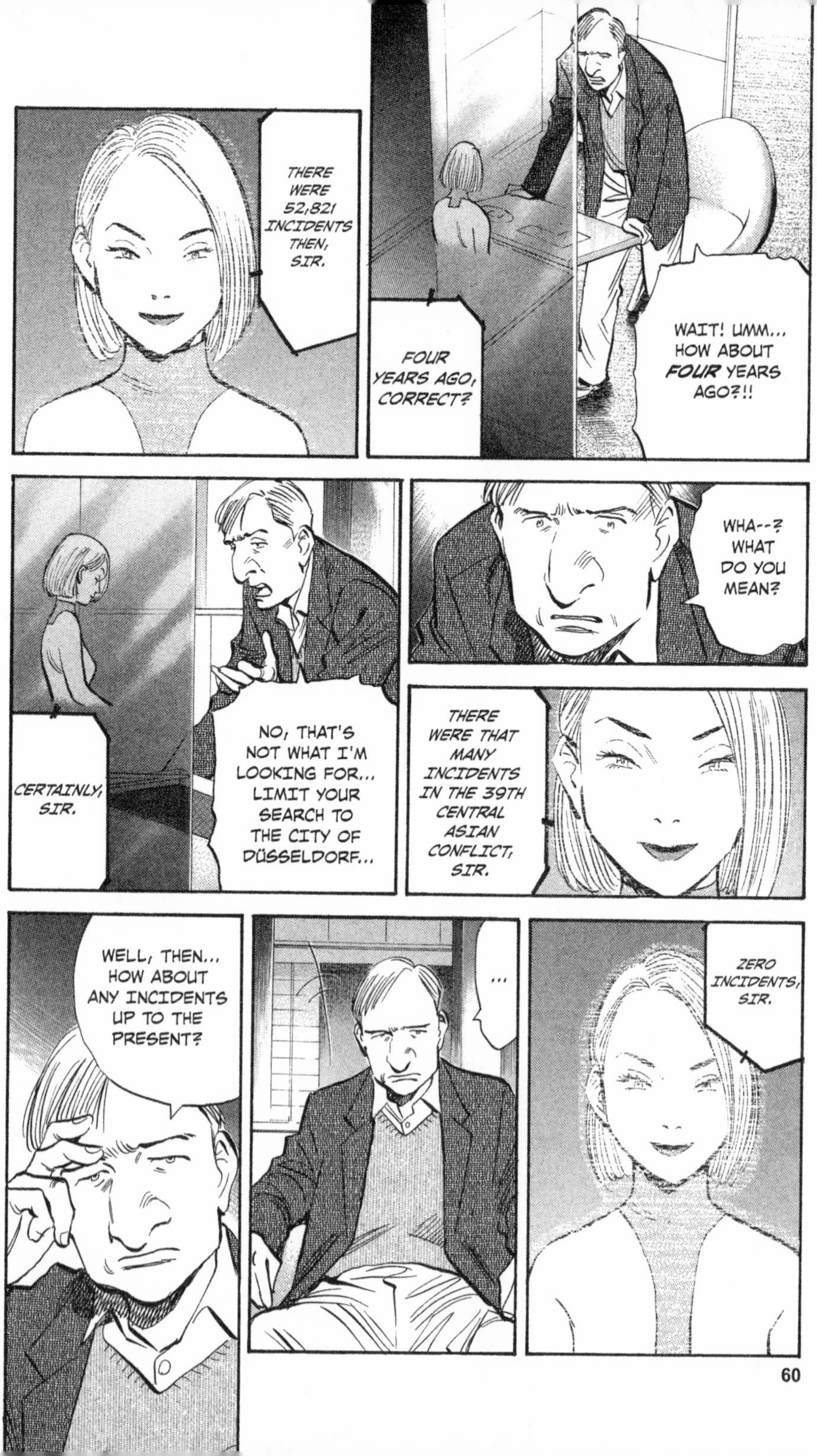
WAIT! UMM... HOW ABOUT FOUR YEARS AGO?!!
FOUR YEARS AGO, CORRECT?
THERE WERE 52,821 INCIDENTS THEN, SIR.
WHA--? WHAT DO YOU MEAN?
THERE WERE THAT MANY INCIDENTS IN THE 39TH CENTRAL ASIAN CONFLICT, SIR.
NO, THAT'S NOT WHAT I'M LOOKING FOR... LIMIT YOUR SEARCH TO THE CITY OF DÜSSELDORF...
CERTAINLY, SIR.
ZERO INCIDENTS, SIR.
...
WELL, THEN... HOW ABOUT ANY INCIDENTS UP TO THE PRESENT?

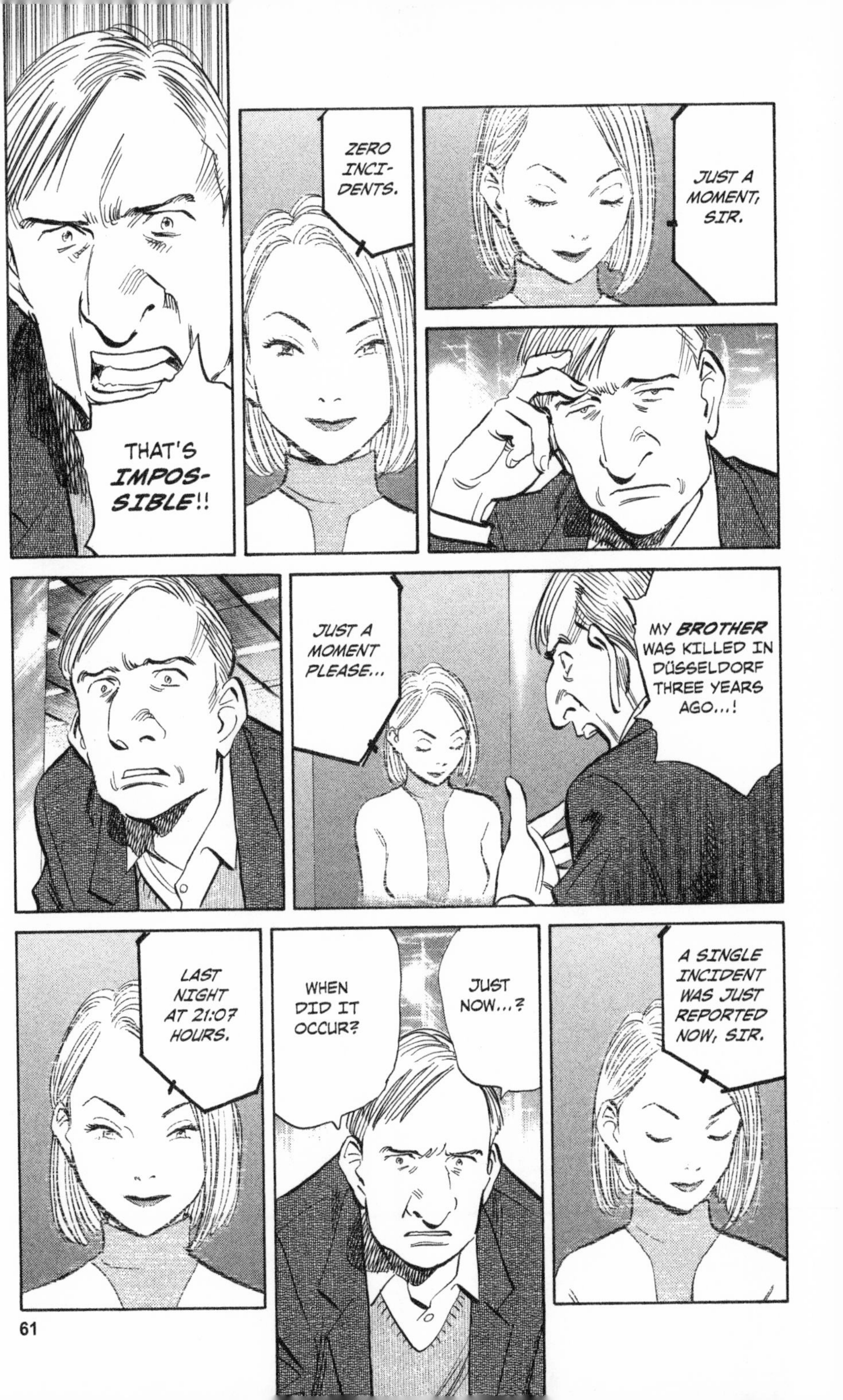
JUST A MOMENT, SIR.
ZERO INCIDENTS.
THAT'S *IMPOSSIBLE*!!
MY **BROTHER** WAS KILLED IN DÜSSELDORF THREE YEARS AGO...!
JUST A MOMENT PLEASE...
A SINGLE INCIDENT WAS JUST REPORTED NOW, SIR.
JUST NOW...?
WHEN DID IT OCCUR?
LAST NIGHT AT 21:07 HOURS.

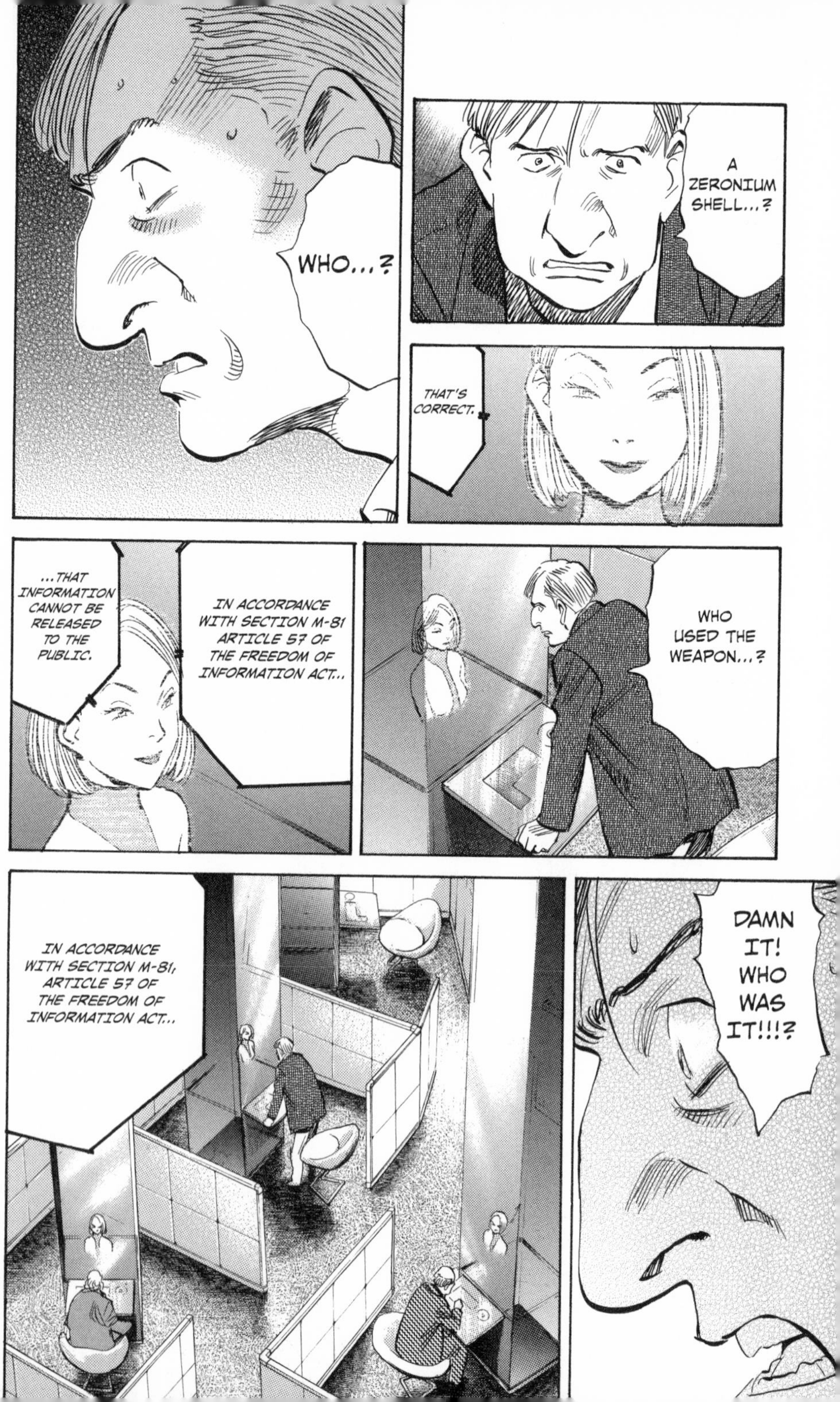
A ZERONIUM SHELL...?
THAT'S CORRECT.
WHO...?
WHO USED THE WEAPON...?
IN ACCORDANCE WITH SECTION M-81 ARTICLE 57 OF THE FREEDOM OF INFORMATION ACT...
...THAT INFORMATION CANNOT BE RELEASED TO THE PUBLIC.
DAMN IT! WHO WAS IT!!!?
IN ACCORDANCE WITH SECTION M-81, ARTICLE 57 OF THE FREEDOM OF INFORMATION ACT...

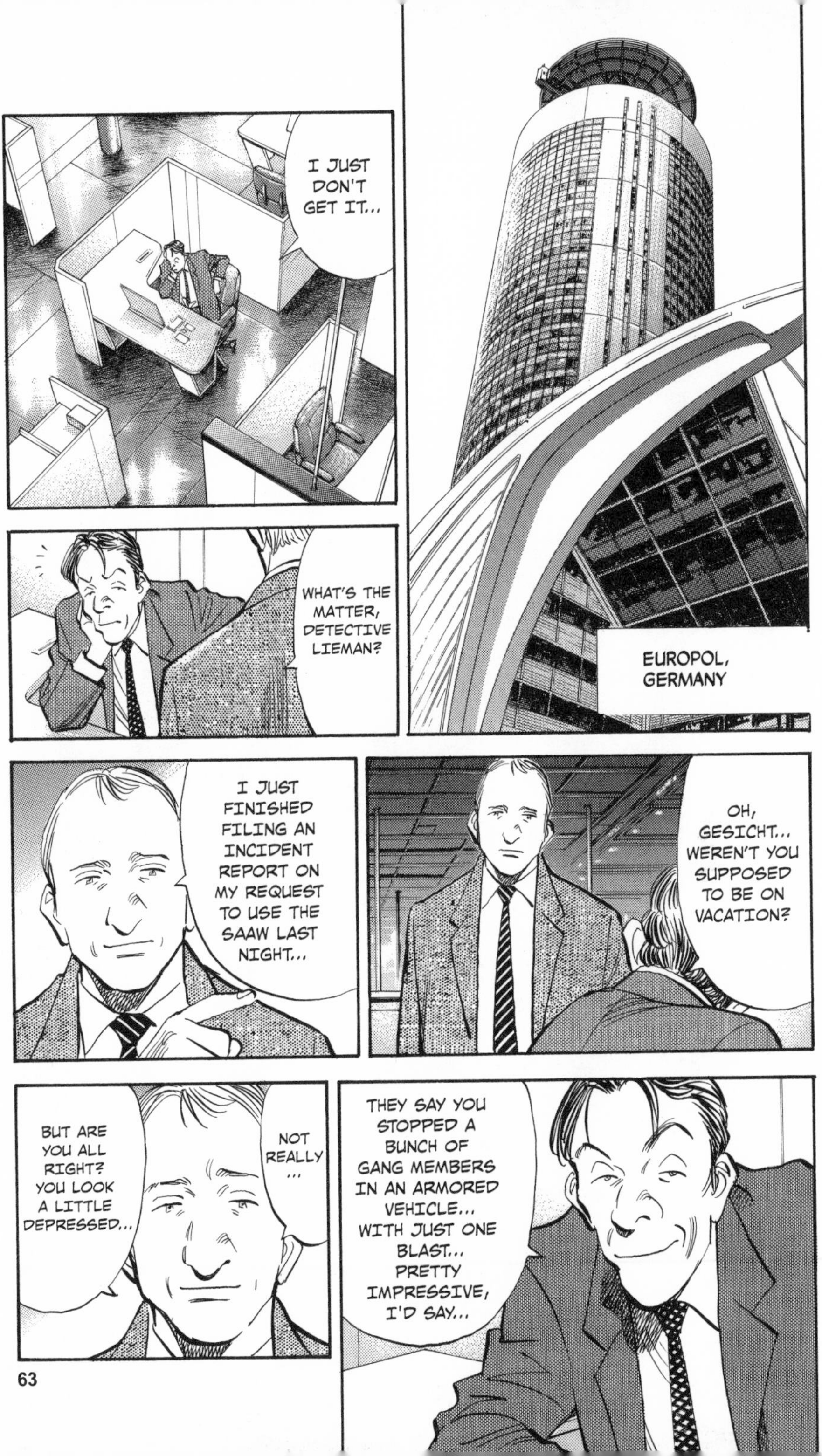
EUROPOL, GERMANY
I JUST DON'T GET IT...
WHAT'S THE MATTER, DETECTIVE LIEMAN?
OH, GESICHT... WEREN'T YOU SUPPOSED TO BE ON VACATION?
I JUST FINISHED FILING AN INCIDENT REPORT ON MY REQUEST TO USE THE SAAW LAST NIGHT...
THEY SAY YOU STOPPED A BUNCH OF GANG MEMBERS IN AN ARMORED VEHICLE... WITH JUST ONE BLAST... PRETTY IMPRESSIVE, I'D SAY...
BUT ARE YOU ALL RIGHT? YOU LOOK A LITTLE DEPRESSED...
NOT REALLY...

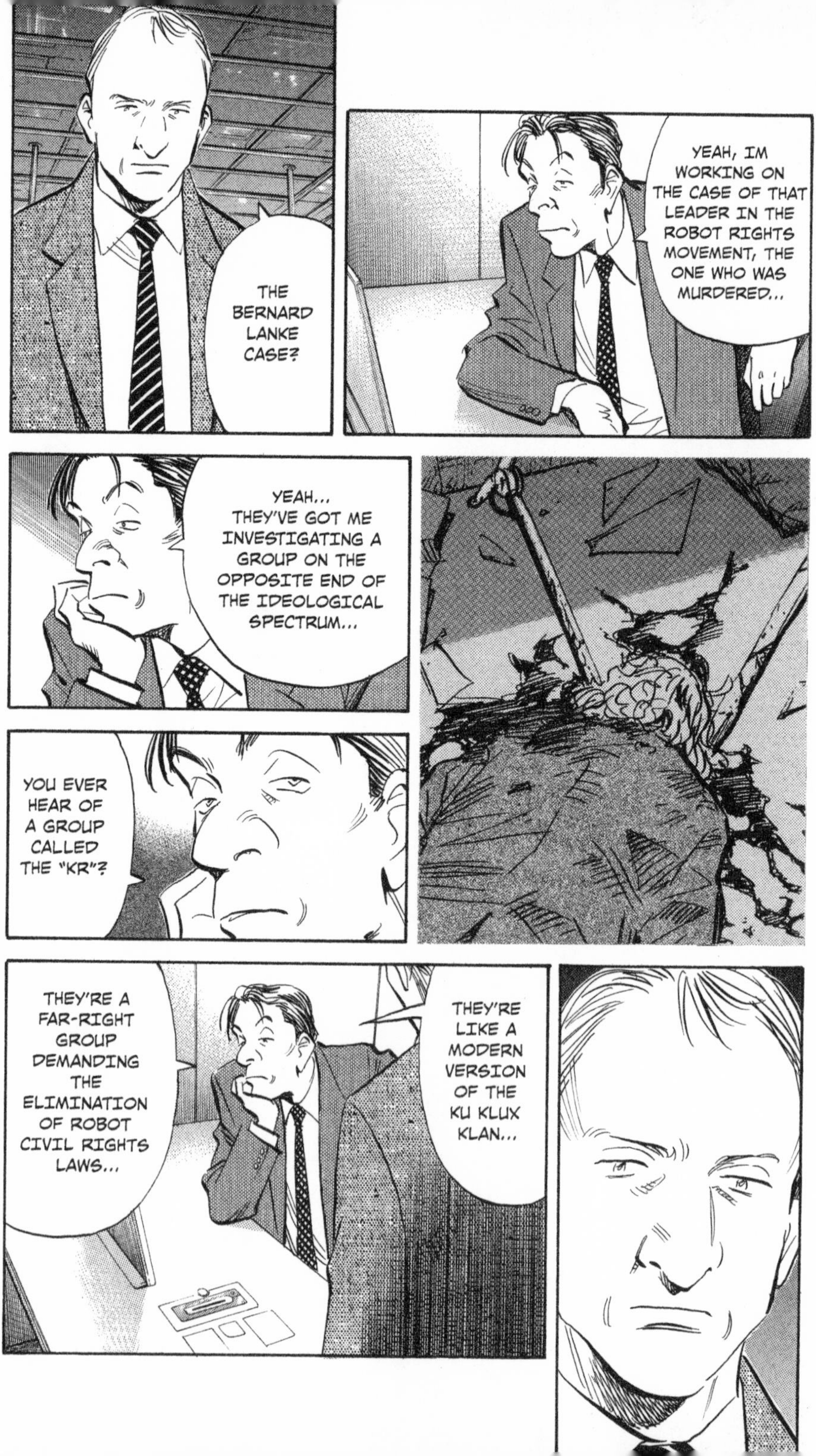
YEAH, IM WORKING ON THE CASE OF THAT LEADER IN THE ROBOT RIGHTS MOVEMENT, THE ONE WHO WAS MURDERED...
THE BERNARD LANKE CASE?
YEAH... THEY'VE GOT ME INVESTIGATING A GROUP ON THE OPPOSITE END OF THE IDEOLOGICAL SPECTRUM...
YOU EVER HEAR OF A GROUP CALLED THE "KR"?
THEY'RE A FAR-RIGHT GROUP DEMANDING THE ELIMINATION OF ROBOT CIVIL RIGHTS LAWS...
THEY'RE LIKE A MODERN VERSION OF THE KU KLUX KLAN...

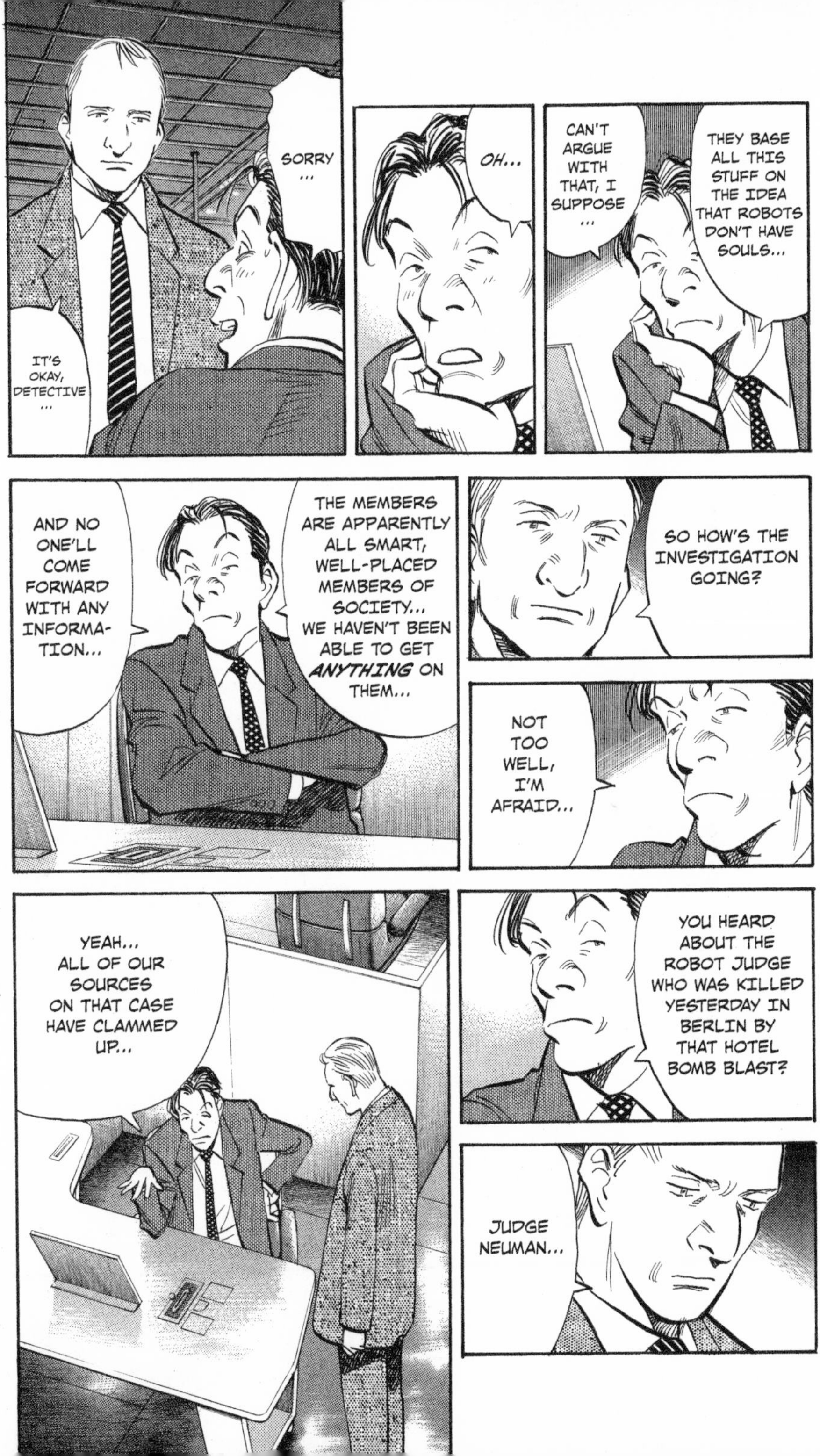
THEY BASE ALL THIS STUFF ON THE IDEA THAT ROBOTS DON'T HAVE SOULS...
CAN'T ARGUE WITH THAT, I SUPPOSE...
OH...
SORRY...
IT'S OKAY, DETECTIVE...
SO HOW'S THE INVESTIGATION GOING?
NOT TOO WELL, I'M AFRAID...
THE MEMBERS ARE APPARENTLY ALL SMART, WELL-PLACED MEMBERS OF SOCIETY... WE HAVEN'T BEEN ABLE TO GET *ANYTHING* ON THEM...
AND NO ONE'LL COME FORWARD WITH ANY INFORMATION...
YOU HEARD ABOUT THE ROBOT JUDGE WHO WAS KILLED YESTERDAY IN BERLIN BY THAT HOTEL BOMB BLAST?
JUDGE NEUMAN...
YEAH... ALL OF OUR SOURCES ON THAT CASE HAVE CLAMMED UP...

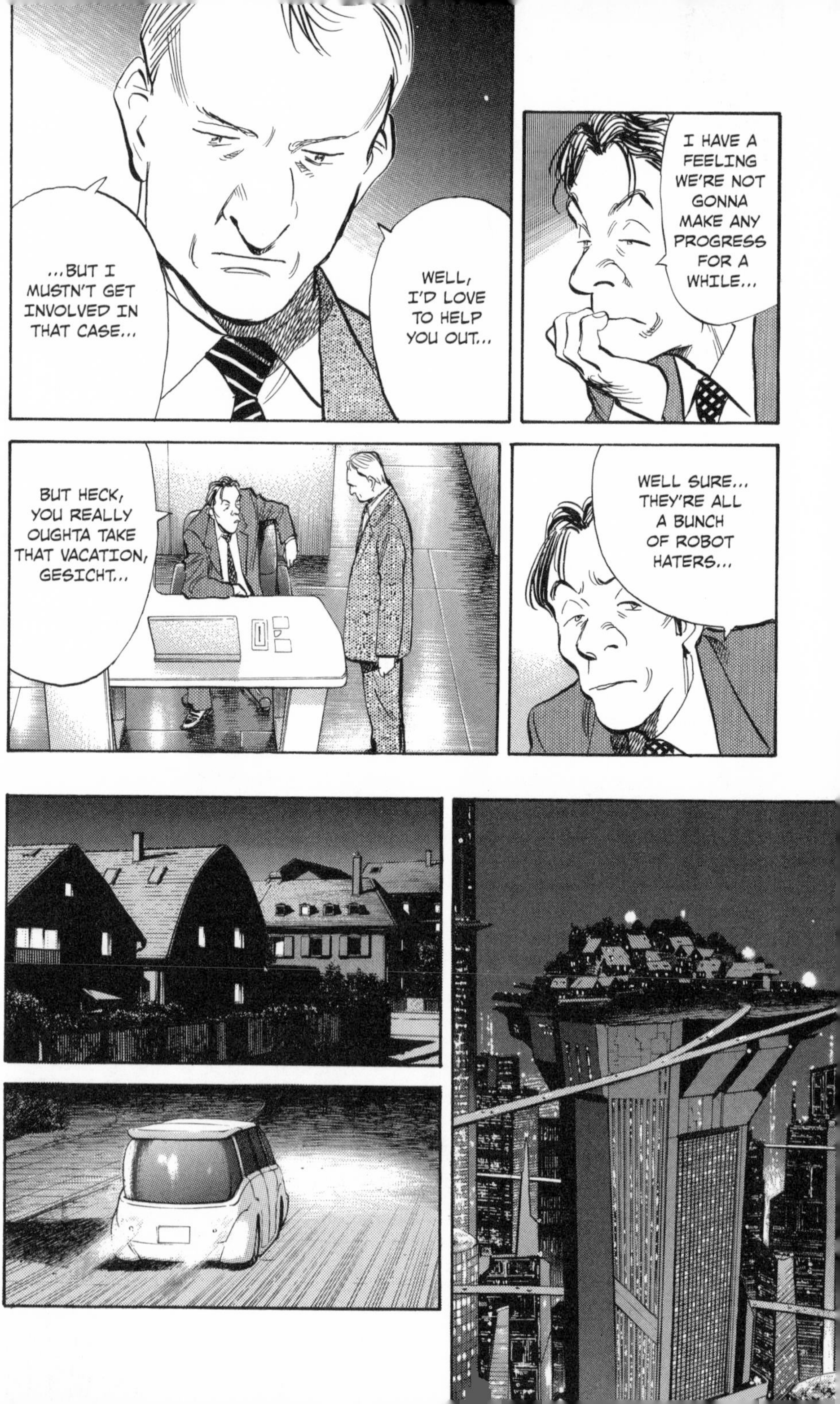
I HAVE A FEELING WE'RE NOT GONNA MAKE ANY PROGRESS FOR A WHILE...
WELL, I'D LOVE TO HELP YOU OUT...
...BUT I MUSTN'T GET INVOLVED IN THAT CASE...
WELL SURE... THEY'RE ALL A BUNCH OF ROBOT HATERS...
BUT HECK, YOU REALLY OUGHTA TAKE THAT VACATION, GESICHT...

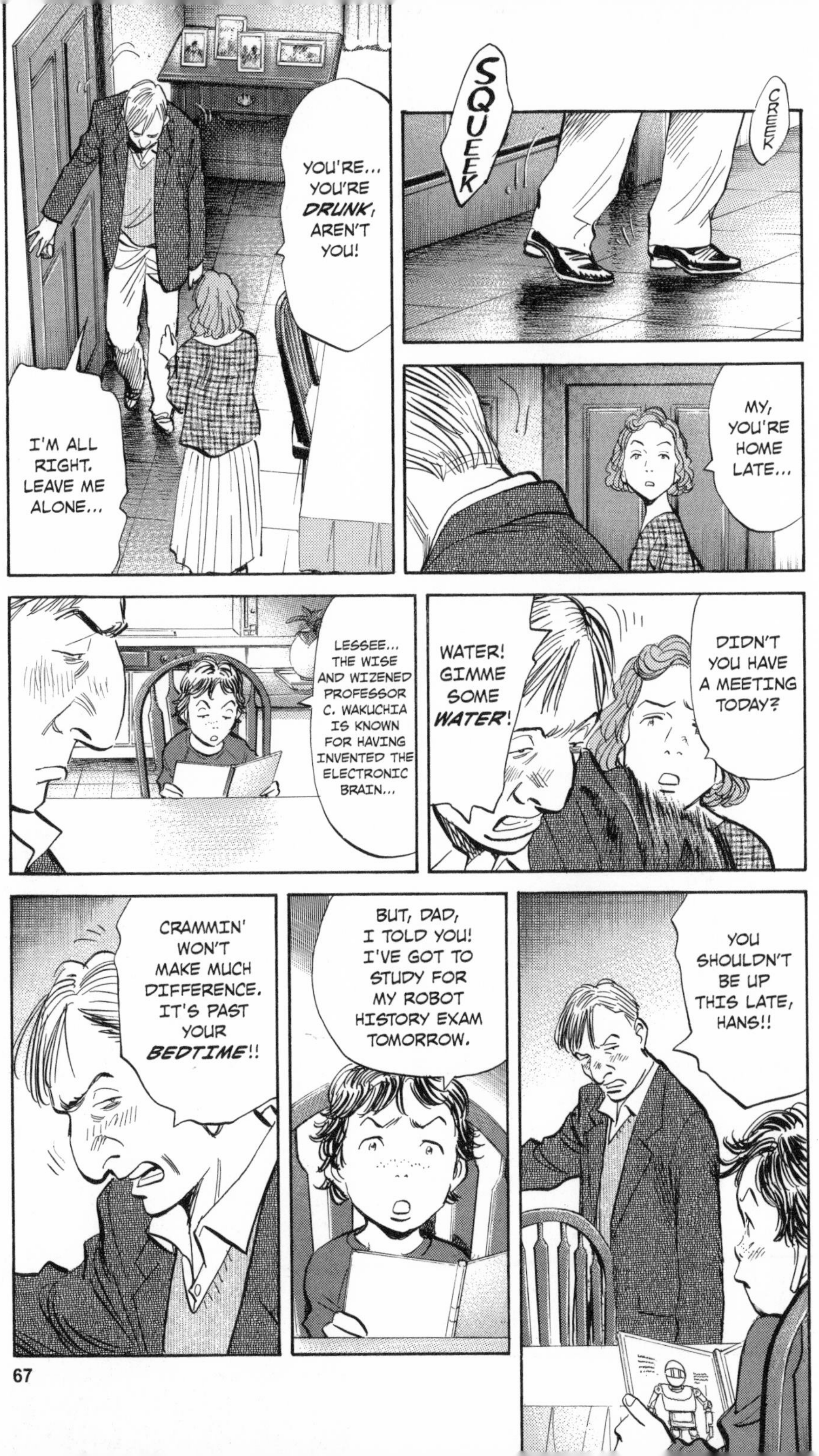
CREEK
SQUEEK
MY, YOU'RE HOME LATE...
YOU'RE... YOU'RE DRUNK, AREN'T YOU!
I'M ALL RIGHT. LEAVE ME ALONE...
DIDN'T YOU HAVE A MEETING TODAY?
WATER! GIMME SOME WATER!
LESSEE... THE WISE AND WIZENED PROFESSOR C. WAKUCHIA IS KNOWN FOR HAVING INVENTED THE ELECTRONIC BRAIN...
YOU SHOULDN'T BE UP THIS LATE, HANS!!
BUT, DAD, I TOLD YOU! I'VE GOT TO STUDY FOR MY ROBOT HISTORY EXAM TOMORROW.
CRAMMIN' WON'T MAKE MUCH DIFFERENCE. IT'S PAST YOUR BEDTIME!!

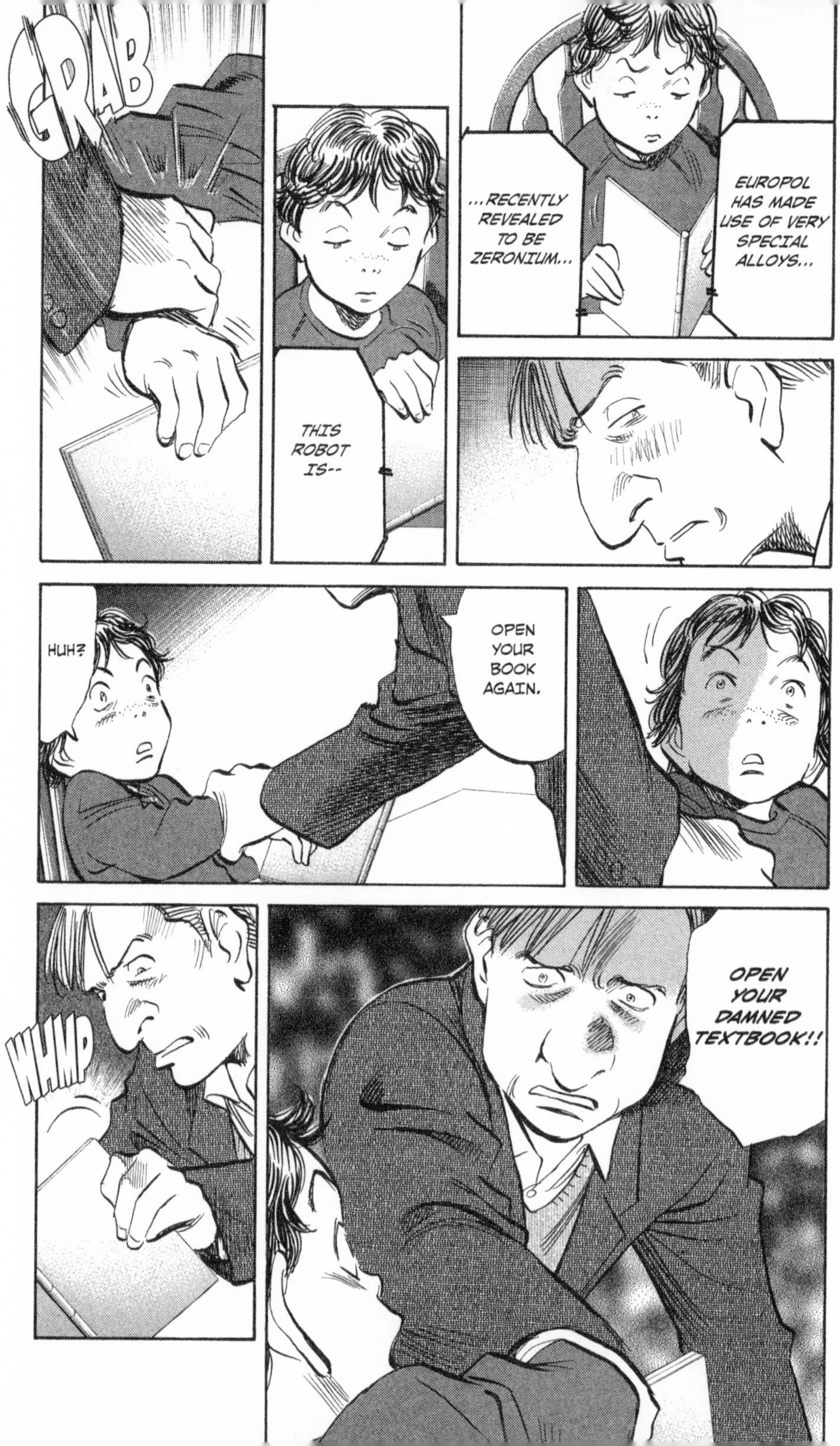
EUROPOL HAS MADE USE OF VERY SPECIAL ALLOYS...
...RECENTLY REVEALED TO BE ZERONIUM...
THIS ROBOT IS--
GRAB
OPEN YOUR BOOK AGAIN.
HUH?
OPEN YOUR DAMNED TEXTBOOK!!
WHMP

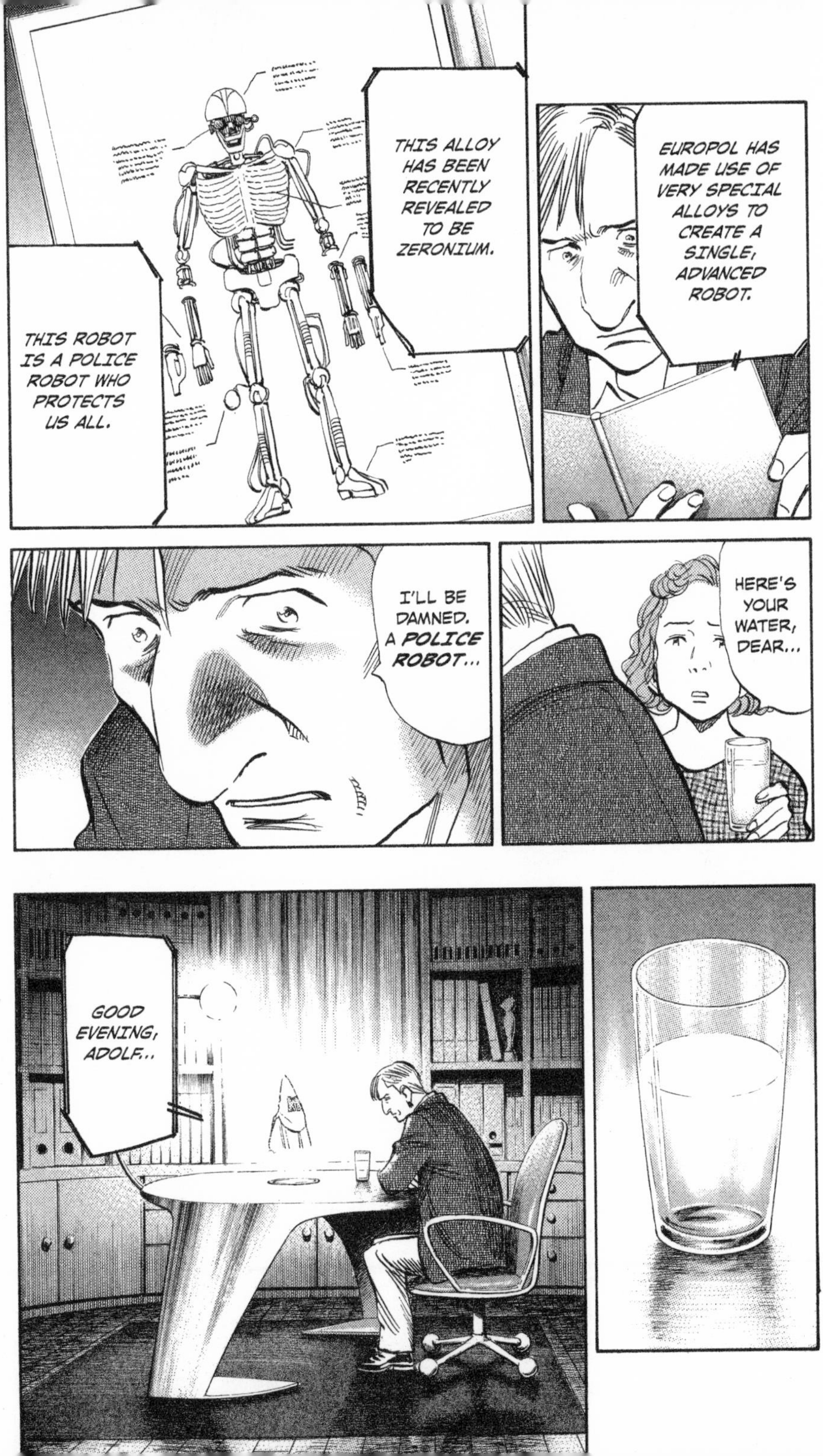
EUROPOL HAS MADE USE OF VERY SPECIAL ALLOYS TO CREATE A SINGLE, ADVANCED ROBOT.
THIS ALLOY HAS BEEN RECENTLY REVEALED TO BE ZERONIUM.
THIS ROBOT IS A POLICE ROBOT WHO PROTECTS US ALL.
HERE'S YOUR WATER, DEAR...
I'LL BE DAMNED. A *POLICE ROBOT*...
GOOD EVENING, ADOLF...

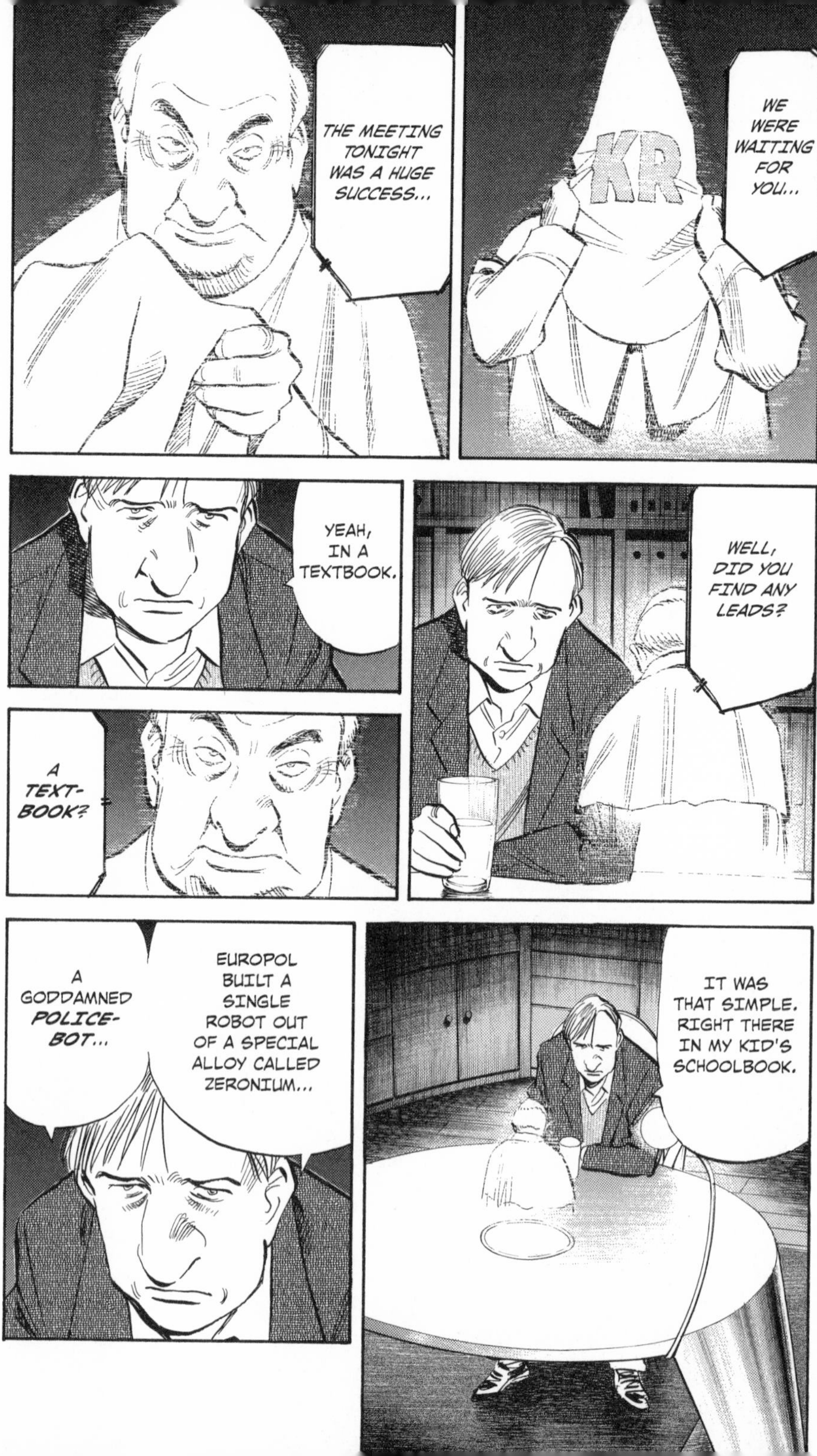
WE WERE WAITING FOR YOU...
THE MEETING TONIGHT WAS A HUGE SUCCESS...
KR
WELL, DID YOU FIND ANY LEADS?
YEAH, IN A TEXTBOOK.
A TEXT-BOOK?
IT WAS THAT SIMPLE. RIGHT THERE IN MY KID'S SCHOOLBOOK.
EUROPOL BUILT A SINGLE ROBOT OUT OF A SPECIAL ALLOY CALLED ZERONIUM...
A GODDAMNED POLICE-BOT...

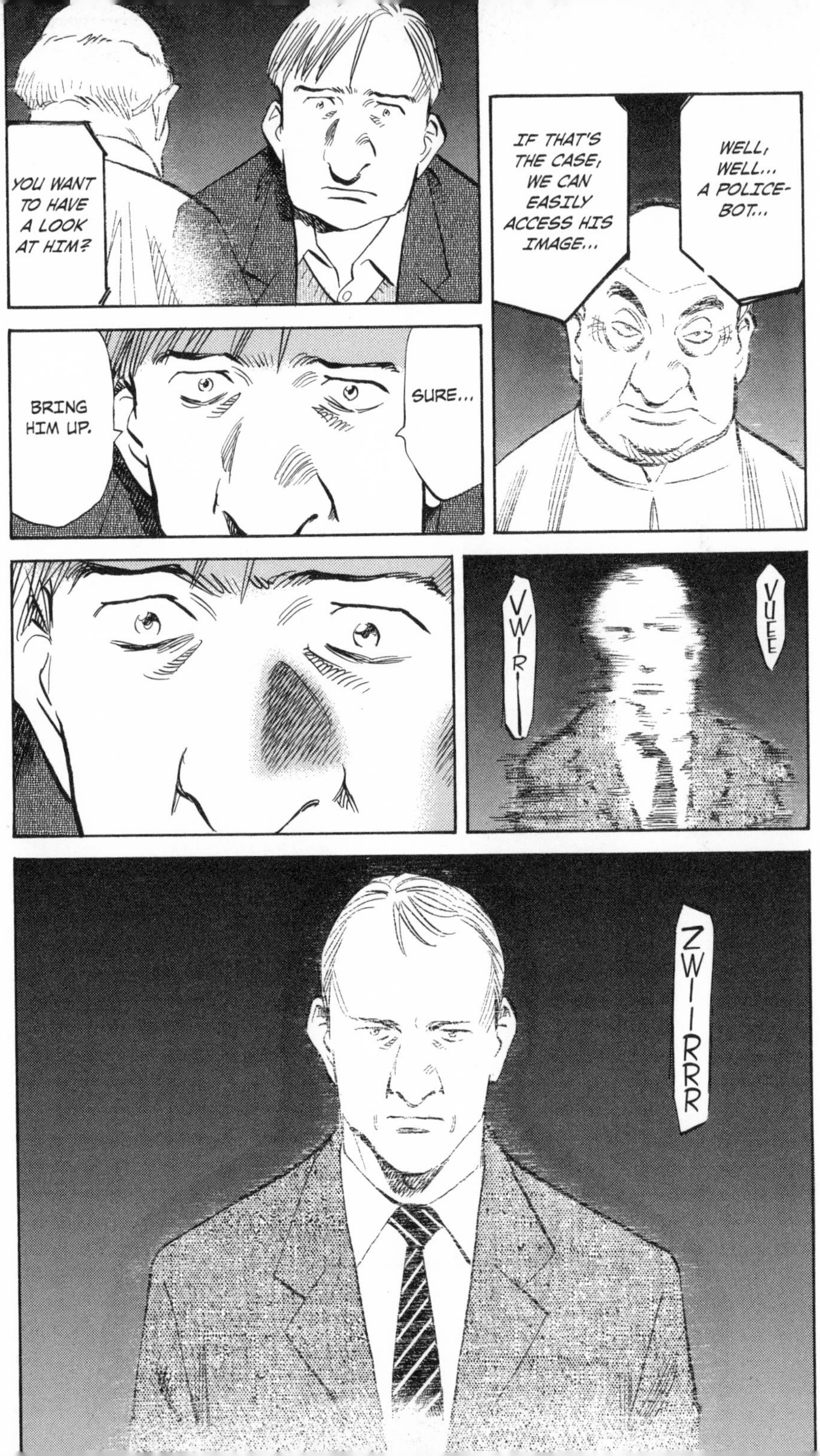
WELL, WELL... A POLICE-BOT...
IF THAT'S THE CASE, WE CAN EASILY ACCESS HIS IMAGE...
YOU WANT TO HAVE A LOOK AT HIM?
SURE...
BRING HIM UP.
VUEE
VWIRI
ZWIIRRR

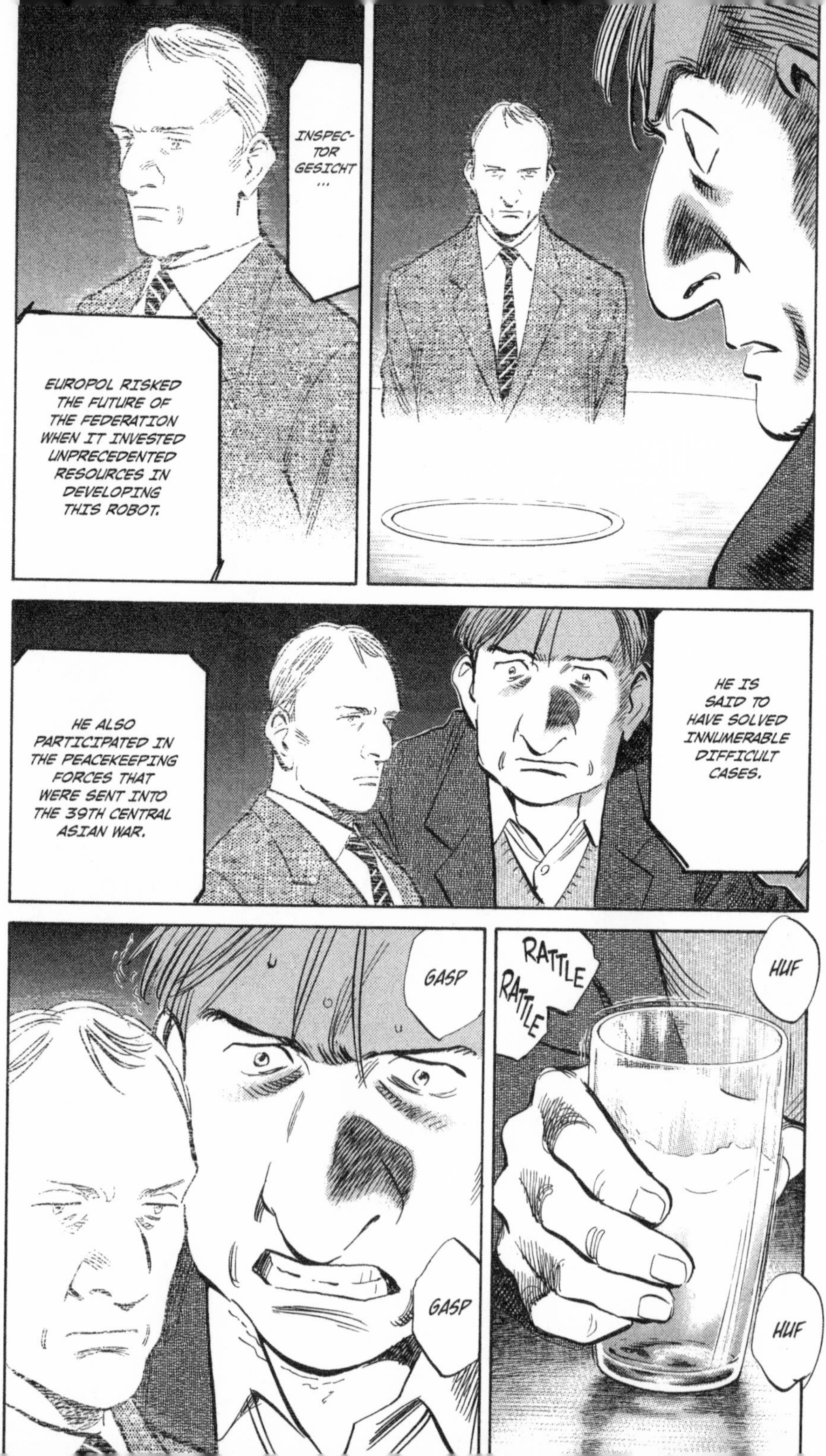
INSPECTOR GESICHT ...
EUROPOL RISKED THE FUTURE OF THE FEDERATION WHEN IT INVESTED UNPRECEDENTED RESOURCES IN DEVELOPING THIS ROBOT.
HE IS SAID TO HAVE SOLVED INNUMERABLE DIFFICULT CASES.
HE ALSO PARTICIPATED IN THE PEACEKEEPING FORCES THAT WERE SENT INTO THE 39TH CENTRAL ASIAN WAR.
HUF
RATTLE
RATTLE
HUF
GASP
GASP

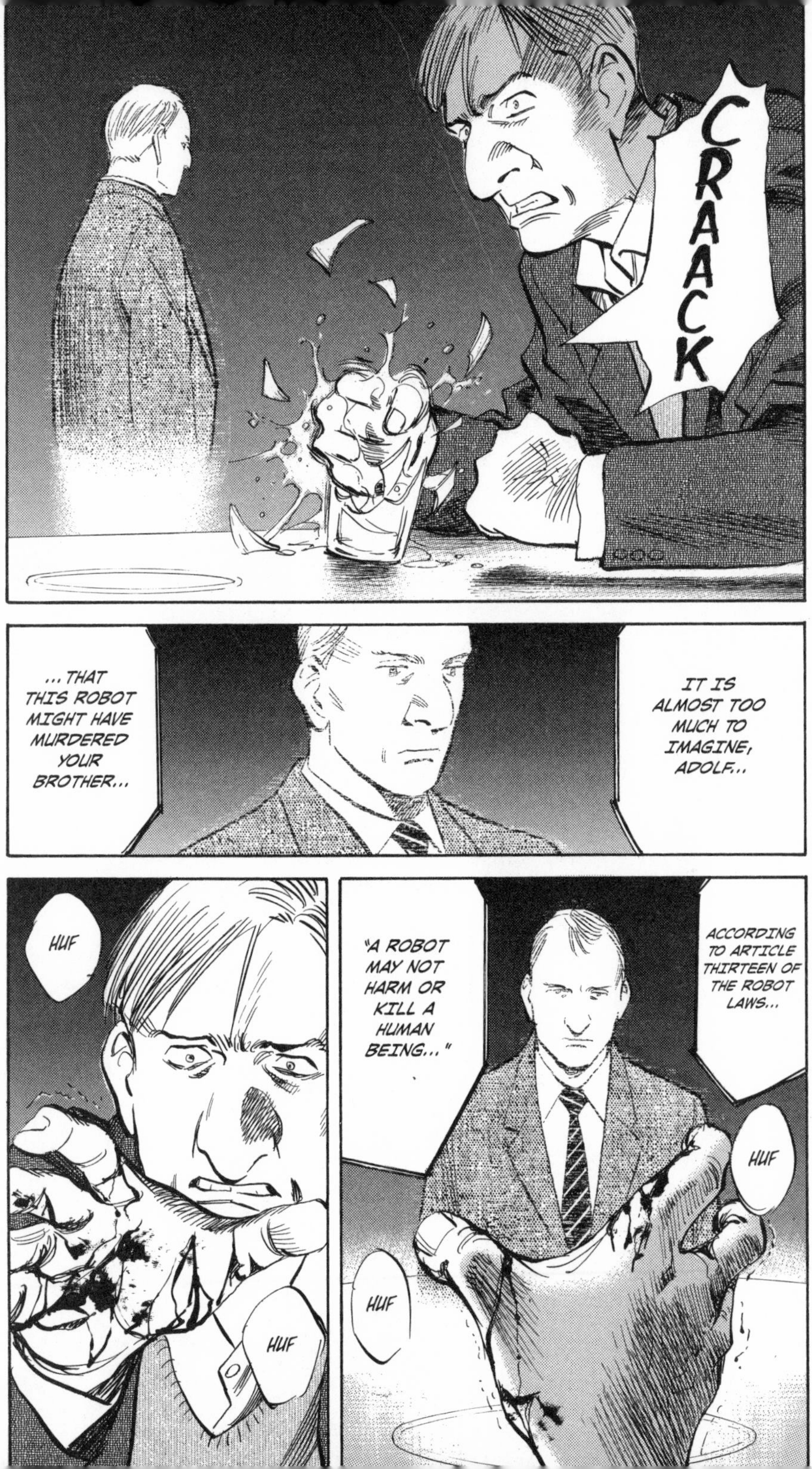
CRAACK
IT IS ALMOST TOO MUCH TO IMAGINE, ADOLF...
...THAT THIS ROBOT MIGHT HAVE MURDERED YOUR BROTHER...
ACCORDING TO ARTICLE THIRTEEN OF THE ROBOT LAWS...
"A ROBOT MAY NOT HARM OR KILL A HUMAN BEING..."
HUF
HUF
HUF
HUF

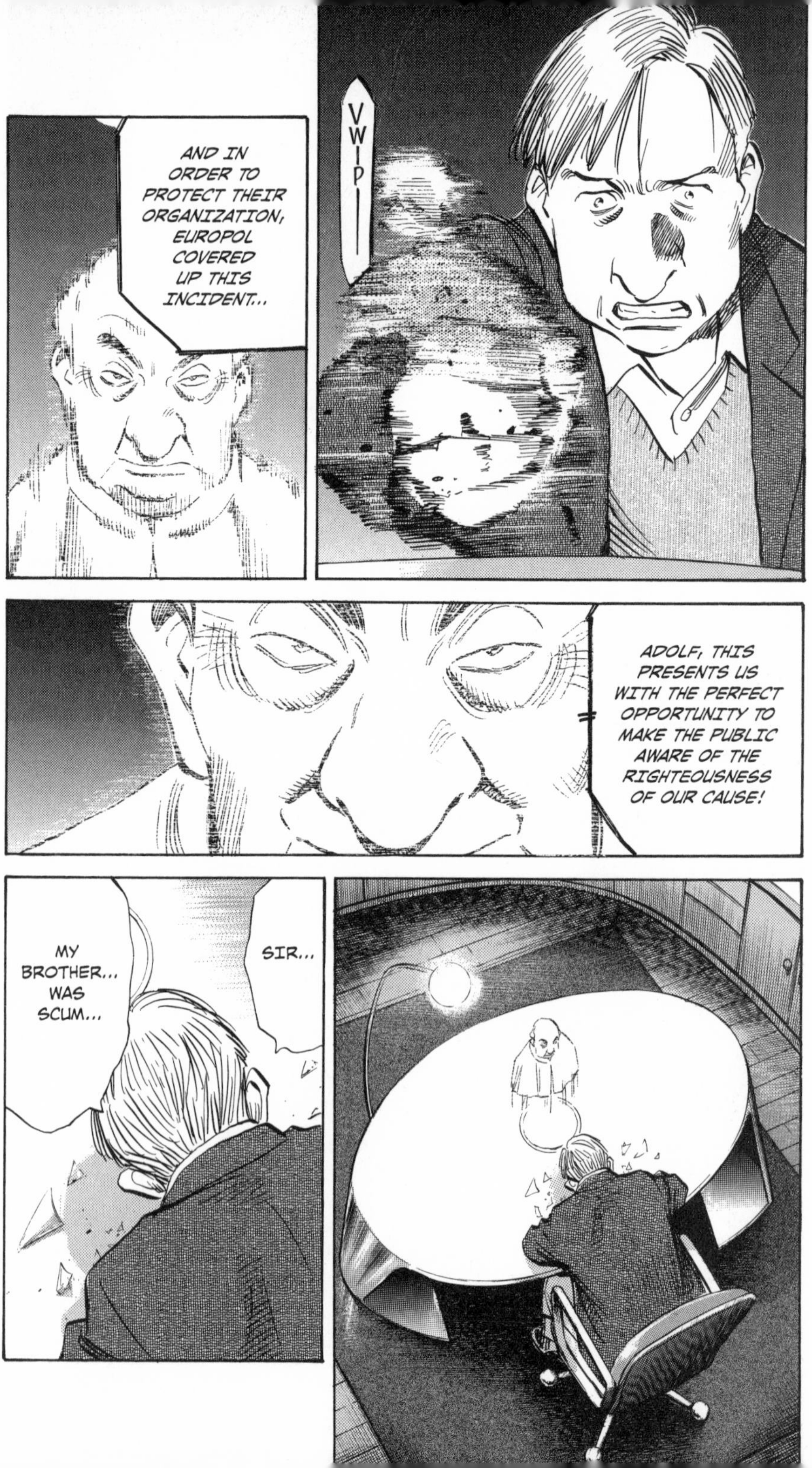
VWIP
AND IN ORDER TO PROTECT THEIR ORGANIZATION, EUROPOL COVERED UP THIS INCIDENT...
ADOLF, THIS PRESENTS US WITH THE PERFECT OPPORTUNITY TO MAKE THE PUBLIC AWARE OF THE RIGHTEOUSNESS OF OUR CAUSE!
SIR...
MY BROTHER... WAS SCUM...

BUT...

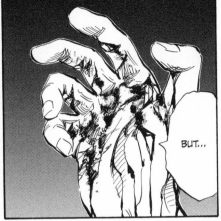
BUT...

...HE DIDN'T DESERVE TO BE PULVERIZED BY A *ROBOT*.

VWIRI

YOU'RE ABSOLUTELY RIGHT, ADOLF...

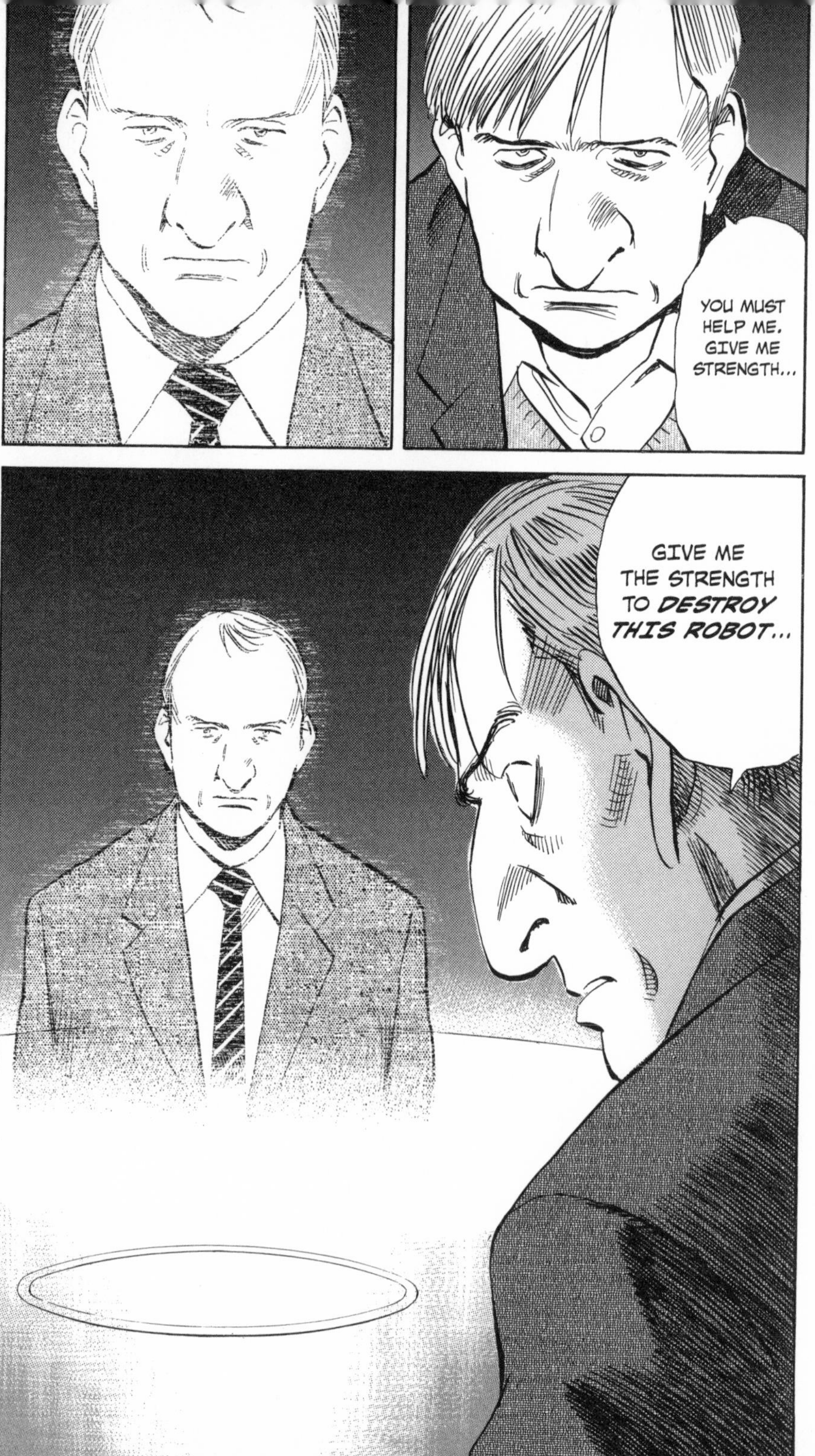
YOU MUST HELP ME. GIVE ME STRENGTH...
GIVE ME THE STRENGTH TO *DESTROY THIS ROBOT*...

Act 19 EPSILON

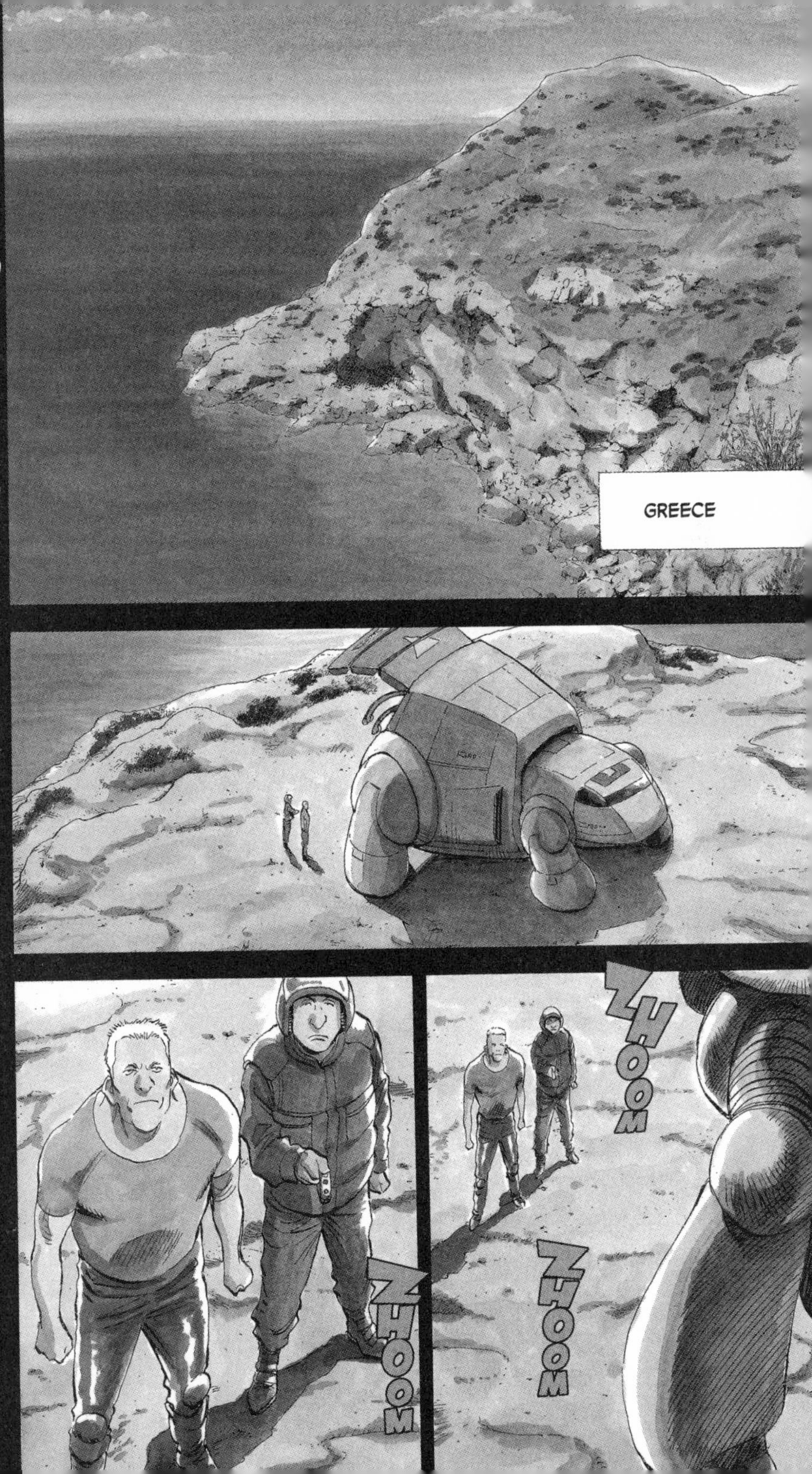
GREECE
ZHOOM
ZHOOM
ZHOOM

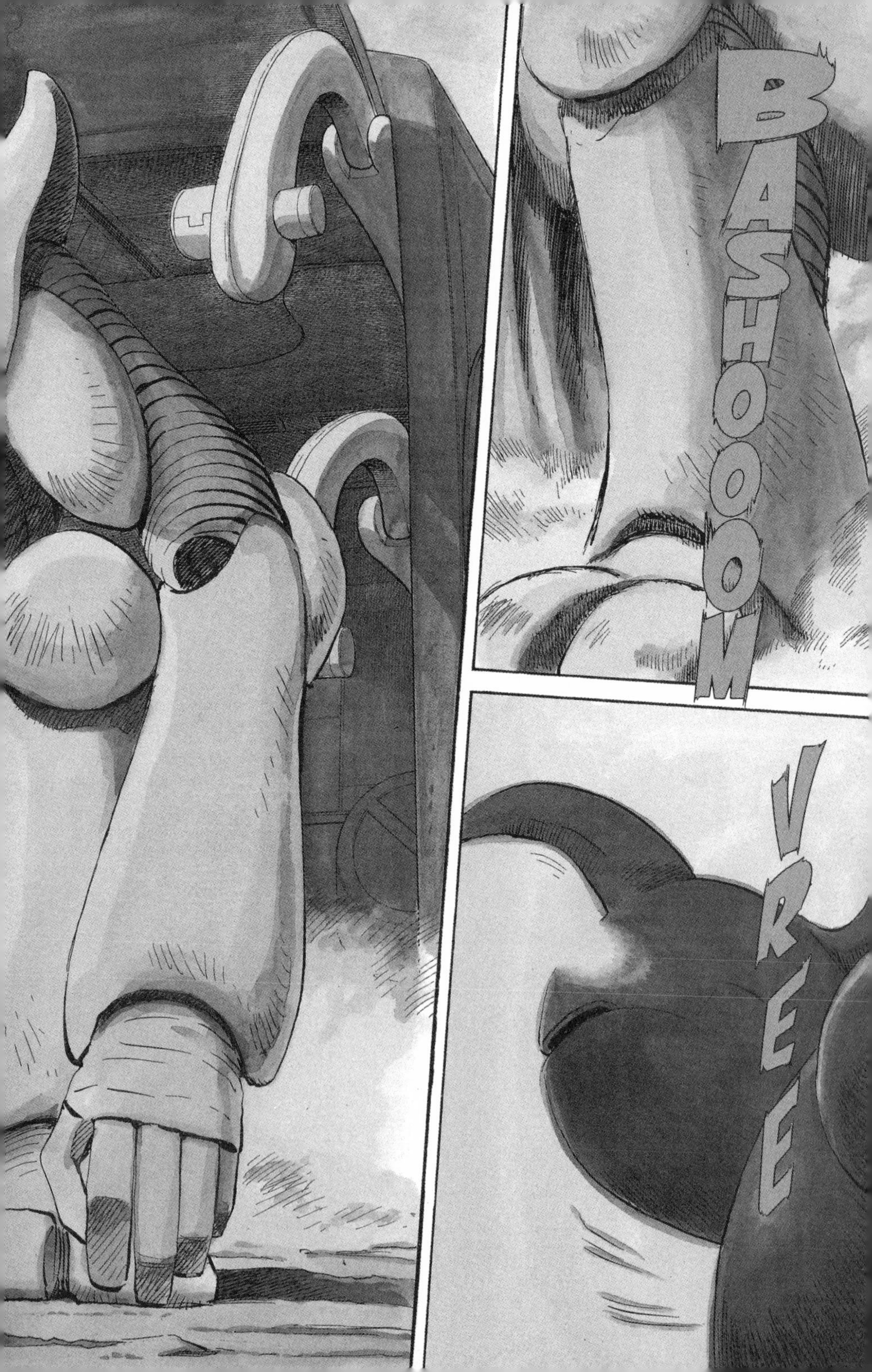
BASHOOOOM
VREEE

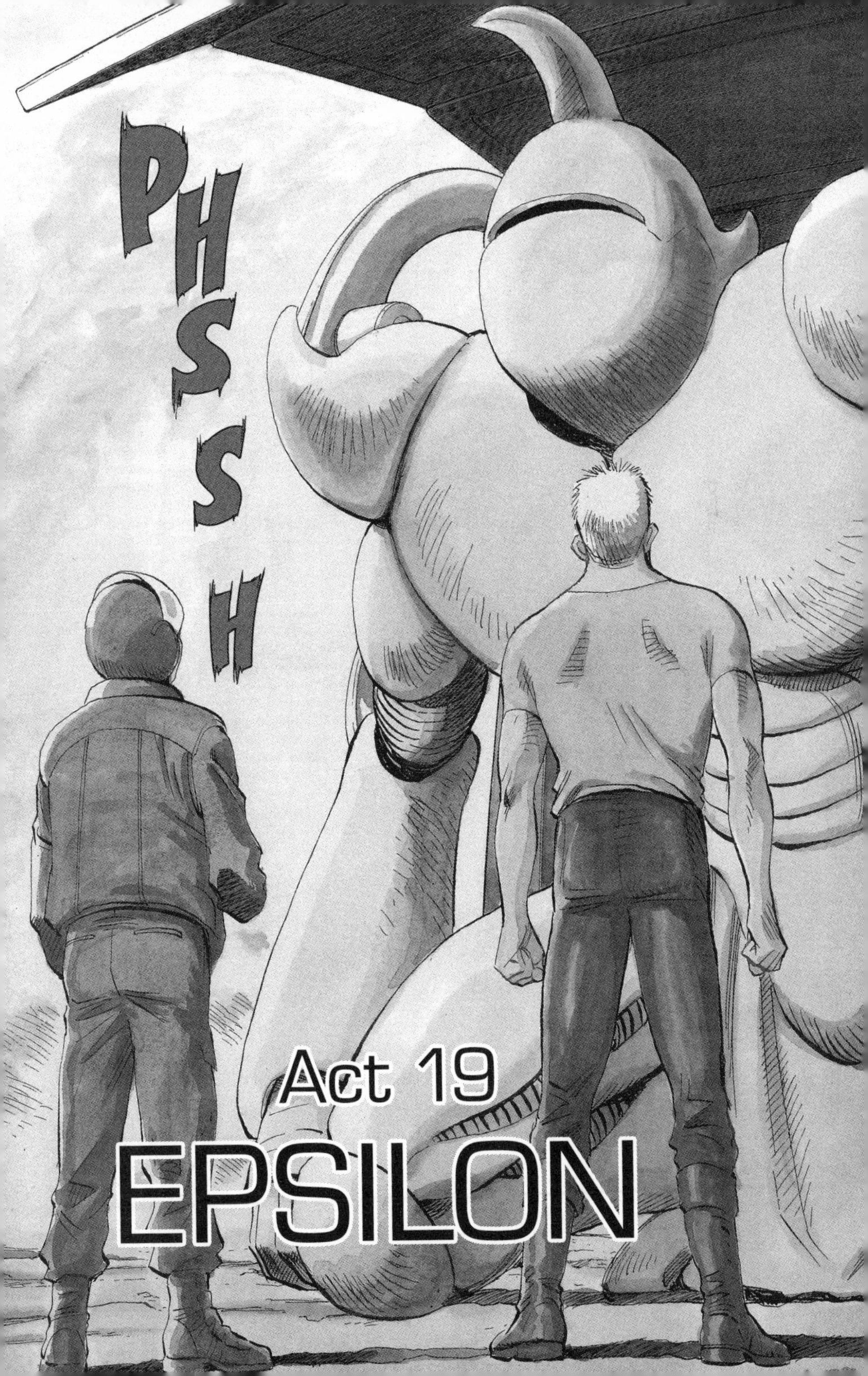
PHSSSH
Act 19
EPSILON

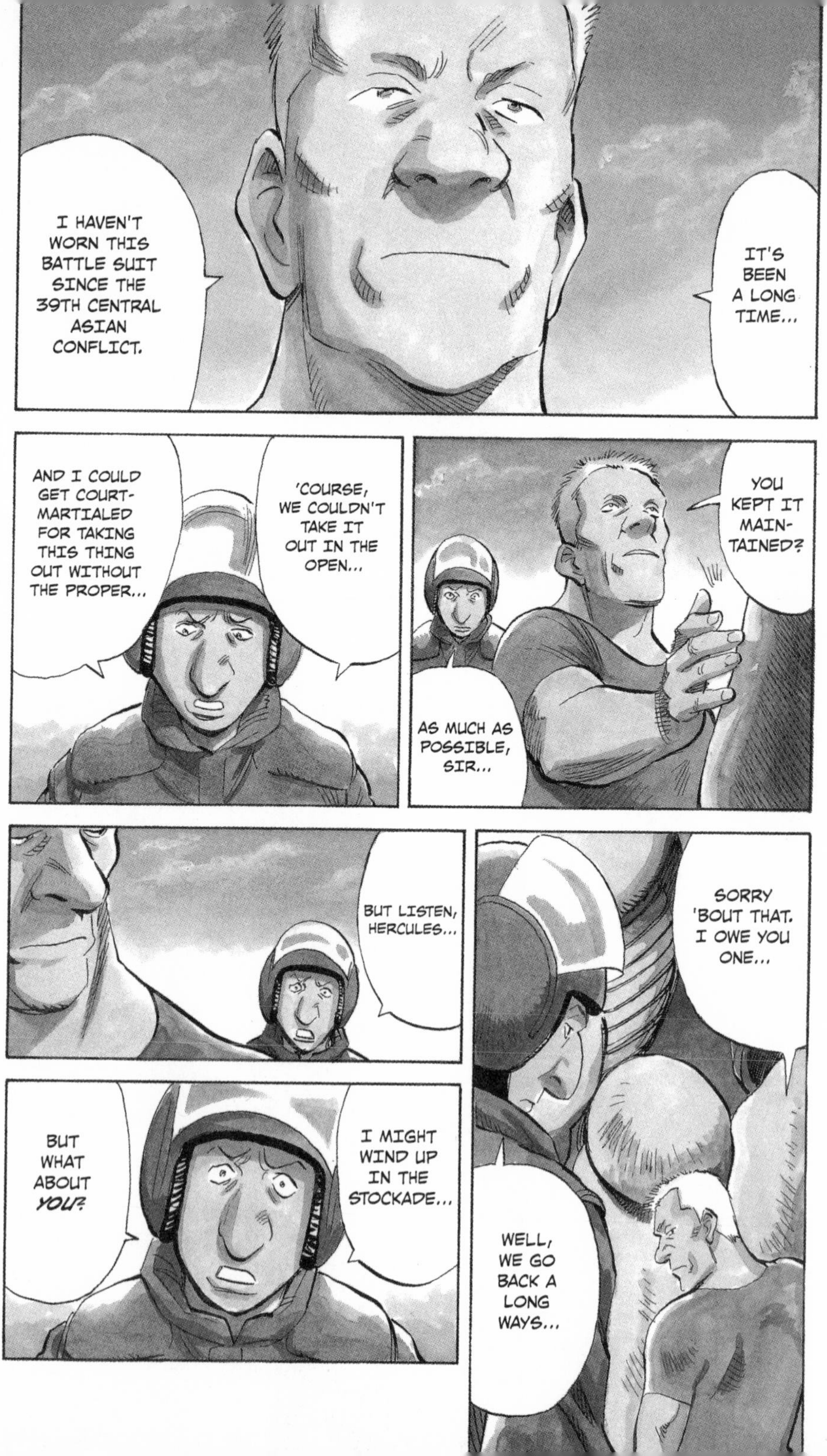
IT'S BEEN A LONG TIME...
I HAVEN'T WORN THIS BATTLE SUIT SINCE THE 39TH CENTRAL ASIAN CONFLICT.
YOU KEPT IT MAIN-TAINED?
AS MUCH AS POSSIBLE, SIR...
'COURSE, WE COULDN'T TAKE IT OUT IN THE OPEN...
AND I COULD GET COURT-MARTIALED FOR TAKING THIS THING OUT WITHOUT THE PROPER...
SORRY 'BOUT THAT. I OWE YOU ONE...
WELL, WE GO BACK A LONG WAYS...
BUT LISTEN, HERCULES...
I MIGHT WIND UP IN THE STOCKADE...
BUT WHAT ABOUT *YOU*?

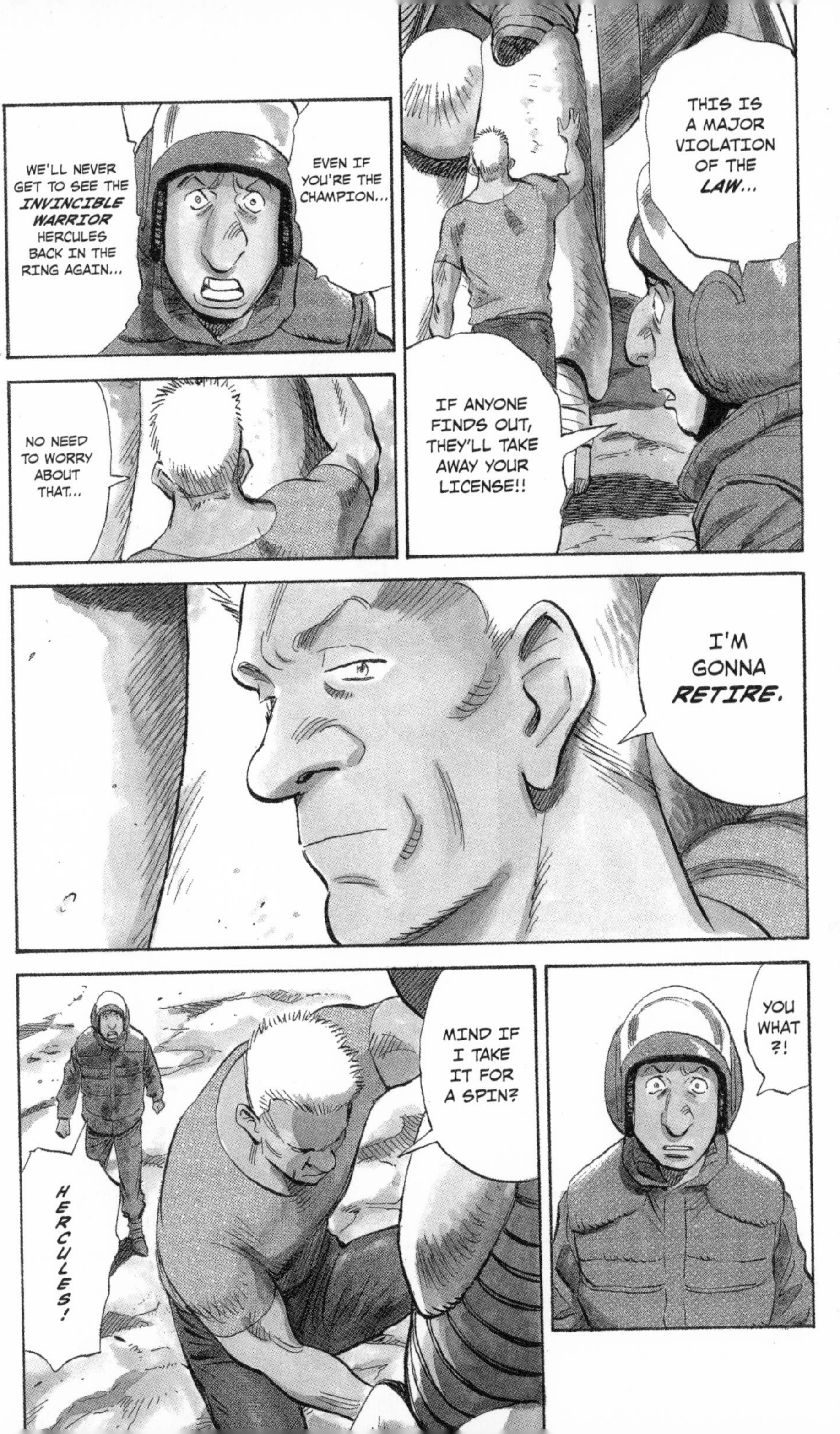
THIS IS A MAJOR VIOLATION OF THE LAW...
IF ANYONE FINDS OUT, THEY'LL TAKE AWAY YOUR LICENSE!!
EVEN IF YOU'RE THE CHAMPION...
WE'LL NEVER GET TO SEE THE INVINCIBLE WARRIOR HERCULES BACK IN THE RING AGAIN...
NO NEED TO WORRY ABOUT THAT...
I'M GONNA RETIRE.
YOU WHAT?!
MIND IF I TAKE IT FOR A SPIN?
HERCULES!

NOTHING LIKE A REAL MILITARY BATTLE SUIT! THIS THING'S GOT WAY MORE HORSEPOWER THAN MY PANKRATION SUIT.

UH-OH...

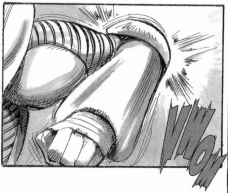

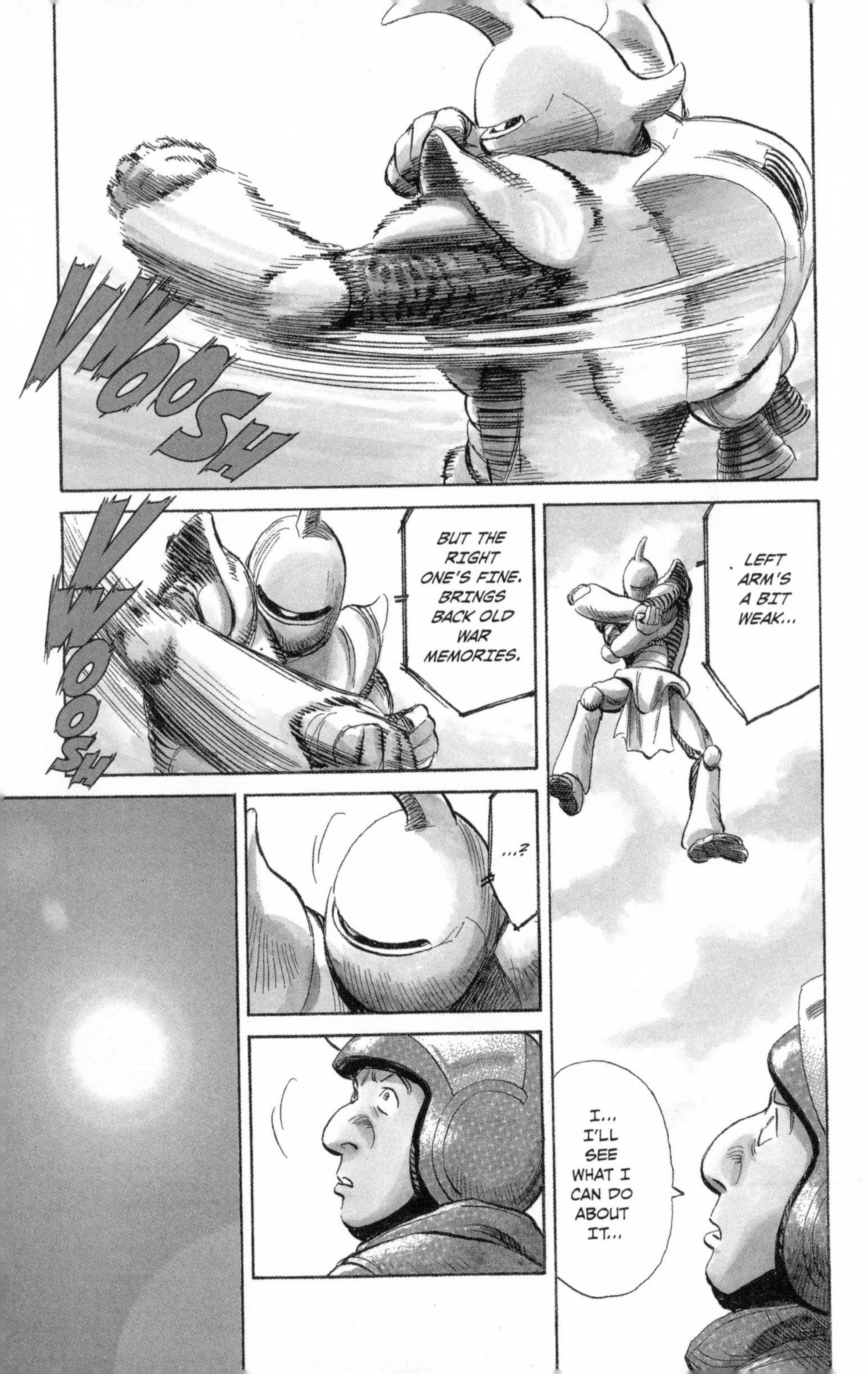
VWOOSH
LEFT ARM'S A BIT WEAK...
BUT THE RIGHT ONE'S FINE. BRINGS BACK OLD WAR MEMORIES.
VWOOSH
...?
I... I'LL SEE WHAT I CAN DO ABOUT IT...

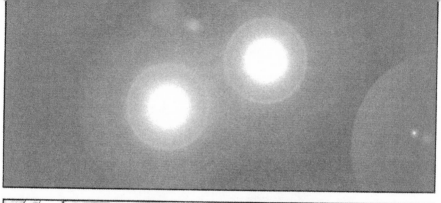

TWO
SUNS
...?!

FLASH

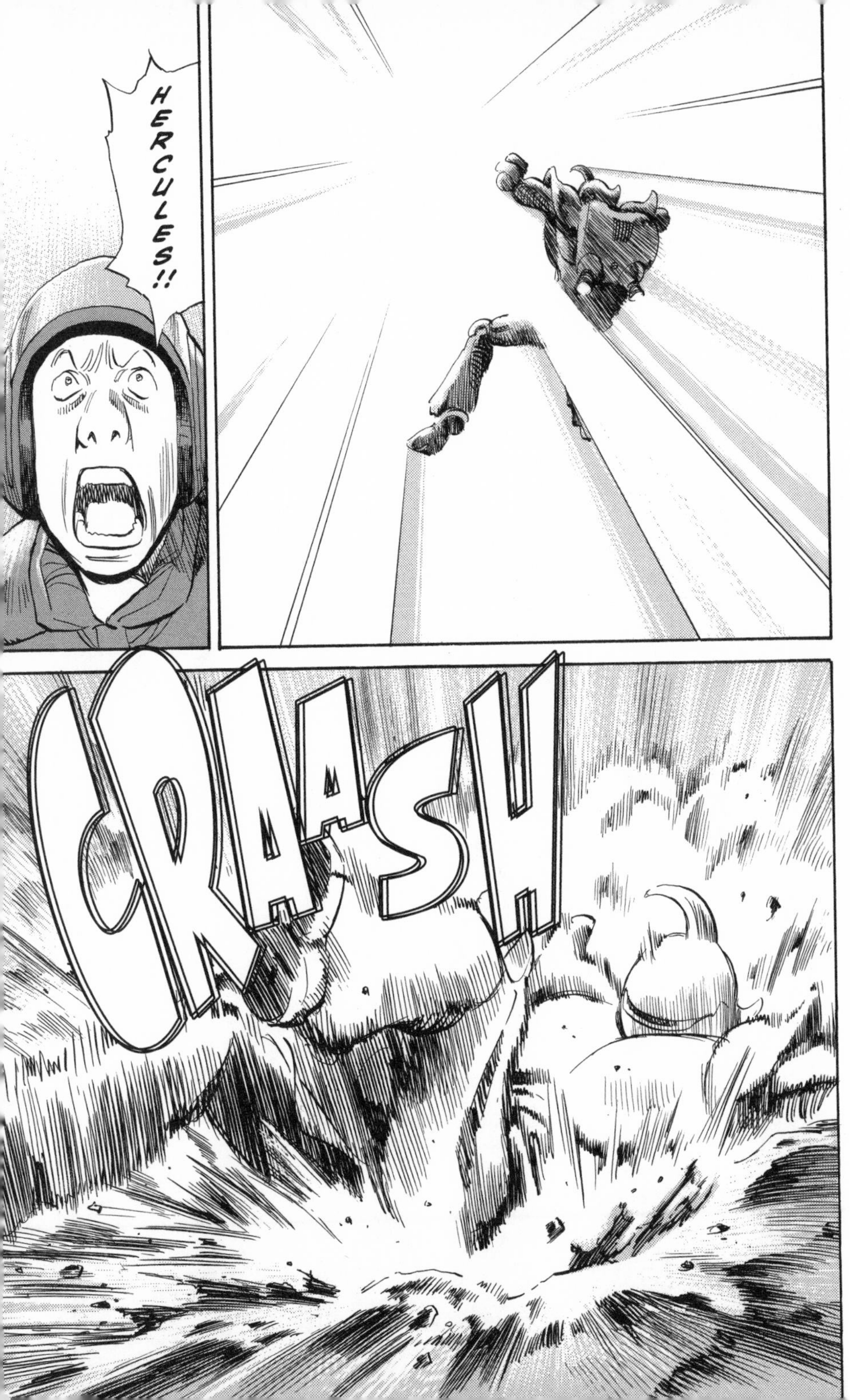
HERCULES!!
CRASH

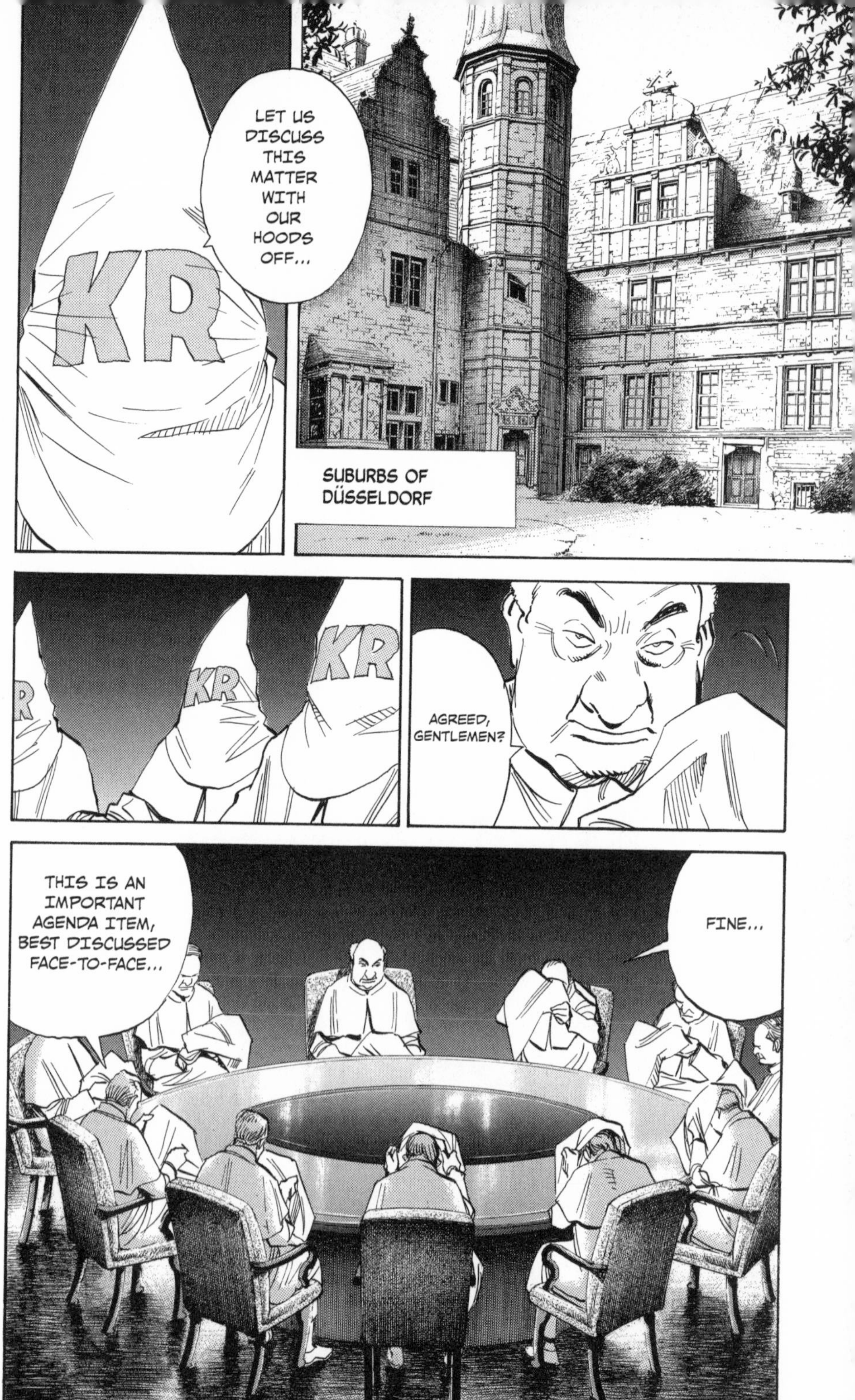
SUBURBS OF DÜSSELDORF
LET US DISCUSS THIS MATTER WITH OUR HOODS OFF...
KR
KR
AGREED, GENTLEMEN?
KR
KR
FINE...
THIS IS AN IMPORTANT AGENDA ITEM, BEST DISCUSSED FACE-TO-FACE...

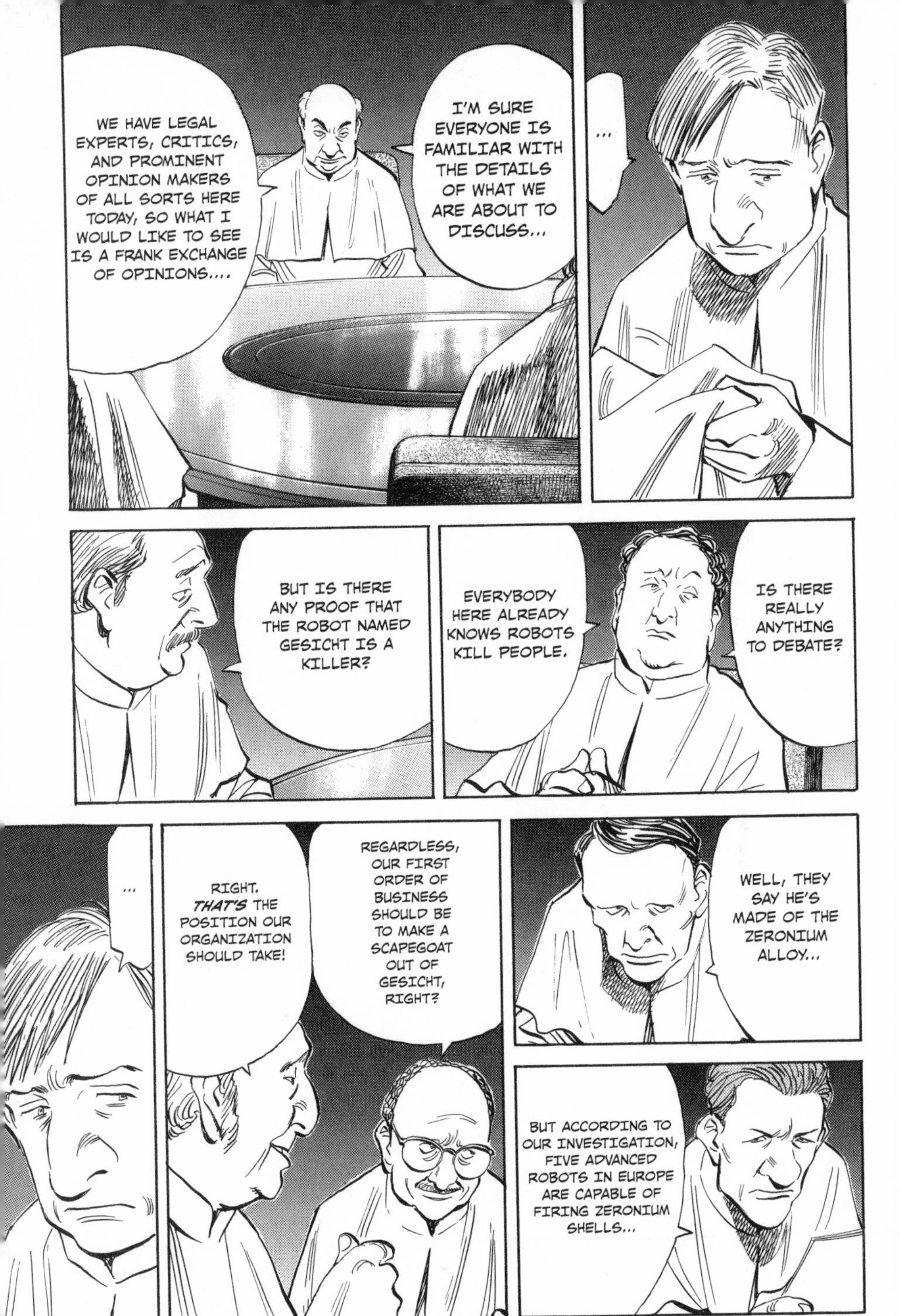
...
I'M SURE EVERYONE IS FAMILIAR WITH THE DETAILS OF WHAT WE ARE ABOUT TO DISCUSS...
WE HAVE LEGAL EXPERTS, CRITICS, AND PROMINENT OPINION MAKERS OF ALL SORTS HERE TODAY, SO WHAT I WOULD LIKE TO SEE IS A FRANK EXCHANGE OF OPINIONS....
IS THERE REALLY ANYTHING TO DEBATE?
EVERYBODY HERE ALREADY KNOWS ROBOTS KILL PEOPLE.
BUT IS THERE ANY PROOF THAT THE ROBOT NAMED GESICHT IS A KILLER?
WELL, THEY SAY HE'S MADE OF THE ZERONIUM ALLOY...
BUT ACCORDING TO OUR INVESTIGATION, FIVE ADVANCED ROBOTS IN EUROPE ARE CAPABLE OF FIRING ZERONIUM SHELLS...
REGARDLESS, OUR FIRST ORDER OF BUSINESS SHOULD BE TO MAKE A SCAPEGOAT OUT OF GESICHT, RIGHT?
RIGHT. *THAT'S* THE POSITION OUR ORGANIZATION SHOULD TAKE!
...

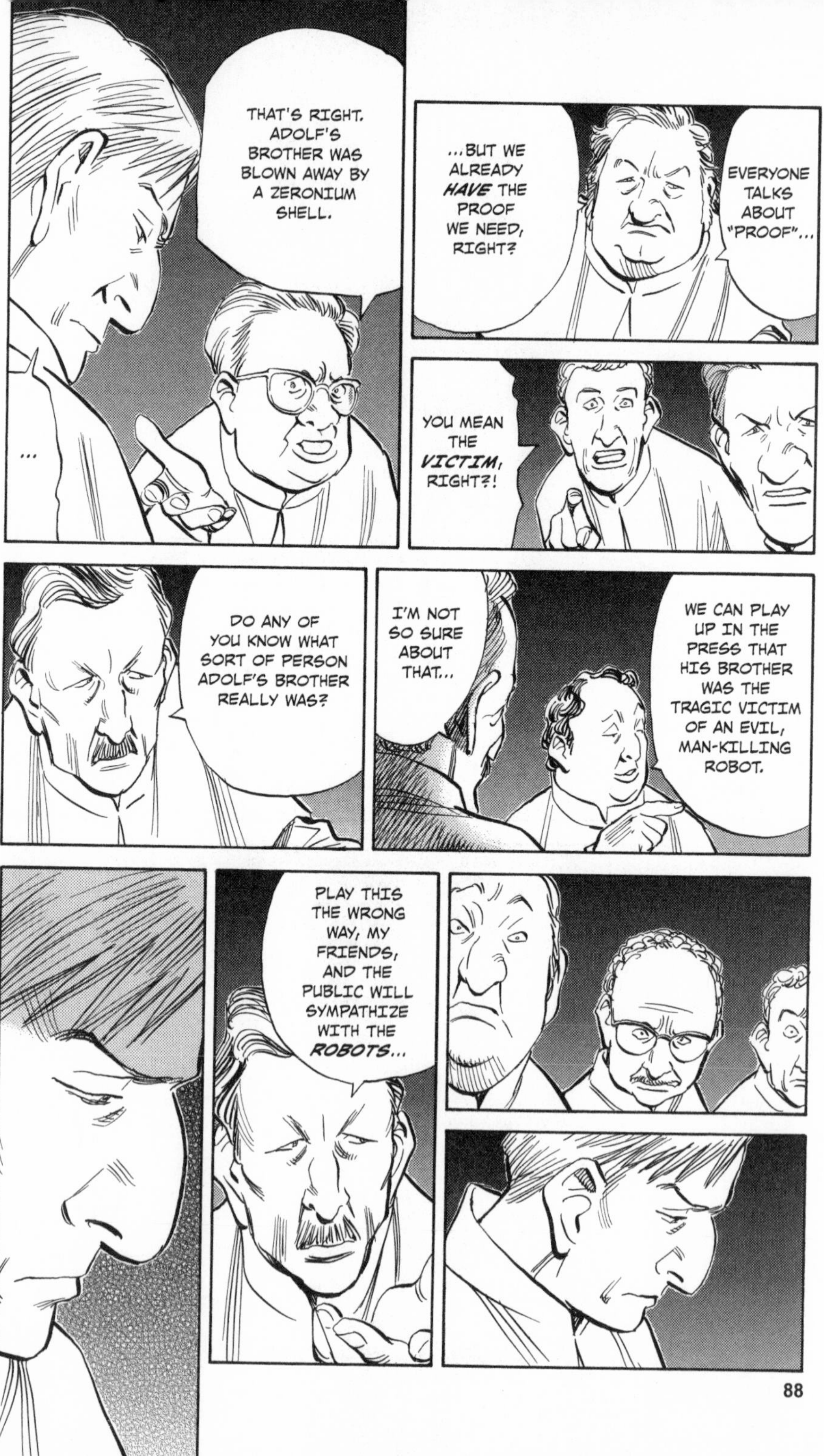
EVERYONE TALKS ABOUT "PROOF"...
...BUT WE ALREADY HAVE THE PROOF WE NEED, RIGHT?
YOU MEAN THE VICTIM, RIGHT?!
THAT'S RIGHT. ADOLF'S BROTHER WAS BLOWN AWAY BY A ZERONIUM SHELL.
...
WE CAN PLAY UP IN THE PRESS THAT HIS BROTHER WAS THE TRAGIC VICTIM OF AN EVIL, MAN-KILLING ROBOT.
I'M NOT SO SURE ABOUT THAT...
DO ANY OF YOU KNOW WHAT SORT OF PERSON ADOLF'S BROTHER REALLY WAS?
PLAY THIS THE WRONG WAY, MY FRIENDS, AND THE PUBLIC WILL SYMPATHIZE WITH THE ROBOTS...

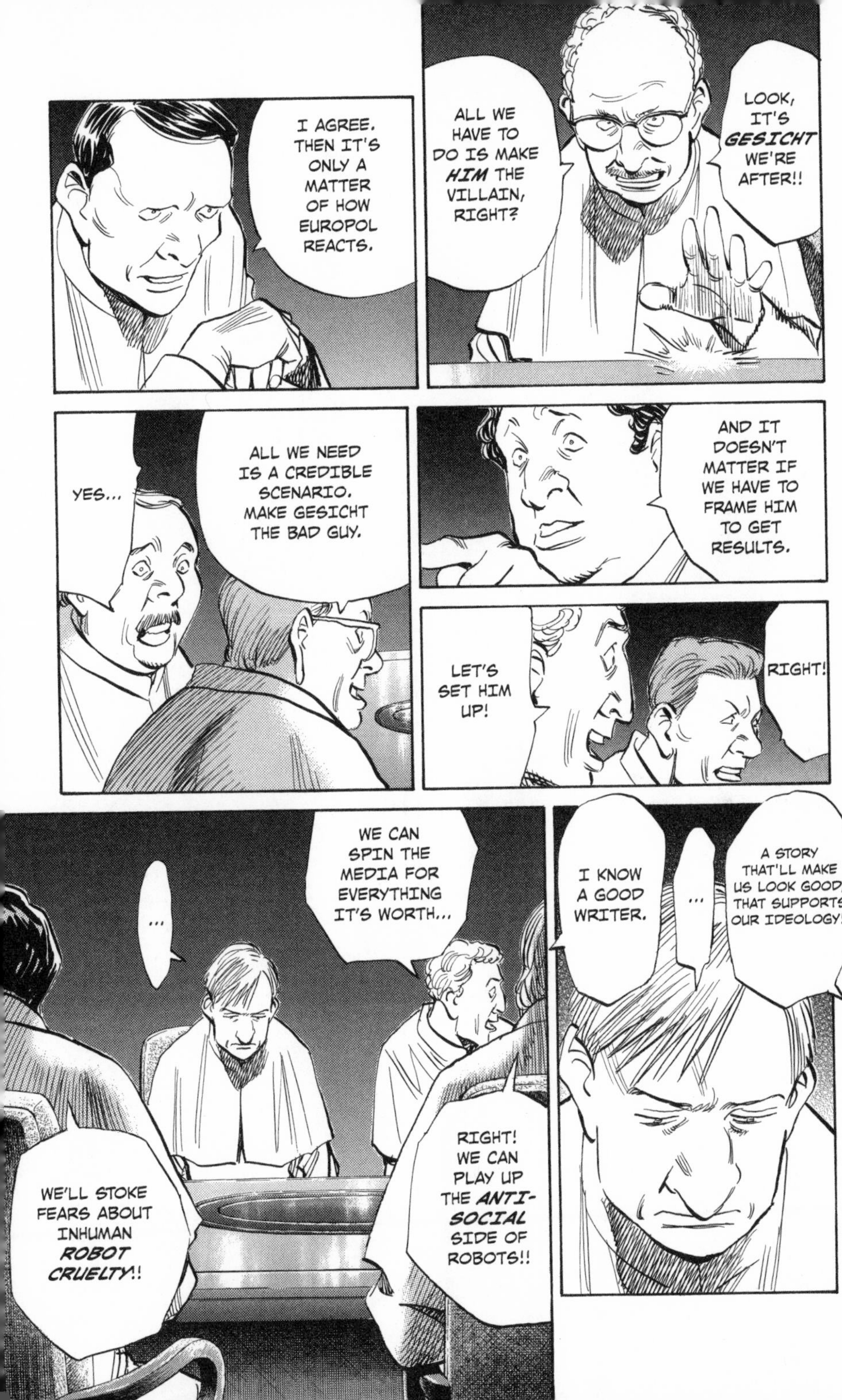
LOOK, IT'S *GESICHT* WE'RE AFTER!!
ALL WE HAVE TO DO IS MAKE *HIM* THE VILLAIN, RIGHT?
I AGREE. THEN IT'S ONLY A MATTER OF HOW EUROPOL REACTS.
AND IT DOESN'T MATTER IF WE HAVE TO FRAME HIM TO GET RESULTS.
RIGHT!
LET'S SET HIM UP!
ALL WE NEED IS A CREDIBLE SCENARIO. MAKE GESICHT THE BAD GUY.
YES...
A STORY THAT'LL MAKE US LOOK GOOD, THAT SUPPORTS OUR IDEOLOGY!!
...
I KNOW A GOOD WRITER.
WE CAN SPIN THE MEDIA FOR EVERYTHING IT'S WORTH...
...
RIGHT! WE CAN PLAY UP THE *ANTI-SOCIAL* SIDE OF ROBOTS!!
WE'LL STOKE FEARS ABOUT INHUMAN *ROBOT CRUELTY*!!

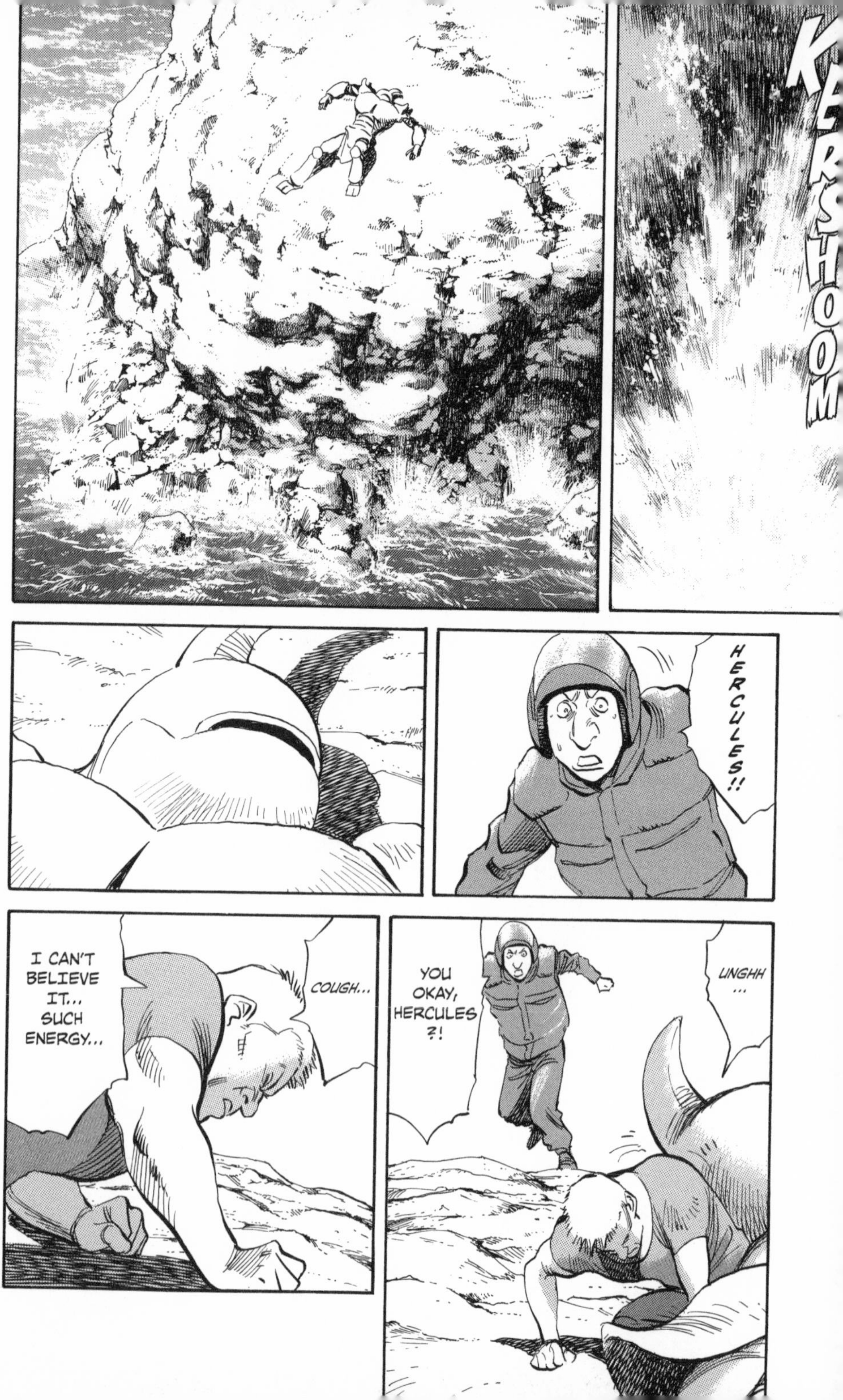
KERSHOOM
HERCULES!!
UNGHH ...
YOU OKAY, HERCULES ?!
COUGH...
I CAN'T BELIEVE IT... SUCH ENERGY...

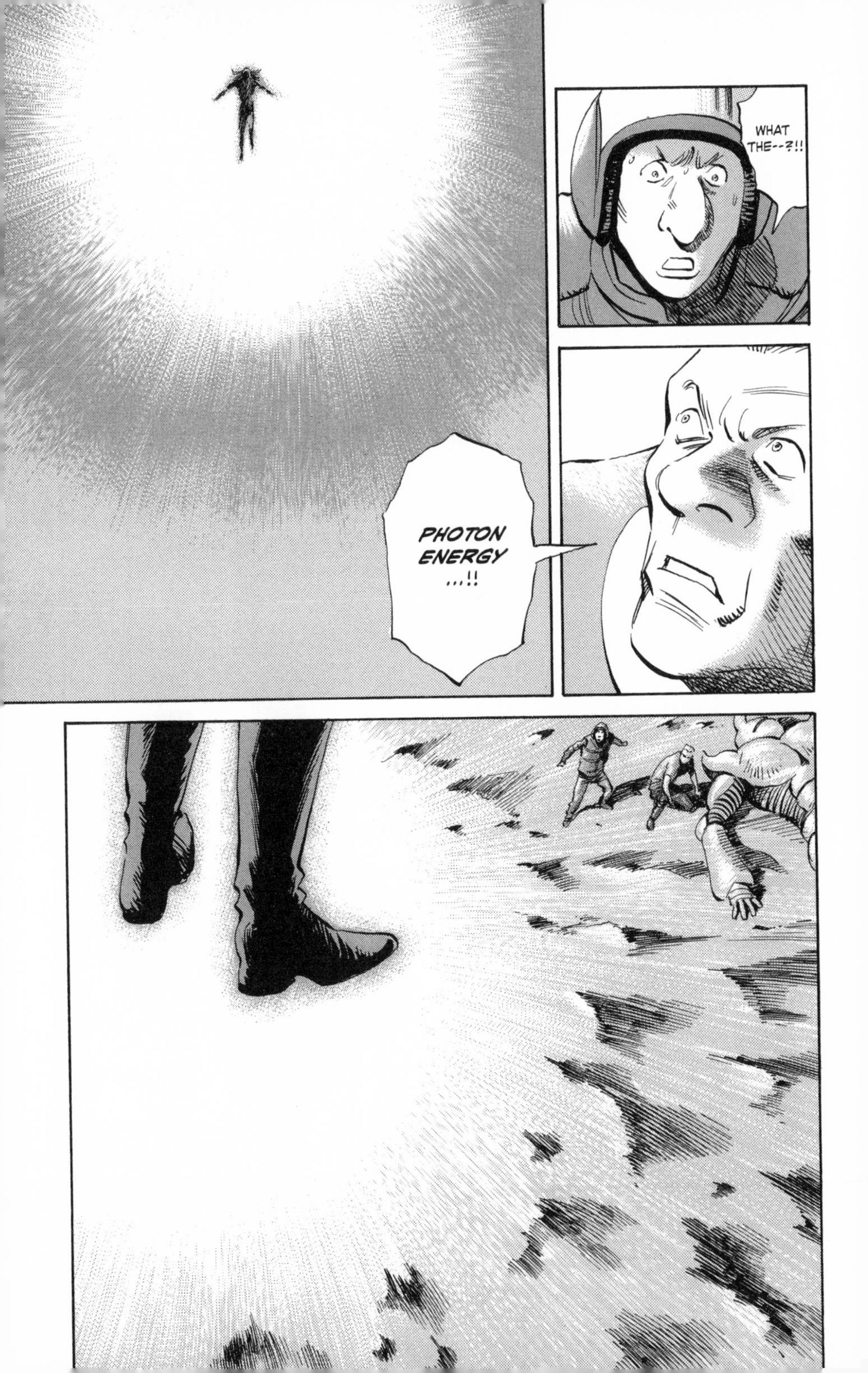
WHAT THE--?!!
PHOTON ENERGY ...!!

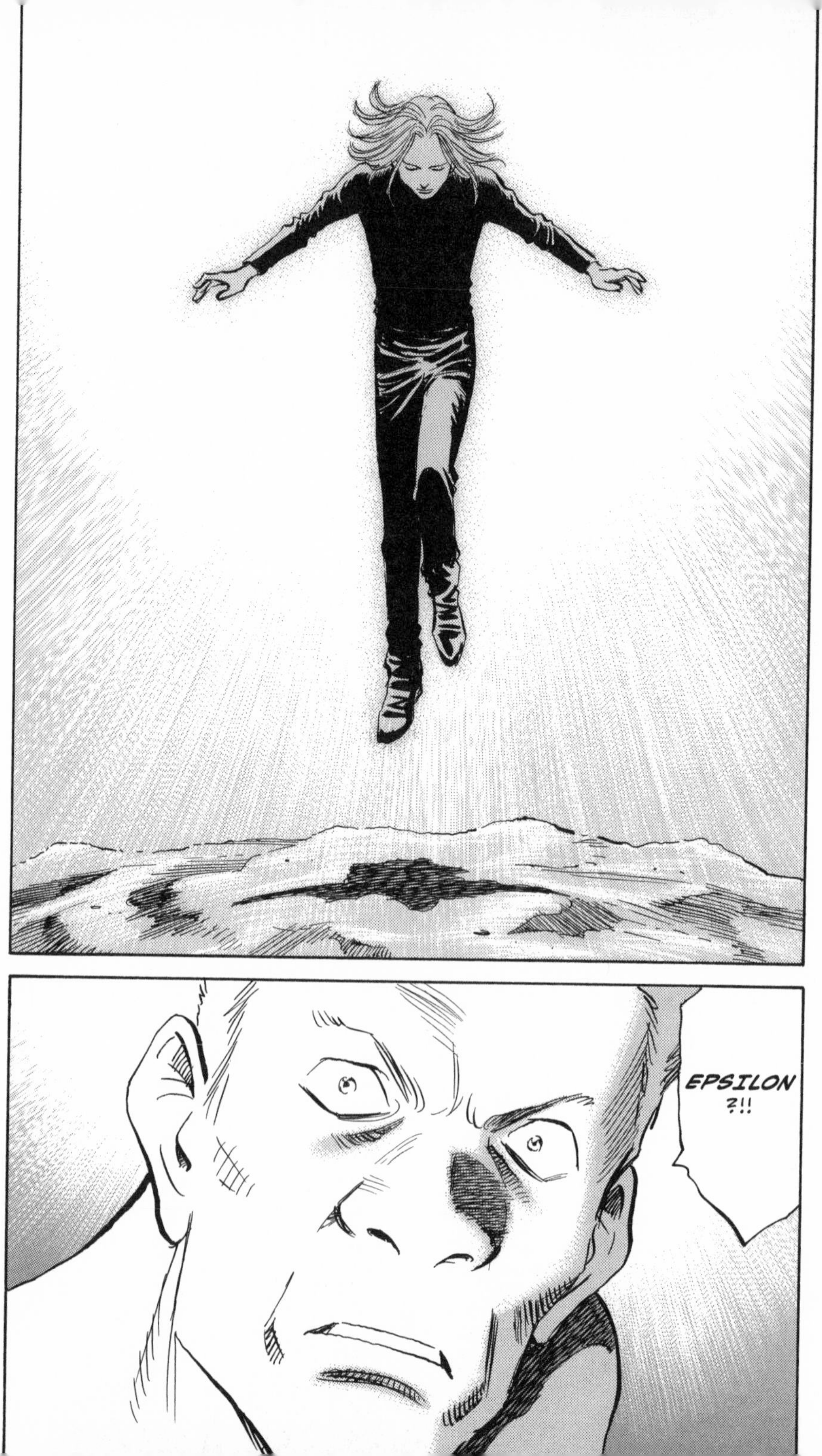
EPSILON ?!!

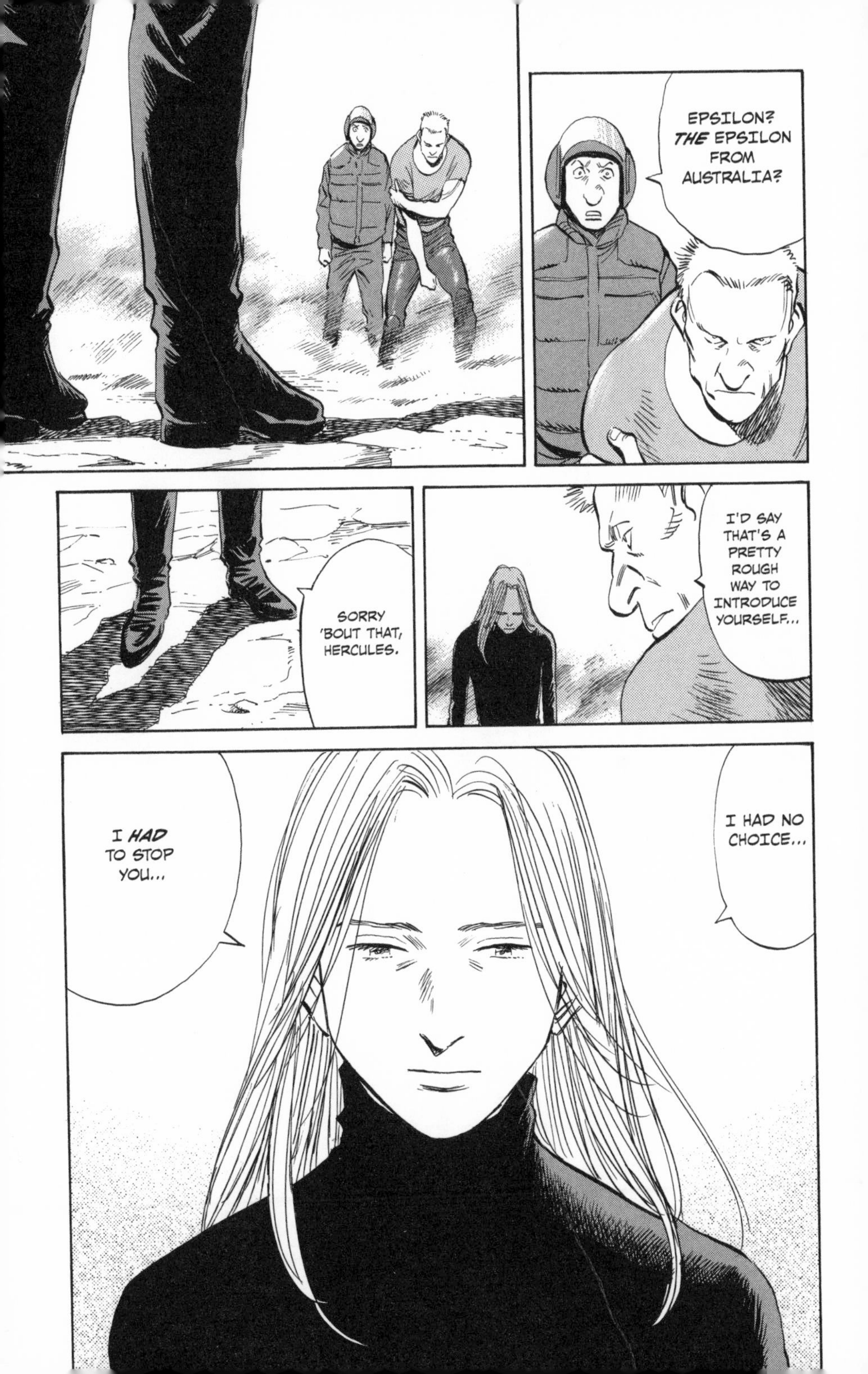
EPSILON? *THE* EPSILON FROM AUSTRALIA?
I'D SAY THAT'S A PRETTY ROUGH WAY TO INTRODUCE YOURSELF...
SORRY 'BOUT THAT, HERCULES.
I HAD NO CHOICE...
I *HAD* TO STOP YOU...

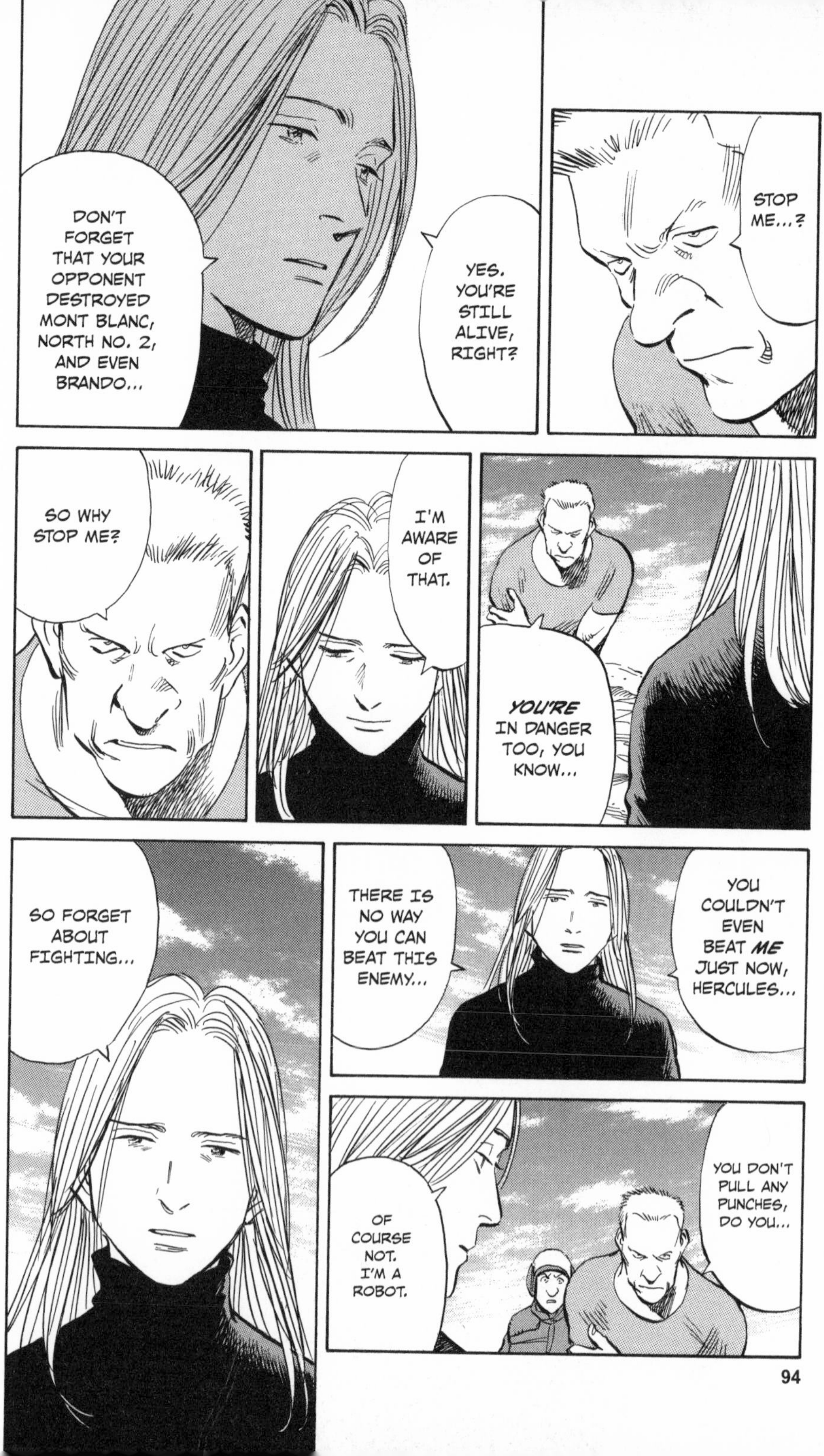
STOP ME...?
YES. YOU'RE STILL ALIVE, RIGHT?
DON'T FORGET THAT YOUR OPPONENT DESTROYED MONT BLANC, NORTH NO. 2, AND EVEN BRANDO...
YOU'RE IN DANGER TOO, YOU KNOW...
I'M AWARE OF THAT.
SO WHY STOP ME?
YOU COULDN'T EVEN BEAT *ME* JUST NOW, HERCULES...
THERE IS NO WAY YOU CAN BEAT THIS ENEMY...
YOU DON'T PULL ANY PUNCHES, DO YOU...
OF COURSE NOT. I'M A ROBOT.
SO FORGET ABOUT FIGHTING...

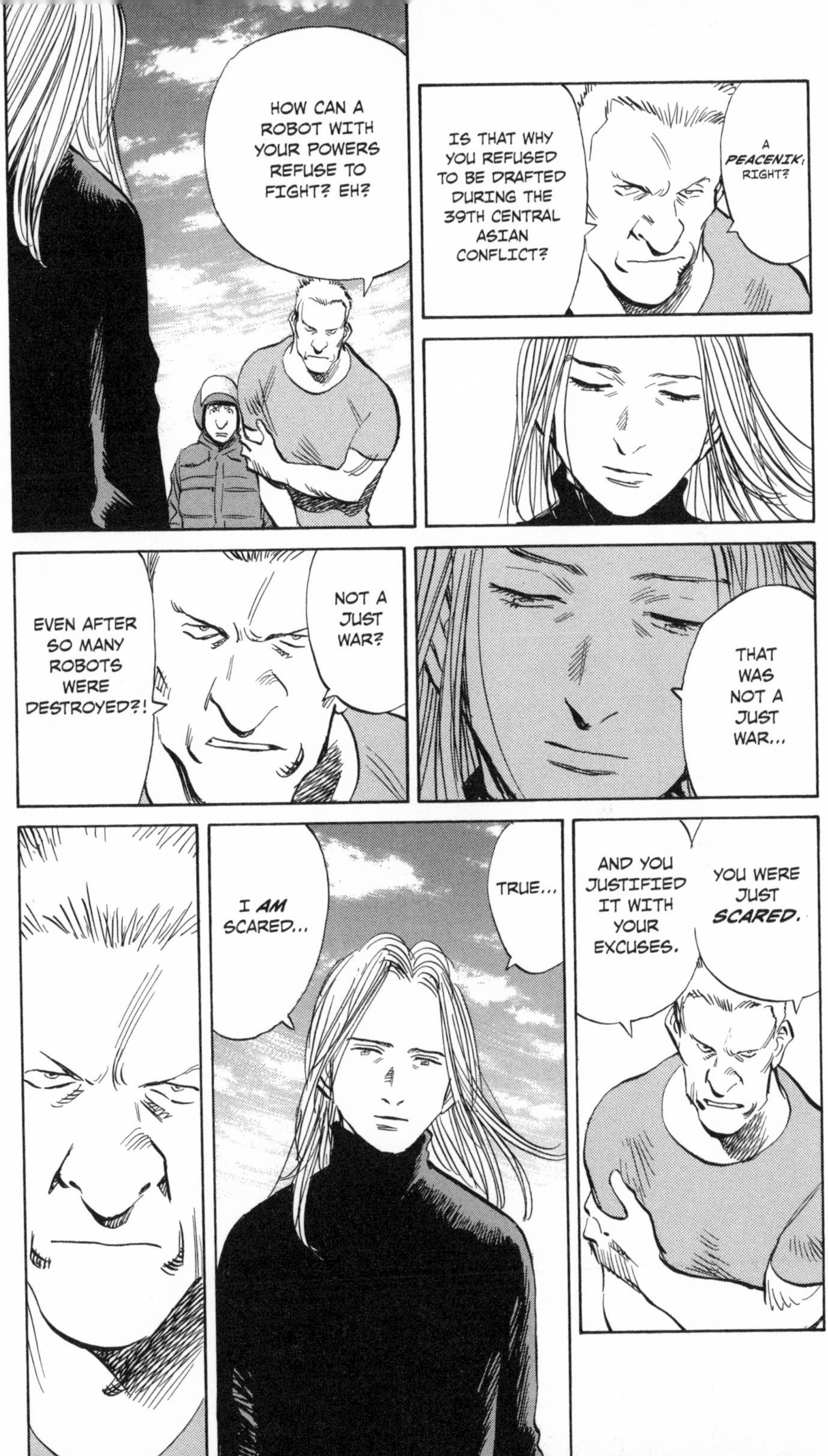
A PEACENIK, RIGHT?
IS THAT WHY YOU REFUSED TO BE DRAFTED DURING THE 39TH CENTRAL ASIAN CONFLICT?
HOW CAN A ROBOT WITH YOUR POWERS REFUSE TO FIGHT? EH?
THAT WAS NOT A JUST WAR...
NOT A JUST WAR?
EVEN AFTER SO MANY ROBOTS WERE DESTROYED?!
YOU WERE JUST SCARED.
AND YOU JUSTIFIED IT WITH YOUR EXCUSES.
TRUE...
I AM SCARED...

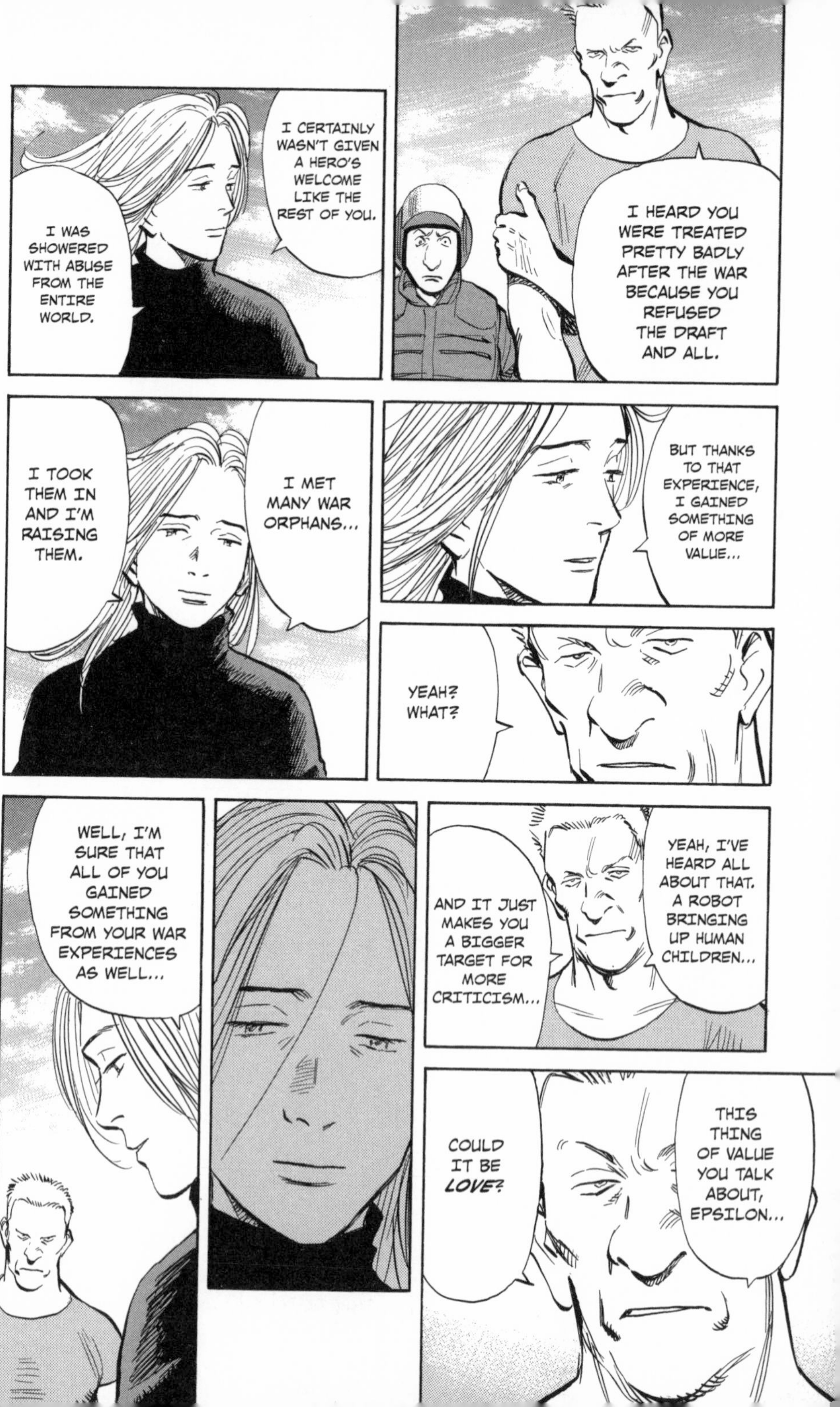
I HEARD YOU WERE TREATED PRETTY BADLY AFTER THE WAR BECAUSE YOU REFUSED THE DRAFT AND ALL.
I CERTAINLY WASN'T GIVEN A HERO'S WELCOME LIKE THE REST OF YOU.
I WAS SHOWERED WITH ABUSE FROM THE ENTIRE WORLD.
BUT THANKS TO THAT EXPERIENCE, I GAINED SOMETHING OF MORE VALUE...
YEAH? WHAT?
I MET MANY WAR ORPHANS...
I TOOK THEM IN AND I'M RAISING THEM.
YEAH, I'VE HEARD ALL ABOUT THAT. A ROBOT BRINGING UP HUMAN CHILDREN...
AND IT JUST MAKES YOU A BIGGER TARGET FOR MORE CRITICISM...
THIS THING OF VALUE YOU TALK ABOUT, EPSILON...
COULD IT BE *LOVE*?
WELL, I'M SURE THAT ALL OF YOU GAINED SOMETHING FROM YOUR WAR EXPERIENCES AS WELL...

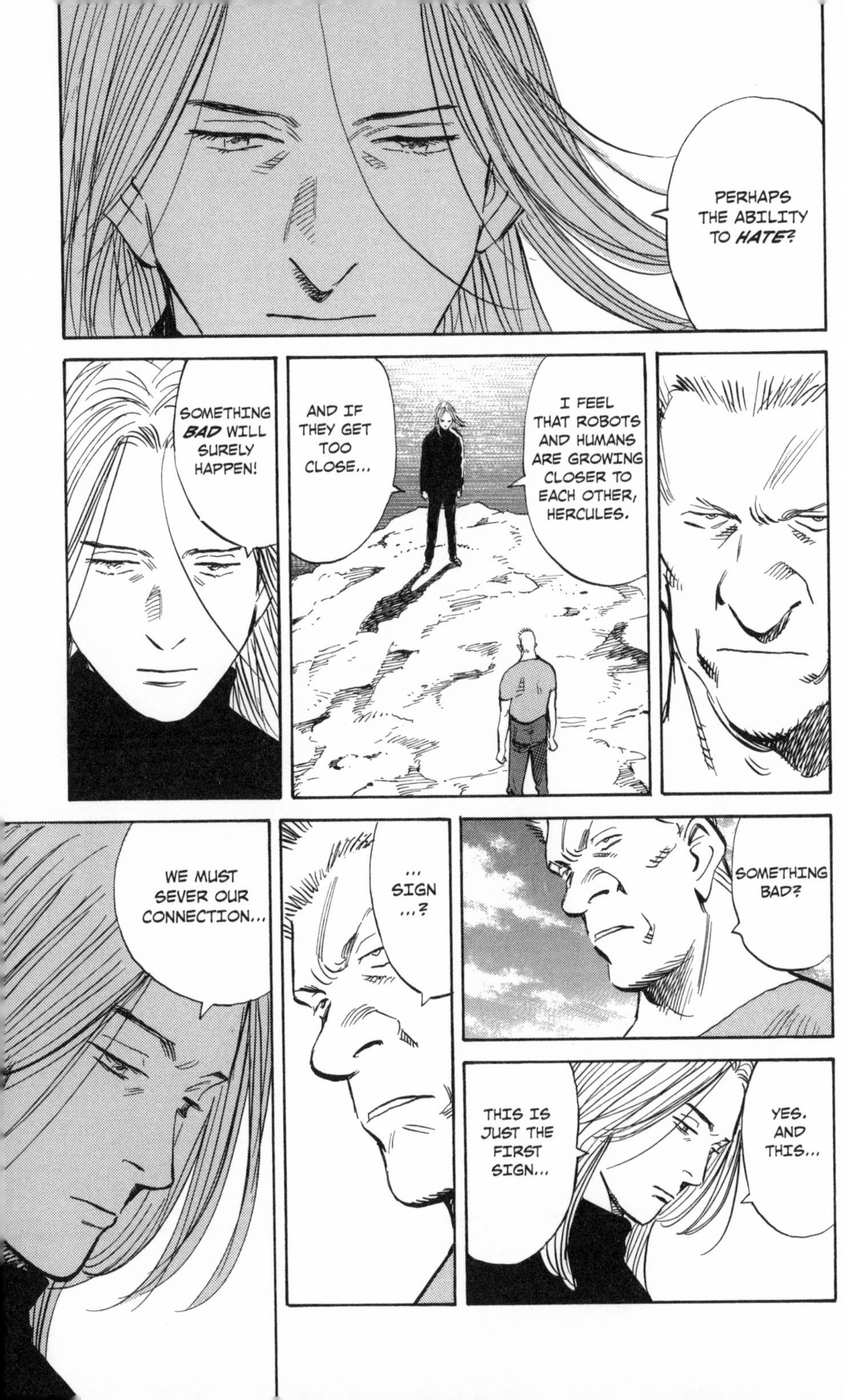
PERHAPS THE ABILITY TO *HATE?*
I FEEL THAT ROBOTS AND HUMANS ARE GROWING CLOSER TO EACH OTHER, HERCULES.
AND IF THEY GET TOO CLOSE...
SOMETHING *BAD* WILL SURELY HAPPEN!
SOMETHING BAD?
YES. AND THIS...
THIS IS JUST THE FIRST SIGN...
... SIGN ...?
WE MUST SEVER OUR CONNECTION...

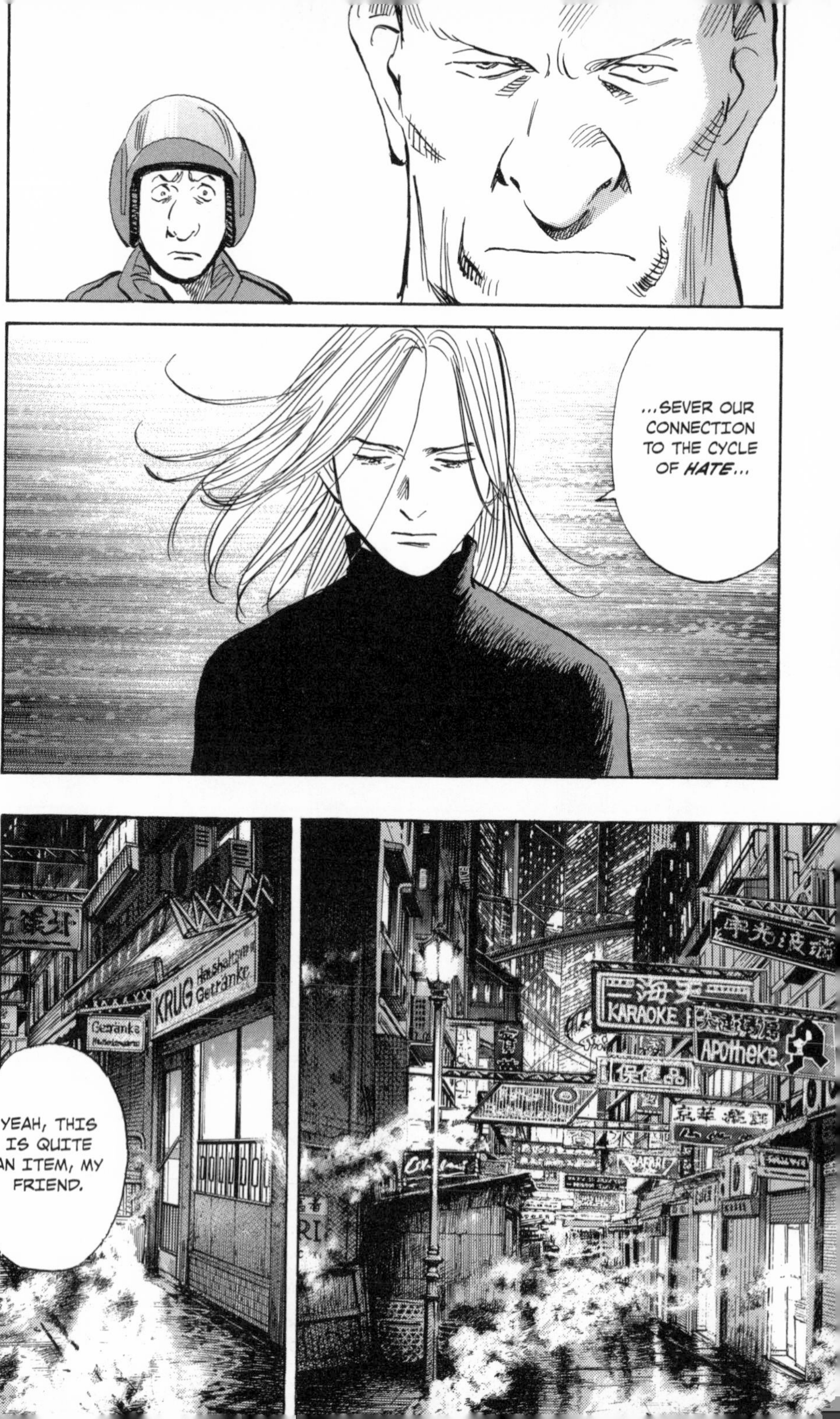
...SEVER OUR CONNECTION TO THE CYCLE OF ***HATE***...
KARAOKE
Apotheke
KRUG
Getränke
YEAH, THIS IS QUITE AN ITEM, MY FRIEND.

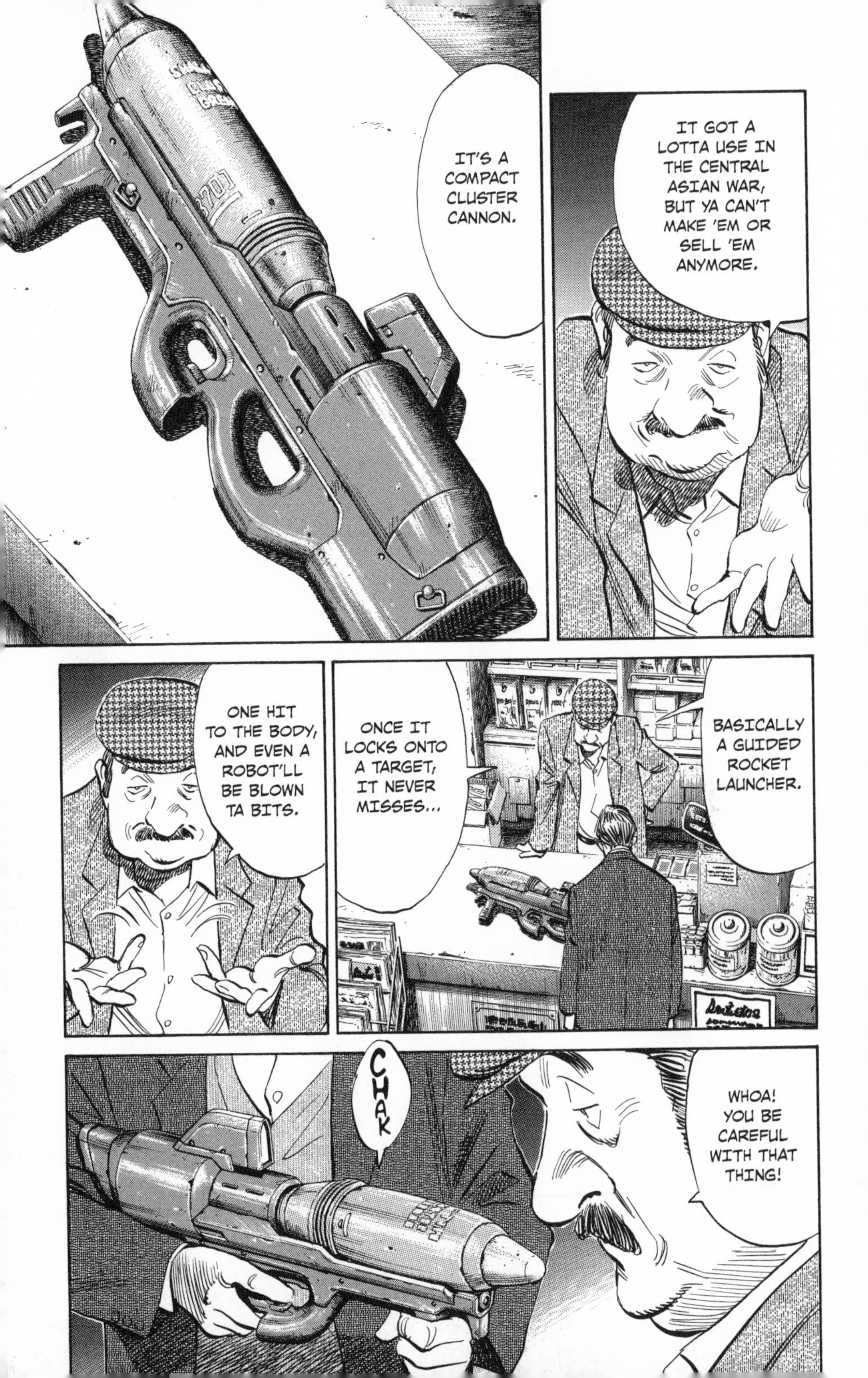
IT GOT A LOTTA USE IN THE CENTRAL ASIAN WAR, BUT YA CAN'T MAKE 'EM OR SELL 'EM ANYMORE.
IT'S A COMPACT CLUSTER CANNON.
BASICALLY A GUIDED ROCKET LAUNCHER.
ONCE IT LOCKS ONTO A TARGET, IT NEVER MISSES...
ONE HIT TO THE BODY, AND EVEN A ROBOT'LL BE BLOWN TA BITS.
WHOA! YOU BE CAREFUL WITH THAT THING!
CHAK

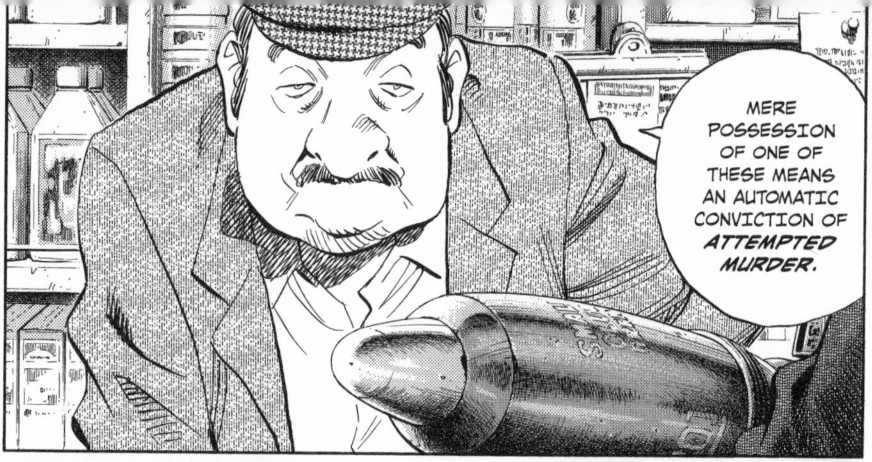
MERE POSSESSION OF ONE OF THESE MEANS AN AUTOMATIC CONVICTION OF ***ATTEMPTED MURDER.***

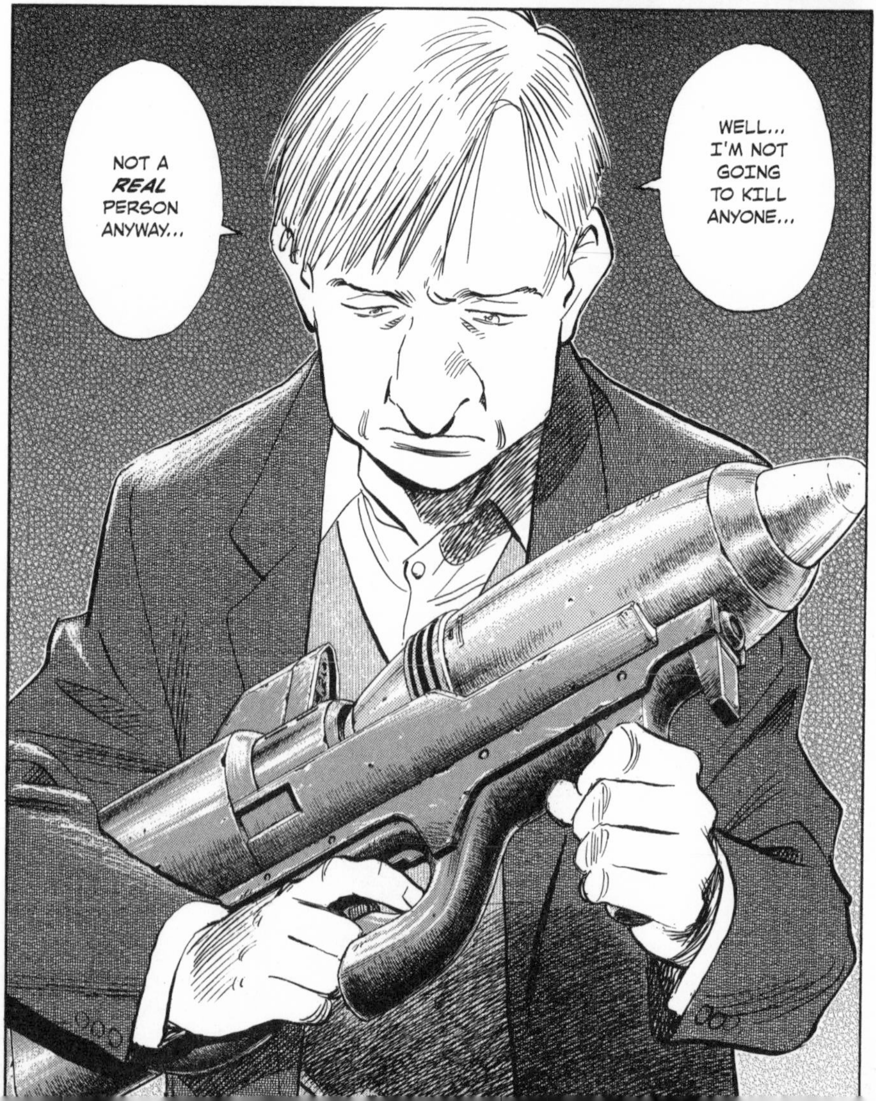
WELL... I'M NOT GOING TO KILL ANYONE...
NOT A ***REAL*** PERSON ANYWAY...

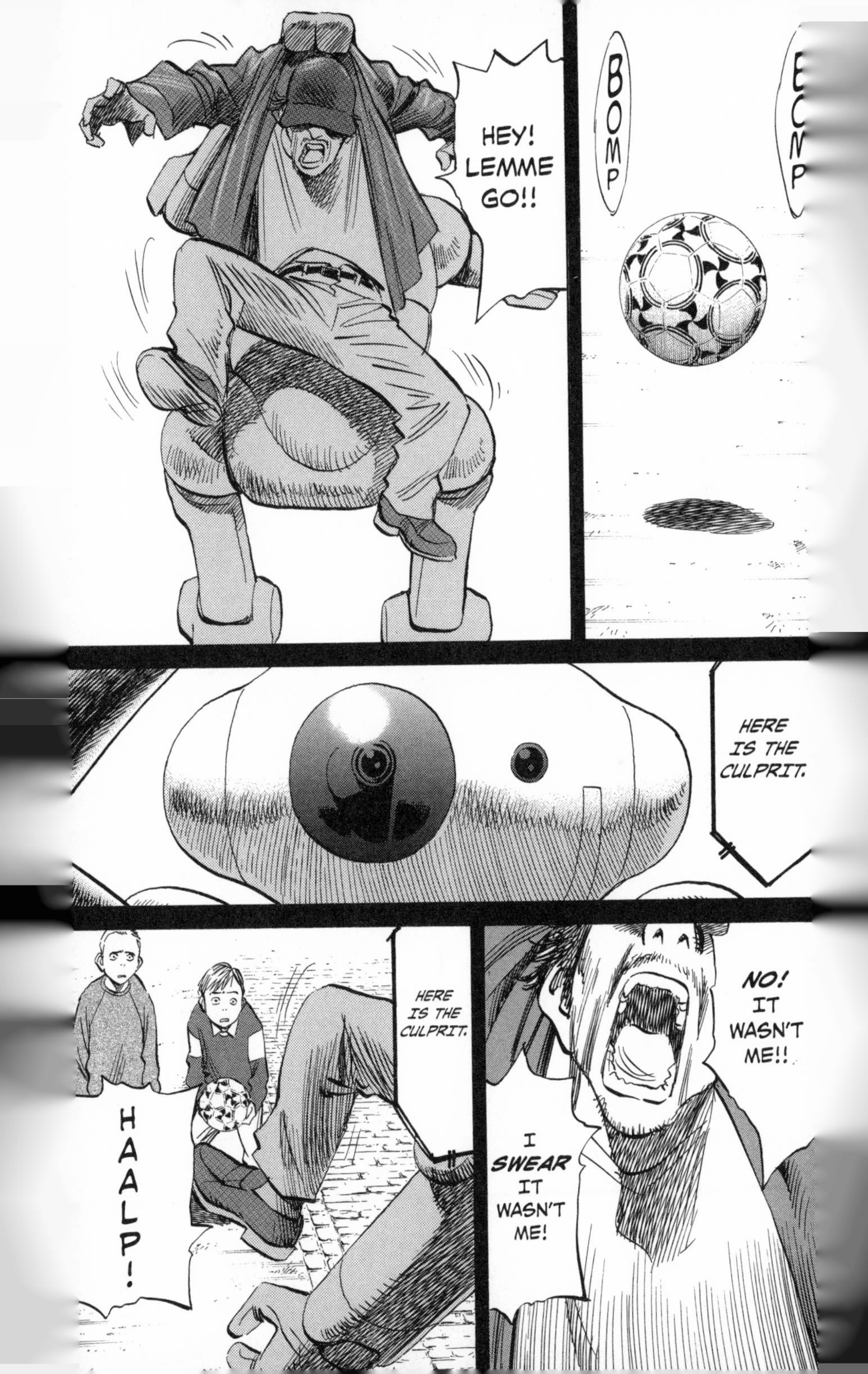
BOMP
HEY! LEMME GO!!
HERE IS THE CULPRIT.
NO! IT WASN'T ME!!
I SWEAR IT WASN'T ME!
HERE IS THE CULPRIT.
HAAALP!

HERE IS THE CULPRIT.

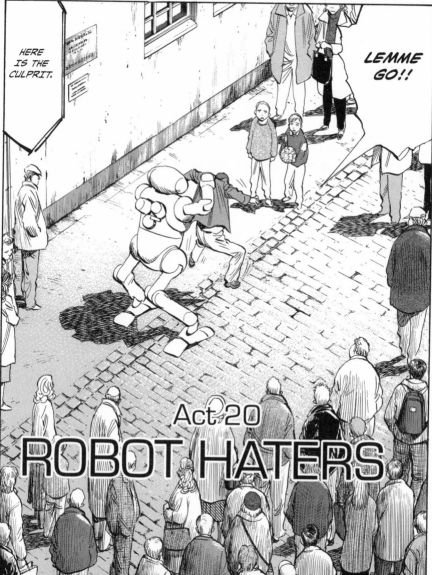

HERE IS THE CULPRIT.

LEMME GO!!

Act.20
ROBOT HATERS

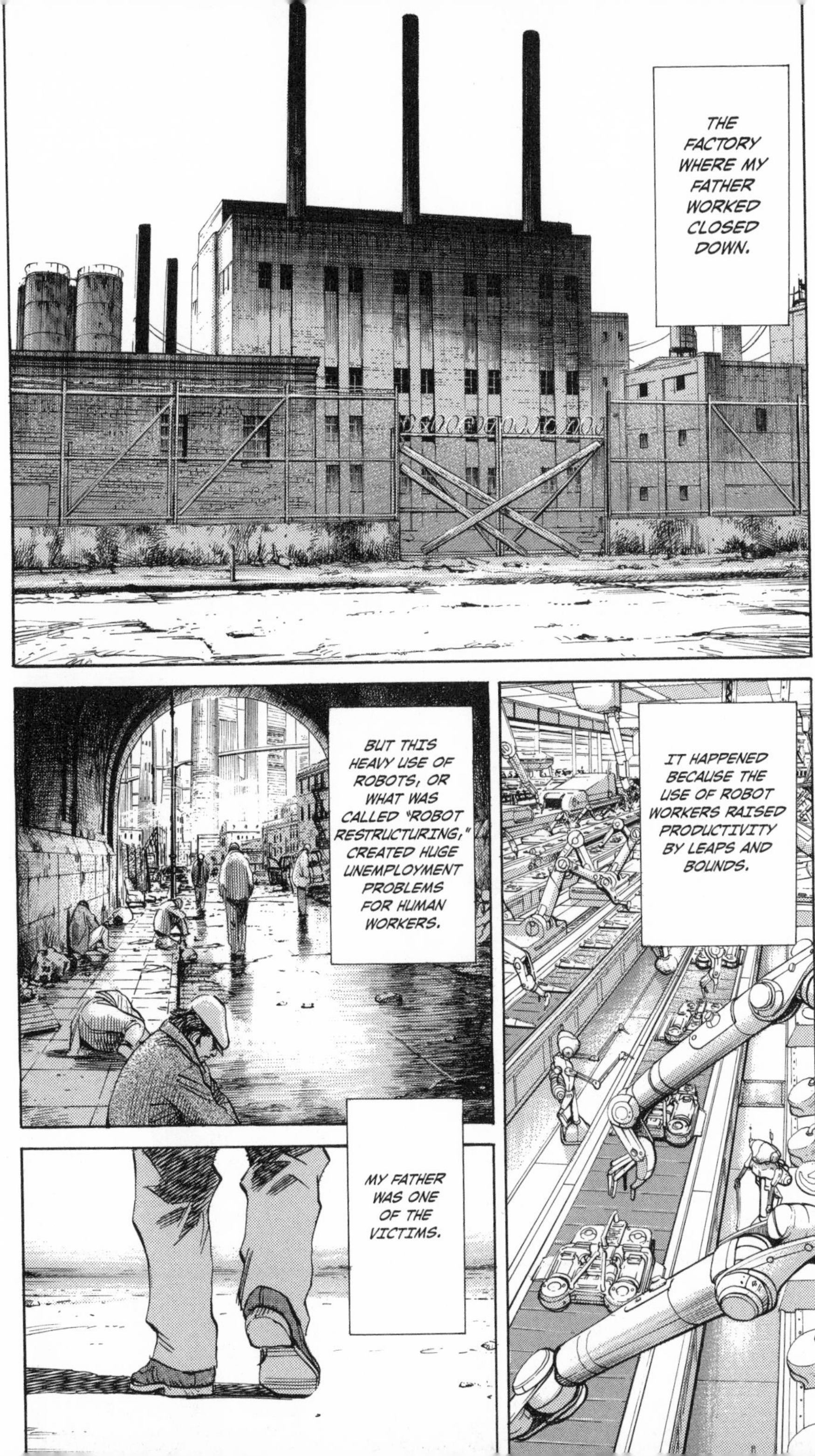
THE FACTORY WHERE MY FATHER WORKED CLOSED DOWN.
IT HAPPENED BECAUSE THE USE OF ROBOT WORKERS RAISED PRODUCTIVITY BY LEAPS AND BOUNDS.
BUT THIS HEAVY USE OF ROBOTS, OR WHAT WAS CALLED "ROBOT RESTRUCTURING," CREATED HUGE UNEMPLOYMENT PROBLEMS FOR HUMAN WORKERS.
MY FATHER WAS ONE OF THE VICTIMS.

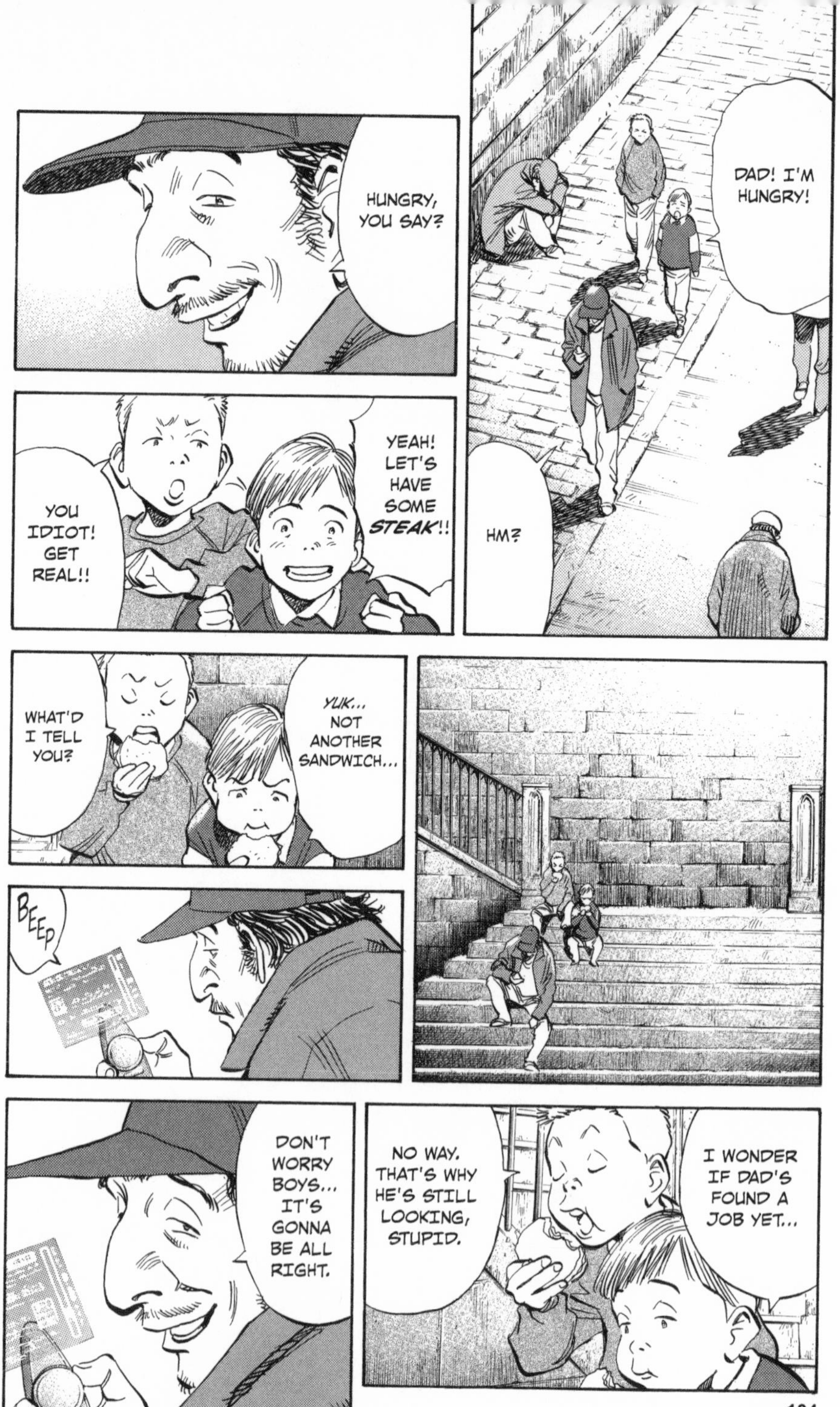
DAD! I'M HUNGRY!
HM?
HUNGRY, YOU SAY?
YEAH! LET'S HAVE SOME *STEAK*!!
YOU IDIOT! GET REAL!!
YUK... NOT ANOTHER SANDWICH...
WHAT'D I TELL YOU?
BEEP
I WONDER IF DAD'S FOUND A JOB YET...
NO WAY. THAT'S WHY HE'S STILL LOOKING, STUPID.
DON'T WORRY BOYS... IT'S GONNA BE ALL RIGHT.

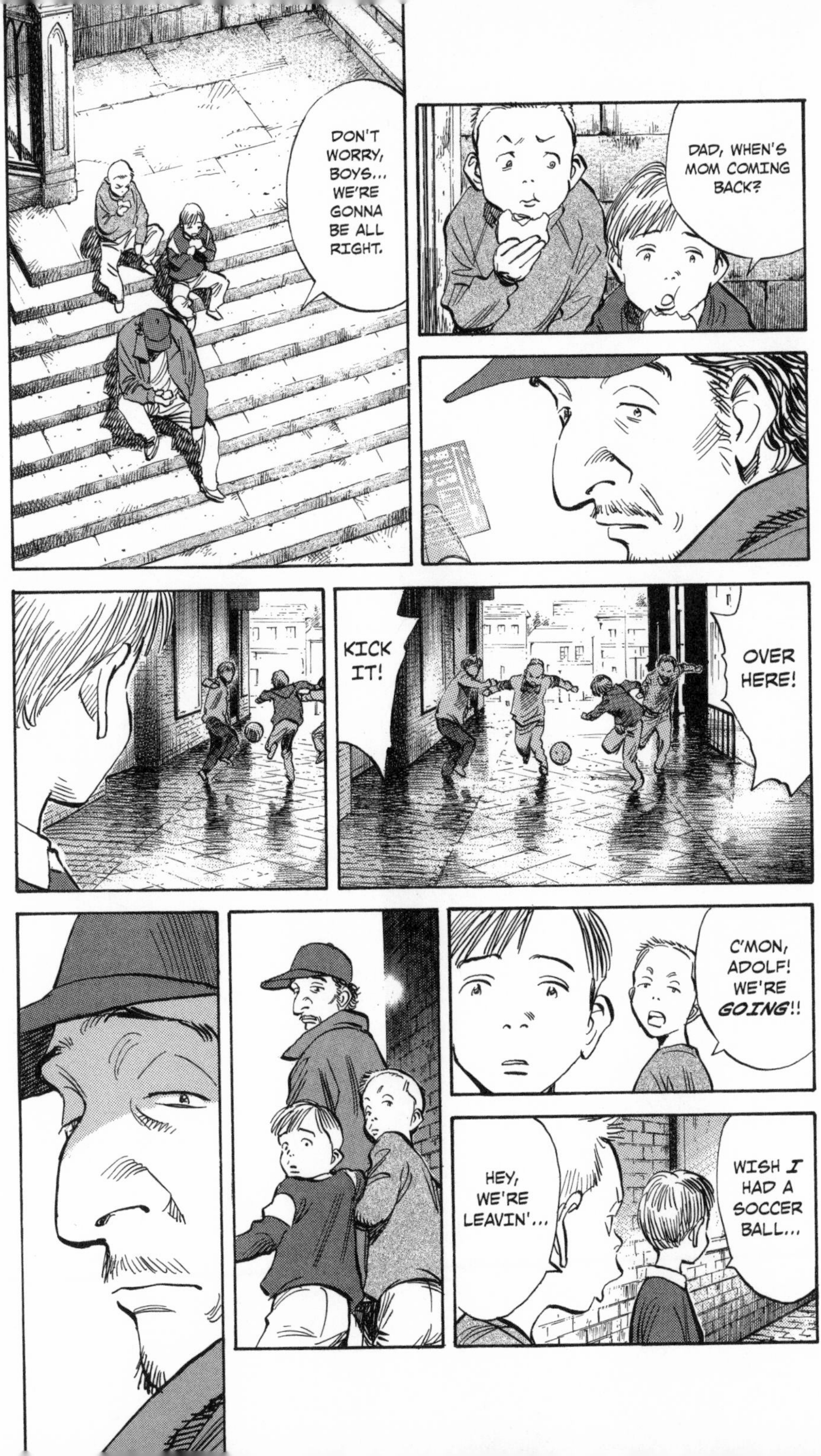
DAD, WHEN'S MOM COMING BACK?
DON'T WORRY, BOYS... WE'RE GONNA BE ALL RIGHT.
OVER HERE!
KICK IT!
C'MON, ADOLF! WE'RE *GOING*!!
WISH *I* HAD A SOCCER BALL...
HEY, WE'RE LEAVIN'...

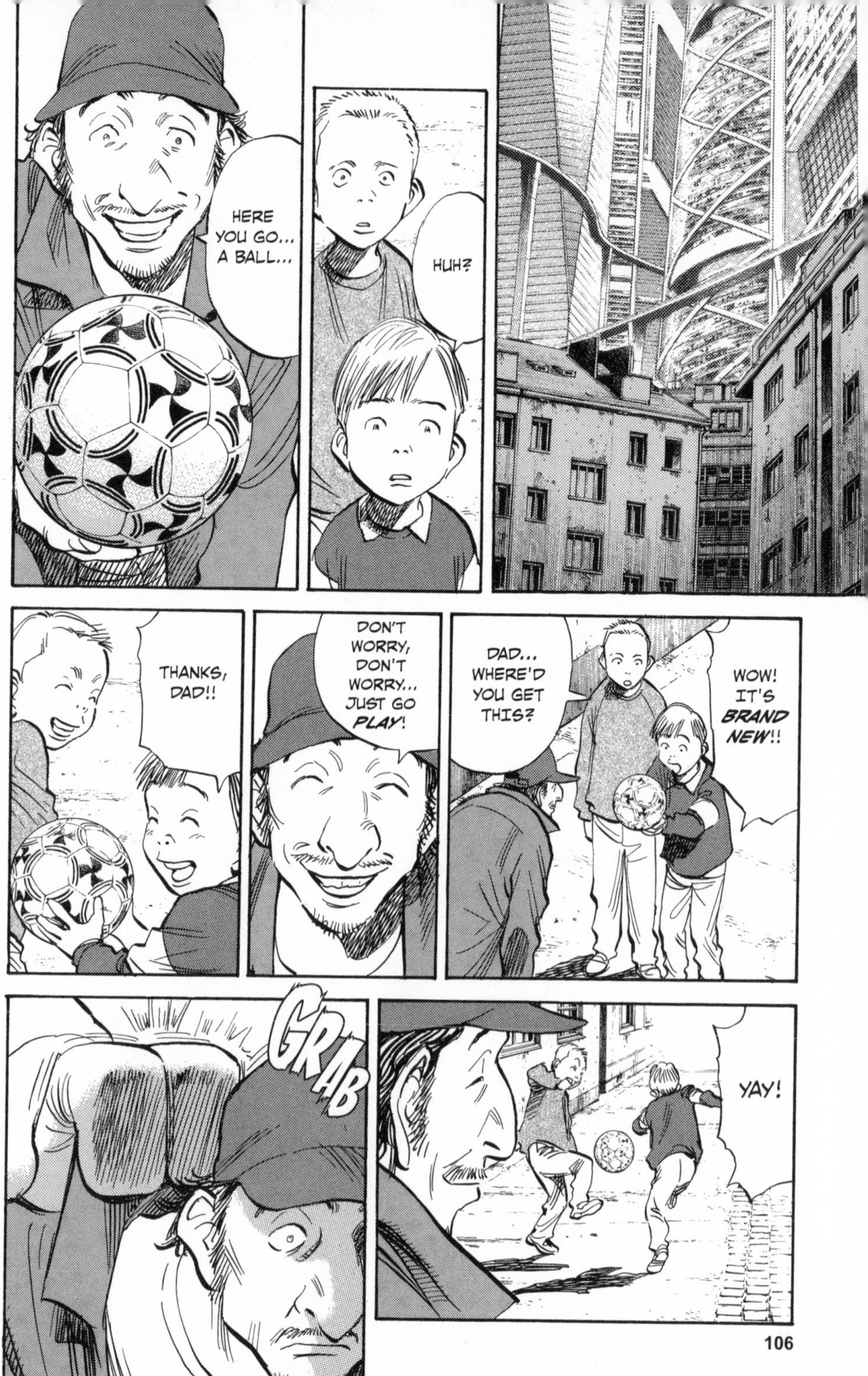
HUH?
HERE YOU GO... A BALL...
WOW! IT'S BRAND NEW!!
DAD... WHERE'D YOU GET THIS?
DON'T WORRY, DON'T WORRY... JUST GO PLAY!
THANKS, DAD!!
YAY!
GRAB

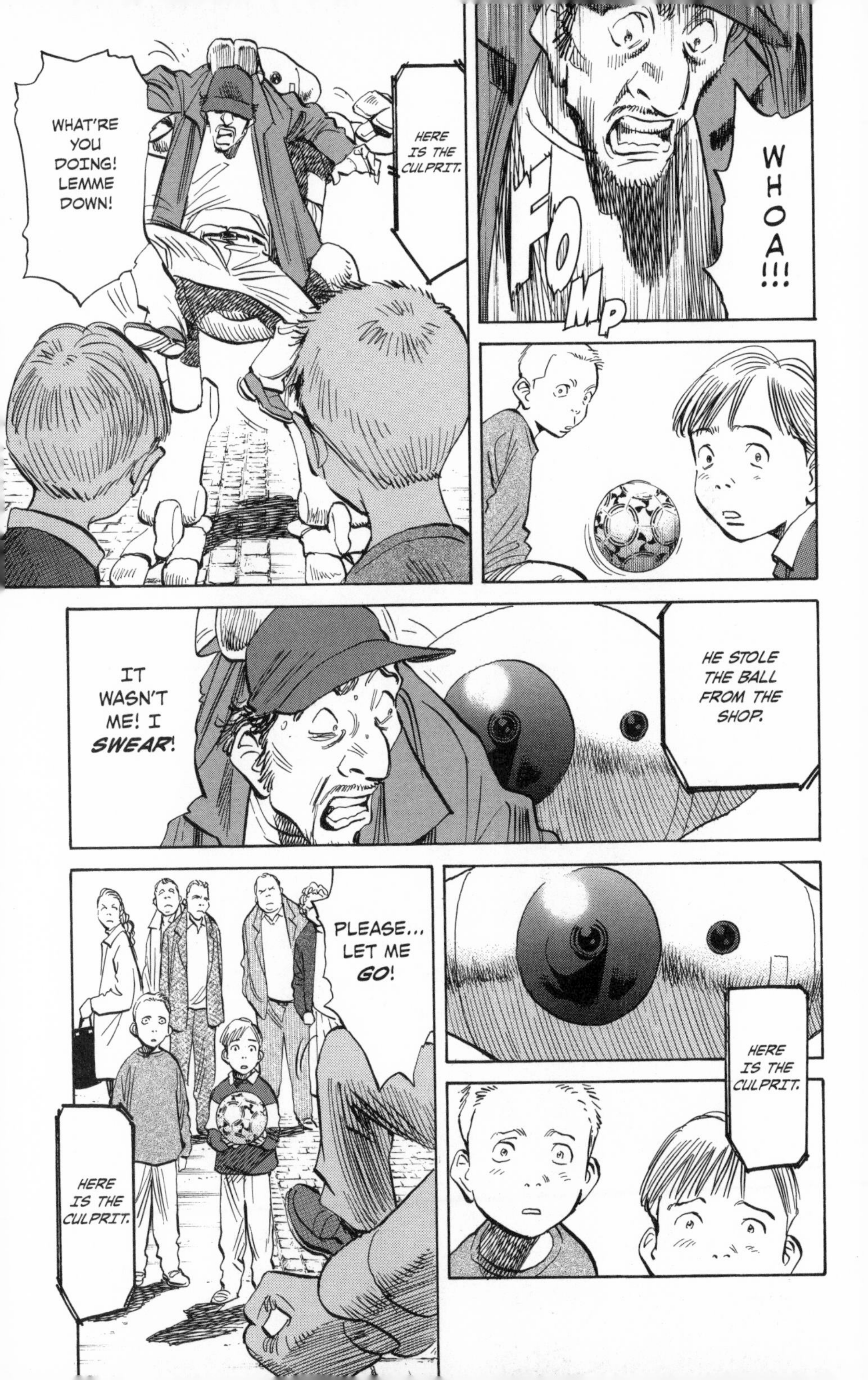
WHOA!!!
FOMP
HERE IS THE CULPRIT.
WHAT'RE YOU DOING! LEMME DOWN!
HE STOLE THE BALL FROM THE SHOP.
IT WASN'T ME! I SWEAR!
HERE IS THE CULPRIT.
PLEASE... LET ME GO!
HERE IS THE CULPRIT.

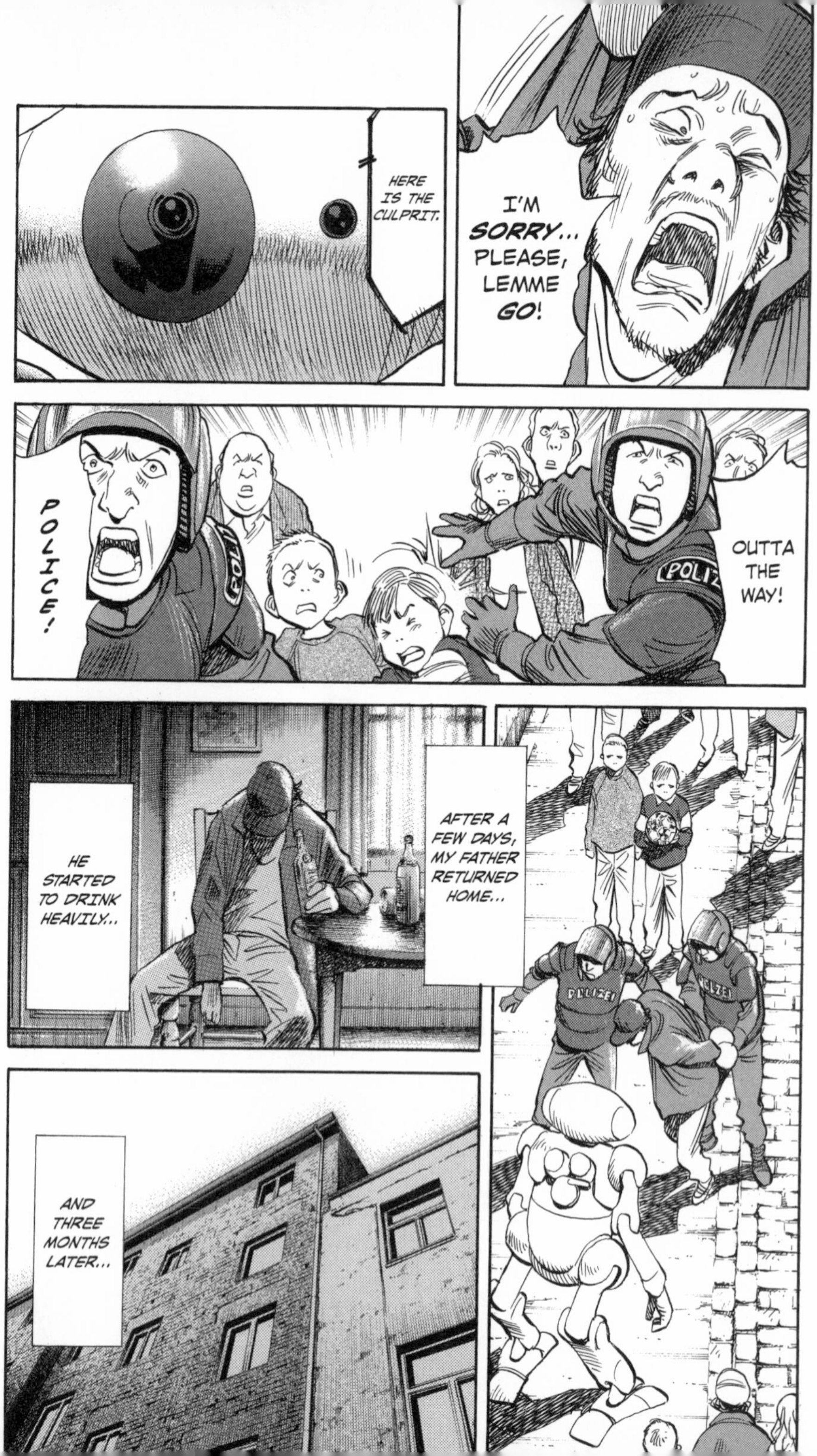
I'M SORRY... PLEASE, LEMME GO!
HERE IS THE CULPRIT.
OUTTA THE WAY!
POLICE!
AFTER A FEW DAYS, MY FATHER RETURNED HOME...
HE STARTED TO DRINK HEAVILY...
AND THREE MONTHS LATER...

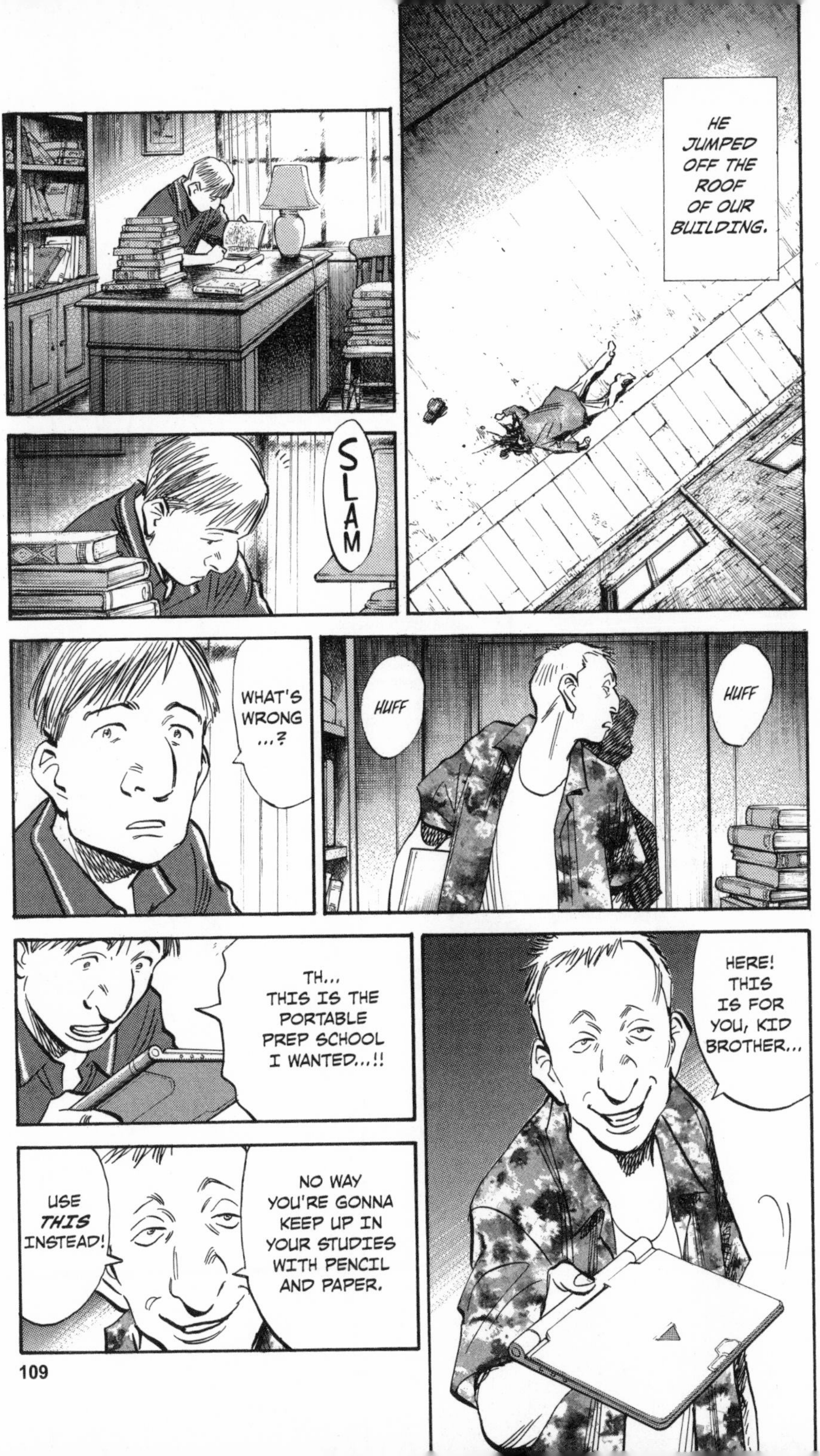
HE JUMPED OFF THE ROOF OF OUR BUILDING.
SLAM
HUFF
HUFF
WHAT'S WRONG ...?
HERE! THIS IS FOR YOU, KID BROTHER...
TH... THIS IS THE PORTABLE PREP SCHOOL I WANTED...!!
NO WAY YOU'RE GONNA KEEP UP IN YOUR STUDIES WITH PENCIL AND PAPER.
USE *THIS* INSTEAD!

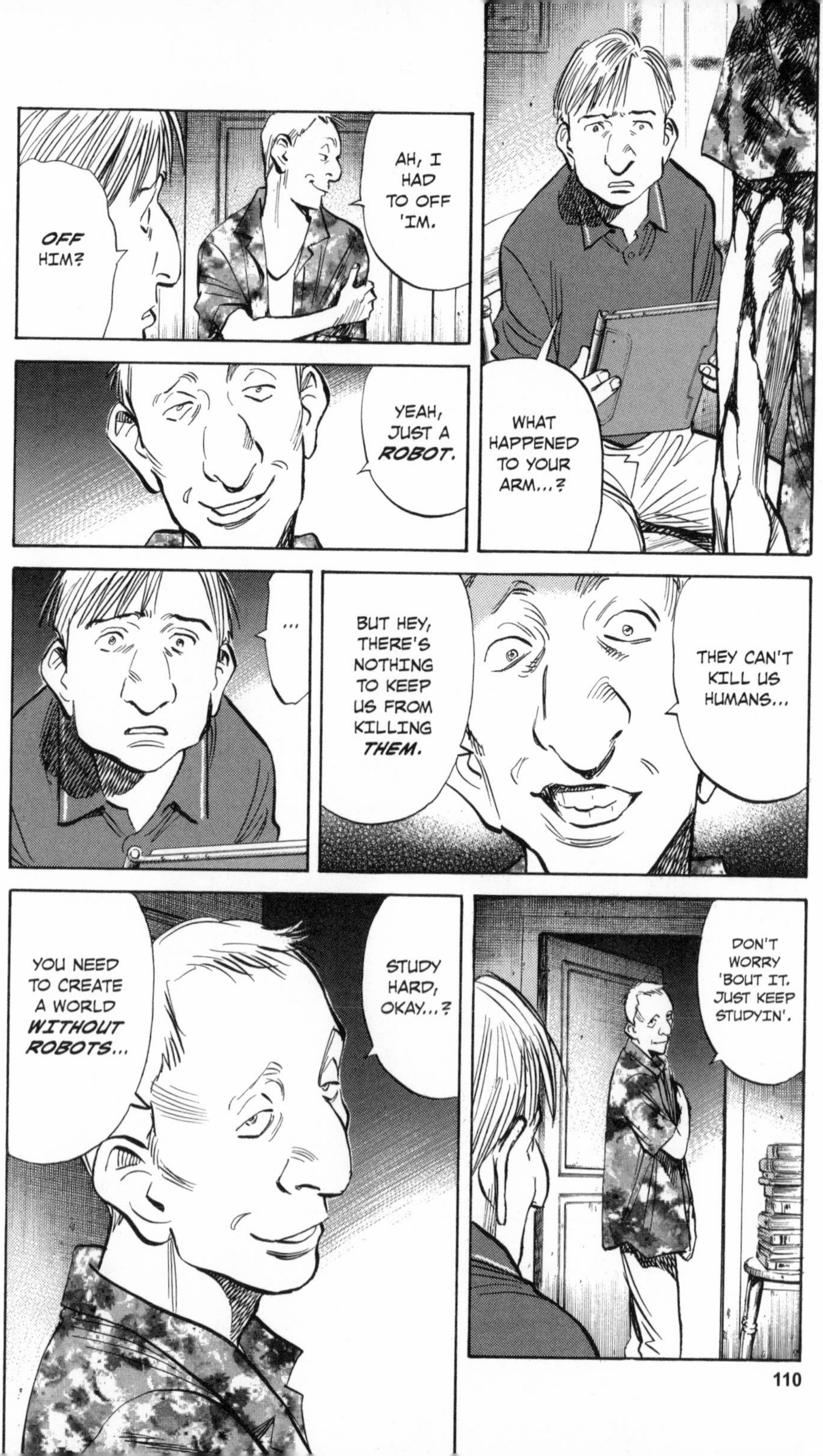
WHAT HAPPENED TO YOUR ARM...?
AH, I HAD TO OFF 'IM.
OFF HIM?
YEAH, JUST A *ROBOT*.
THEY CAN'T KILL US HUMANS...
BUT HEY, THERE'S NOTHING TO KEEP US FROM KILLING *THEM*.
...
DON'T WORRY 'BOUT IT. JUST KEEP STUDYIN'.
STUDY HARD, OKAY...?
YOU NEED TO CREATE A WORLD *WITHOUT ROBOTS*...

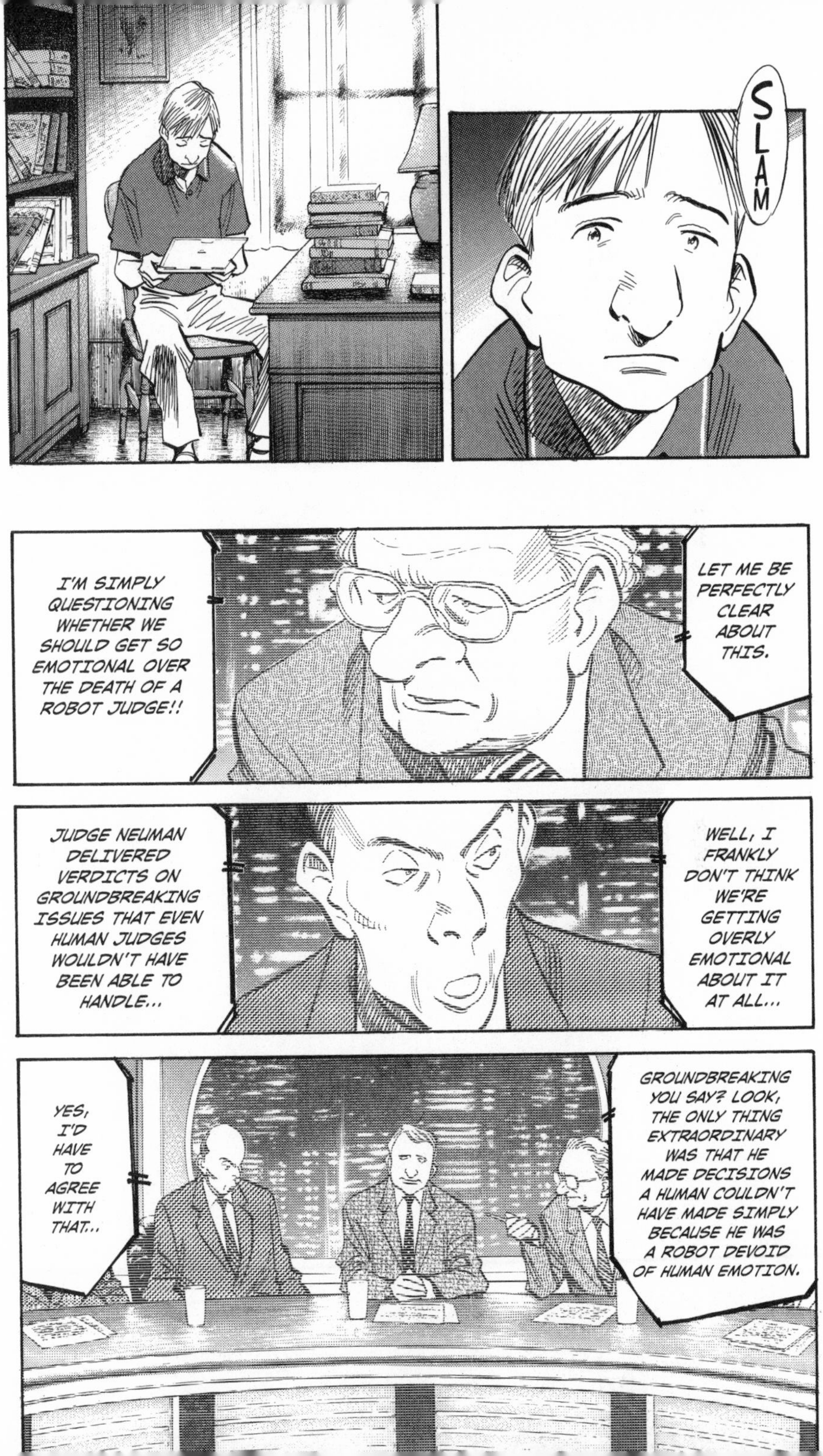
SLAM
LET ME BE PERFECTLY CLEAR ABOUT THIS.
I'M SIMPLY QUESTIONING WHETHER WE SHOULD GET SO EMOTIONAL OVER THE DEATH OF A ROBOT JUDGE!!
WELL, I FRANKLY DON'T THINK WE'RE GETTING OVERLY EMOTIONAL ABOUT IT AT ALL...
JUDGE NEUMAN DELIVERED VERDICTS ON GROUNDBREAKING ISSUES THAT EVEN HUMAN JUDGES WOULDN'T HAVE BEEN ABLE TO HANDLE...
GROUNDBREAKING YOU SAY? LOOK, THE ONLY THING EXTRAORDINARY WAS THAT HE MADE DECISIONS A HUMAN COULDN'T HAVE MADE SIMPLY BECAUSE HE WAS A ROBOT DEVOID OF HUMAN EMOTION.
YES, I'D HAVE TO AGREE WITH THAT...

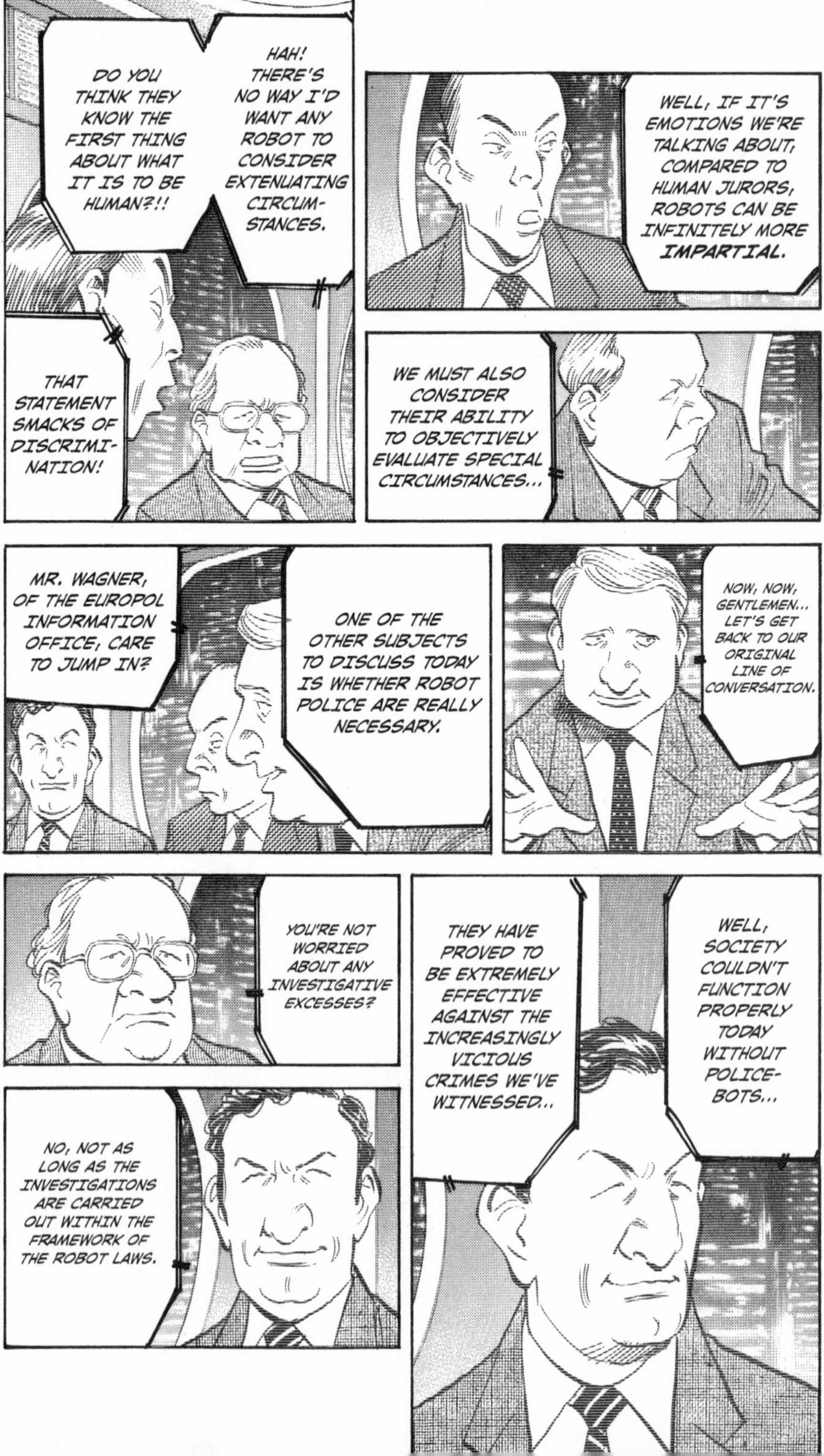
WELL, IF IT'S EMOTIONS WE'RE TALKING ABOUT, COMPARED TO HUMAN JURORS, ROBOTS CAN BE INFINITELY MORE IMPARTIAL.
WE MUST ALSO CONSIDER THEIR ABILITY TO OBJECTIVELY EVALUATE SPECIAL CIRCUMSTANCES...
HAH! THERE'S NO WAY I'D WANT ANY ROBOT TO CONSIDER EXTENUATING CIRCUM-STANCES.
DO YOU THINK THEY KNOW THE FIRST THING ABOUT WHAT IT IS TO BE HUMAN?!!
THAT STATEMENT SMACKS OF DISCRIMI-NATION!
NOW, NOW, GENTLEMEN... LET'S GET BACK TO OUR ORIGINAL LINE OF CONVERSATION.
ONE OF THE OTHER SUBJECTS TO DISCUSS TODAY IS WHETHER ROBOT POLICE ARE REALLY NECESSARY.
MR. WAGNER, OF THE EUROPOL INFORMATION OFFICE, CARE TO JUMP IN?
WELL, SOCIETY COULDN'T FUNCTION PROPERLY TODAY WITHOUT POLICE-BOTS...
THEY HAVE PROVED TO BE EXTREMELY EFFECTIVE AGAINST THE INCREASINGLY VICIOUS CRIMES WE'VE WITNESSED...
YOU'RE NOT WORRIED ABOUT ANY INVESTIGATIVE EXCESSES?
NO, NOT AS LONG AS THE INVESTIGATIONS ARE CARRIED OUT WITHIN THE FRAMEWORK OF THE ROBOT LAWS.

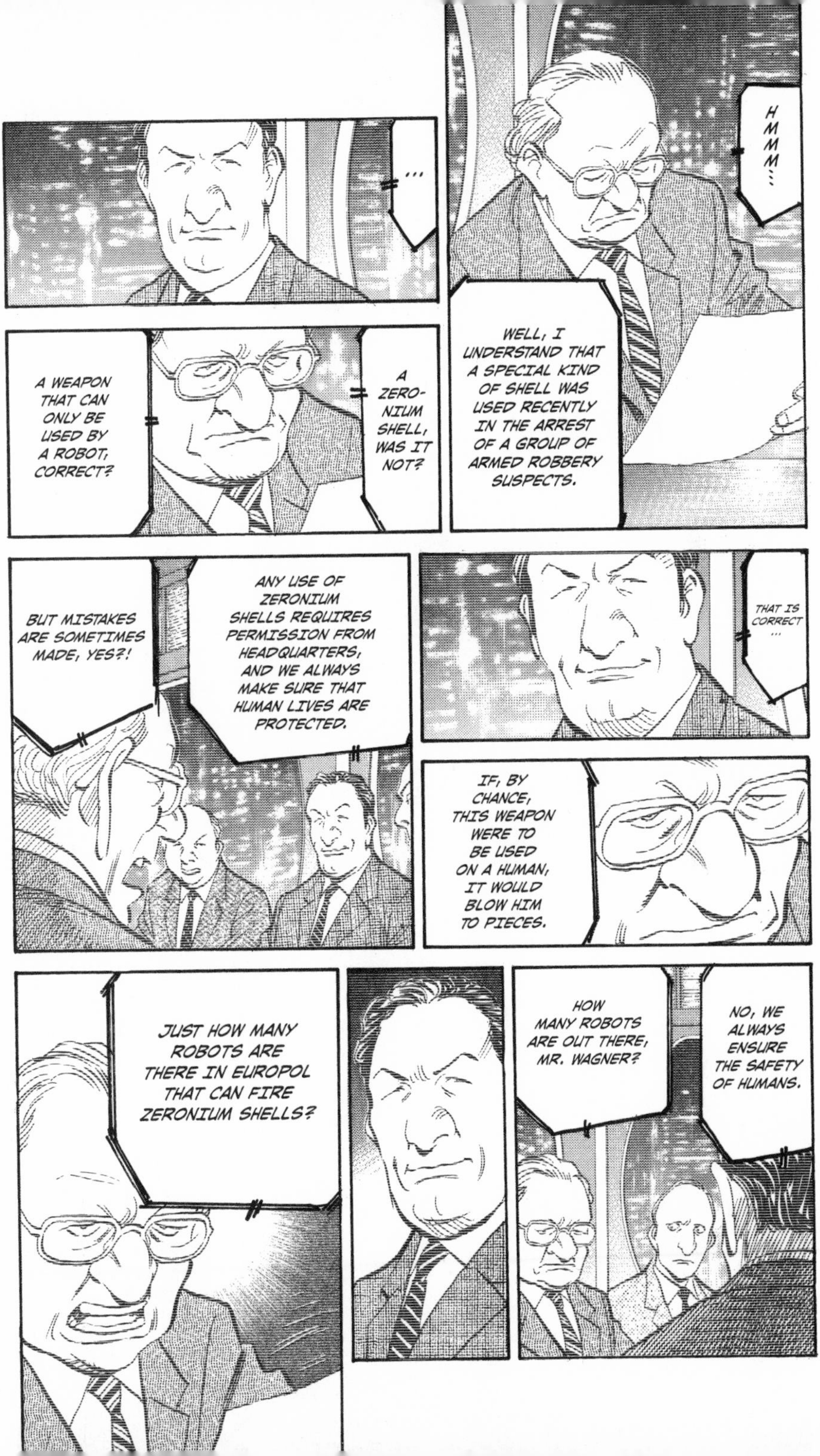
HMMM...
WELL, I UNDERSTAND THAT A SPECIAL KIND OF SHELL WAS USED RECENTLY IN THE ARREST OF A GROUP OF ARMED ROBBERY SUSPECTS.
...
A ZERONIUM SHELL, WAS IT NOT?
A WEAPON THAT CAN ONLY BE USED BY A ROBOT, CORRECT?
THAT IS CORRECT...
IF, BY CHANCE, THIS WEAPON WERE TO BE USED ON A HUMAN, IT WOULD BLOW HIM TO PIECES.
ANY USE OF ZERONIUM SHELLS REQUIRES PERMISSION FROM HEADQUARTERS, AND WE ALWAYS MAKE SURE THAT HUMAN LIVES ARE PROTECTED.
BUT MISTAKES ARE SOMETIMES MADE, YES?!
NO, WE ALWAYS ENSURE THE SAFETY OF HUMANS.
HOW MANY ROBOTS ARE OUT THERE, MR. WAGNER?
JUST HOW MANY ROBOTS ARE THERE IN EUROPOL THAT CAN FIRE ZERONIUM SHELLS?

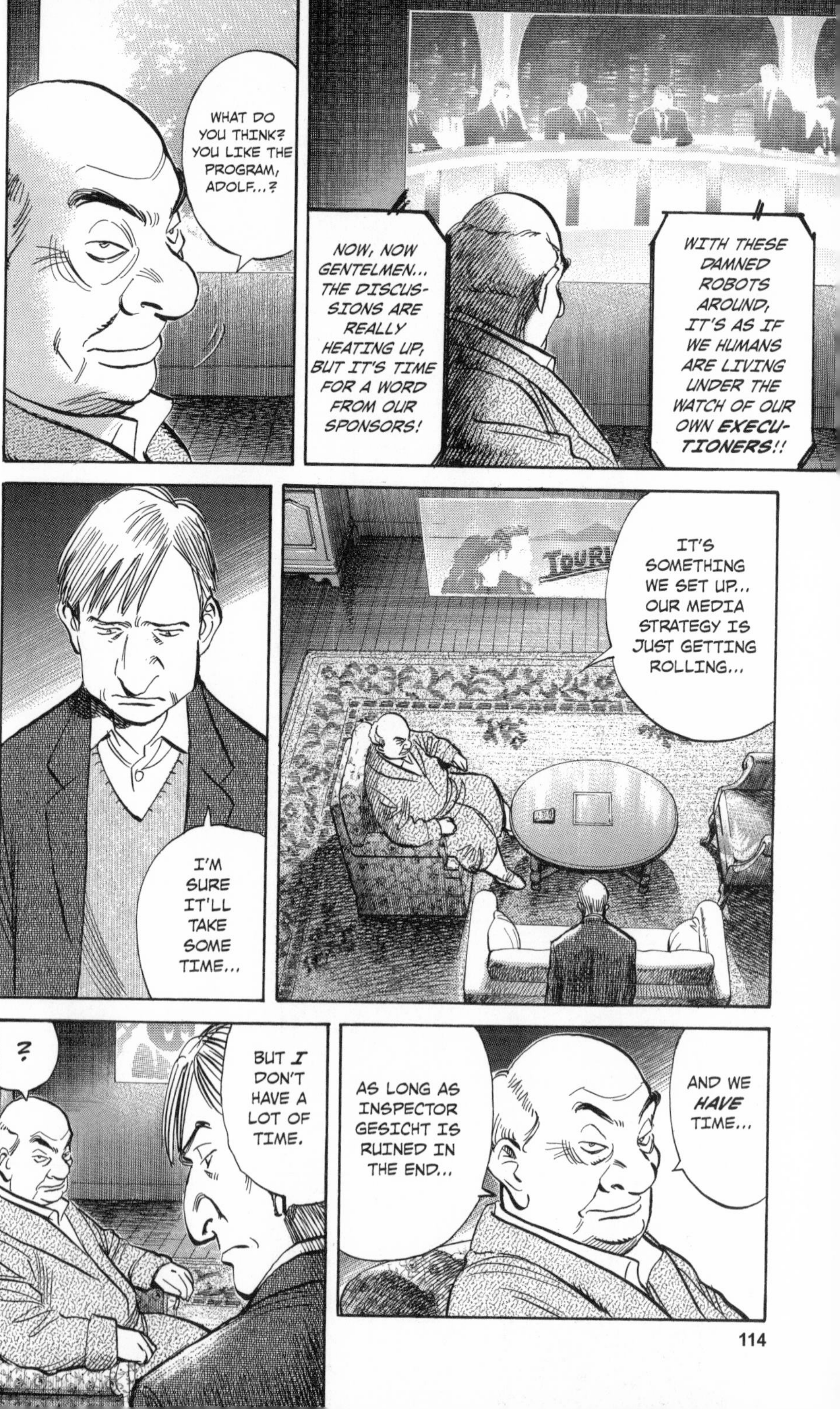
WITH THESE DAMNED ROBOTS AROUND, IT'S AS IF WE HUMANS ARE LIVING UNDER THE WATCH OF OUR OWN **EXECUTIONERS**!!
NOW, NOW GENTELMEN... THE DISCUSSIONS ARE REALLY HEATING UP, BUT IT'S TIME FOR A WORD FROM OUR SPONSORS!
WHAT DO YOU THINK? YOU LIKE THE PROGRAM, ADOLF...?
TOURI
IT'S SOMETHING WE SET UP... OUR MEDIA STRATEGY IS JUST GETTING ROLLING...
I'M SURE IT'LL TAKE SOME TIME...
AND WE *HAVE* TIME...
AS LONG AS INSPECTOR GESICHT IS RUINED IN THE END...
BUT *I* DON'T HAVE A LOT OF TIME.
?

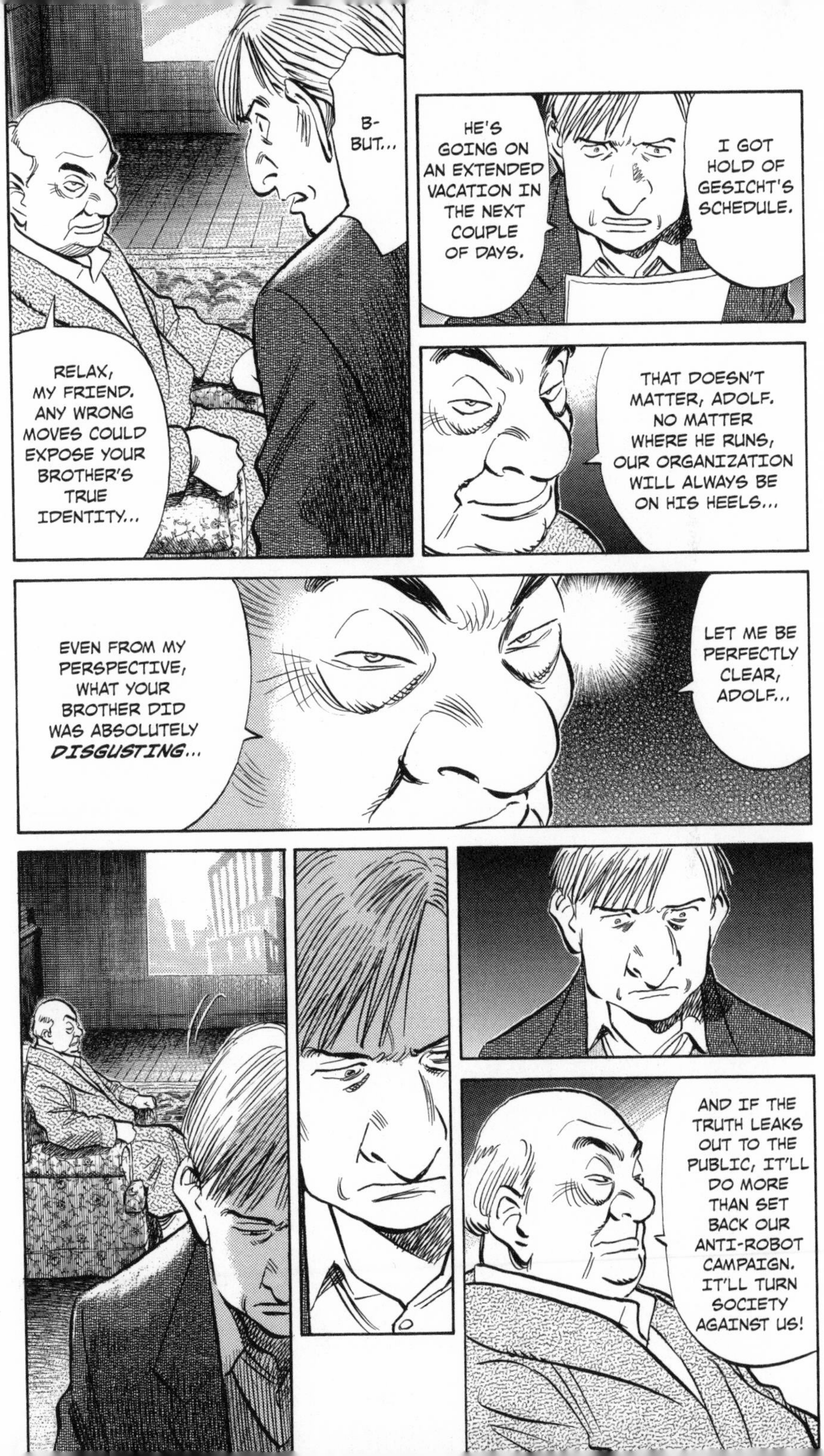
I GOT HOLD OF GESICHT'S SCHEDULE.
HE'S GOING ON AN EXTENDED VACATION IN THE NEXT COUPLE OF DAYS.
THAT DOESN'T MATTER, ADOLF. NO MATTER WHERE HE RUNS, OUR ORGANIZATION WILL ALWAYS BE ON HIS HEELS...
B-BUT...
RELAX, MY FRIEND. ANY WRONG MOVES COULD EXPOSE YOUR BROTHER'S TRUE IDENTITY...
LET ME BE PERFECTLY CLEAR, ADOLF...
EVEN FROM MY PERSPECTIVE, WHAT YOUR BROTHER DID WAS ABSOLUTELY *DISGUSTING*...
AND IF THE TRUTH LEAKS OUT TO THE PUBLIC, IT'LL DO MORE THAN SET BACK OUR ANTI-ROBOT CAMPAIGN. IT'LL TURN SOCIETY AGAINST US!

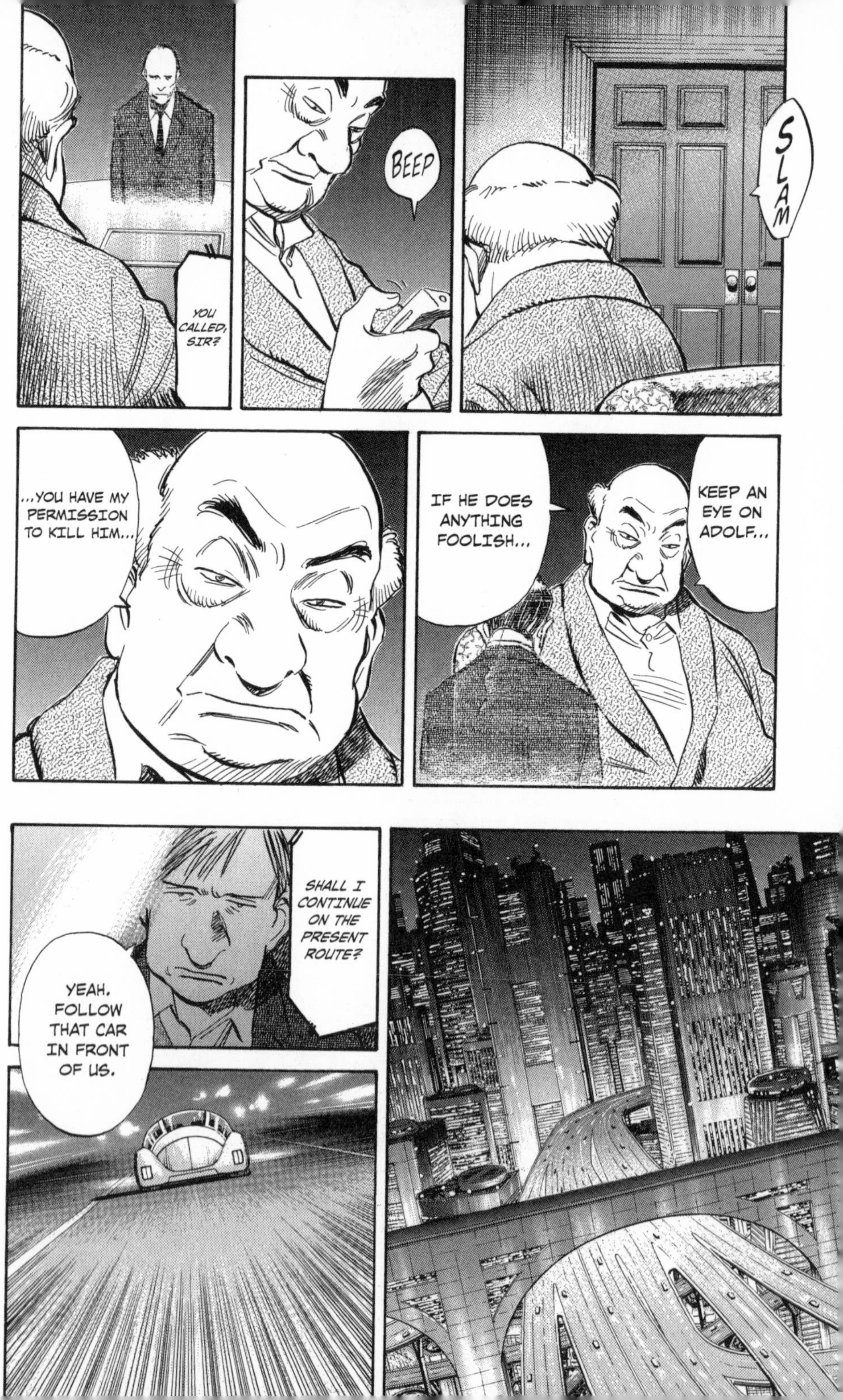
SLAM
BEEP
YOU CALLED, SIR?
KEEP AN EYE ON ADOLF...
IF HE DOES ANYTHING FOOLISH...
...YOU HAVE MY PERMISSION TO KILL HIM...
SHALL I CONTINUE ON THE PRESENT ROUTE?
YEAH. FOLLOW THAT CAR IN FRONT OF US.

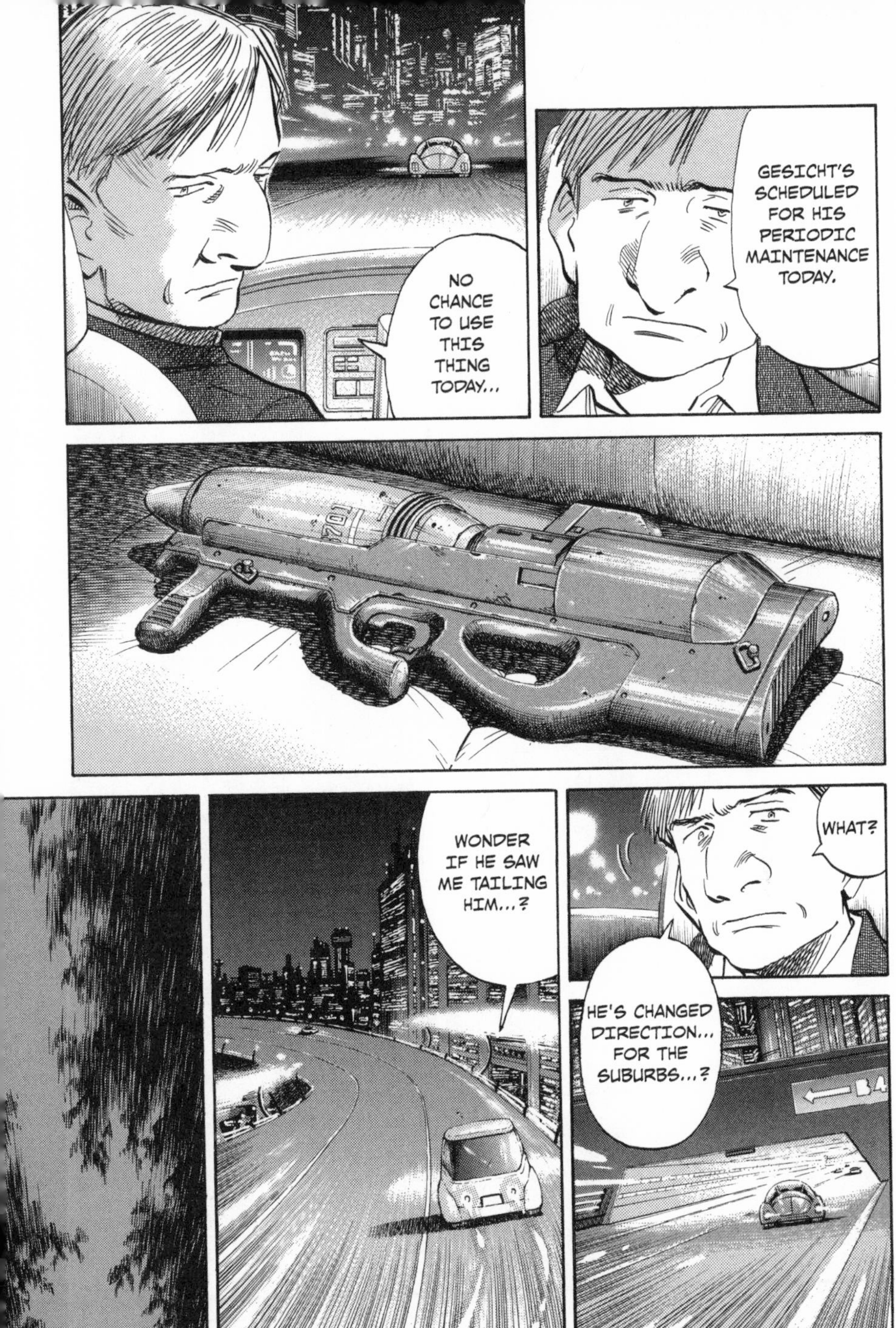
GESICHT'S SCHEDULED FOR HIS PERIODIC MAINTENANCE TODAY.
NO CHANCE TO USE THIS THING TODAY...
WHAT?
HE'S CHANGED DIRECTION... FOR THE SUBURBS...?
WONDER IF HE SAW ME TAILING HIM...?

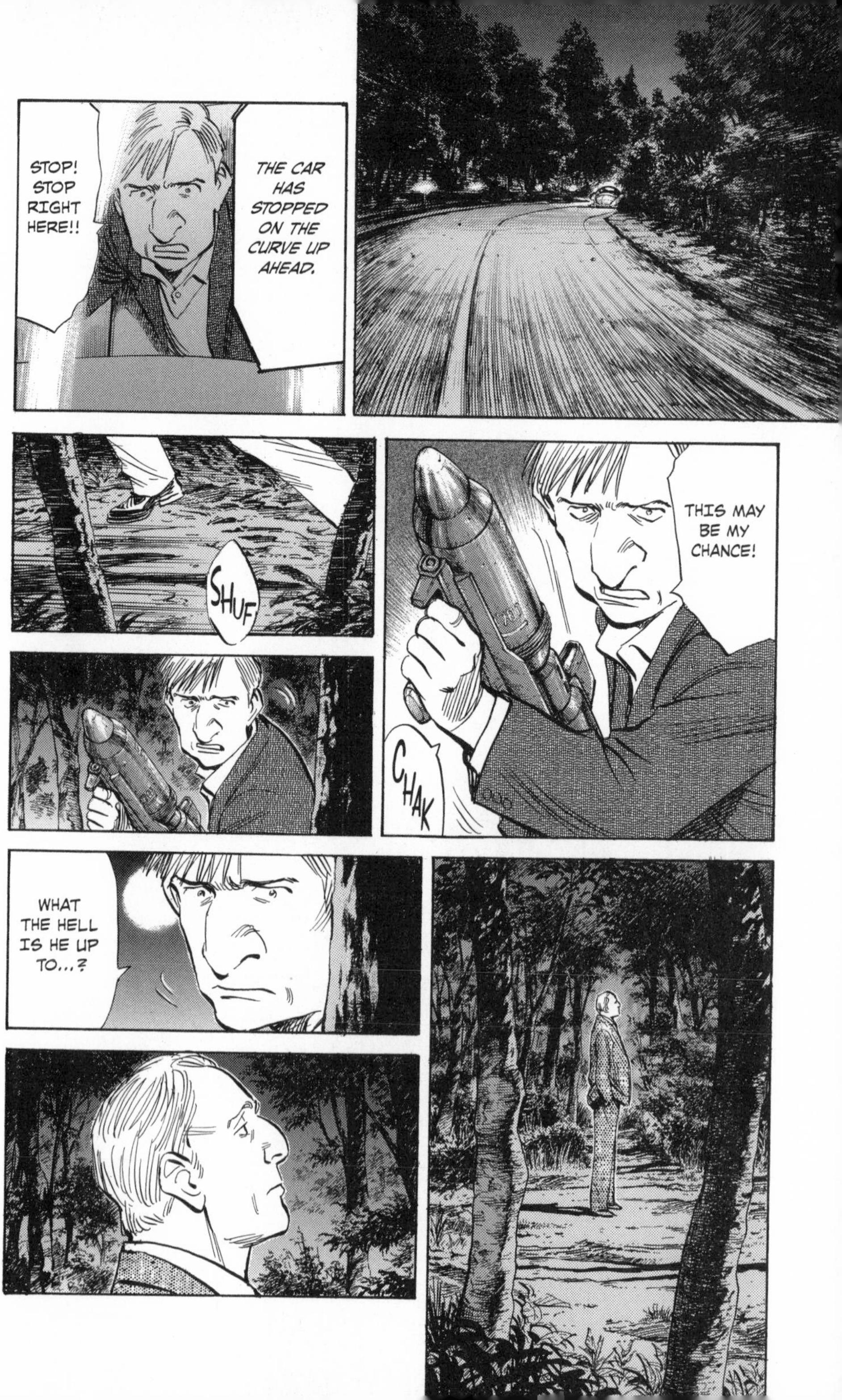
THE CAR HAS STOPPED ON THE CURVE UP AHEAD.
STOP! STOP RIGHT HERE!!
THIS MAY BE MY CHANCE!
CHAK
SHUF
WHAT THE HELL IS HE UP TO...?

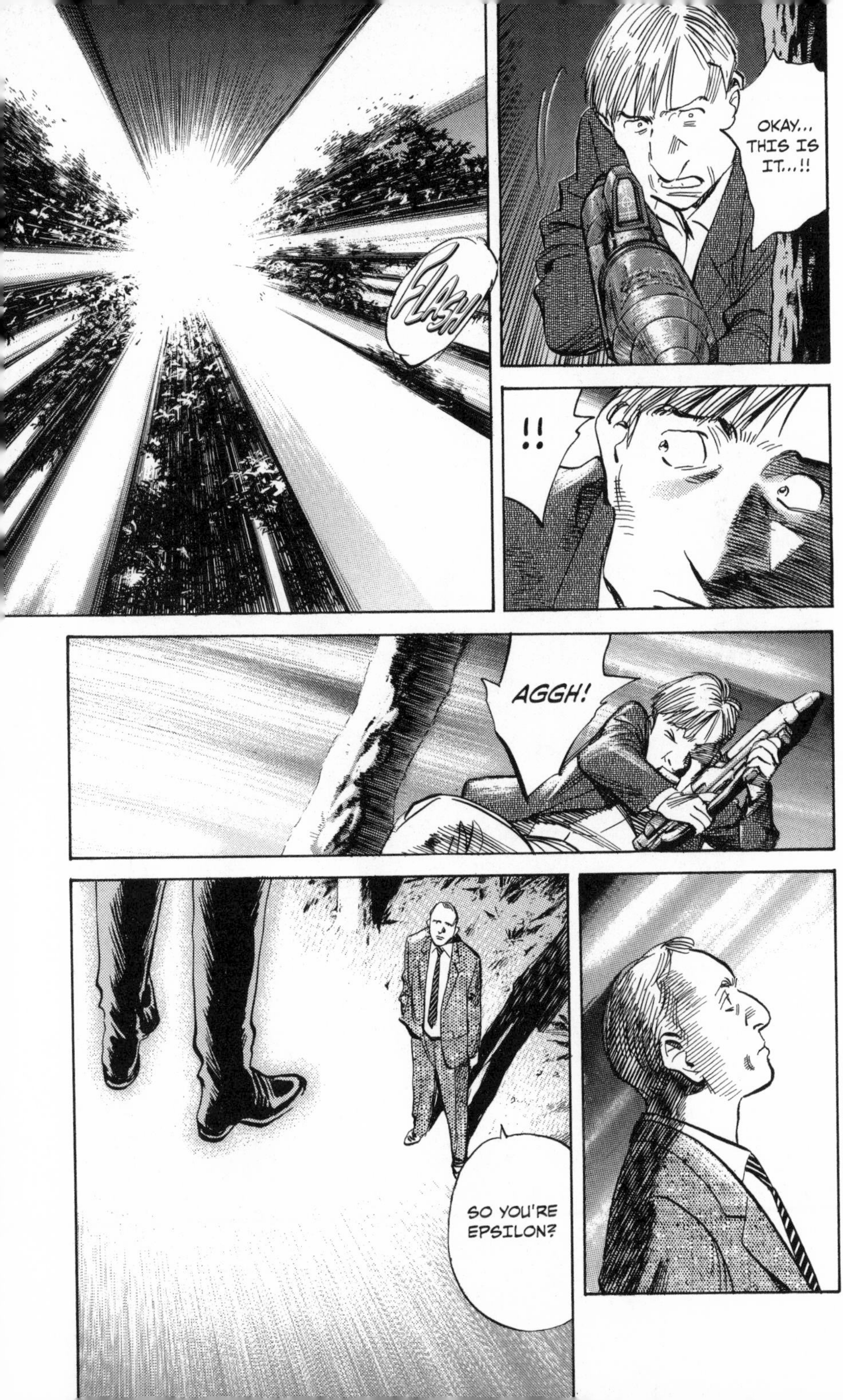
OKAY... THIS IS IT...!!
!!
FLASH
AGGH!
SO YOU'RE EPSILON?

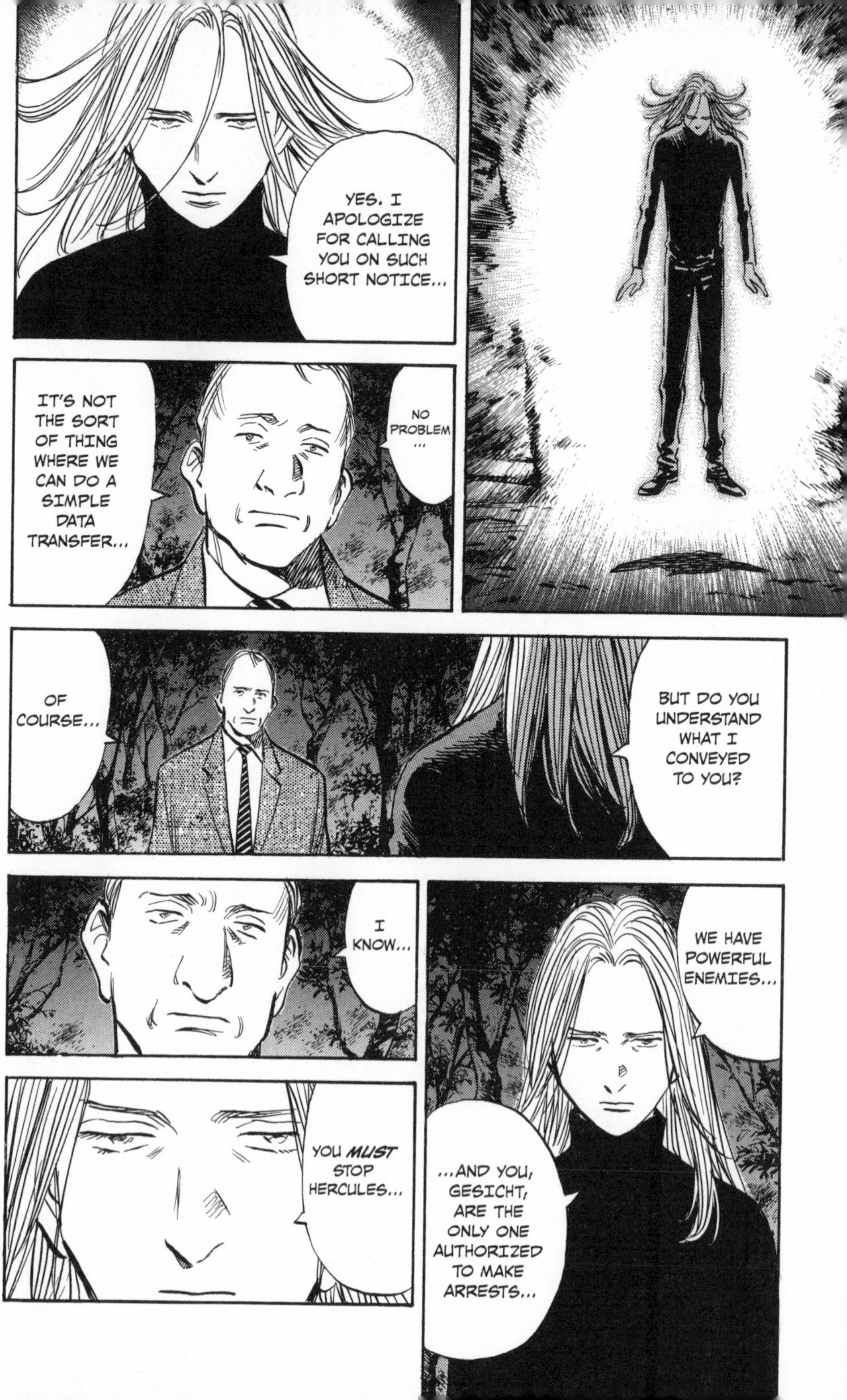
YES. I APOLOGIZE FOR CALLING YOU ON SUCH SHORT NOTICE...
NO PROBLEM...
IT'S NOT THE SORT OF THING WHERE WE CAN DO A SIMPLE DATA TRANSFER...
BUT DO YOU UNDERSTAND WHAT I CONVEYED TO YOU?
OF COURSE...
WE HAVE POWERFUL ENEMIES...
...AND YOU, GESICHT, ARE THE ONLY ONE AUTHORIZED TO MAKE ARRESTS...
I KNOW...
YOU *MUST* STOP HERCULES...

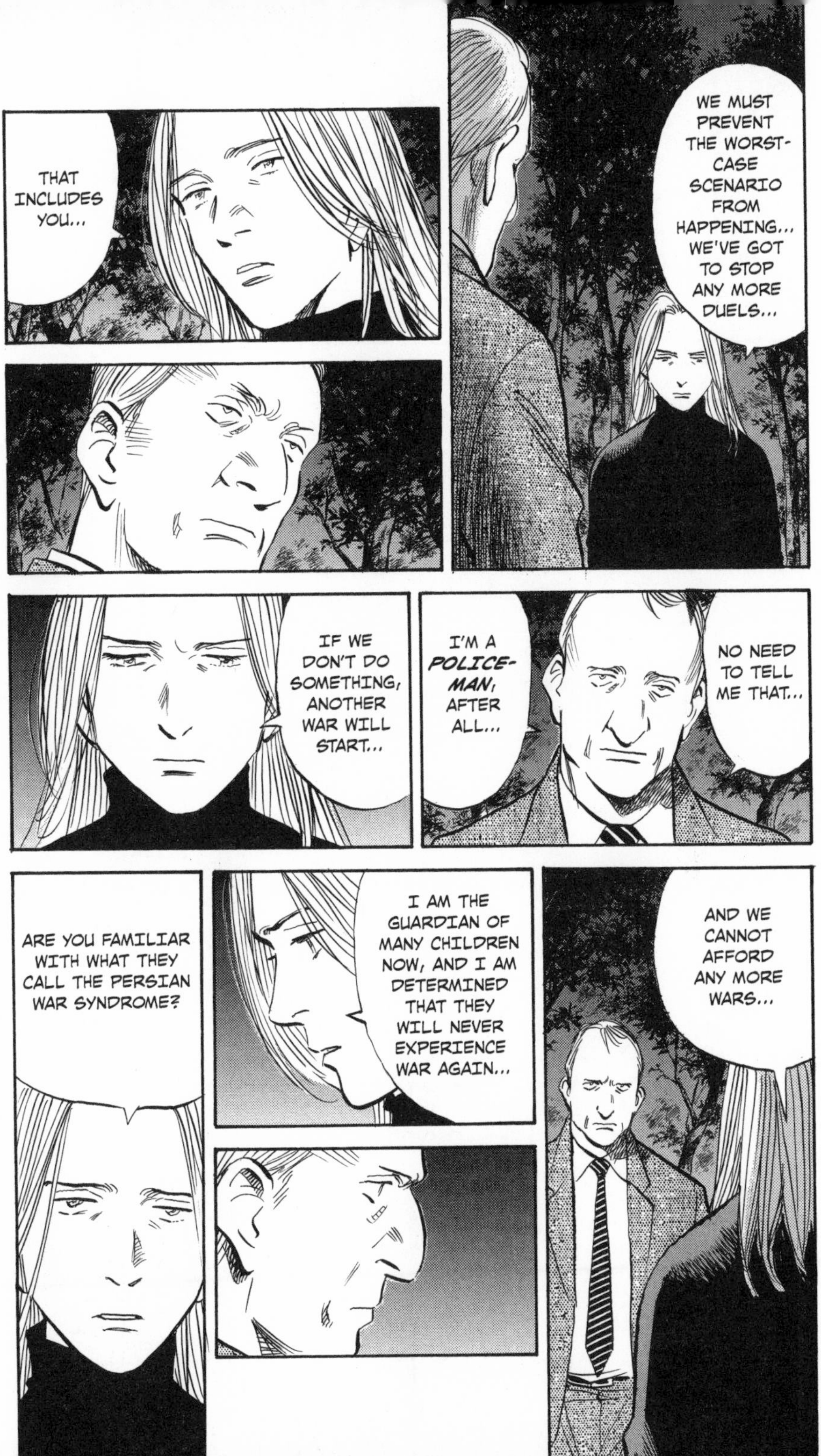
WE MUST PREVENT THE WORST-CASE SCENARIO FROM HAPPENING... WE'VE GOT TO STOP ANY MORE DUELS...
THAT INCLUDES YOU...
NO NEED TO TELL ME THAT...
I'M A *POLICEMAN*, AFTER ALL...
IF WE DON'T DO SOMETHING, ANOTHER WAR WILL START...
AND WE CANNOT AFFORD ANY MORE WARS...
I AM THE GUARDIAN OF MANY CHILDREN NOW, AND I AM DETERMINED THAT THEY WILL NEVER EXPERIENCE WAR AGAIN...
ARE YOU FAMILIAR WITH WHAT THEY CALL THE PERSIAN WAR SYNDROME?

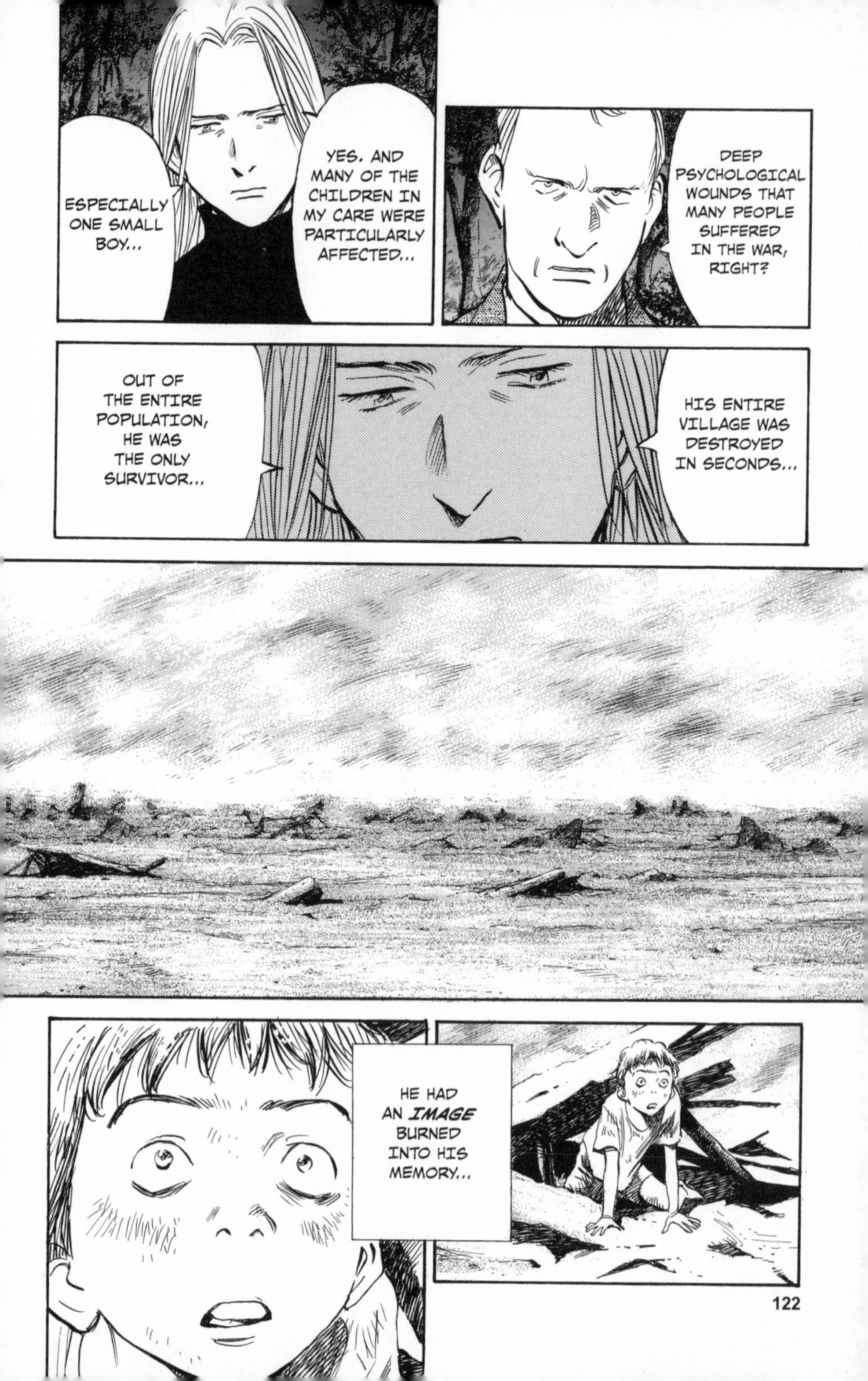
DEEP PSYCHOLOGICAL WOUNDS THAT MANY PEOPLE SUFFERED IN THE WAR, RIGHT?
YES. AND MANY OF THE CHILDREN IN MY CARE WERE PARTICULARLY AFFECTED...
ESPECIALLY ONE SMALL BOY...
HIS ENTIRE VILLAGE WAS DESTROYED IN SECONDS...
OUT OF THE ENTIRE POPULATION, HE WAS THE ONLY SURVIVOR...
HE HAD AN *IMAGE* BURNED INTO HIS MEMORY...

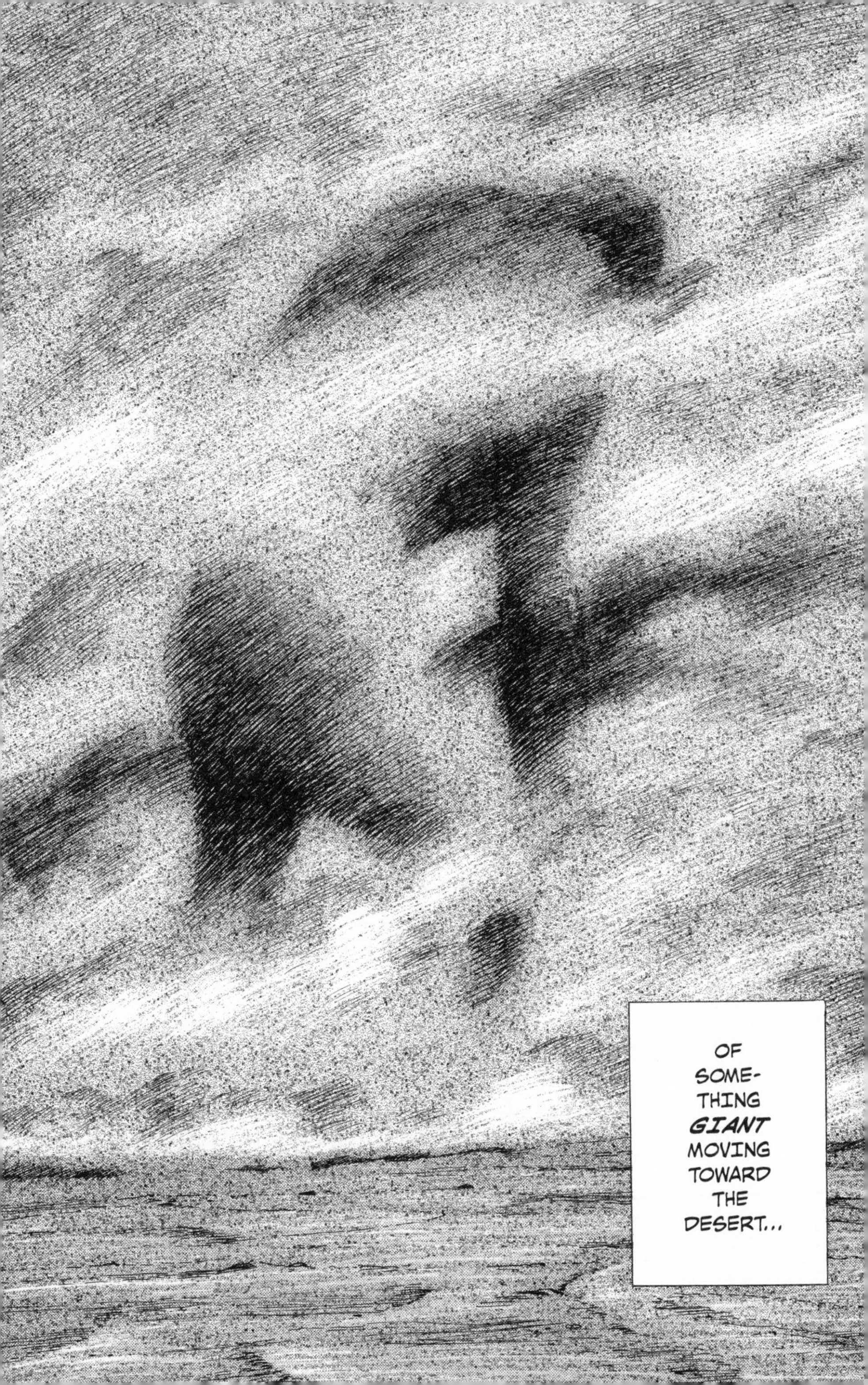
OF SOME-THING ***GIANT*** MOVING TOWARD THE DESERT...

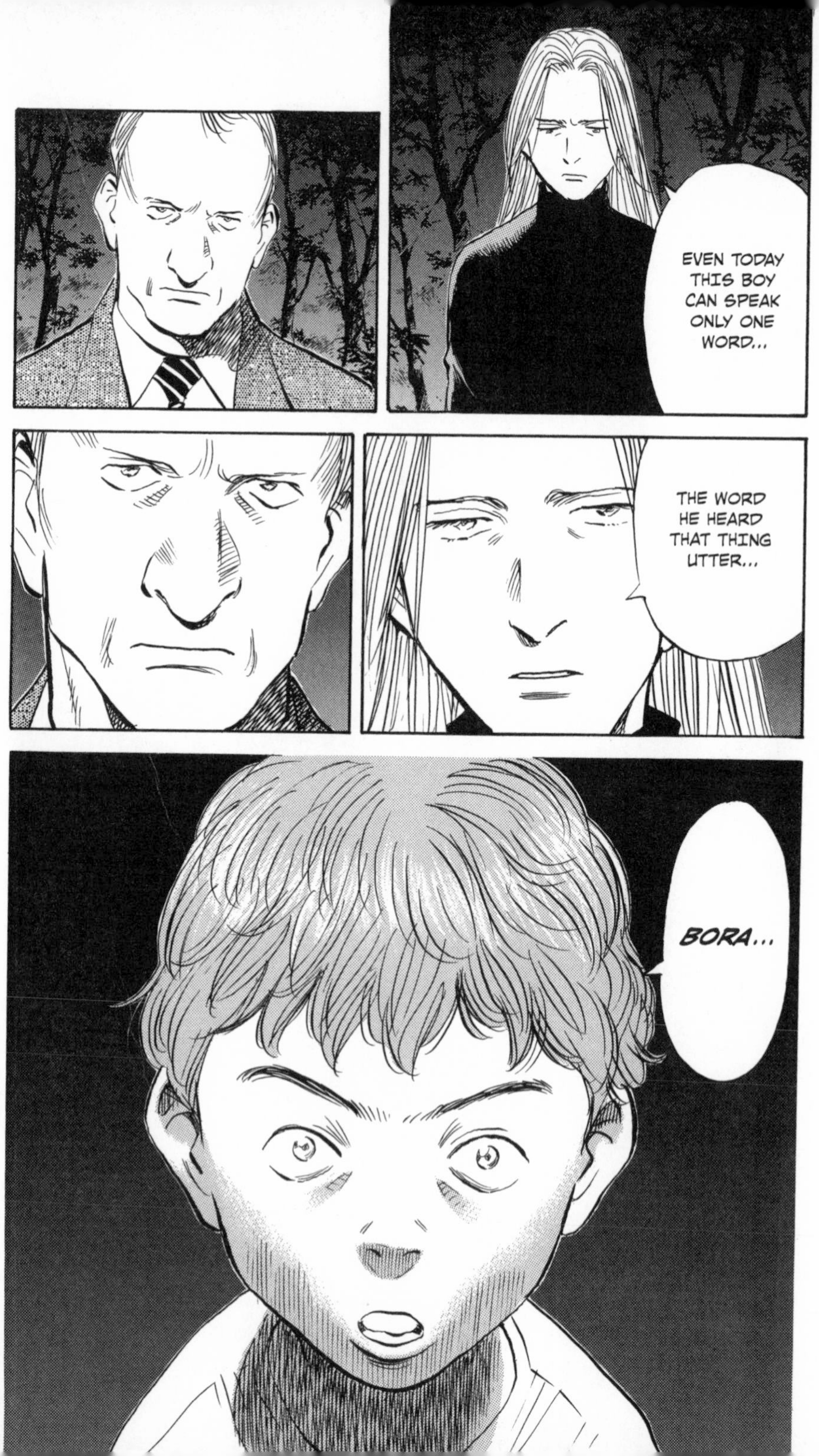
EVEN TODAY THIS BOY CAN SPEAK ONLY ONE WORD...
THE WORD HE HEARD THAT THING UTTER...
BORA...

Act 21 Uran's Search

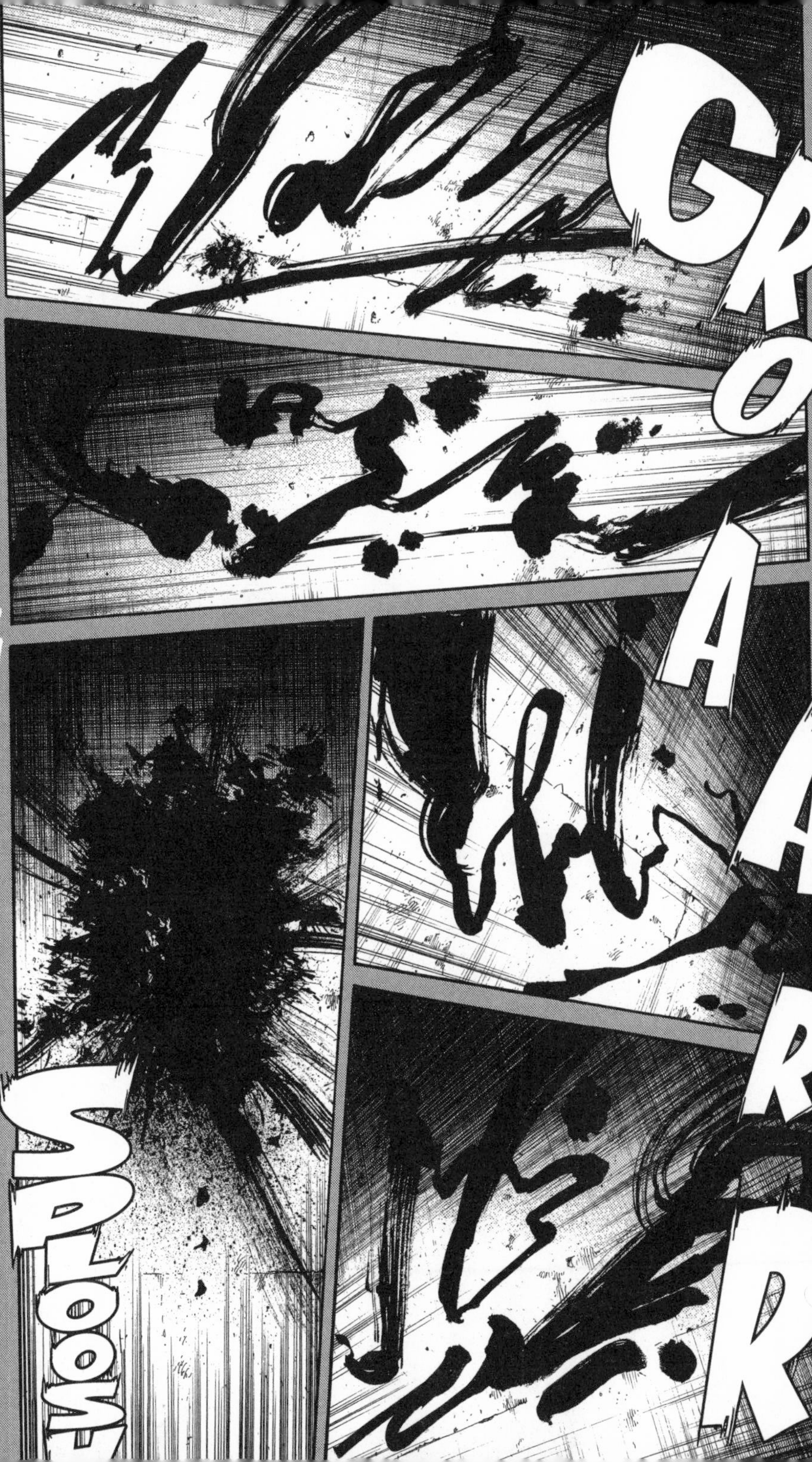
GROAARR
SPLOOS

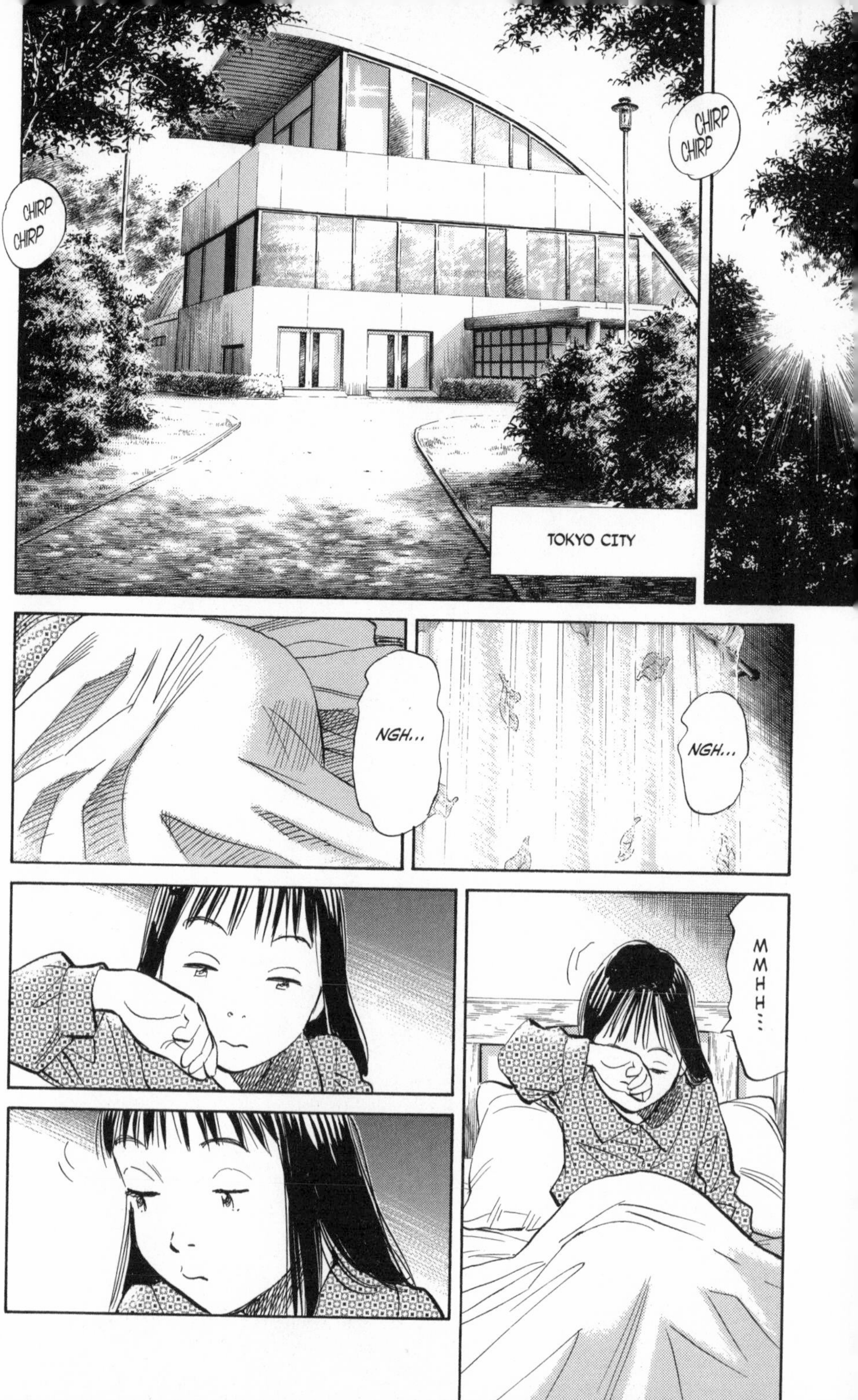
CHIRP CHIRP
CHIRP CHIRP
TOKYO CITY
NGH...
NGH...
MMHH...

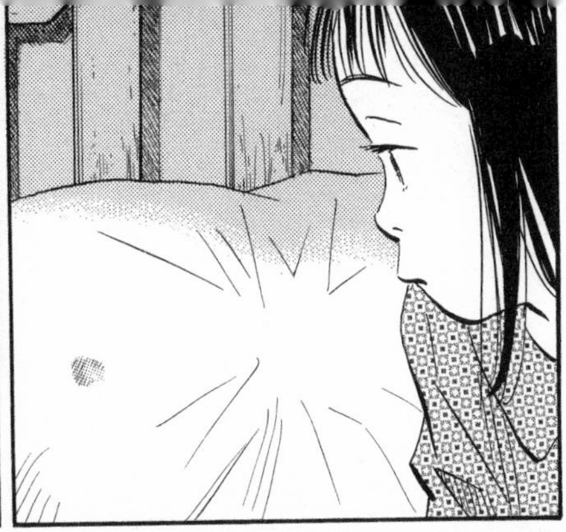

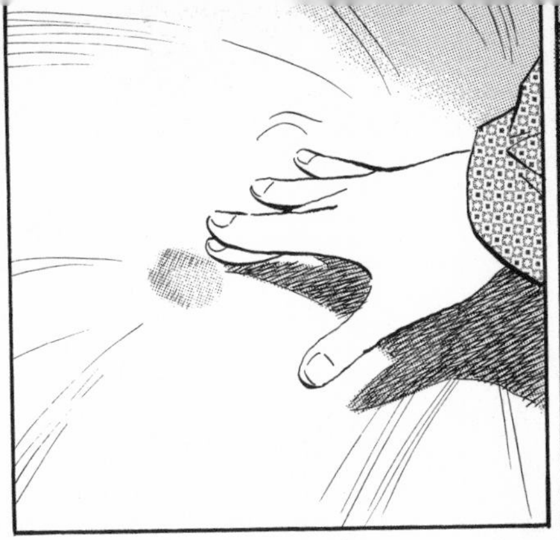

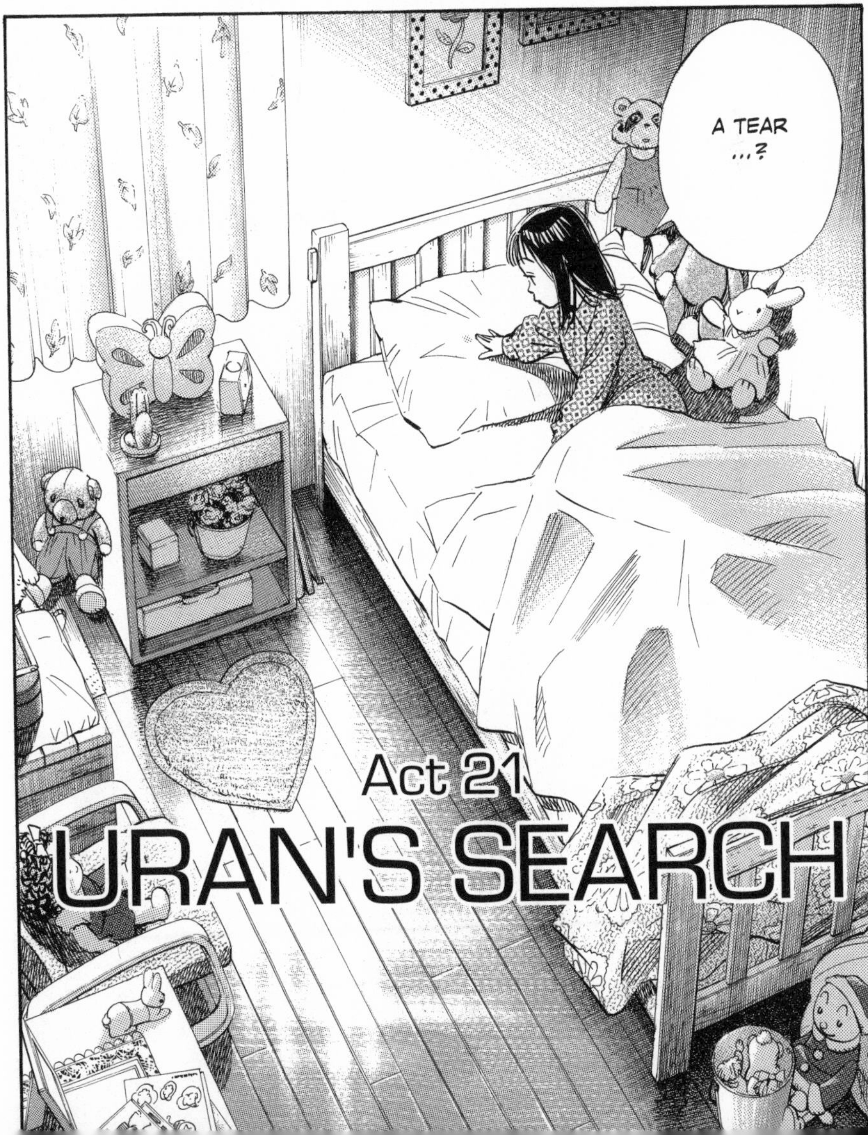
A TEAR ...?
Act 21
URAN'S SEARCH

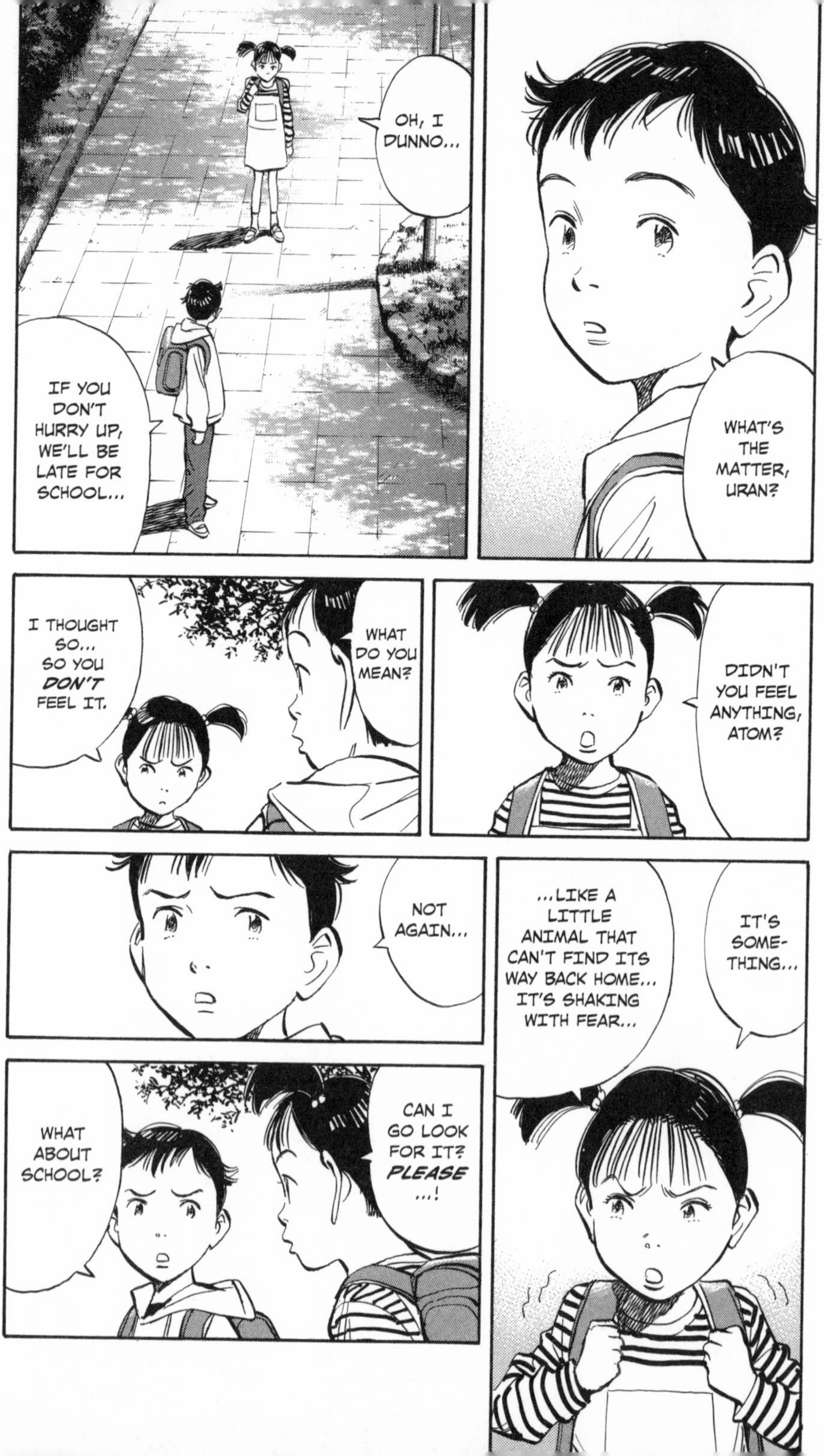
WHAT'S THE MATTER, URAN?
OH, I DUNNO...
IF YOU DON'T HURRY UP, WE'LL BE LATE FOR SCHOOL...
DIDN'T YOU FEEL ANYTHING, ATOM?
WHAT DO YOU MEAN?
I THOUGHT SO... SO YOU *DON'T* FEEL IT.
IT'S SOME-THING...
...LIKE A LITTLE ANIMAL THAT CAN'T FIND ITS WAY BACK HOME... IT'S SHAKING WITH FEAR...
NOT AGAIN...
CAN I GO LOOK FOR IT? *PLEASE* ...!
WHAT ABOUT SCHOOL?

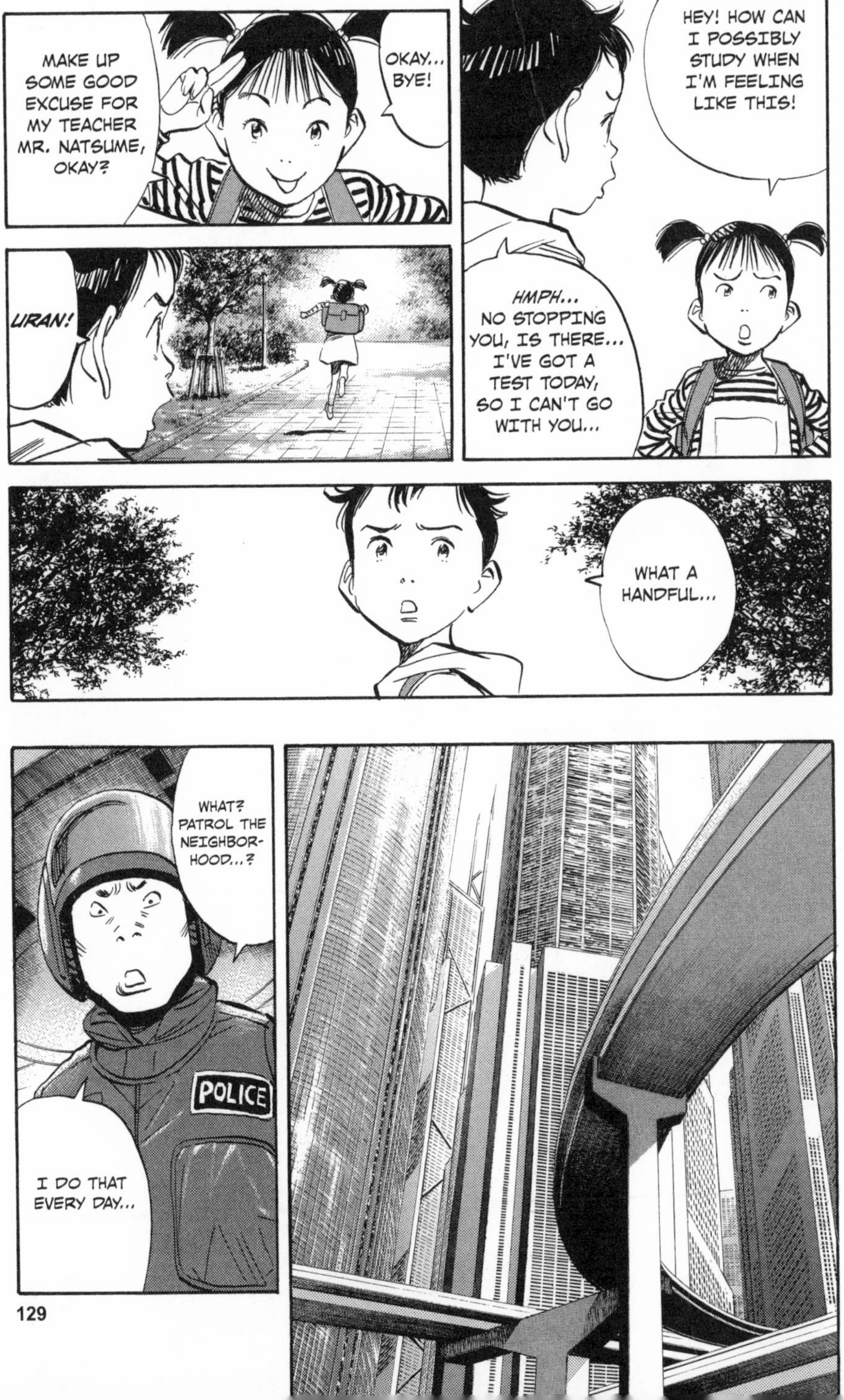
HEY! HOW CAN I POSSIBLY STUDY WHEN I'M FEELING LIKE THIS!
HMPH... NO STOPPING YOU, IS THERE... I'VE GOT A TEST TODAY, SO I CAN'T GO WITH YOU...
OKAY... BYE!
MAKE UP SOME GOOD EXCUSE FOR MY TEACHER MR. NATSUME, OKAY?
URAN!
WHAT A HANDFUL...
WHAT? PATROL THE NEIGHBOR-HOOD...?
POLICE
I DO THAT EVERY DAY...

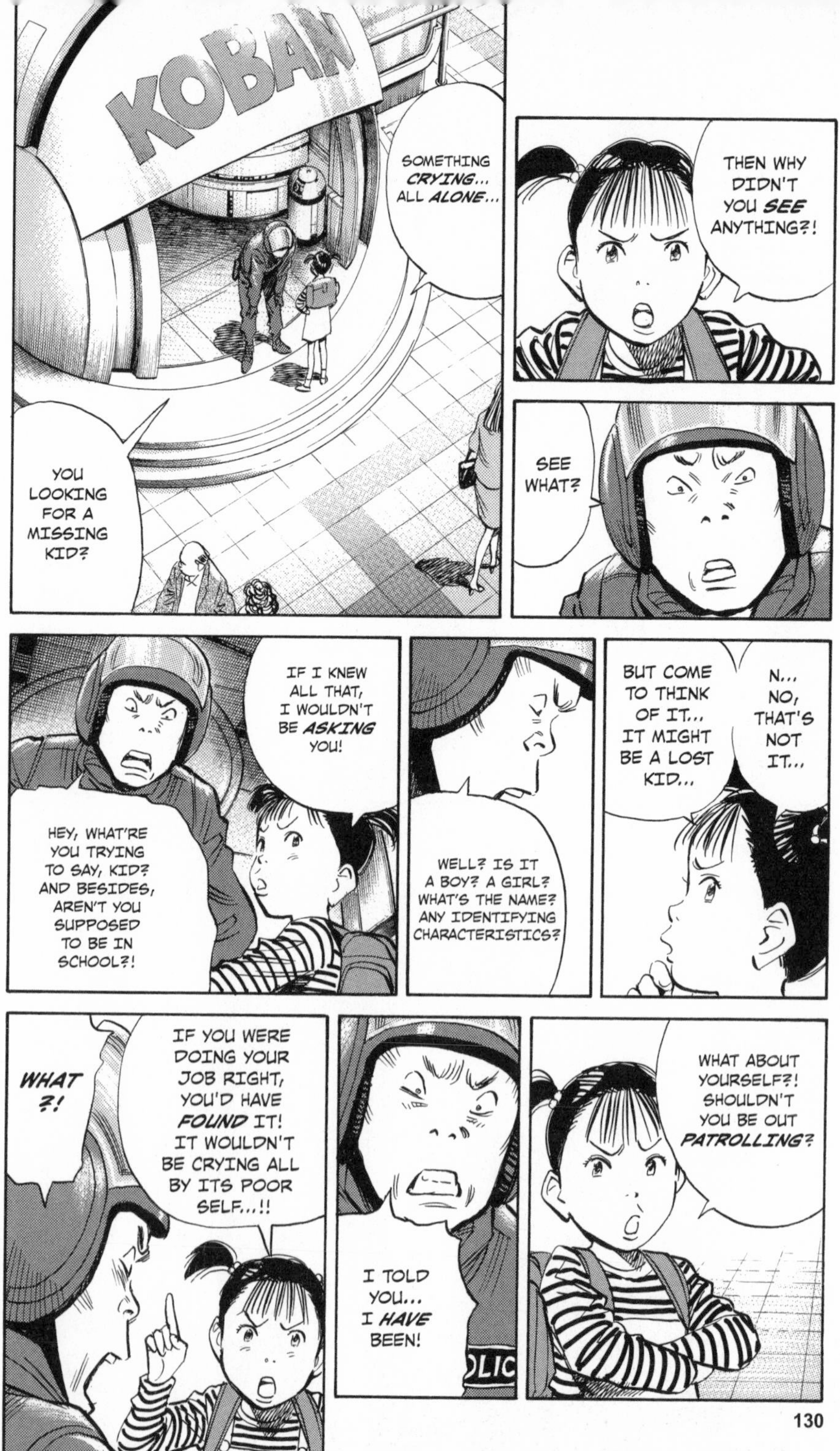
THEN WHY DIDN'T YOU SEE ANYTHING?!
SEE WHAT?
KOBAN
SOMETHING CRYING... ALL ALONE...
YOU LOOKING FOR A MISSING KID?
N... NO, THAT'S NOT IT...
BUT COME TO THINK OF IT... IT MIGHT BE A LOST KID...
WELL? IS IT A BOY? A GIRL? WHAT'S THE NAME? ANY IDENTIFYING CHARACTERISTICS?
IF I KNEW ALL THAT, I WOULDN'T BE ASKING YOU!
HEY, WHAT'RE YOU TRYING TO SAY, KID? AND BESIDES, AREN'T YOU SUPPOSED TO BE IN SCHOOL?!
WHAT ABOUT YOURSELF?! SHOULDN'T YOU BE OUT PATROLLING?
I TOLD YOU... I HAVE BEEN!
POLIC
IF YOU WERE DOING YOUR JOB RIGHT, YOU'D HAVE FOUND IT! IT WOULDN'T BE CRYING ALL BY ITS POOR SELF...!!
WHAT?!

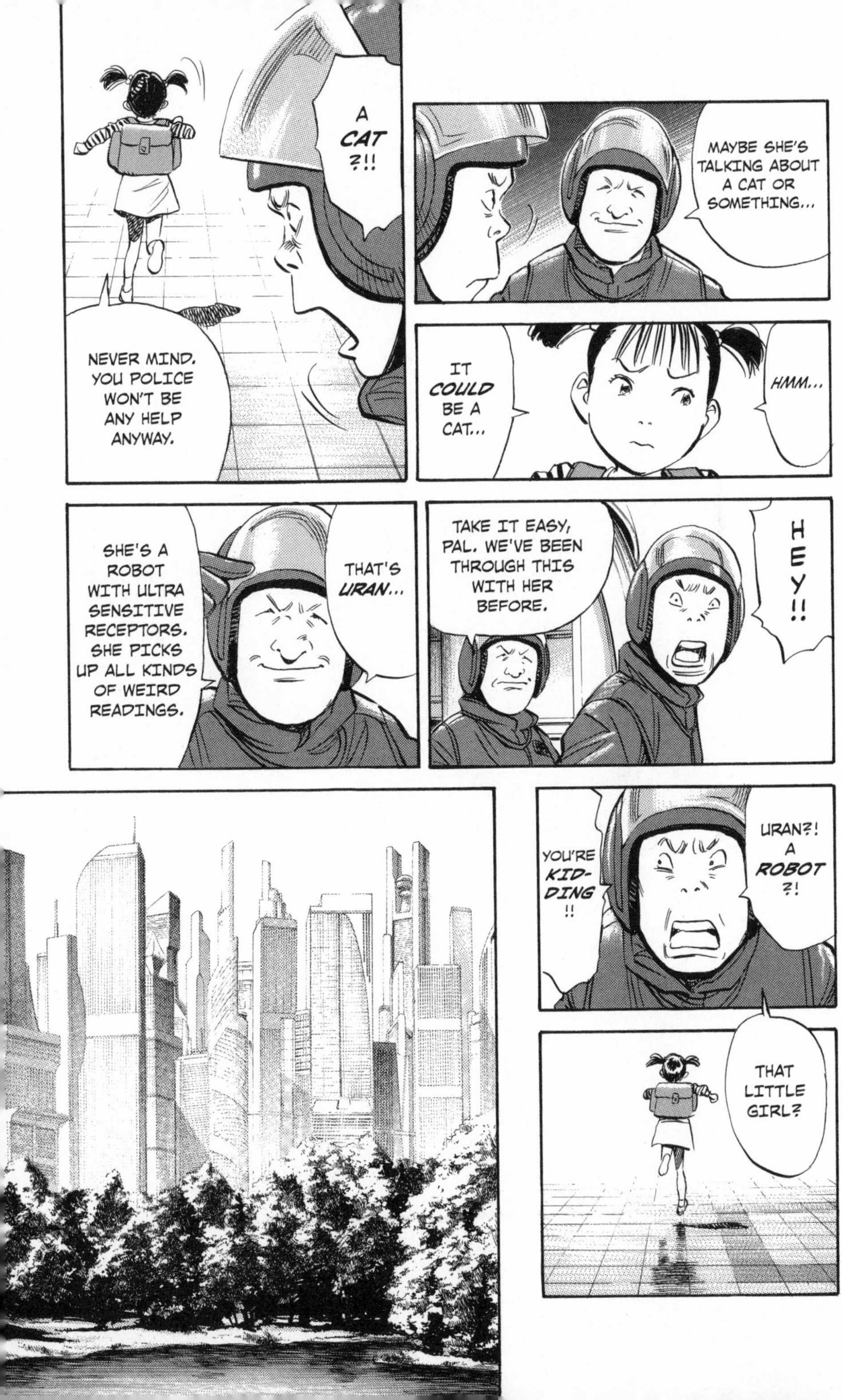
MAYBE SHE'S TALKING ABOUT A CAT OR SOMETHING...
HMM...
IT COULD BE A CAT...
A CAT?!!
NEVER MIND. YOU POLICE WON'T BE ANY HELP ANYWAY.
HEY!!
TAKE IT EASY, PAL. WE'VE BEEN THROUGH THIS WITH HER BEFORE.
THAT'S URAN...
SHE'S A ROBOT WITH ULTRA SENSITIVE RECEPTORS. SHE PICKS UP ALL KINDS OF WEIRD READINGS.
URAN?! A ROBOT?!
YOU'RE KIDDING!!
THAT LITTLE GIRL?

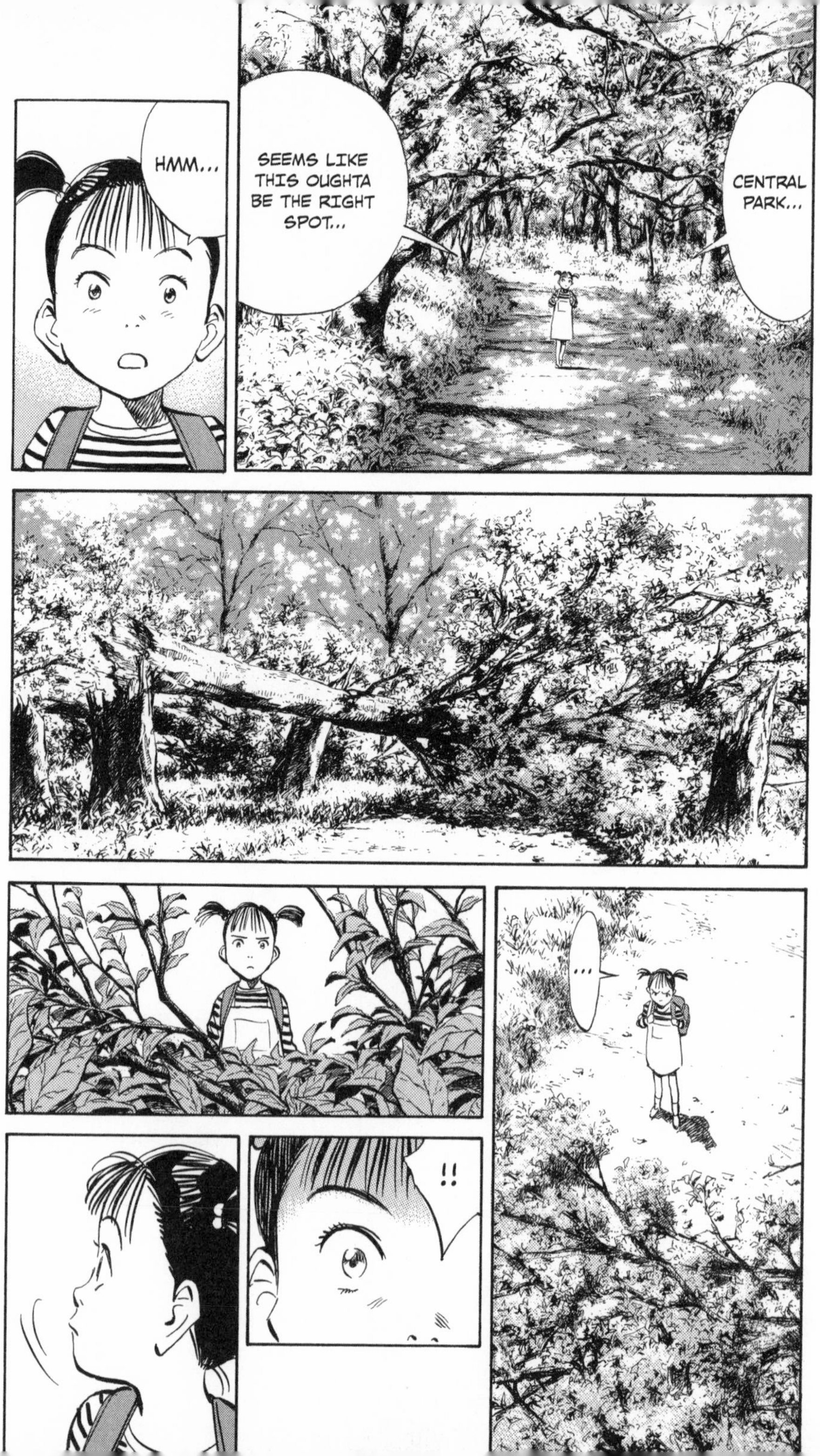
CENTRAL PARK...
SEEMS LIKE THIS OUGHTA BE THE RIGHT SPOT...
HMM...
...
!!

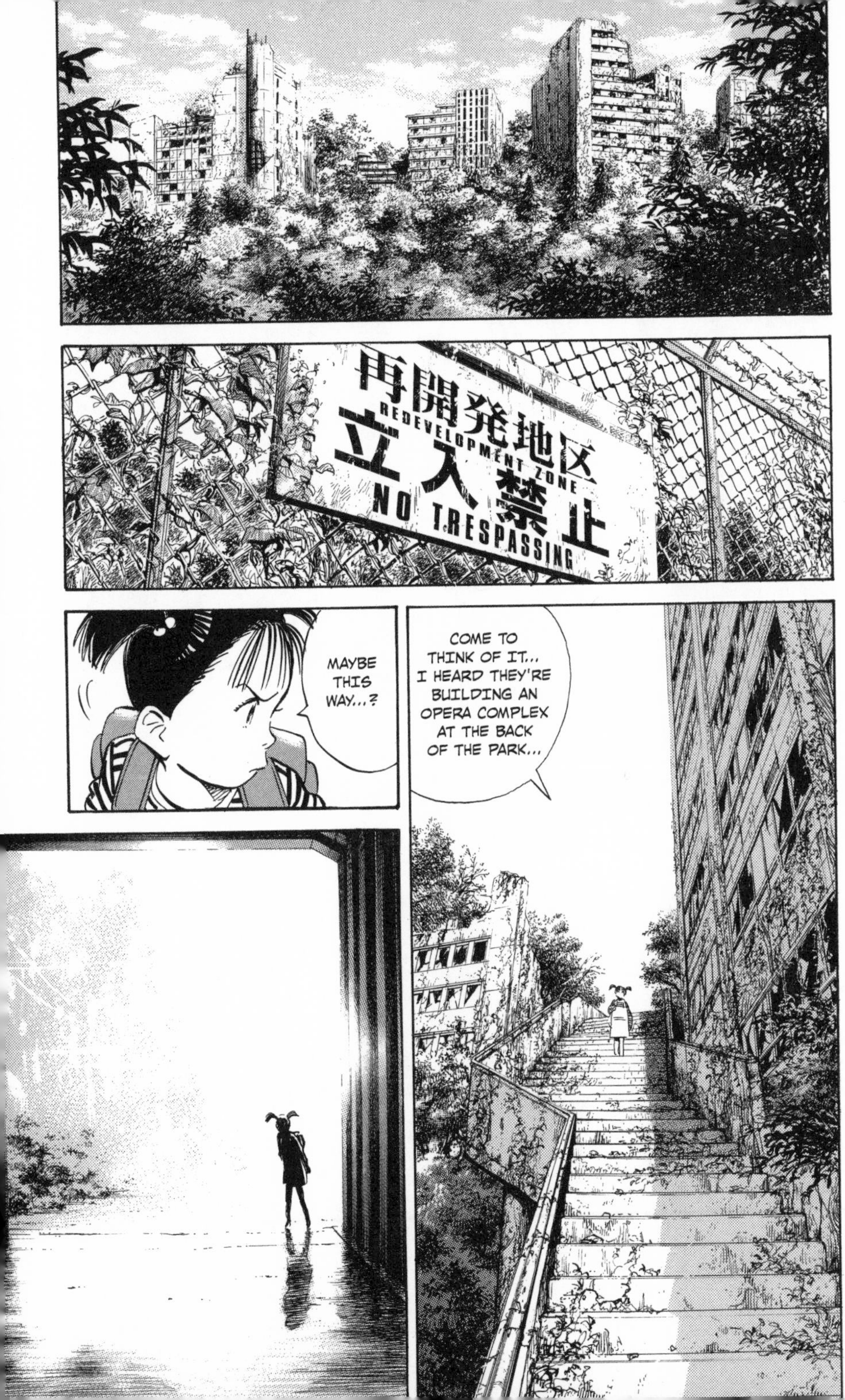
再開発地区
REDEVELOPMENT ZONE
立入禁止
NO TRESPASSING
COME TO THINK OF IT... I HEARD THEY'RE BUILDING AN OPERA COMPLEX AT THE BACK OF THE PARK...
MAYBE THIS WAY...?

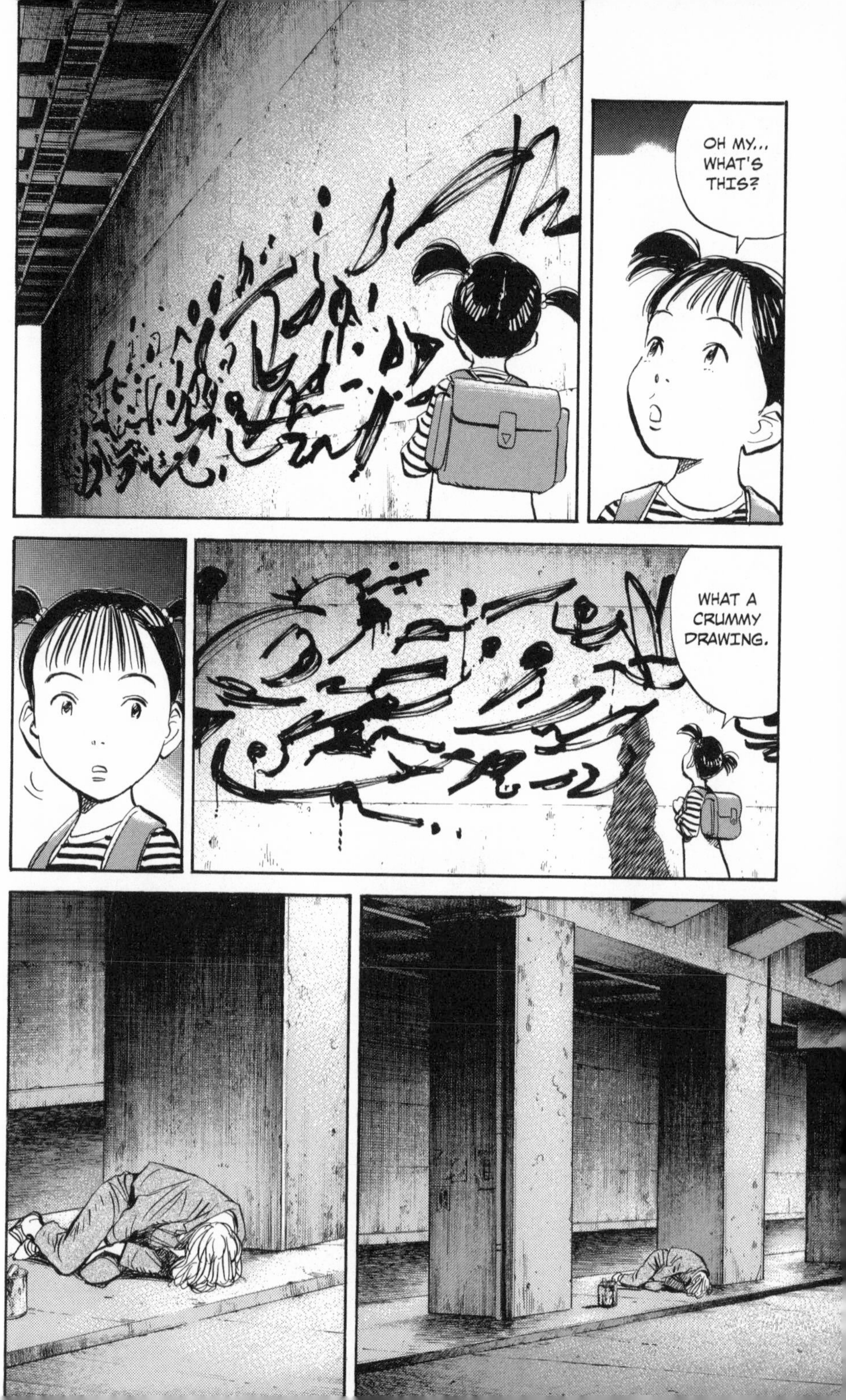
OH MY... WHAT'S THIS?
WHAT A CRUMMY DRAWING.

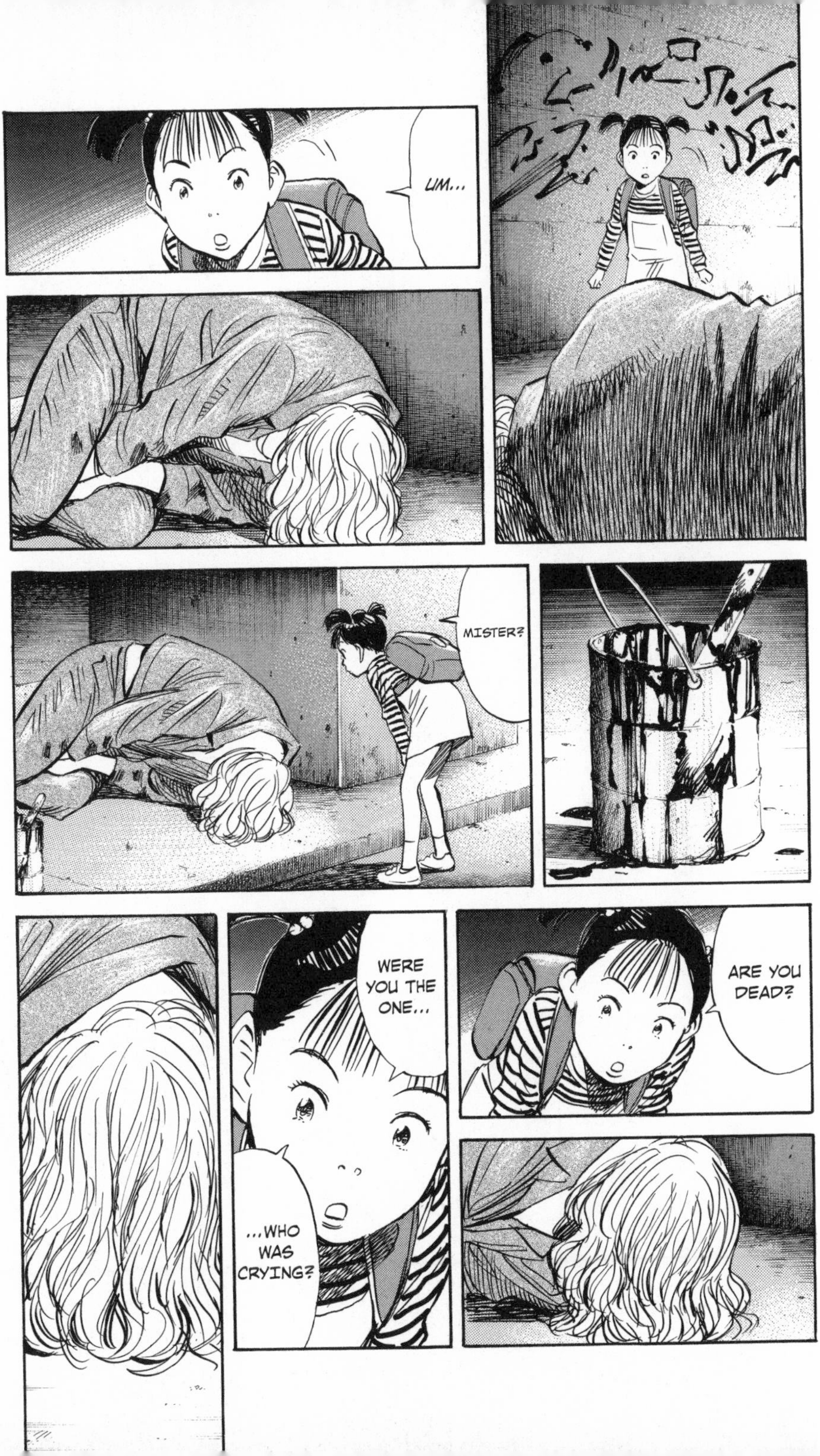
UM...
MISTER?
ARE YOU DEAD?
WERE YOU THE ONE...
...WHO WAS CRYING?

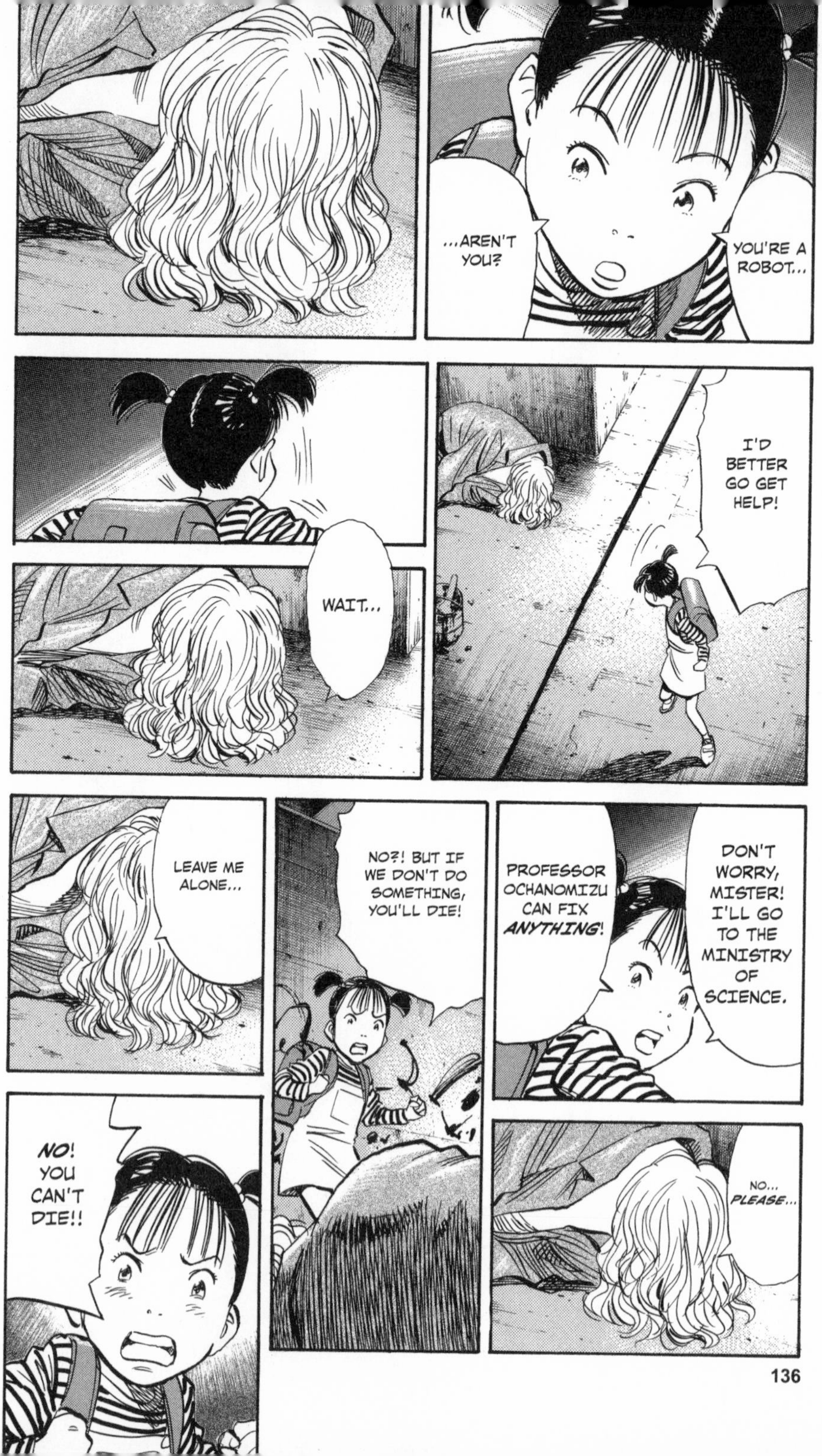
YOU'RE A ROBOT...
...AREN'T YOU?
I'D BETTER GO GET HELP!
WAIT...
DON'T WORRY, MISTER! I'LL GO TO THE MINISTRY OF SCIENCE.
PROFESSOR OCHANOMIZU CAN FIX *ANYTHING*!
NO... *PLEASE*...
NO?! BUT IF WE DON'T DO SOMETHING, YOU'LL DIE!
LEAVE ME ALONE...
NO! YOU CAN'T DIE!!

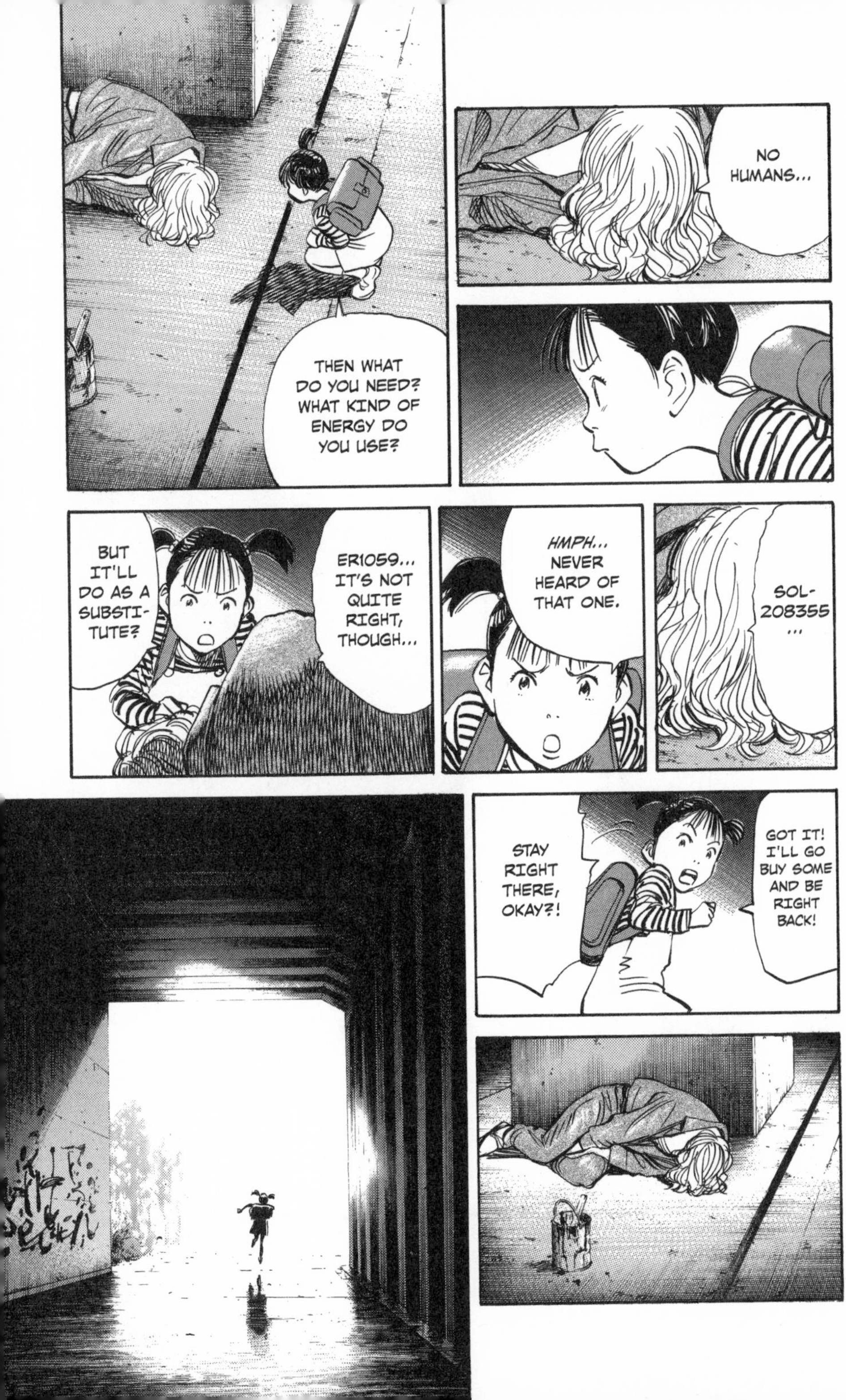
NO HUMANS...
THEN WHAT DO YOU NEED? WHAT KIND OF ENERGY DO YOU USE?
SOL-208355 ...
HMPH... NEVER HEARD OF THAT ONE.
ER1059... IT'S NOT QUITE RIGHT, THOUGH...
BUT IT'LL DO AS A SUBSTITUTE?
GOT IT! I'LL GO BUY SOME AND BE RIGHT BACK!
STAY RIGHT THERE, OKAY?!

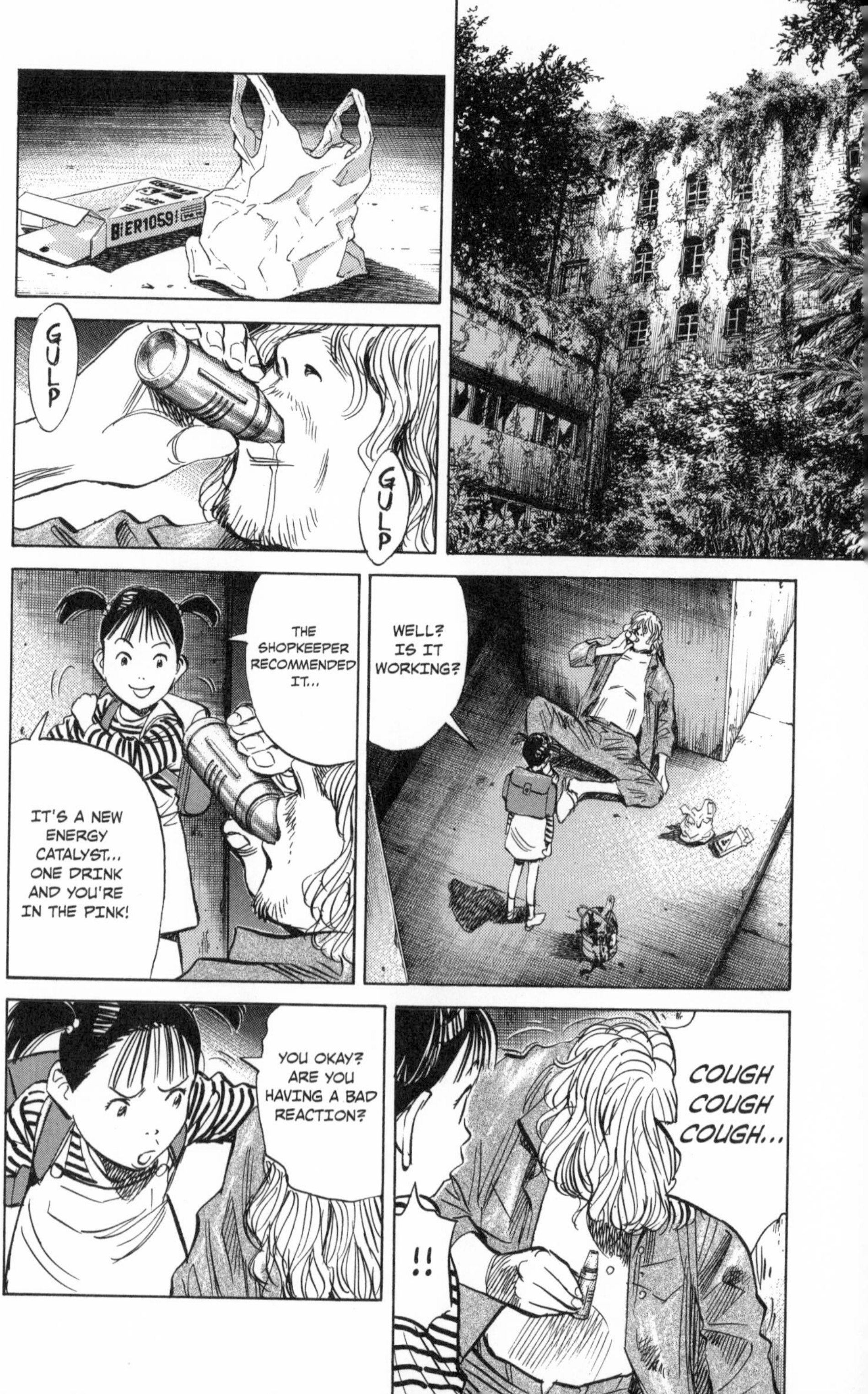
BIER1059!
GULP
GULP
WELL? IS IT WORKING?
THE SHOPKEEPER RECOMMENDED IT...
IT'S A NEW ENERGY CATALYST... ONE DRINK AND YOU'RE IN THE PINK!
COUGH COUGH COUGH...
!!
YOU OKAY? ARE YOU HAVING A BAD REACTION?

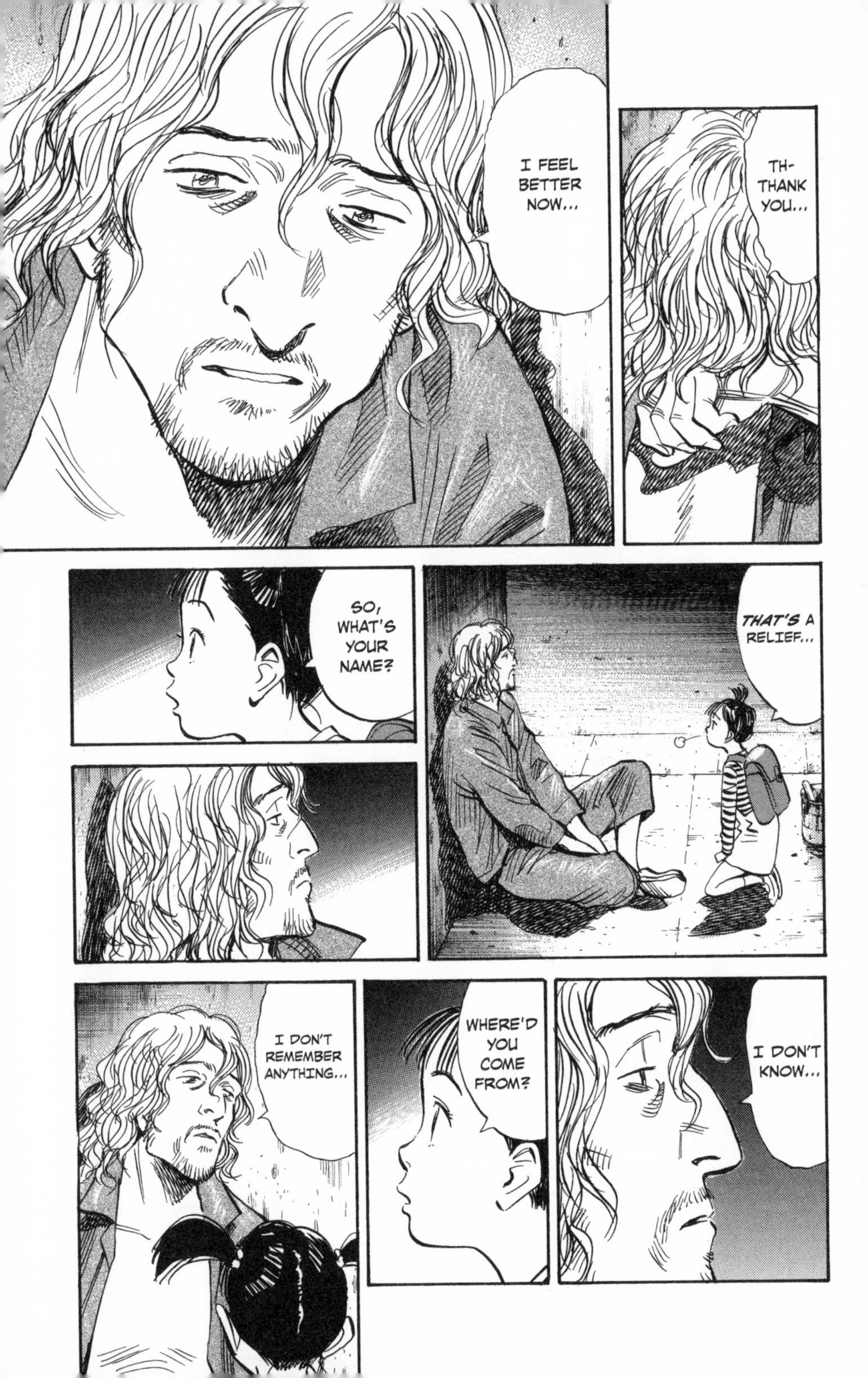
TH-THANK YOU...
I FEEL BETTER NOW...
THAT'S A RELIEF...
SO, WHAT'S YOUR NAME?
I DON'T KNOW...
WHERE'D YOU COME FROM?
I DON'T REMEMBER ANYTHING...

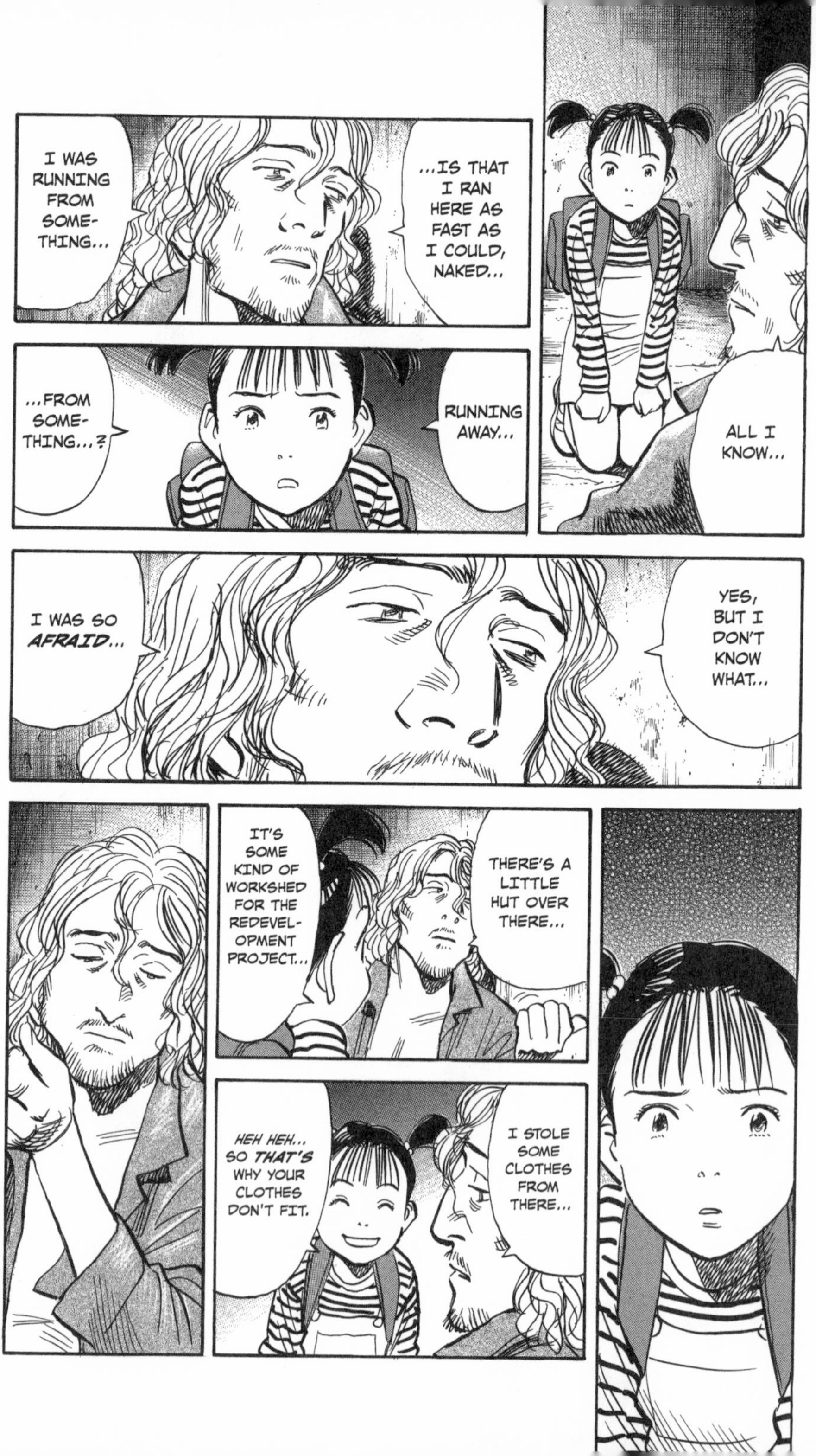
ALL I KNOW...
...IS THAT I RAN HERE AS FAST AS I COULD, NAKED...
I WAS RUNNING FROM SOME-THING...
RUNNING AWAY...
...FROM SOME-THING...?
YES, BUT I DON'T KNOW WHAT...
I WAS SO *AFRAID*...
THERE'S A LITTLE HUT OVER THERE...
IT'S SOME KIND OF WORKSHED FOR THE REDEVEL-OPMENT PROJECT...
I STOLE SOME CLOTHES FROM THERE...
HEH HEH... SO ***THAT'S*** WHY YOUR CLOTHES DON'T FIT.

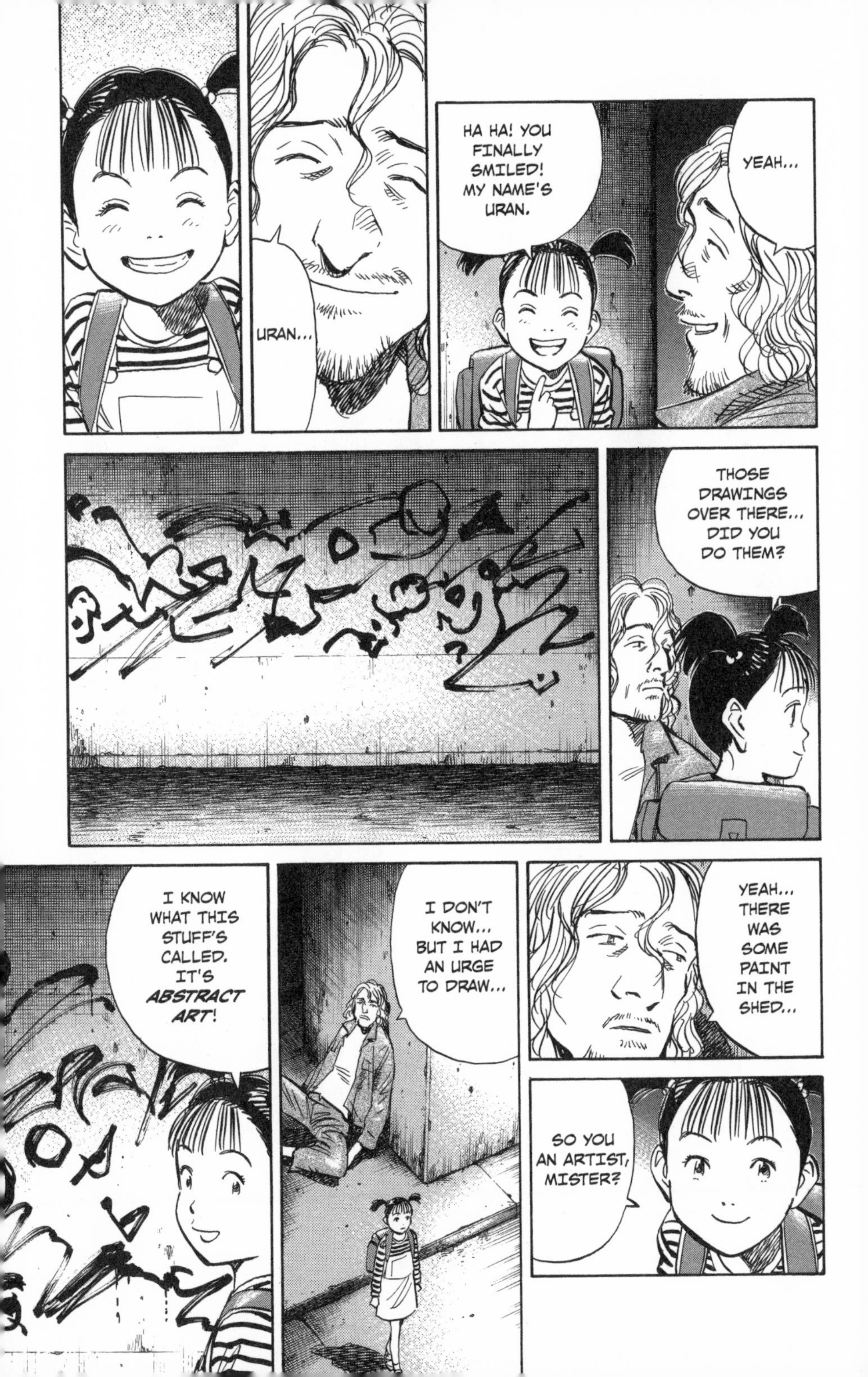
HA HA! YOU FINALLY SMILED! MY NAME'S URAN.
YEAH...
URAN...
THOSE DRAWINGS OVER THERE... DID YOU DO THEM?
YEAH... THERE WAS SOME PAINT IN THE SHED...
SO YOU AN ARTIST, MISTER?
I DON'T KNOW... BUT I HAD AN URGE TO DRAW...
I KNOW WHAT THIS STUFF'S CALLED. IT'S *ABSTRACT ART*!

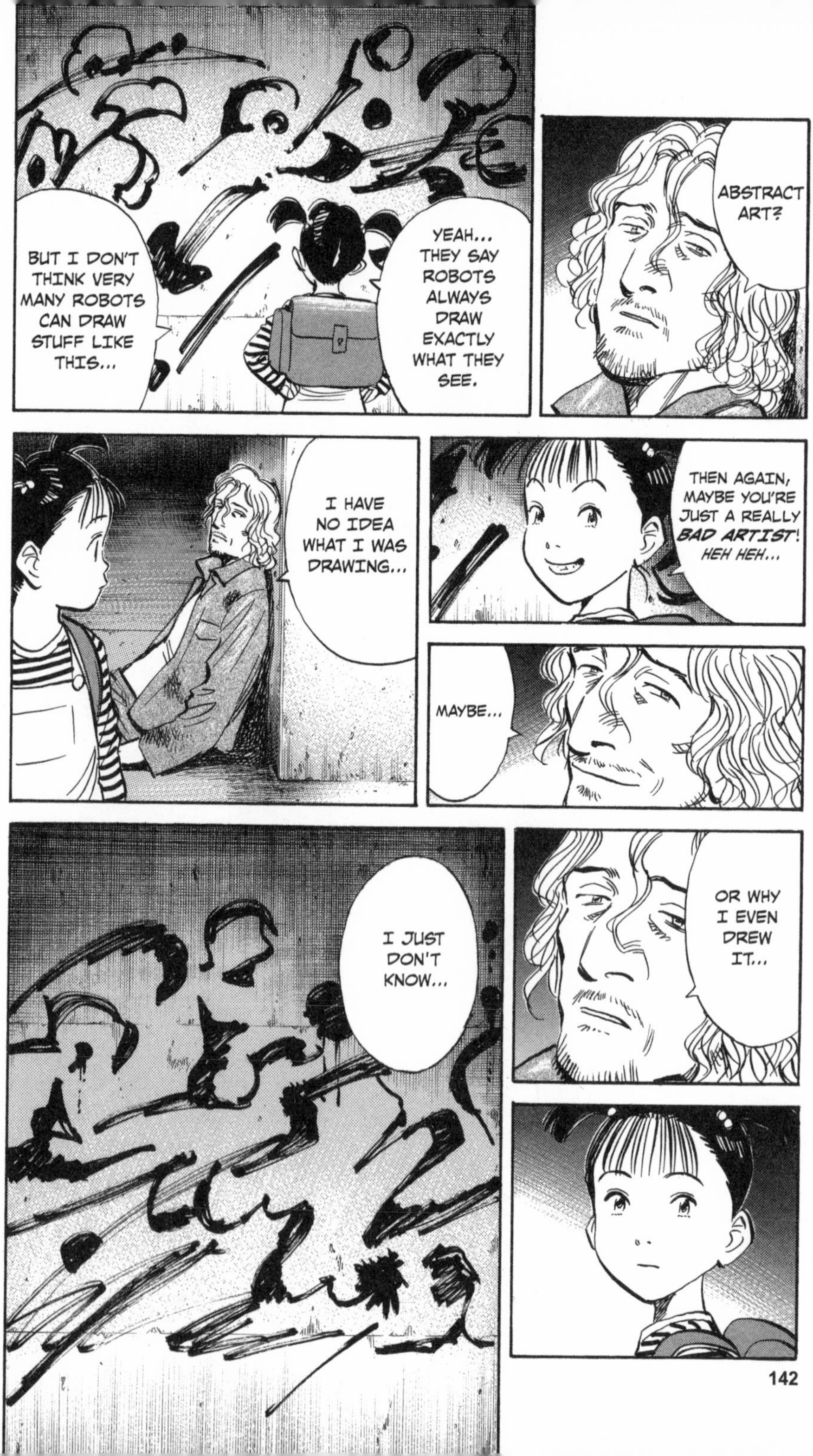
ABSTRACT ART?
YEAH... THEY SAY ROBOTS ALWAYS DRAW EXACTLY WHAT THEY SEE.
BUT I DON'T THINK VERY MANY ROBOTS CAN DRAW STUFF LIKE THIS...
THEN AGAIN, MAYBE YOU'RE JUST A REALLY ***BAD ARTIST***! *HEH HEH...*
MAYBE...
I HAVE NO IDEA WHAT I WAS DRAWING...
OR WHY I EVEN DREW IT...
I JUST DON'T KNOW...

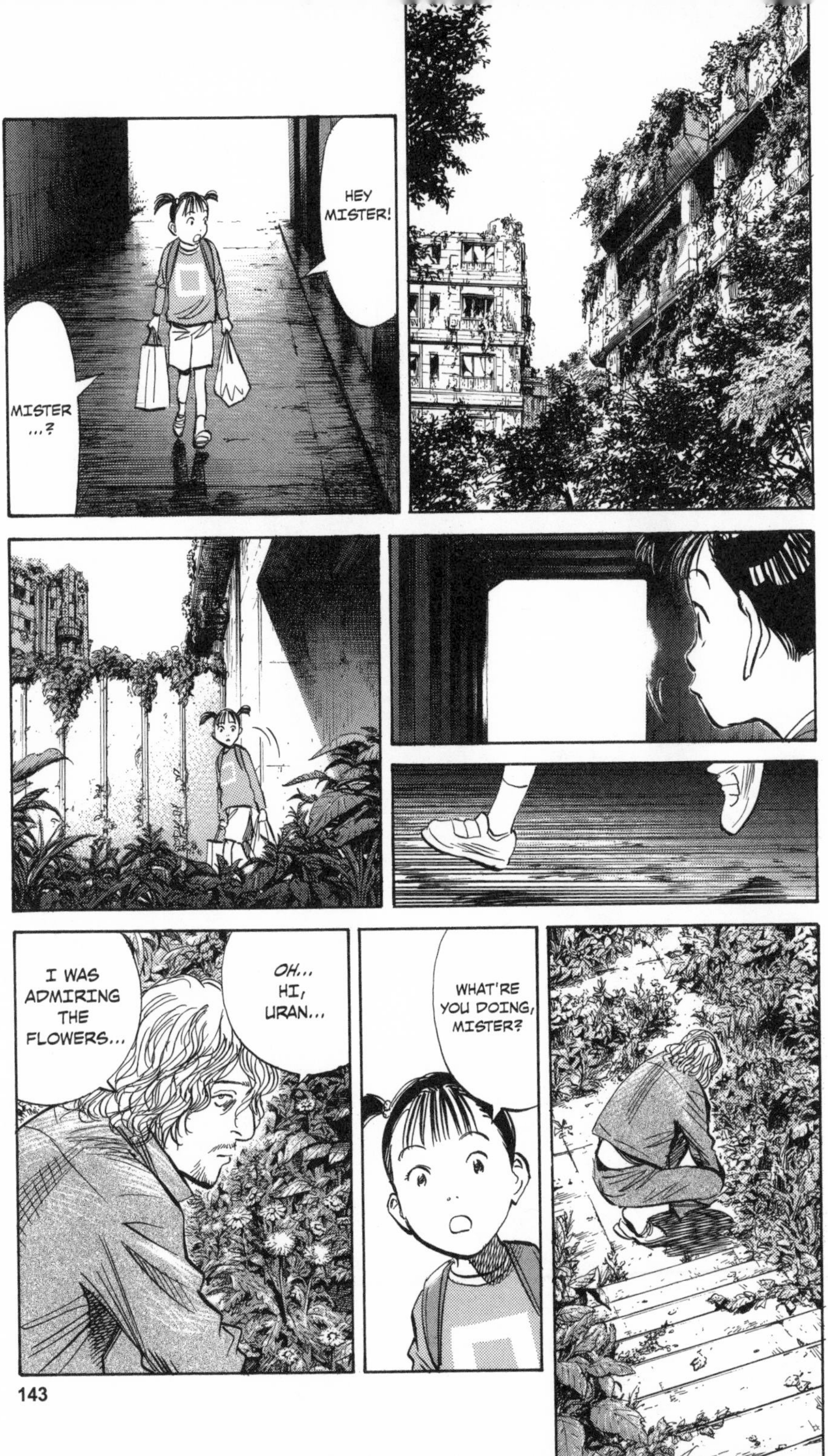
HEY MISTER!
MISTER ...?
WHAT'RE YOU DOING, MISTER?
OH... HI, URAN...
I WAS ADMIRING THE FLOWERS...

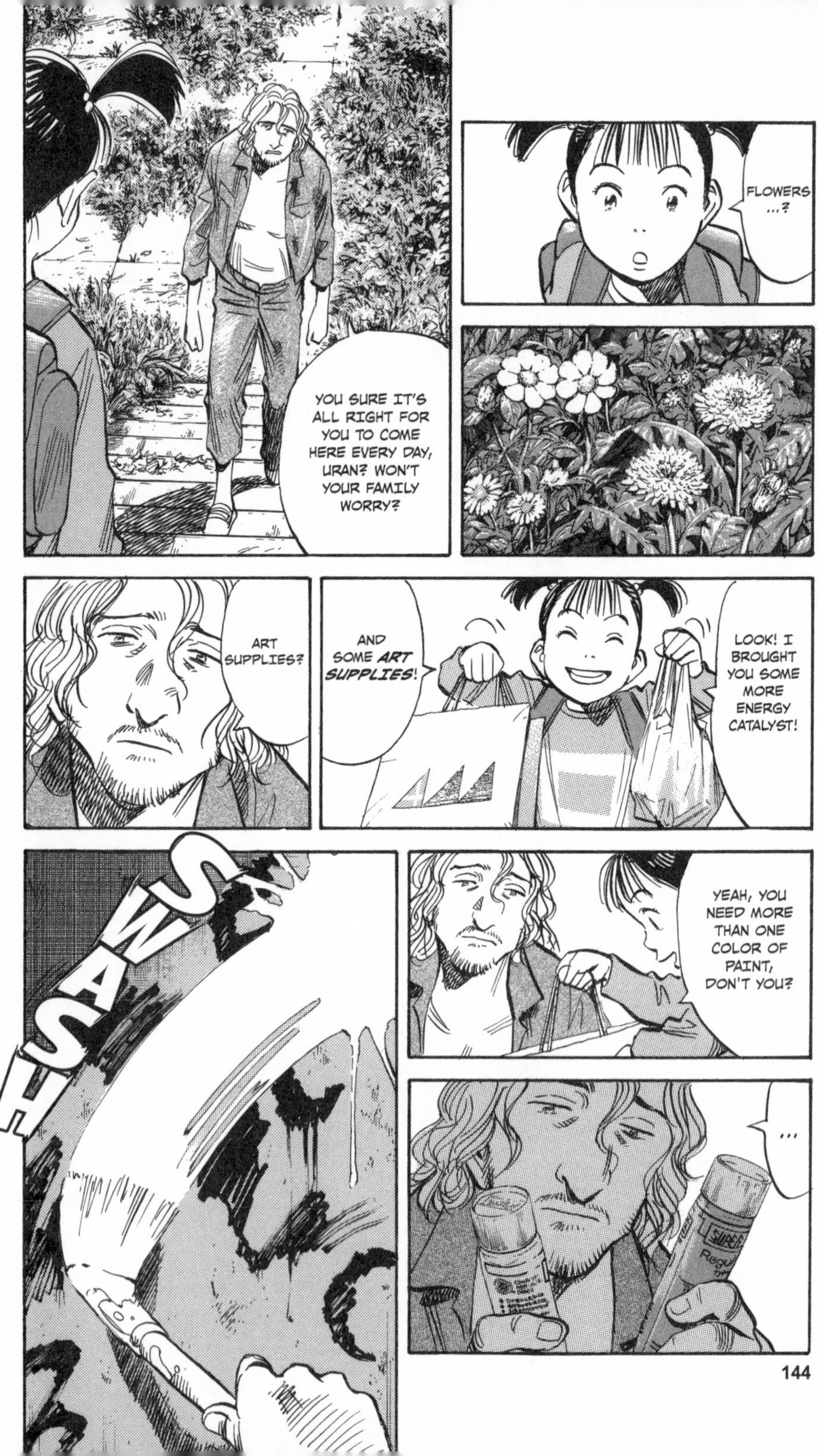
FLOWERS ...?
YOU SURE IT'S ALL RIGHT FOR YOU TO COME HERE EVERY DAY, URAN? WON'T YOUR FAMILY WORRY?
LOOK! I BROUGHT YOU SOME MORE ENERGY CATALYST!
AND SOME ART SUPPLIES!
ART SUPPLIES?
YEAH, YOU NEED MORE THAN ONE COLOR OF PAINT, DON'T YOU?
...
SWASH

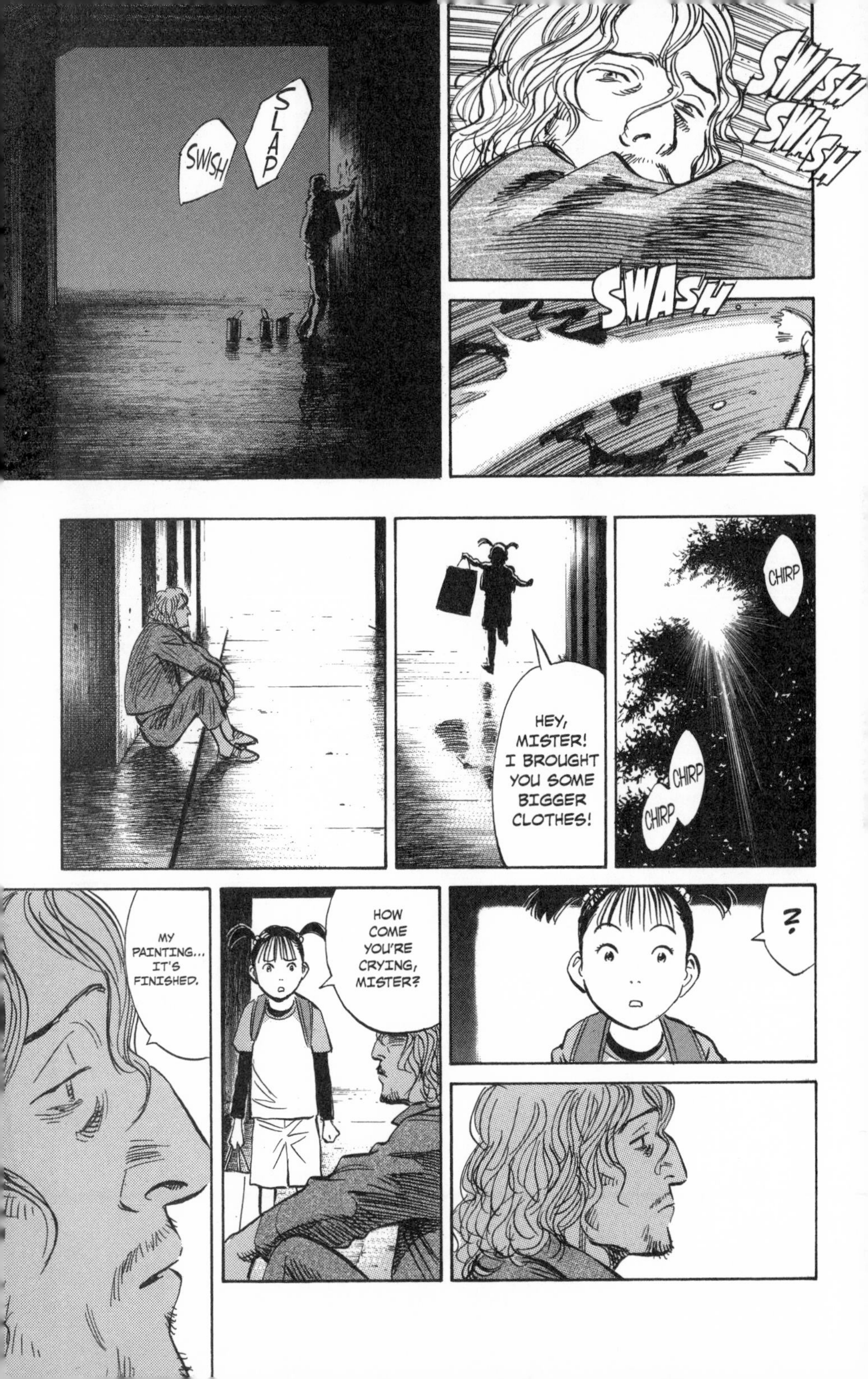
SWISH
SWASH
SWASH
SWISH
SLAP
CHIRP
CHIRP
CHIRP
HEY, MISTER! I BROUGHT YOU SOME BIGGER CLOTHES!
?
HOW COME YOU'RE CRYING, MISTER?
MY PAINTING... IT'S FINISHED.

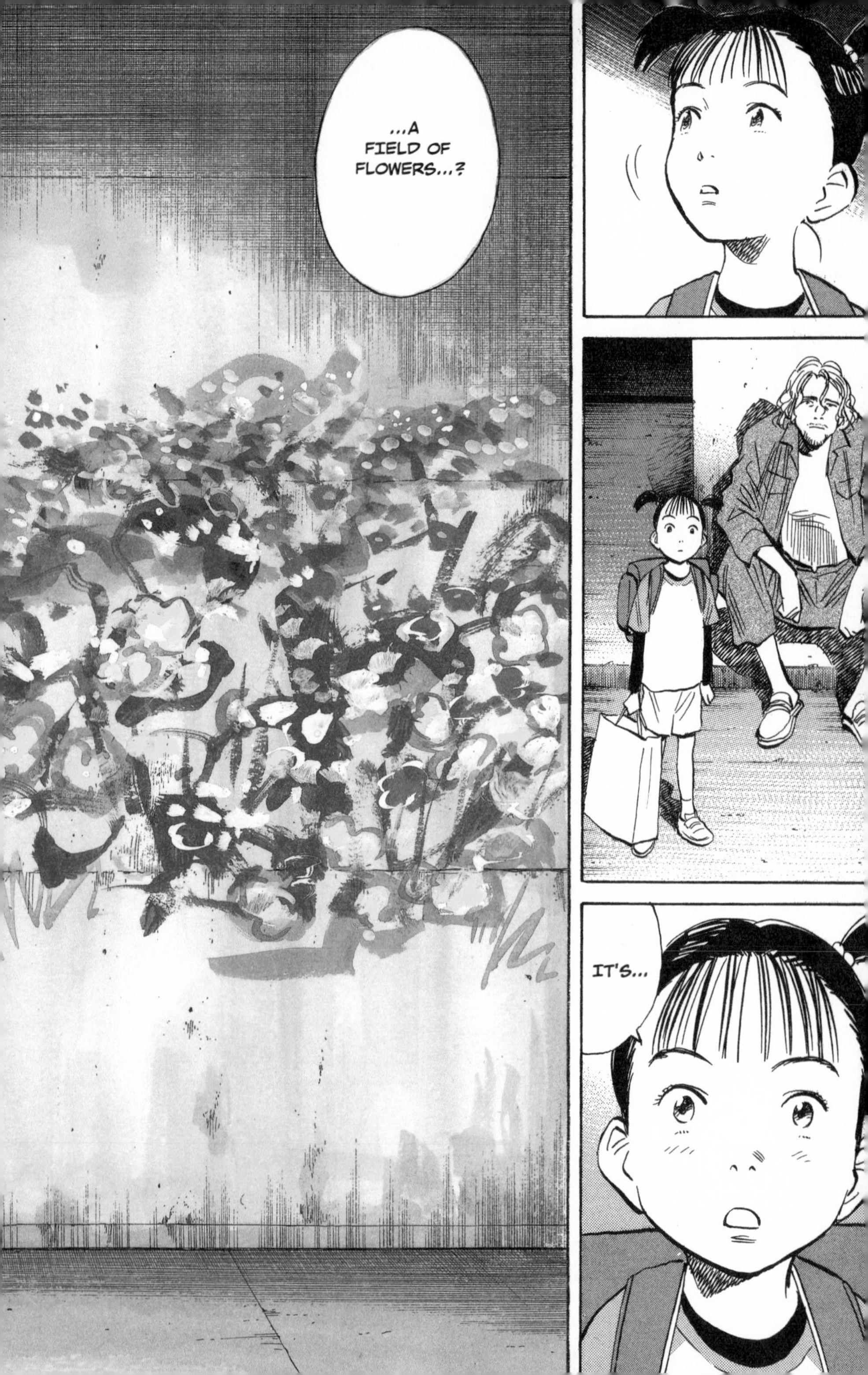
IT'S...
...A FIELD OF FLOWERS...?

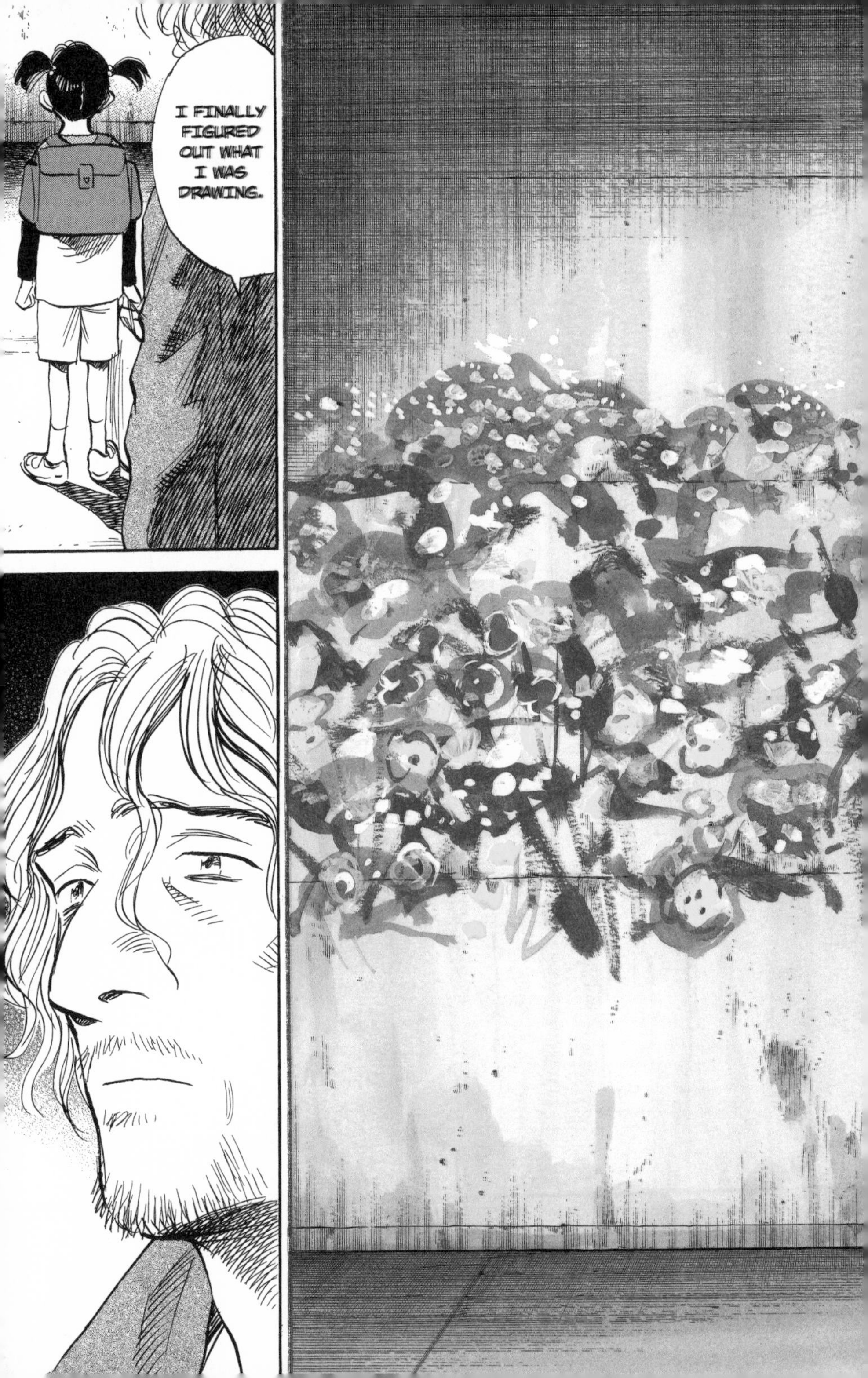
I FINALLY FIGURED OUT WHAT I WAS DRAWING.

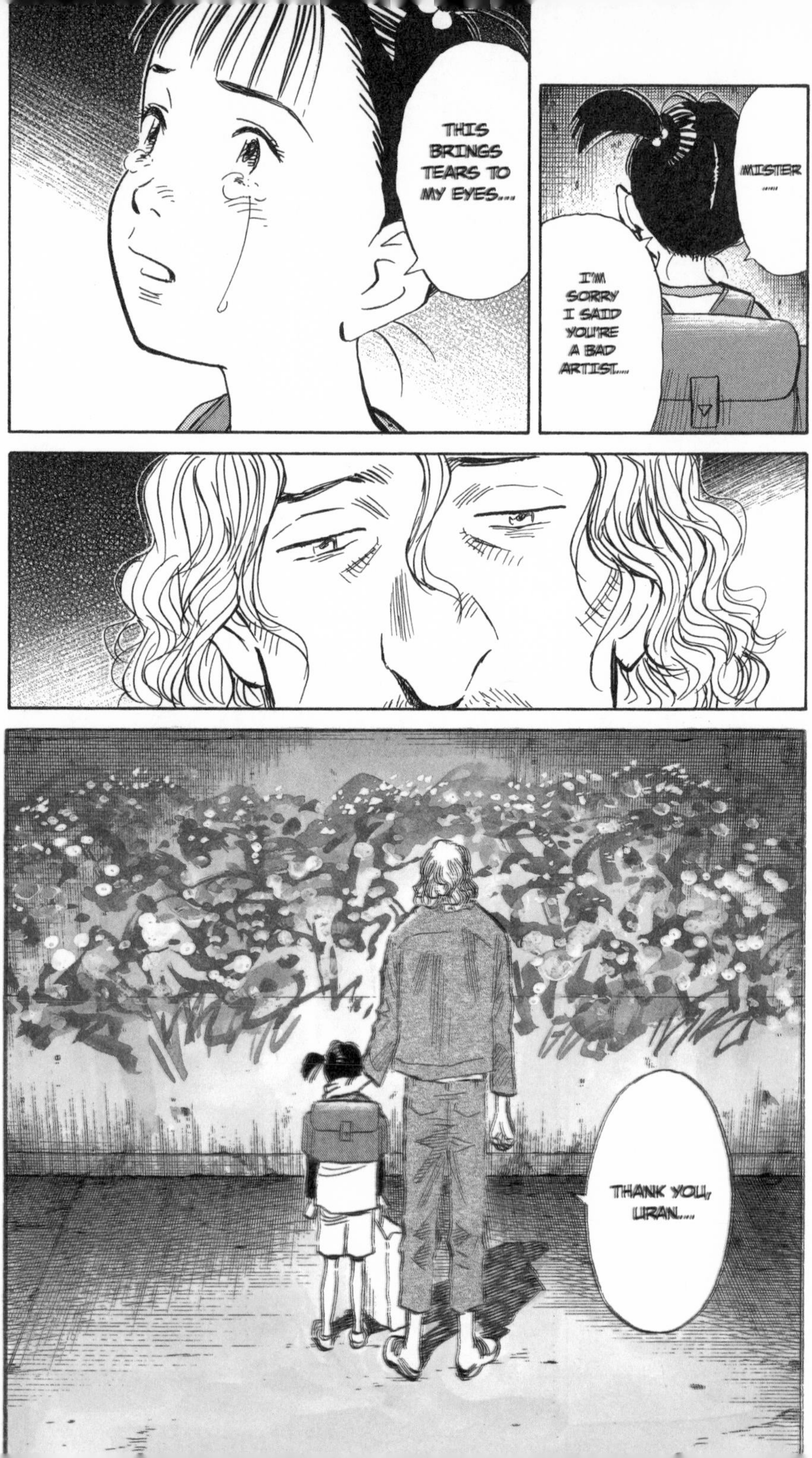
MISTER ....
I'M SORRY I SAID YOU'RE A BAD ARTIST....
THIS BRINGS TEARS TO MY EYES....
THANK YOU, URAN....

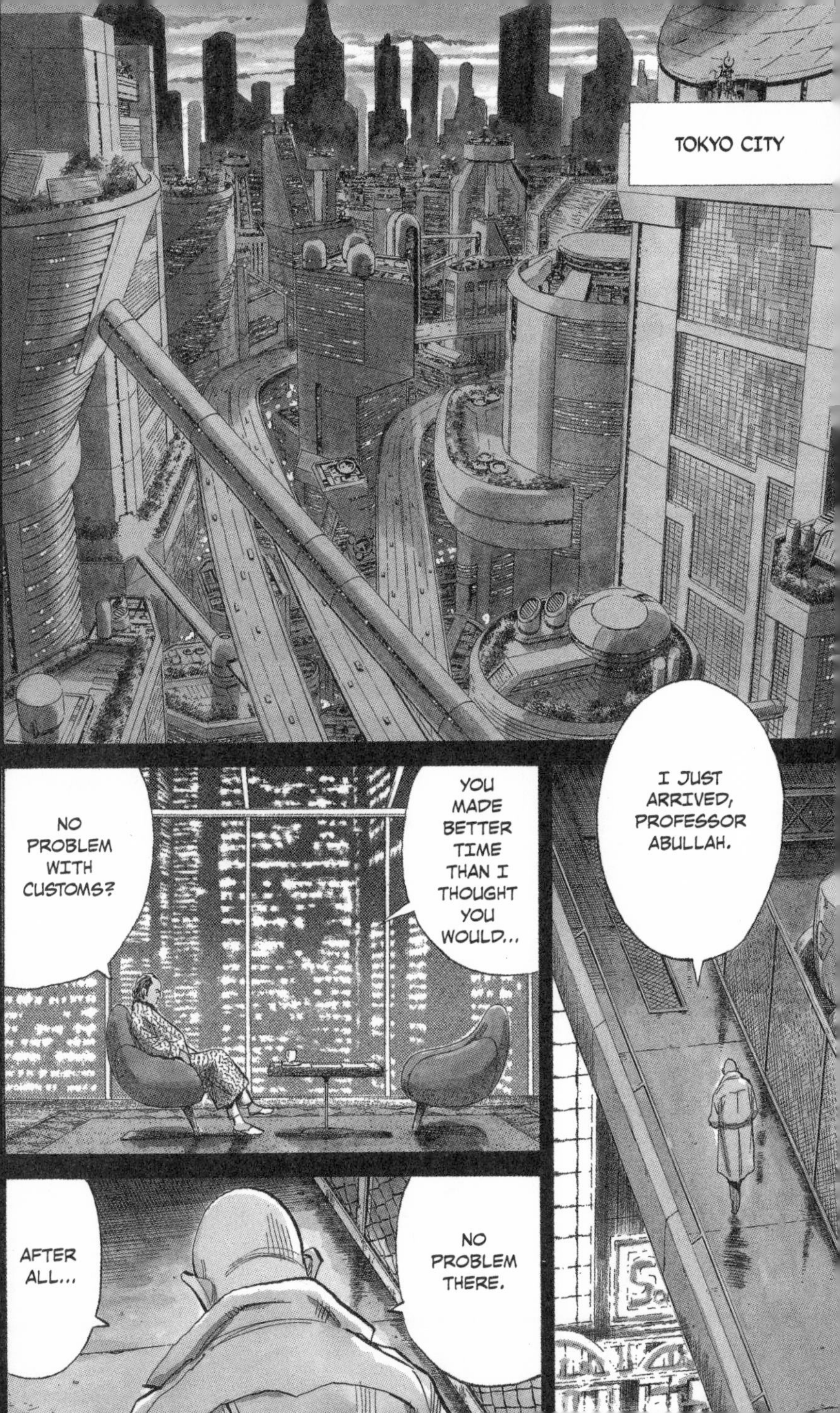
TOKYO CITY
I JUST ARRIVED, PROFESSOR ABULLAH.
YOU MADE BETTER TIME THAN I THOUGHT YOU WOULD...
NO PROBLEM WITH CUSTOMS?
NO PROBLEM THERE.
AFTER ALL...

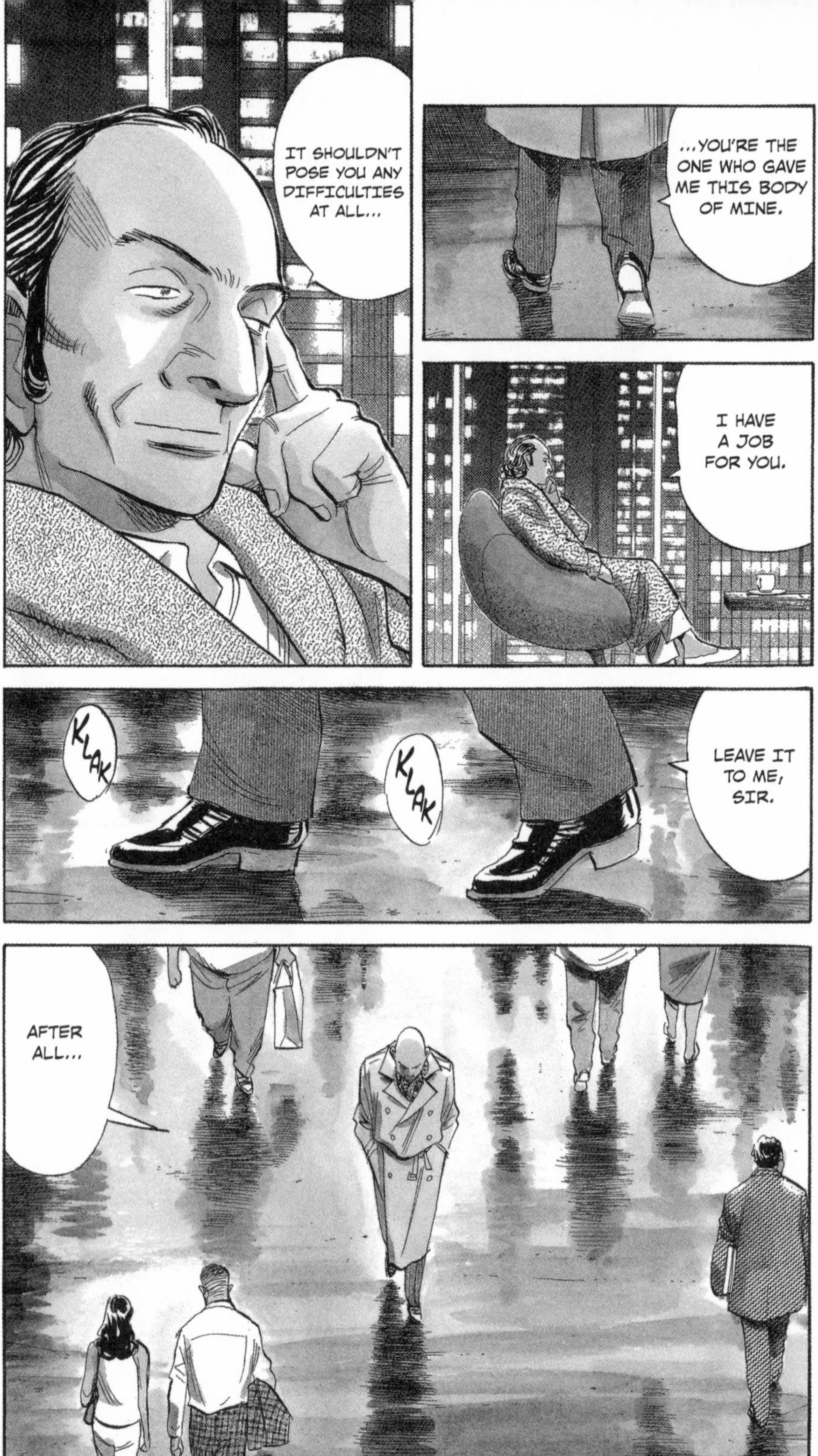
...YOU'RE THE ONE WHO GAVE ME THIS BODY OF MINE.
I HAVE A JOB FOR YOU.
IT SHOULDN'T POSE YOU ANY DIFFICULTIES AT ALL...
LEAVE IT TO ME, SIR.
KLAK
KLAK
AFTER ALL...

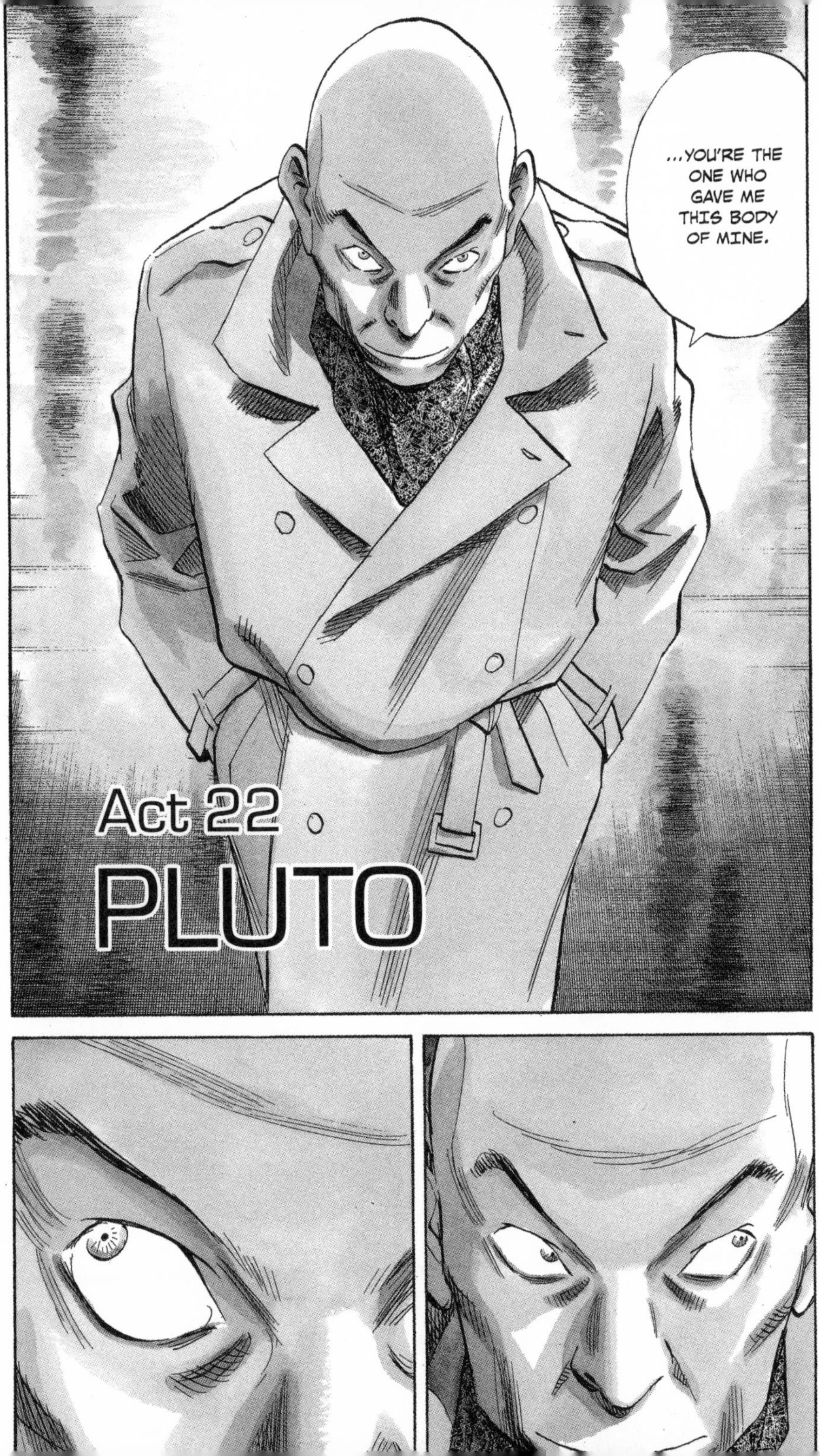
...YOU'RE THE ONE WHO GAVE ME THIS BODY OF MINE.
Act 22
PLUTO

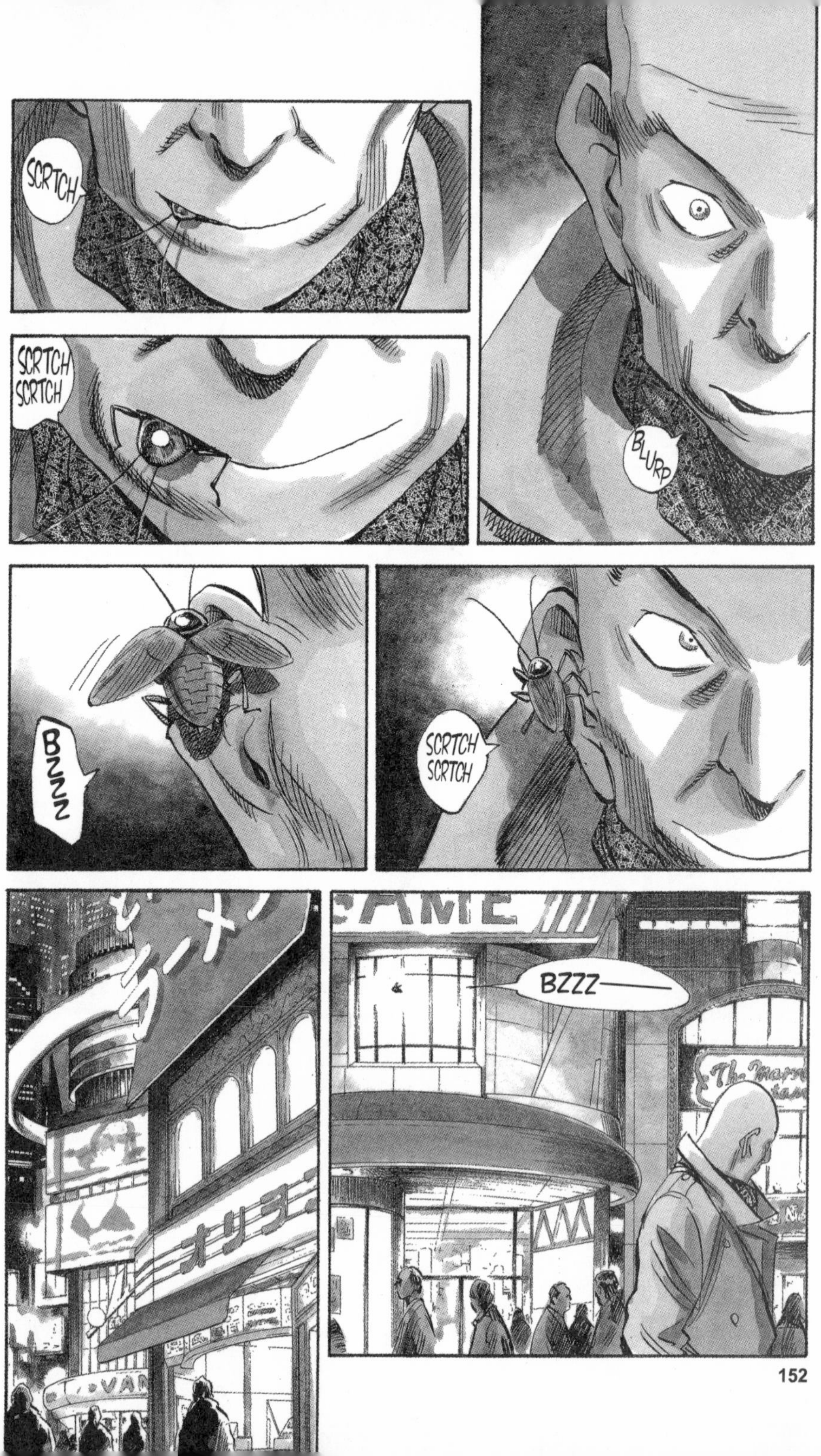
BLURP
SCRTCH
SCRTCH SCRTCH
SCRTCH SCRTCH
BZZZ
BZZZ———

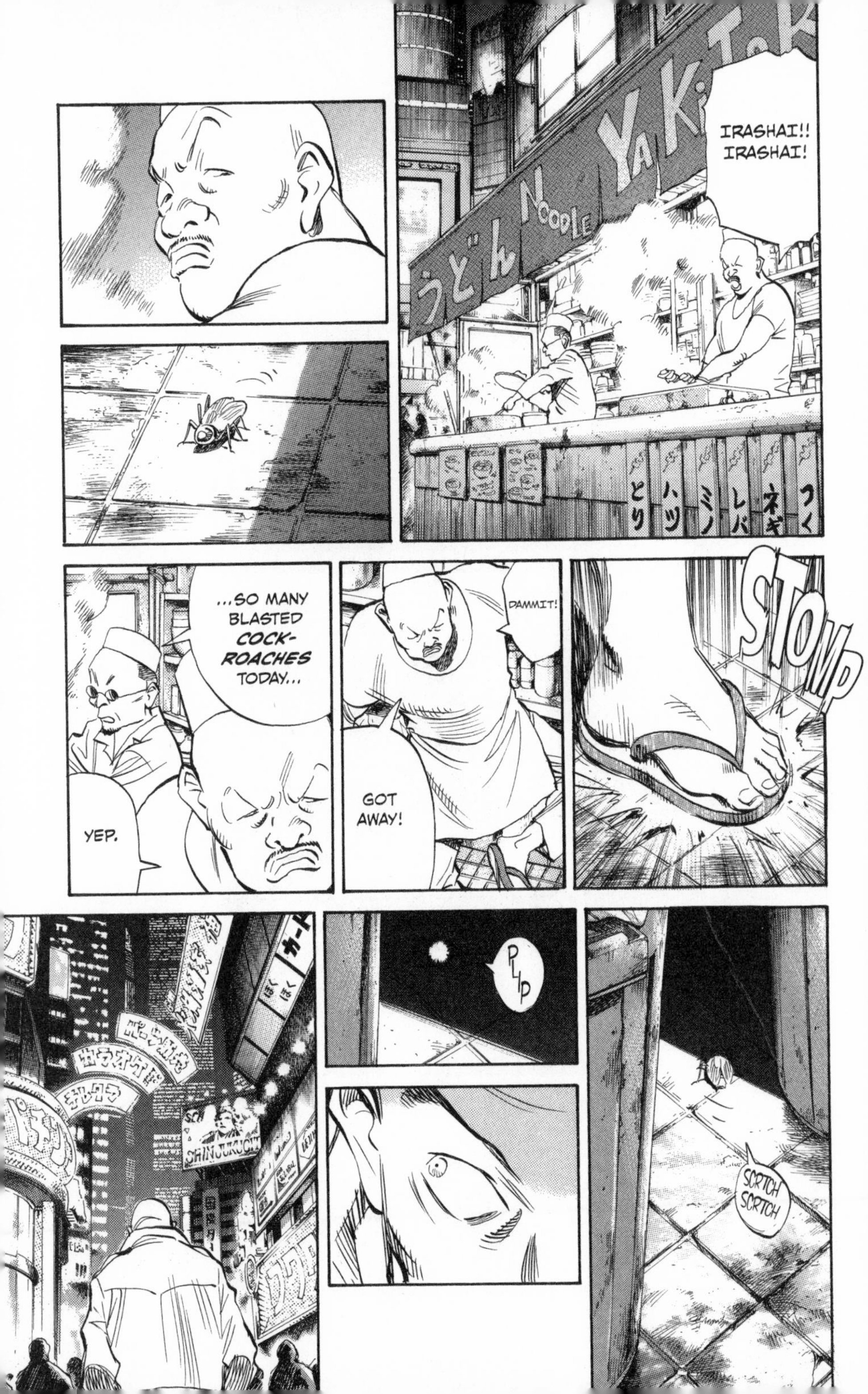
IRASHAI!! IRASHAI!
うどん
NOODLE
つく
ネギ
レバ
ミノ
ハツ
とり
STOMP
DAMMIT!
GOT AWAY!
...SO MANY BLASTED COCK-ROACHES TODAY...
YEP.
SCRTCH SCRTCH
PLIP

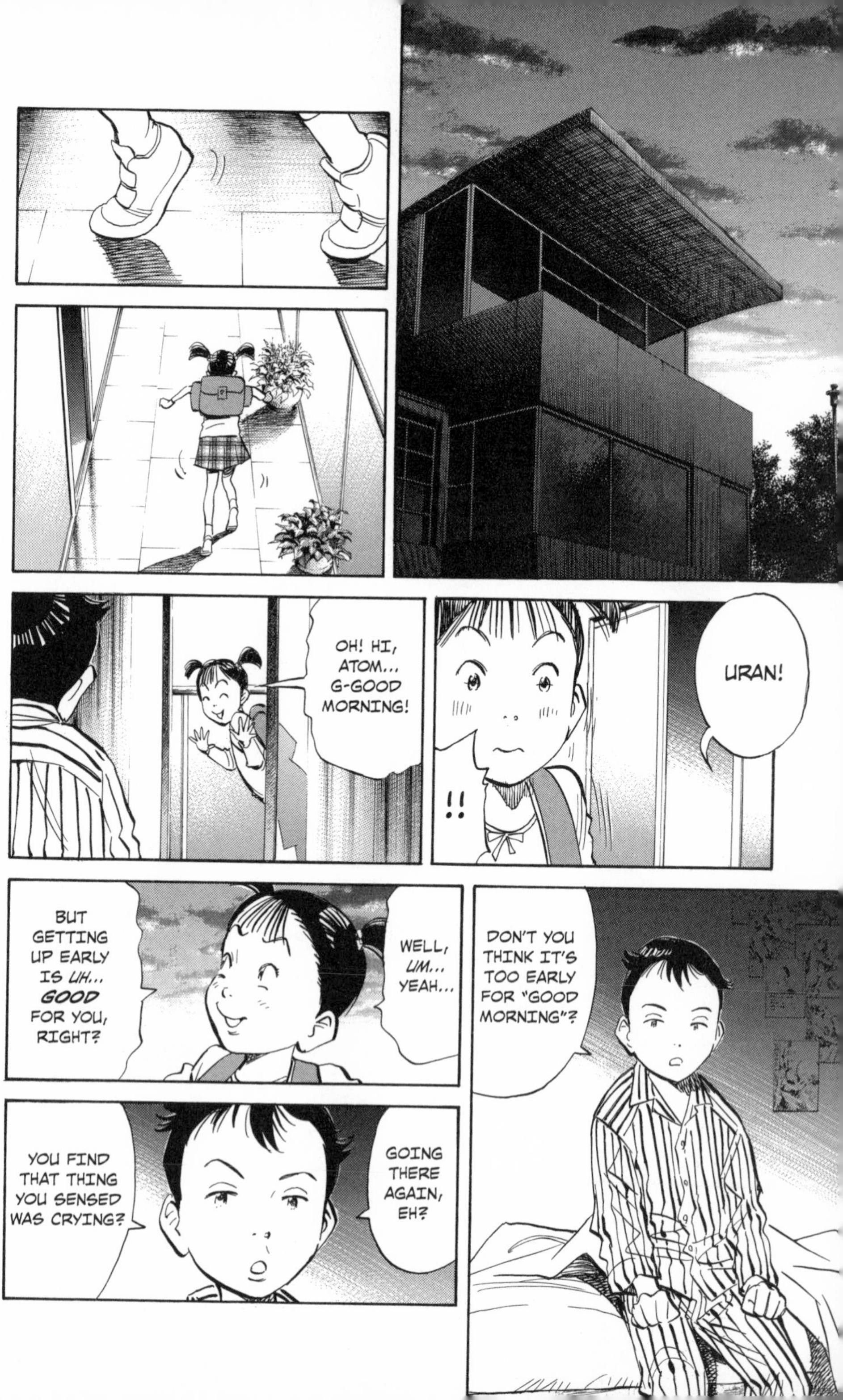
URAN!
!!
OH! HI, ATOM... G-GOOD MORNING!
DON'T YOU THINK IT'S TOO EARLY FOR "GOOD MORNING"?
WELL, *UM*... YEAH...
BUT GETTING UP EARLY IS *UH*... ***GOOD*** FOR YOU, RIGHT?
GOING THERE AGAIN, EH?
YOU FIND THAT THING YOU SENSED WAS CRYING?

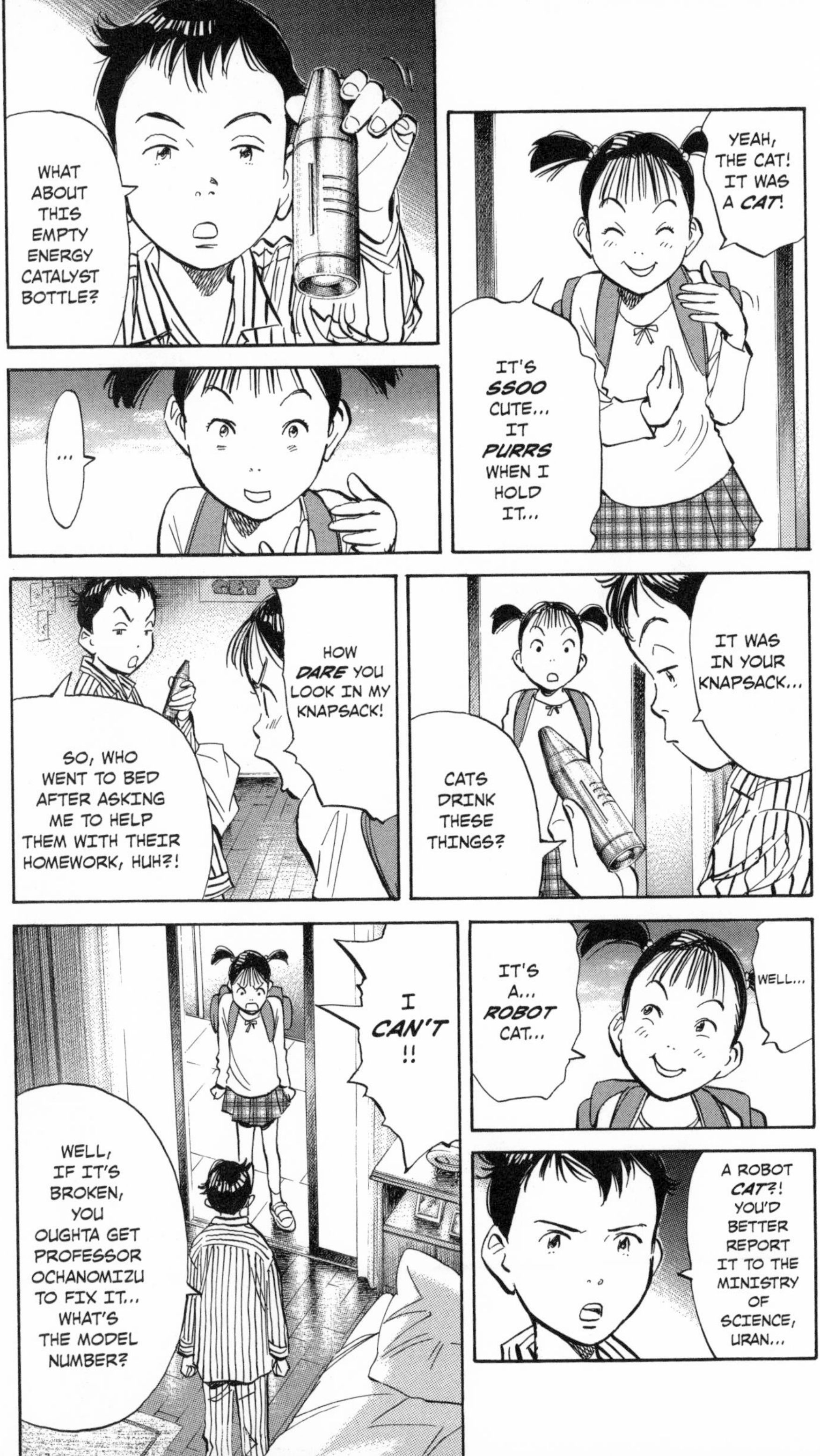

YEAH, THE CAT! IT WAS A *CAT*!
IT'S ***SSOO*** CUTE... IT ***PURRS*** WHEN I HOLD IT...
WHAT ABOUT THIS EMPTY ENERGY CATALYST BOTTLE?
...
IT WAS IN YOUR KNAPSACK...
CATS DRINK THESE THINGS?
HOW ***DARE*** YOU LOOK IN MY KNAPSACK!
SO, WHO WENT TO BED AFTER ASKING ME TO HELP THEM WITH THEIR HOMEWORK, HUH?!
WELL...
IT'S A... ***ROBOT*** CAT...
A ROBOT ***CAT***?! YOU'D BETTER REPORT IT TO THE MINISTRY OF SCIENCE, URAN...
I ***CAN'T*** !!
WELL, IF IT'S BROKEN, YOU OUGHTA GET PROFESSOR OCHANOMIZU TO FIX IT... WHAT'S THE MODEL NUMBER?

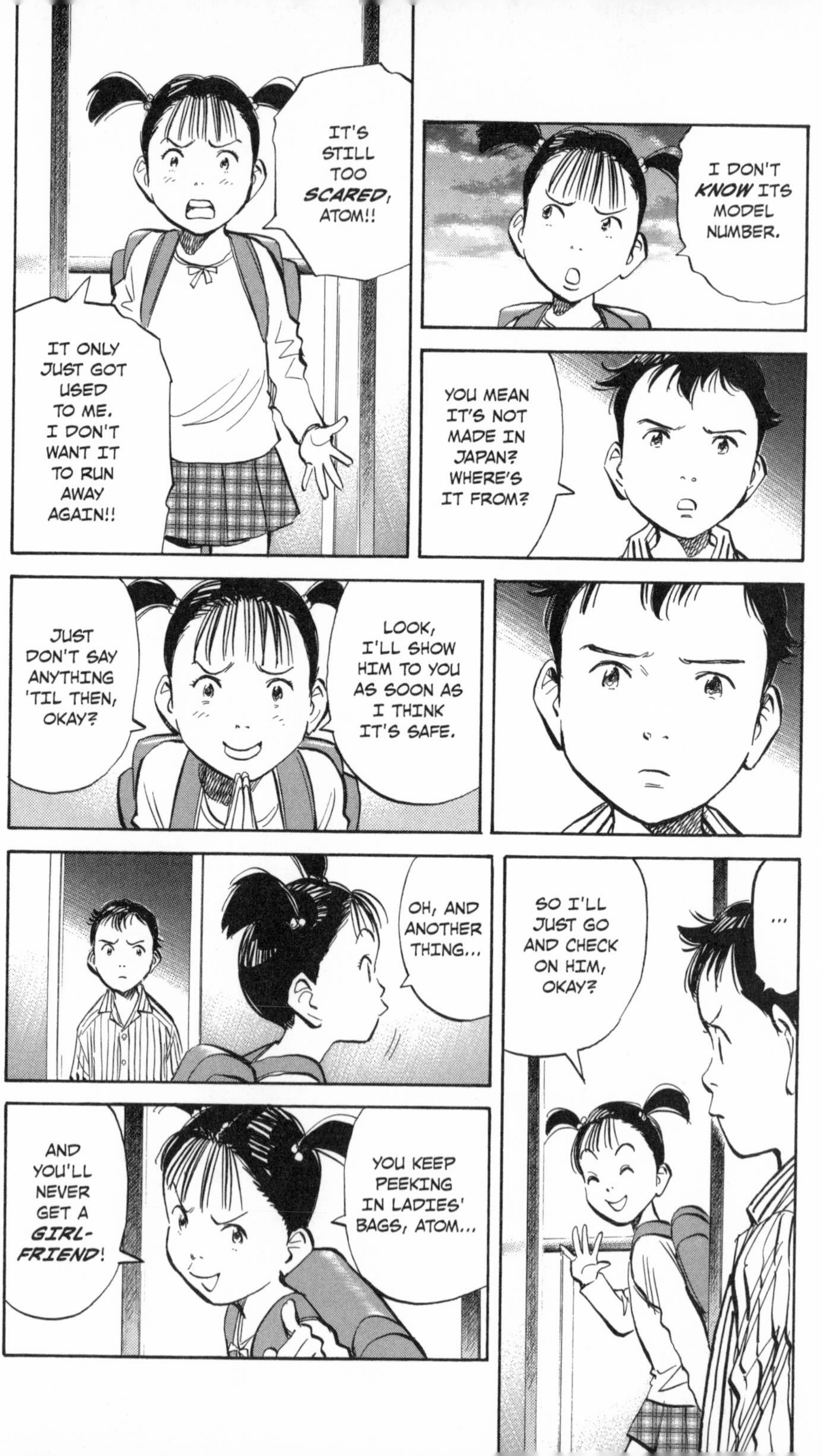

I DON'T *KNOW* ITS MODEL NUMBER.
YOU MEAN IT'S NOT MADE IN JAPAN? WHERE'S IT FROM?
IT'S STILL TOO *SCARED*, ATOM!!
IT ONLY JUST GOT USED TO ME. I DON'T WANT IT TO RUN AWAY AGAIN!!
LOOK, I'LL SHOW HIM TO YOU AS SOON AS I THINK IT'S SAFE.
JUST DON'T SAY ANYTHING 'TIL THEN, OKAY?
...
SO I'LL JUST GO AND CHECK ON HIM, OKAY?
OH, AND ANOTHER THING...
YOU KEEP PEEKING IN LADIES' BAGS, ATOM...
AND YOU'LL NEVER GET A *GIRL-FRIEND*!

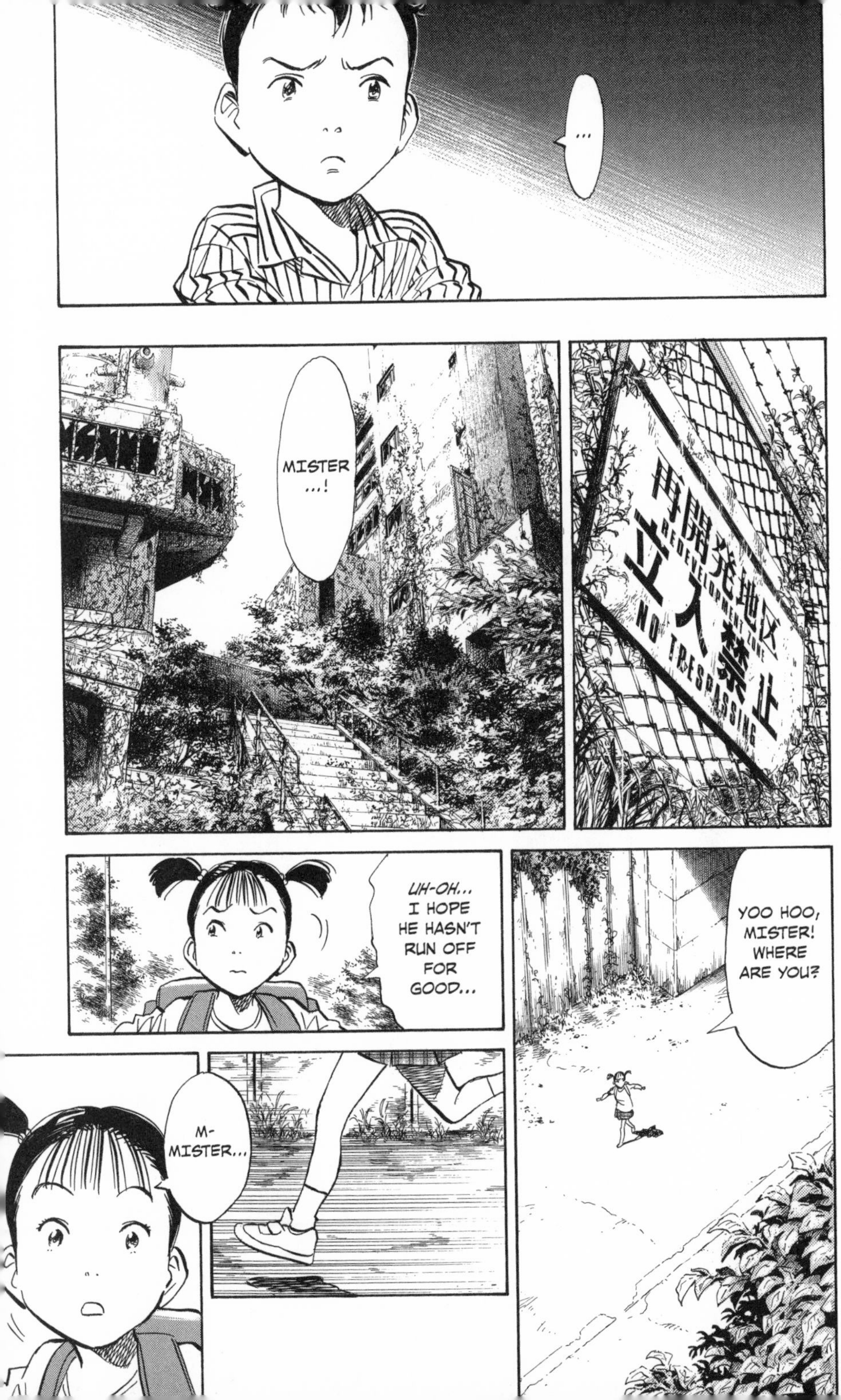
...
再開発地区
REDEVELOPMENT ZONE
立入禁止
NO TRESPASSING
MISTER ...!
YOO HOO, MISTER! WHERE ARE YOU?
UH-OH... I HOPE HE HASN'T RUN OFF FOR GOOD...
M-MISTER...

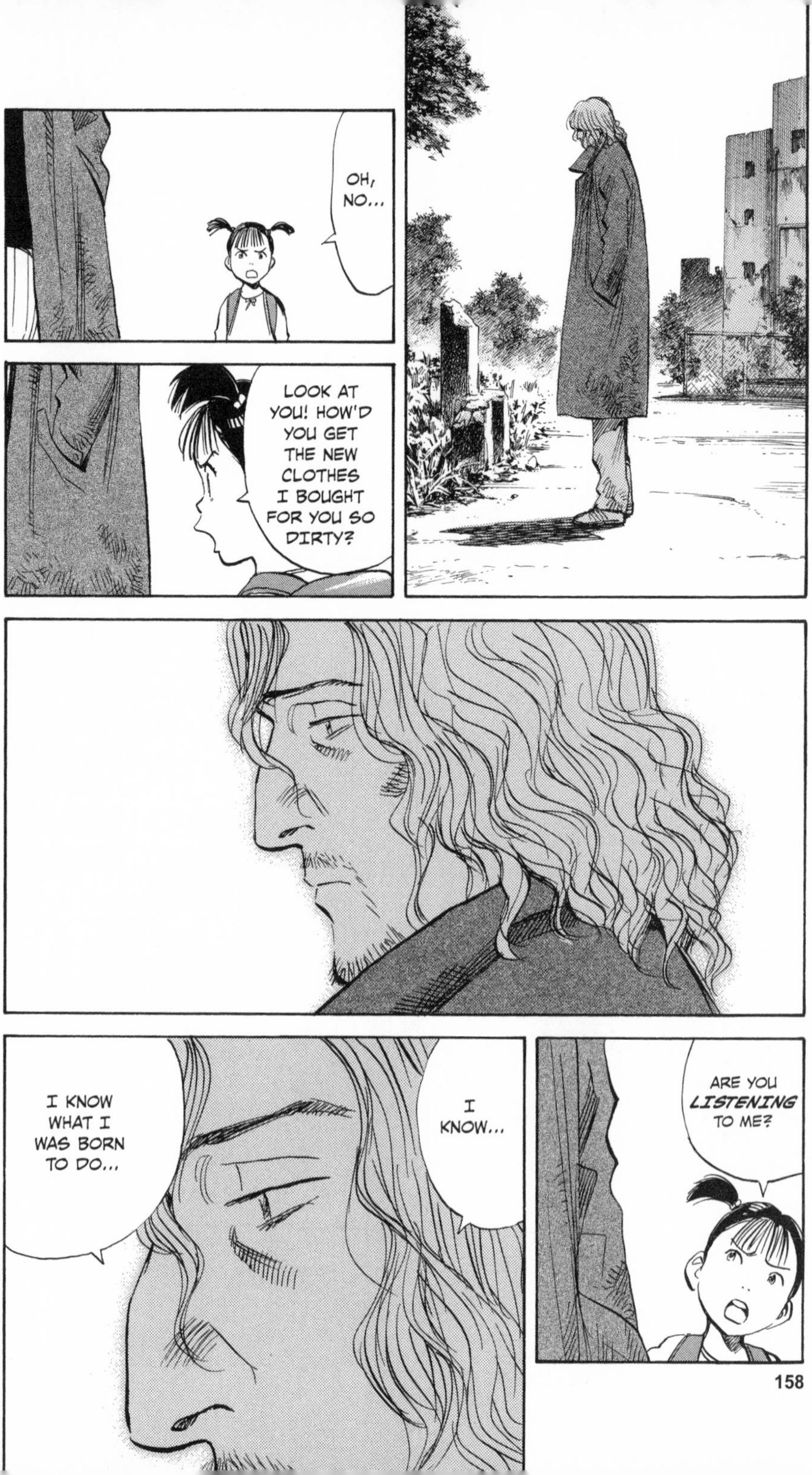
OH, NO...
LOOK AT YOU! HOW'D YOU GET THE NEW CLOTHES I BOUGHT FOR YOU SO DIRTY?
ARE YOU *LISTENING* TO ME?
I KNOW...
I KNOW WHAT I WAS BORN TO DO...

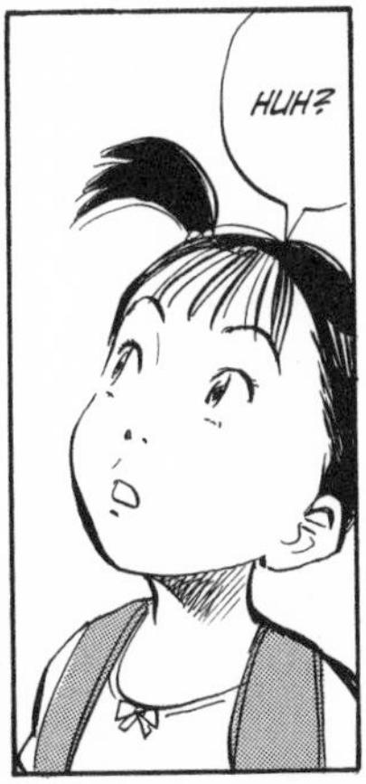
HUH?
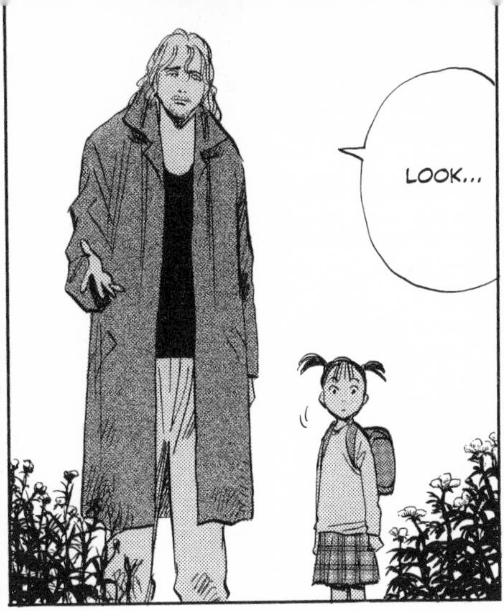
LOOK...
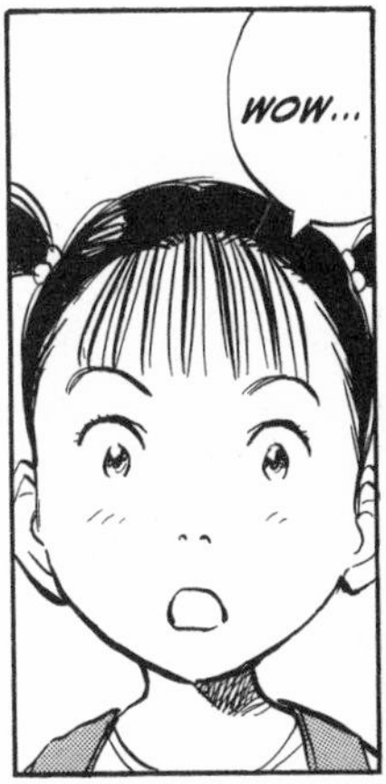
WOW...
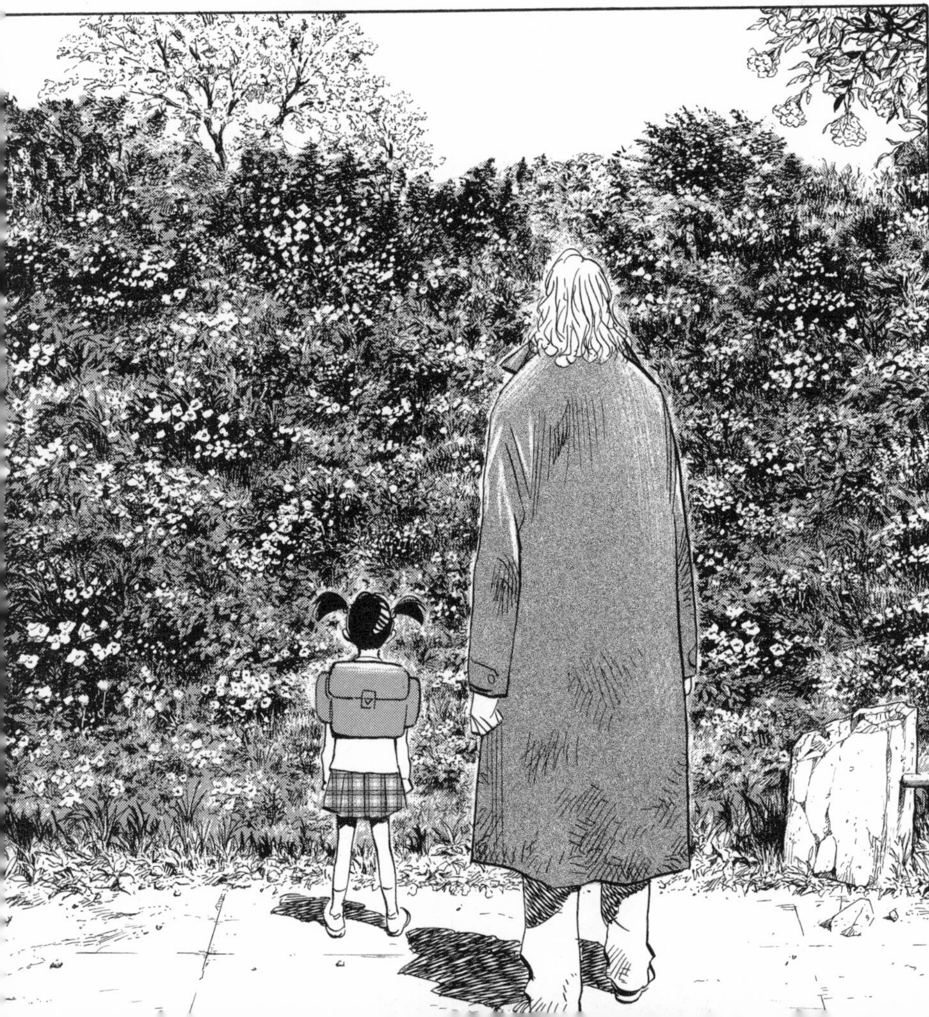

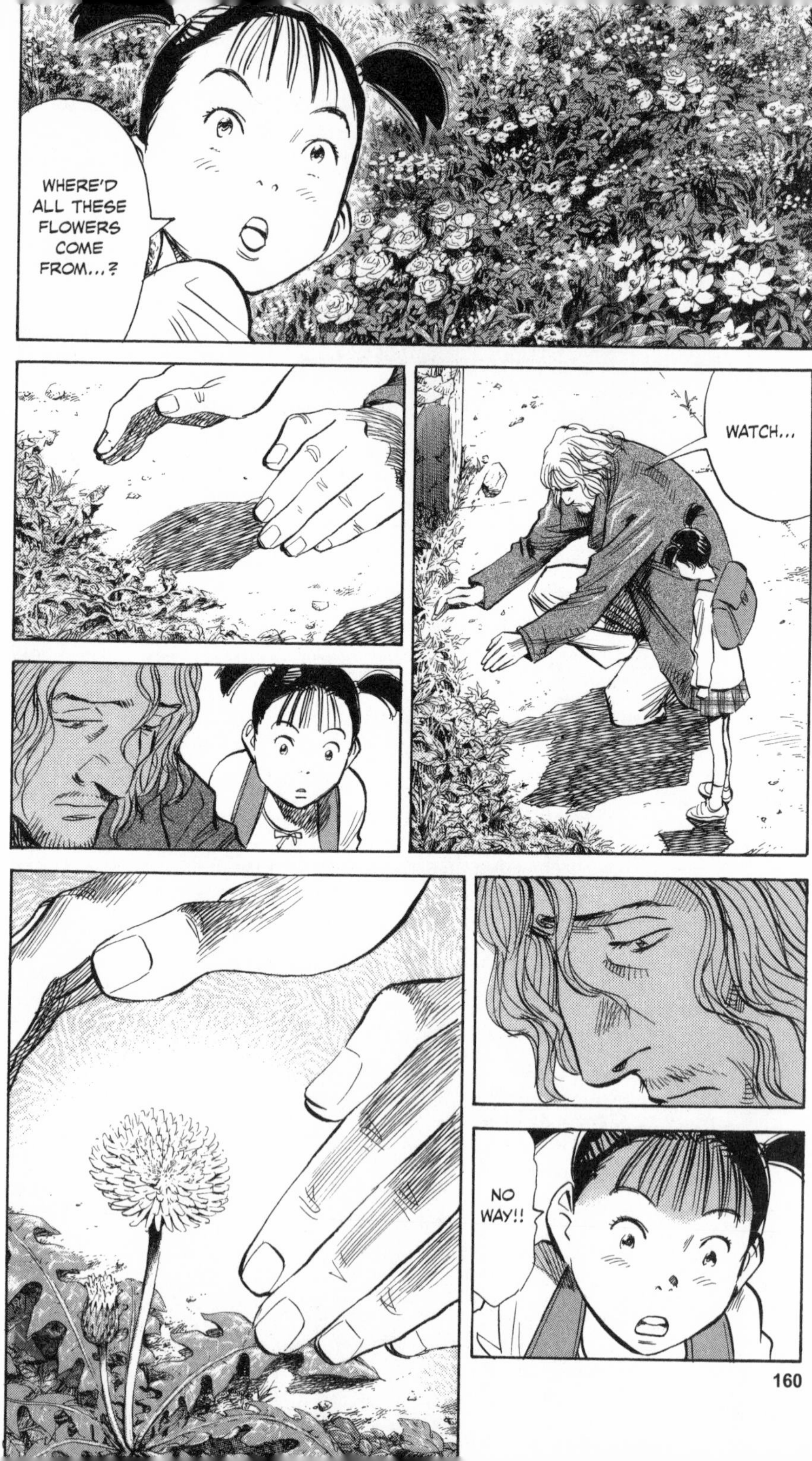
WHERE'D ALL THESE FLOWERS COME FROM...?
WATCH...
NO WAY!!

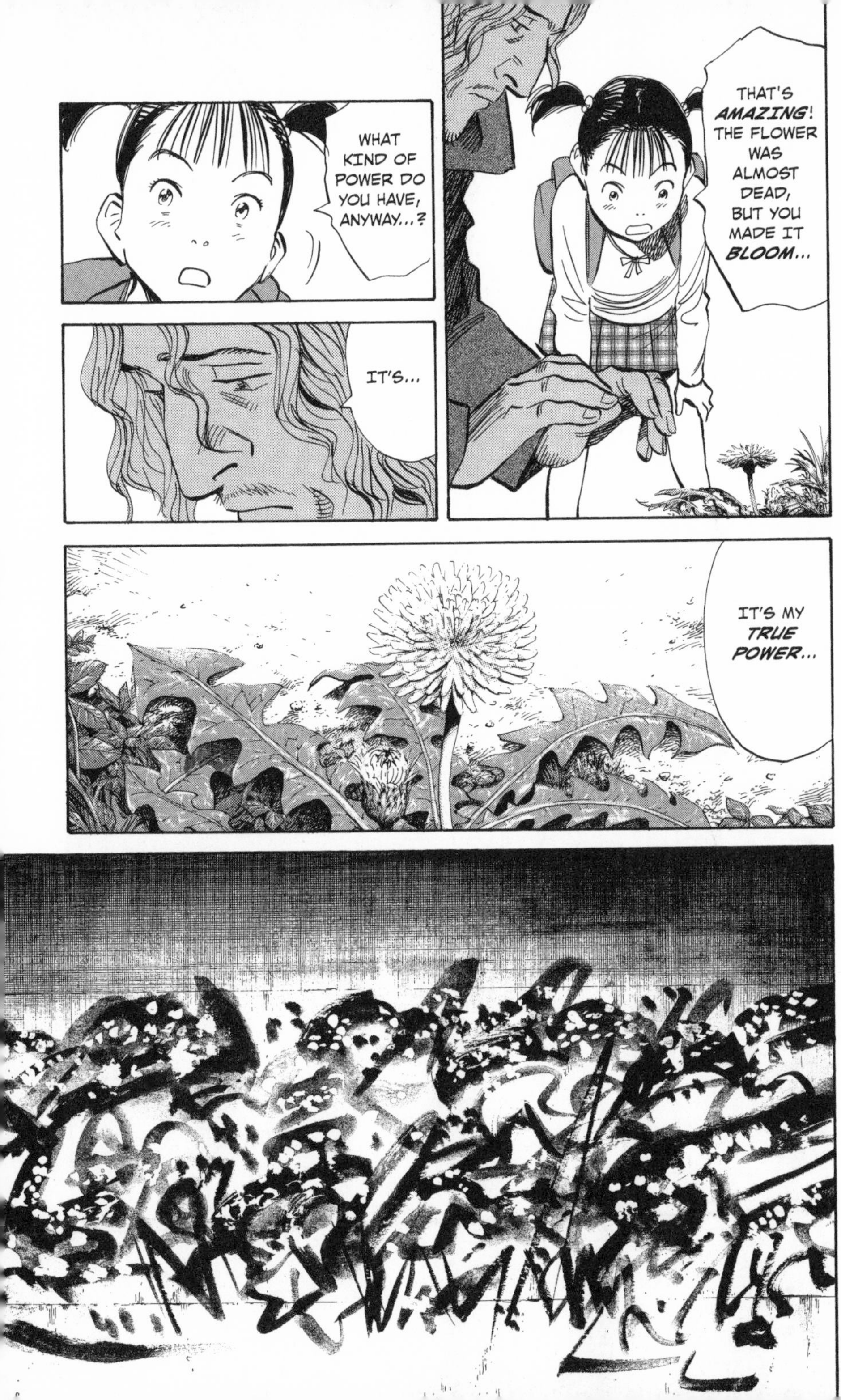
THAT'S **AMAZING**! THE FLOWER WAS ALMOST DEAD, BUT YOU MADE IT **BLOOM**...
WHAT KIND OF POWER DO YOU HAVE, ANYWAY...?
IT'S...
IT'S MY **TRUE POWER**...

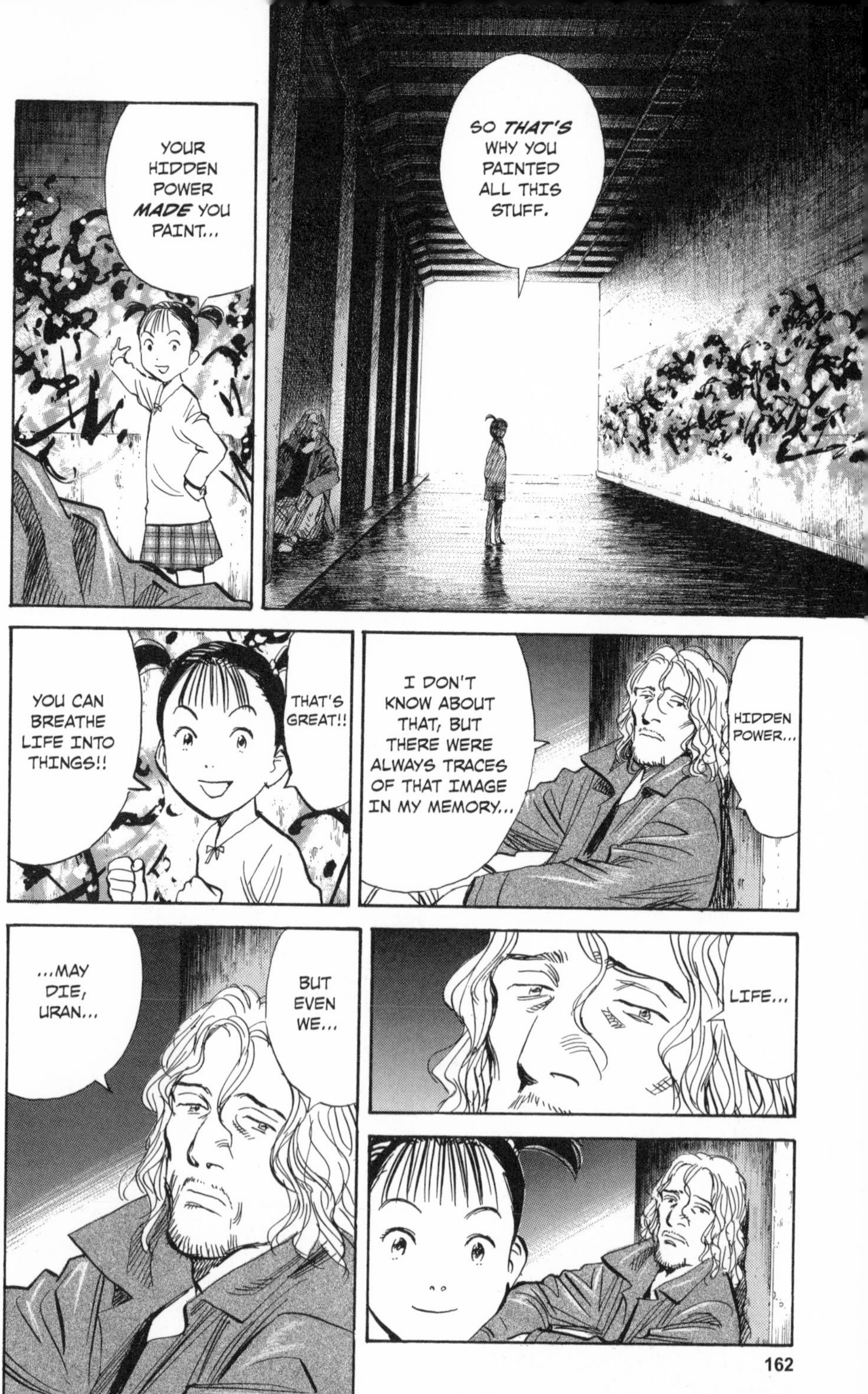
SO *THAT'S* WHY YOU PAINTED ALL THIS STUFF.
YOUR HIDDEN POWER *MADE* YOU PAINT...
HIDDEN POWER...
I DON'T KNOW ABOUT THAT, BUT THERE WERE ALWAYS TRACES OF THAT IMAGE IN MY MEMORY...
THAT'S GREAT!!
YOU CAN BREATHE LIFE INTO THINGS!!
LIFE...
BUT EVEN WE...
...MAY DIE, URAN...

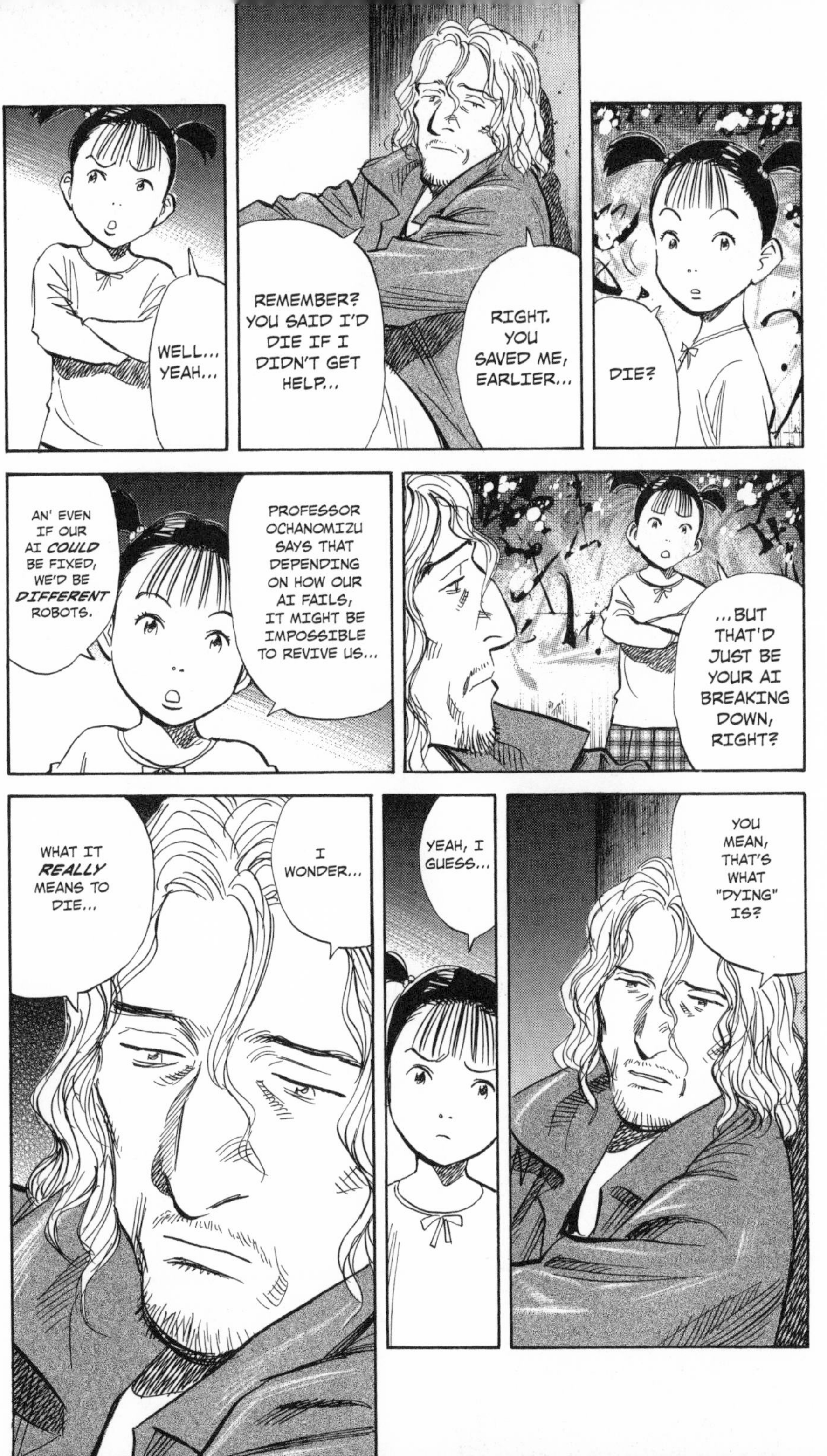
DIE?
RIGHT. YOU SAVED ME, EARLIER...
REMEMBER? YOU SAID I'D DIE IF I DIDN'T GET HELP...
WELL... YEAH...
...BUT THAT'D JUST BE YOUR AI BREAKING DOWN, RIGHT?
PROFESSOR OCHANOMIZU SAYS THAT DEPENDING ON HOW OUR AI FAILS, IT MIGHT BE IMPOSSIBLE TO REVIVE US...
AN' EVEN IF OUR AI *COULD* BE FIXED, WE'D BE *DIFFERENT* ROBOTS.
YOU MEAN, THAT'S WHAT "DYING" IS?
YEAH, I GUESS...
I WONDER...
WHAT IT *REALLY* MEANS TO DIE...

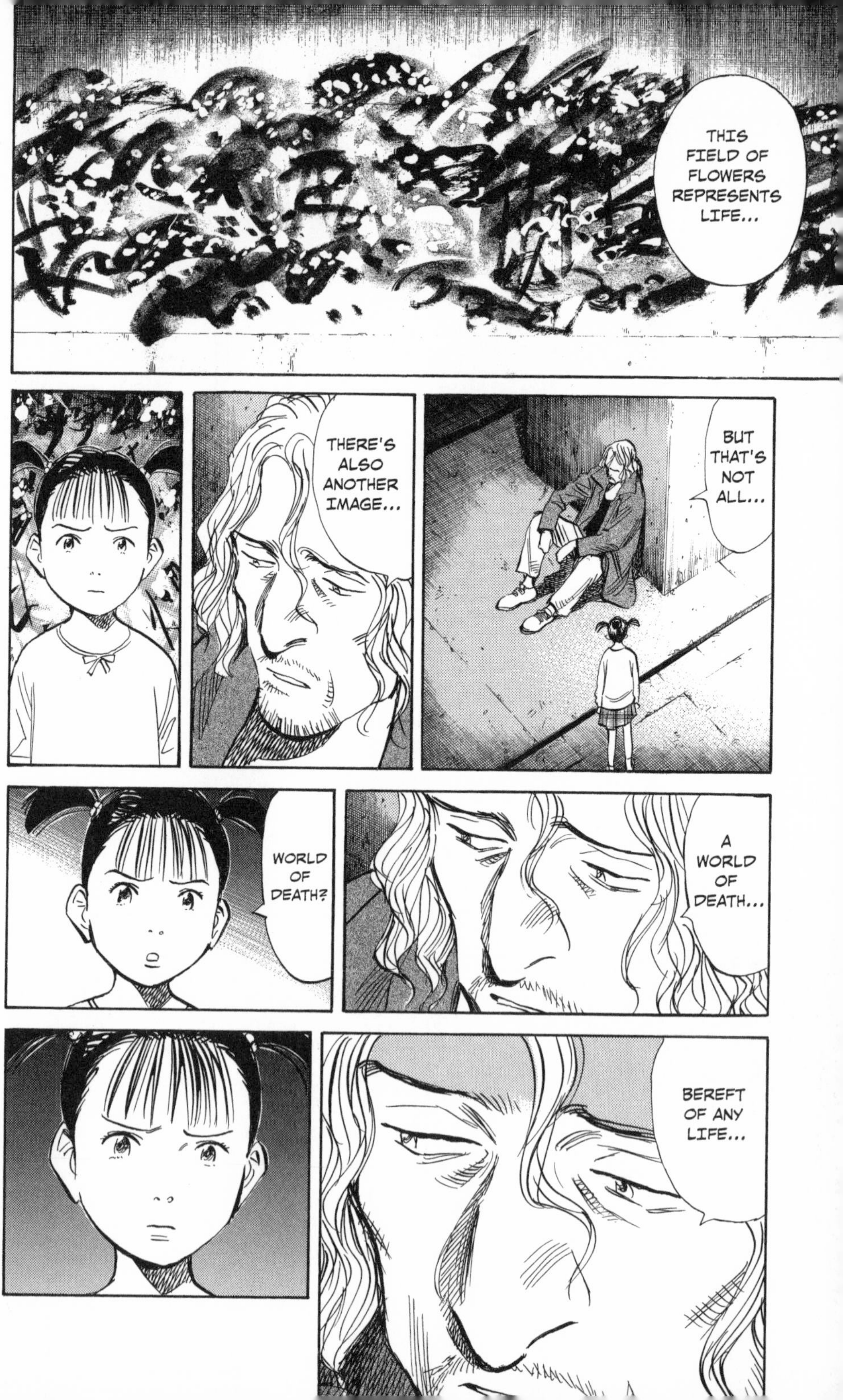
THIS FIELD OF FLOWERS REPRESENTS LIFE...
BUT THAT'S NOT ALL...
THERE'S ALSO ANOTHER IMAGE...
A WORLD OF DEATH...
WORLD OF DEATH?
BEREFT OF ANY LIFE...

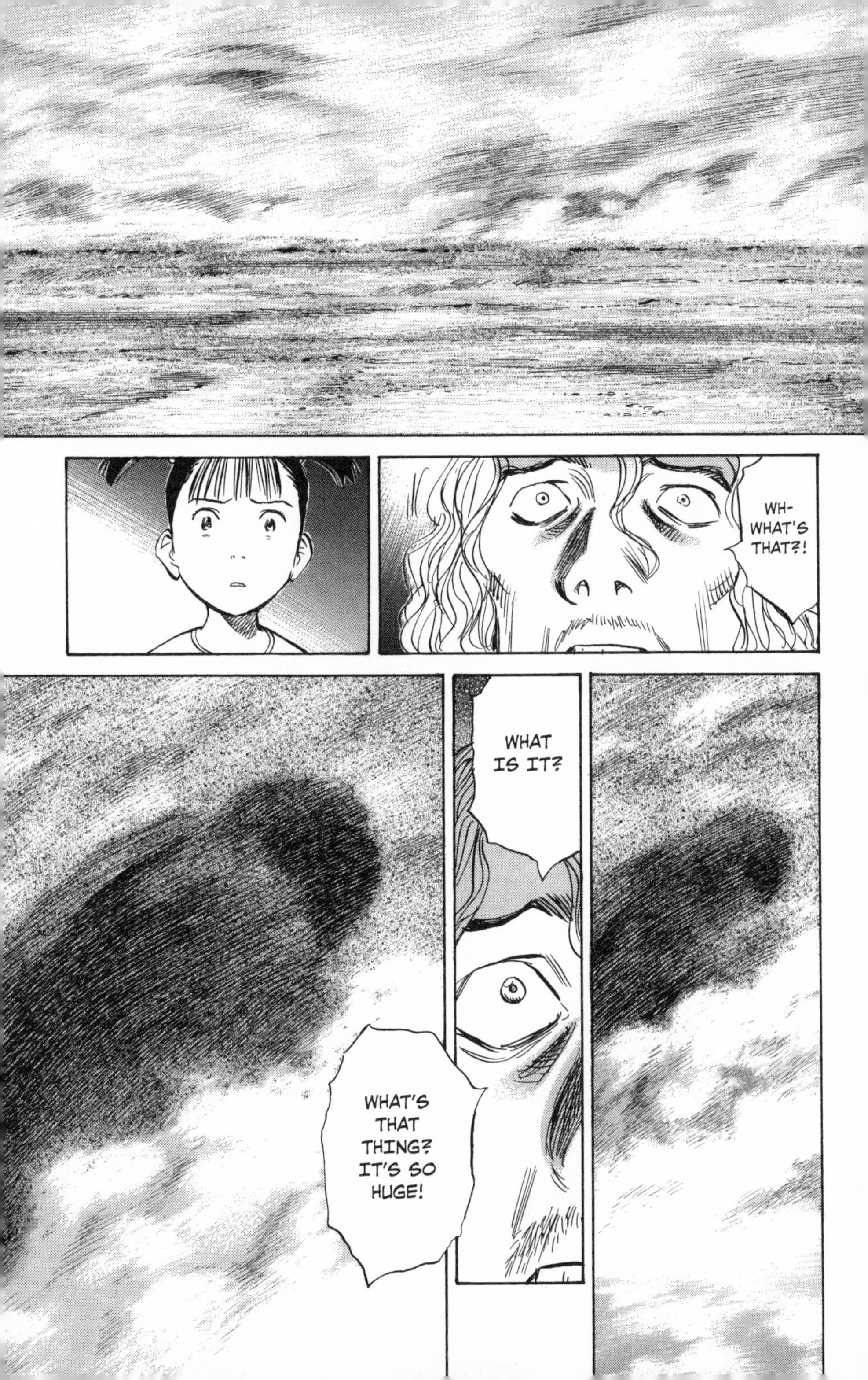
WH- WHAT'S THAT?!
WHAT IS IT?
WHAT'S THAT THING? IT'S SO HUGE!

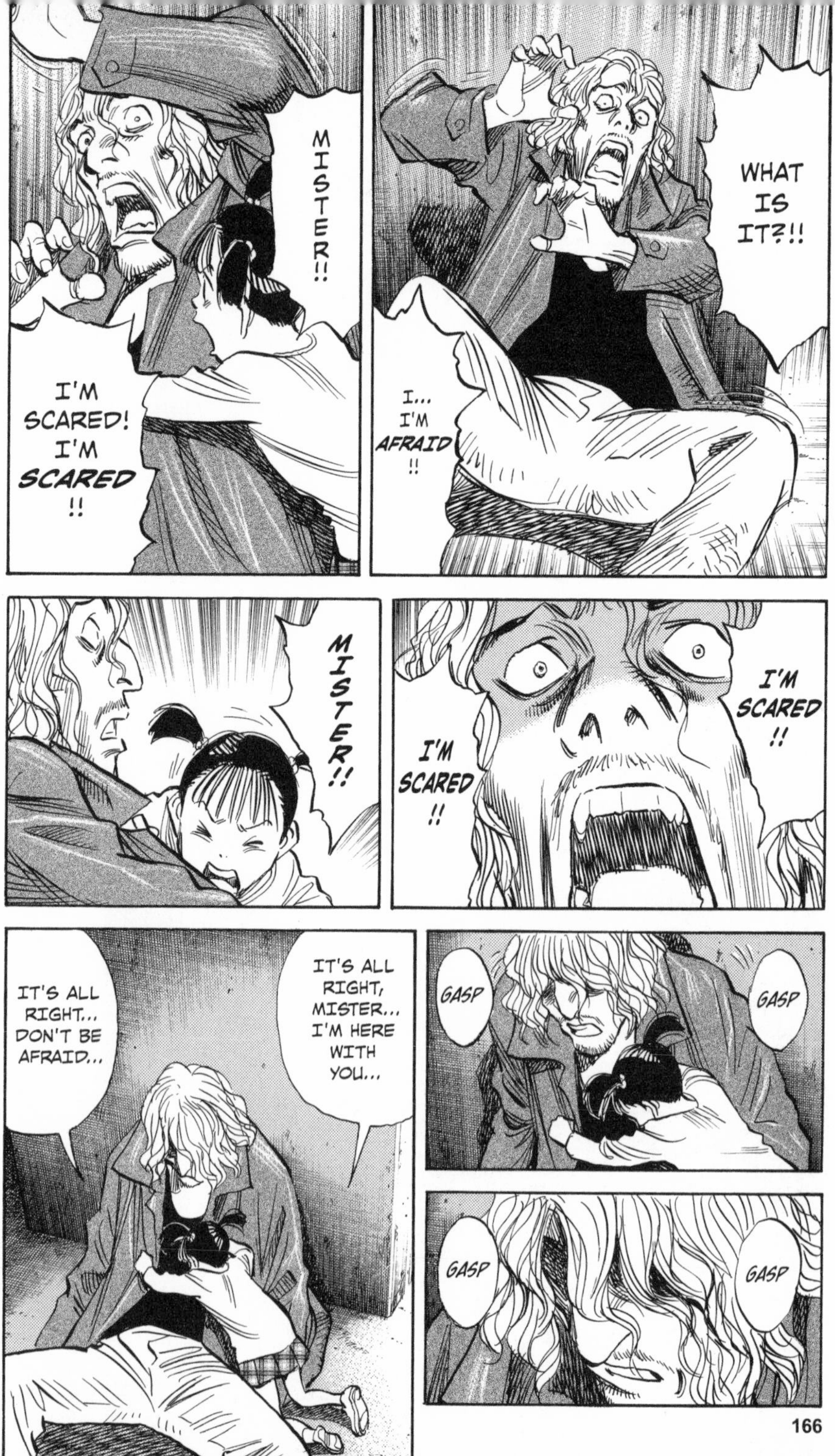
WHAT IS IT?!!
I... I'M AFRAID !!
MISTER!!
I'M SCARED! I'M SCARED !!
I'M SCARED !!
I'M SCARED !!
MISTER!!
GASP
GASP
GASP
GASP
IT'S ALL RIGHT, MISTER... I'M HERE WITH YOU...
IT'S ALL RIGHT... DON'T BE AFRAID...

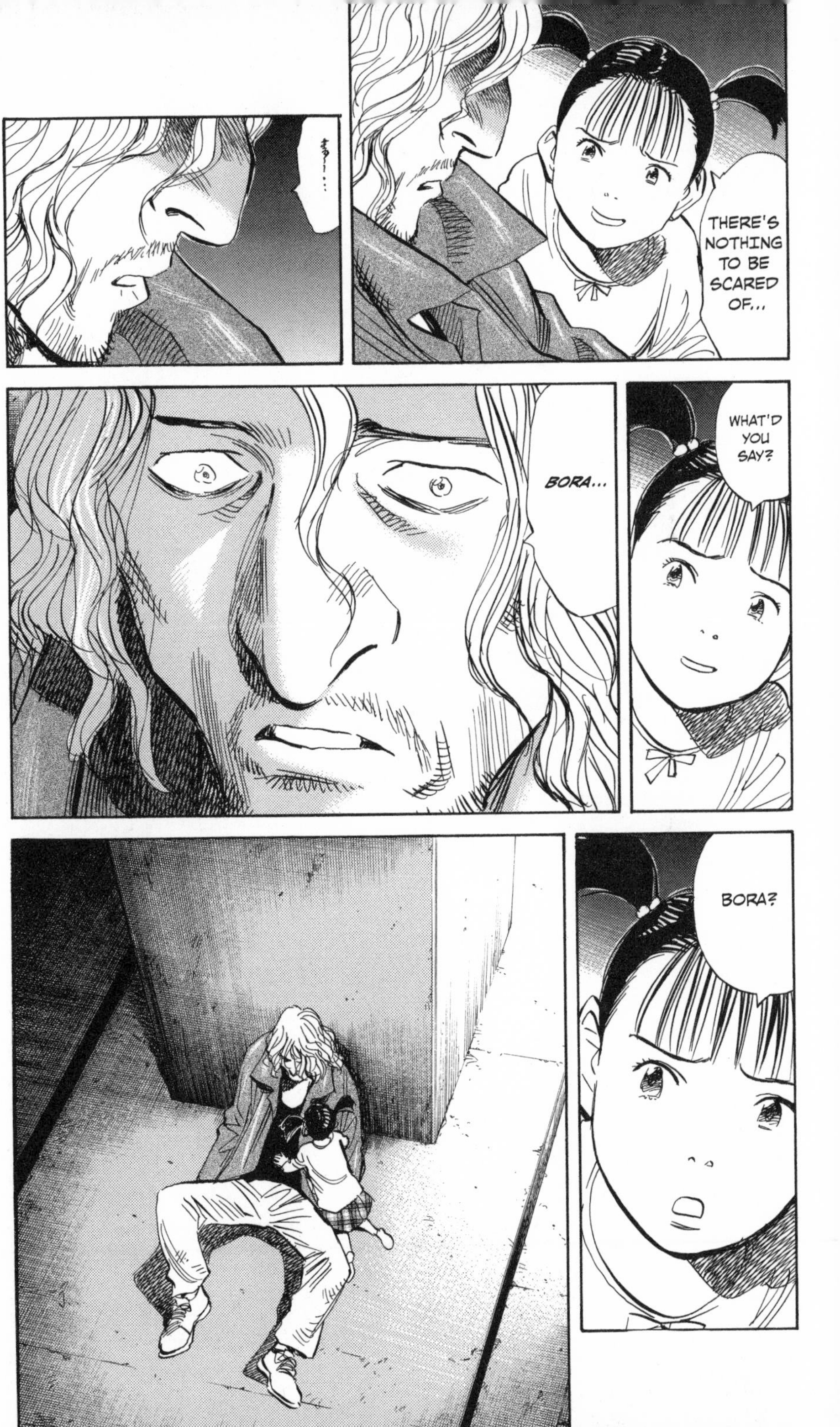
THERE'S NOTHING TO BE SCARED OF...
WHAT'D YOU SAY?
BORA...
BORA?

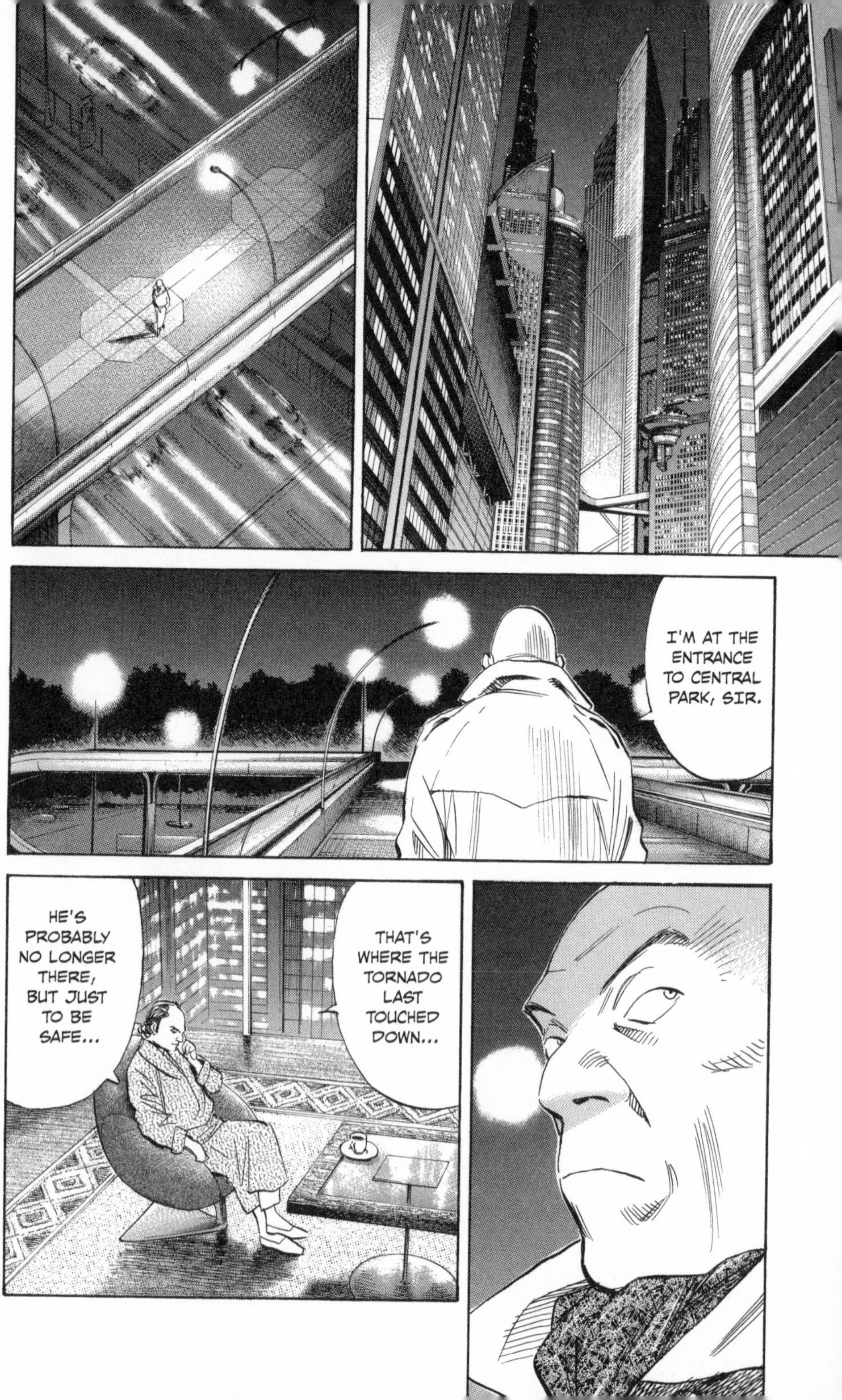
I'M AT THE ENTRANCE TO CENTRAL PARK, SIR.
THAT'S WHERE THE TORNADO LAST TOUCHED DOWN...
HE'S PROBABLY NO LONGER THERE, BUT JUST TO BE SAFE...

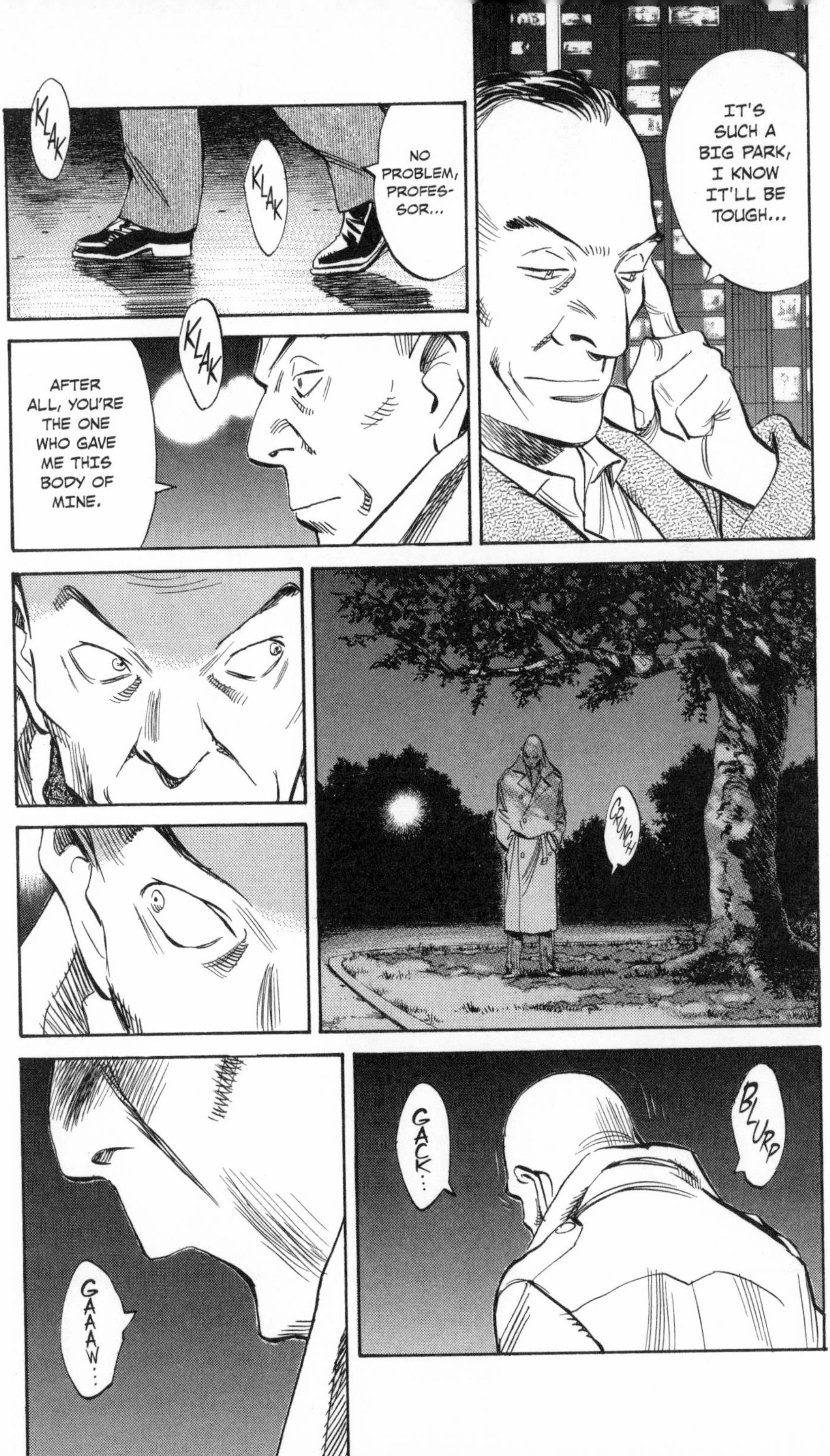
IT'S SUCH A BIG PARK, I KNOW IT'LL BE TOUGH...
NO PROBLEM, PROFES-SOR...
KLAK
KLAK
KLAK
AFTER ALL, YOU'RE THE ONE WHO GAVE ME THIS BODY OF MINE.
CRUNCH
BLURP
GACK...
GAAAW...

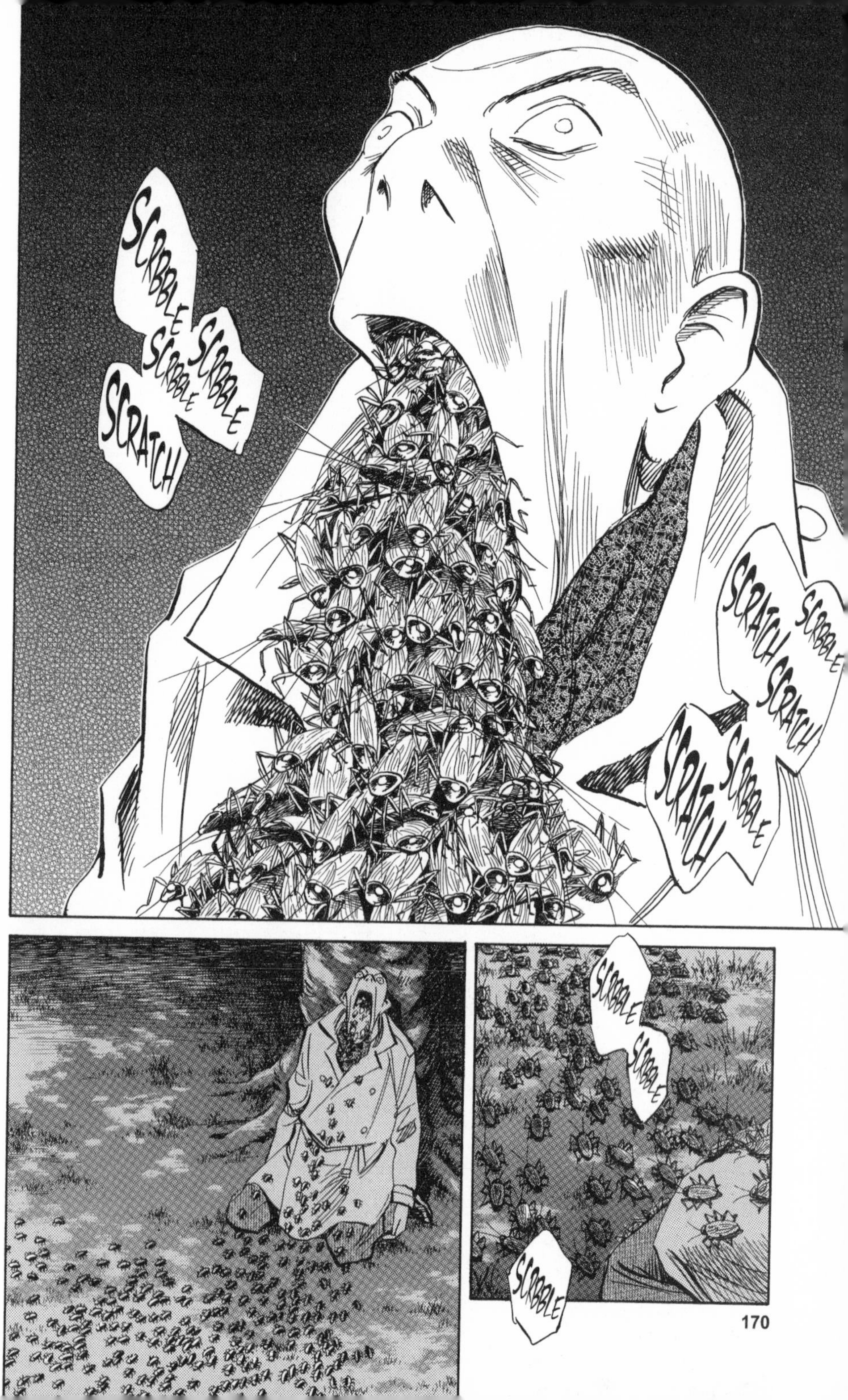
SCRBBLE
SCRATCH
SCRATCH
SCRBBLE
SCRATCH
SCRBBLE
SCRBBLE
SCRBBLE
SCRATCH
SCRBBLE
SCRBBLE
SCRBBLE

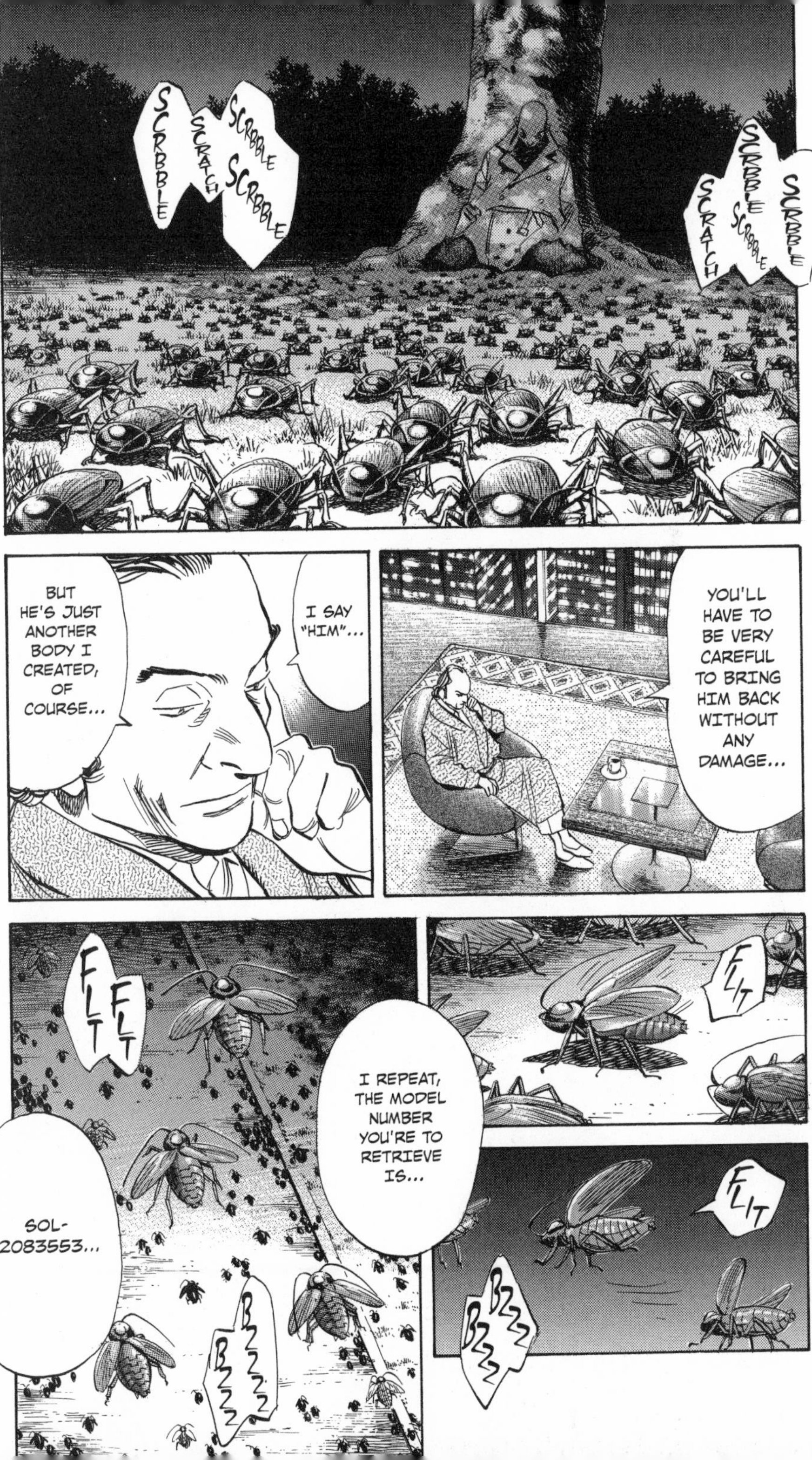
SCRBBLE
SCRBBLE
SCRBBLE
SCRATCH
SCRBBLE
SCRBBLE
SCRATCH
SCRBBLE
YOU'LL HAVE TO BE VERY CAREFUL TO BRING HIM BACK WITHOUT ANY DAMAGE...
I SAY "HIM"...
BUT HE'S JUST ANOTHER BODY I CREATED, OF COURSE...
FLIT
FLIT
BZZZ
BZZZ
FLT FLT
I REPEAT, THE MODEL NUMBER YOU'RE TO RETRIEVE IS...
SOL-2083553...
BZZZZ
BZZZ

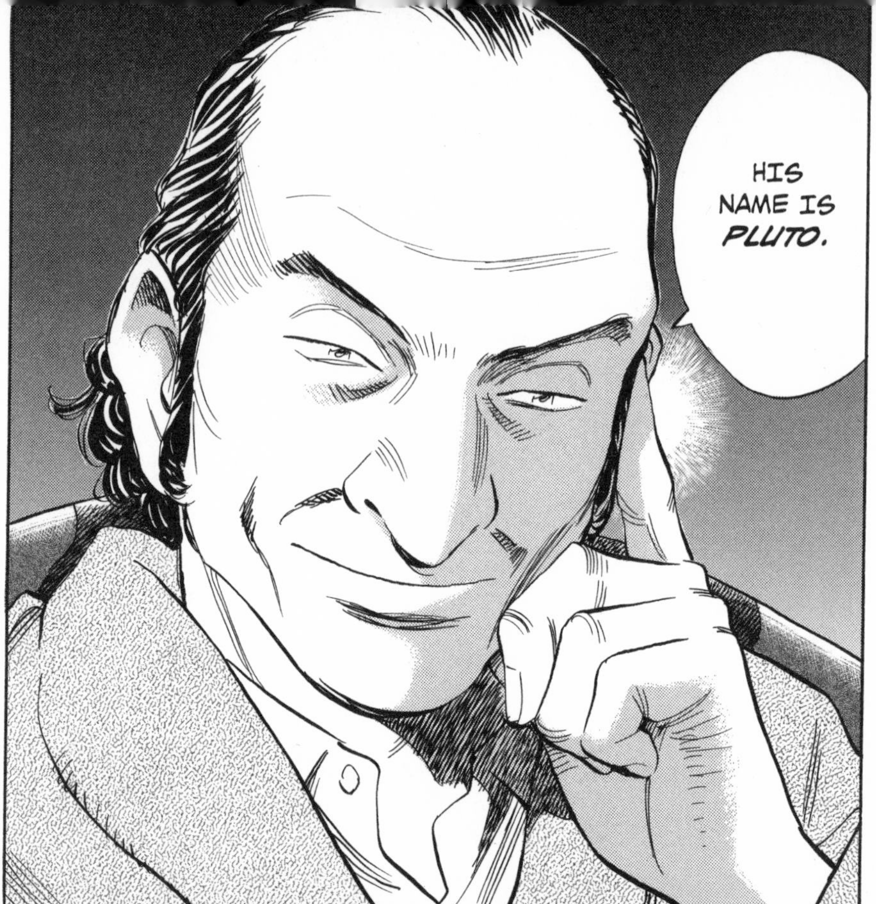
HIS NAME IS *PLUTO.*

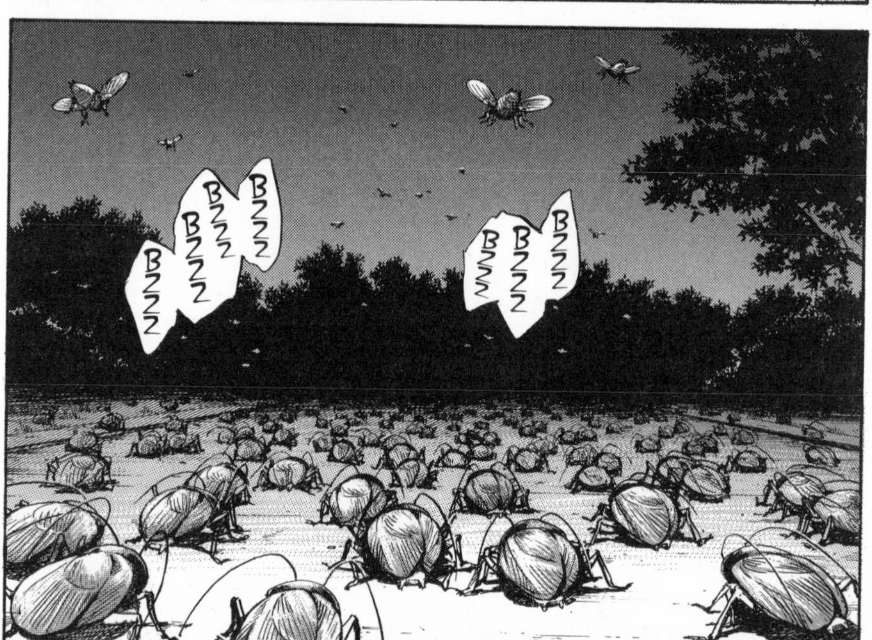
BZZZ BZZZ BZZZ
BZZZ BZZZ BZZZ BZZZ

Act 23 Wandering Soul

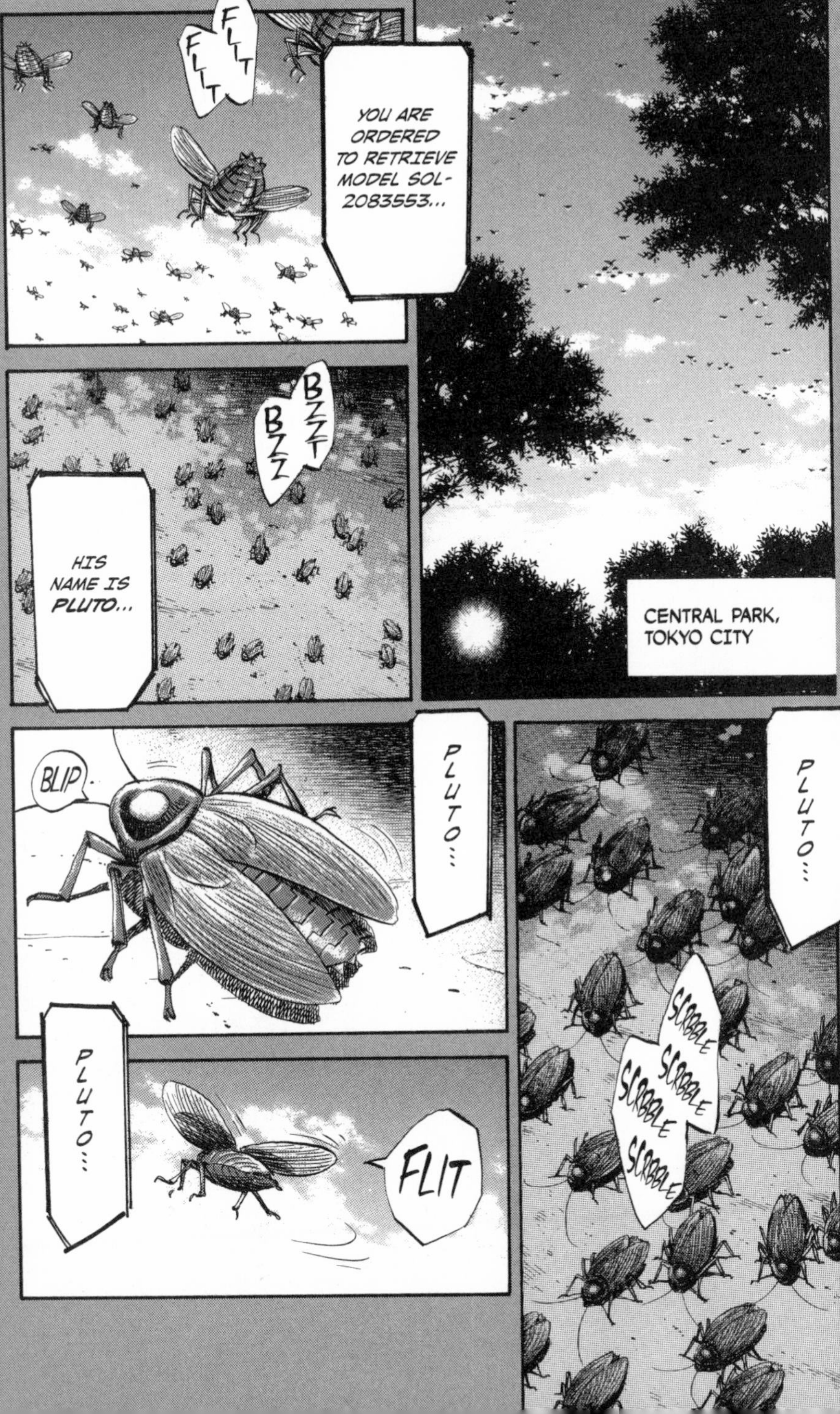
CENTRAL PARK, TOKYO CITY
FLIIT FLIIT
YOU ARE ORDERED TO RETRIEVE MODEL SOL-2083553...
BZZT BZZ
HIS NAME IS PLUTO...
PLUTO...
SCRBBLE SCRBBLE SCRBBLE SCRBBLE
PLUTO...
BLIP
PLUTO...
FLIT

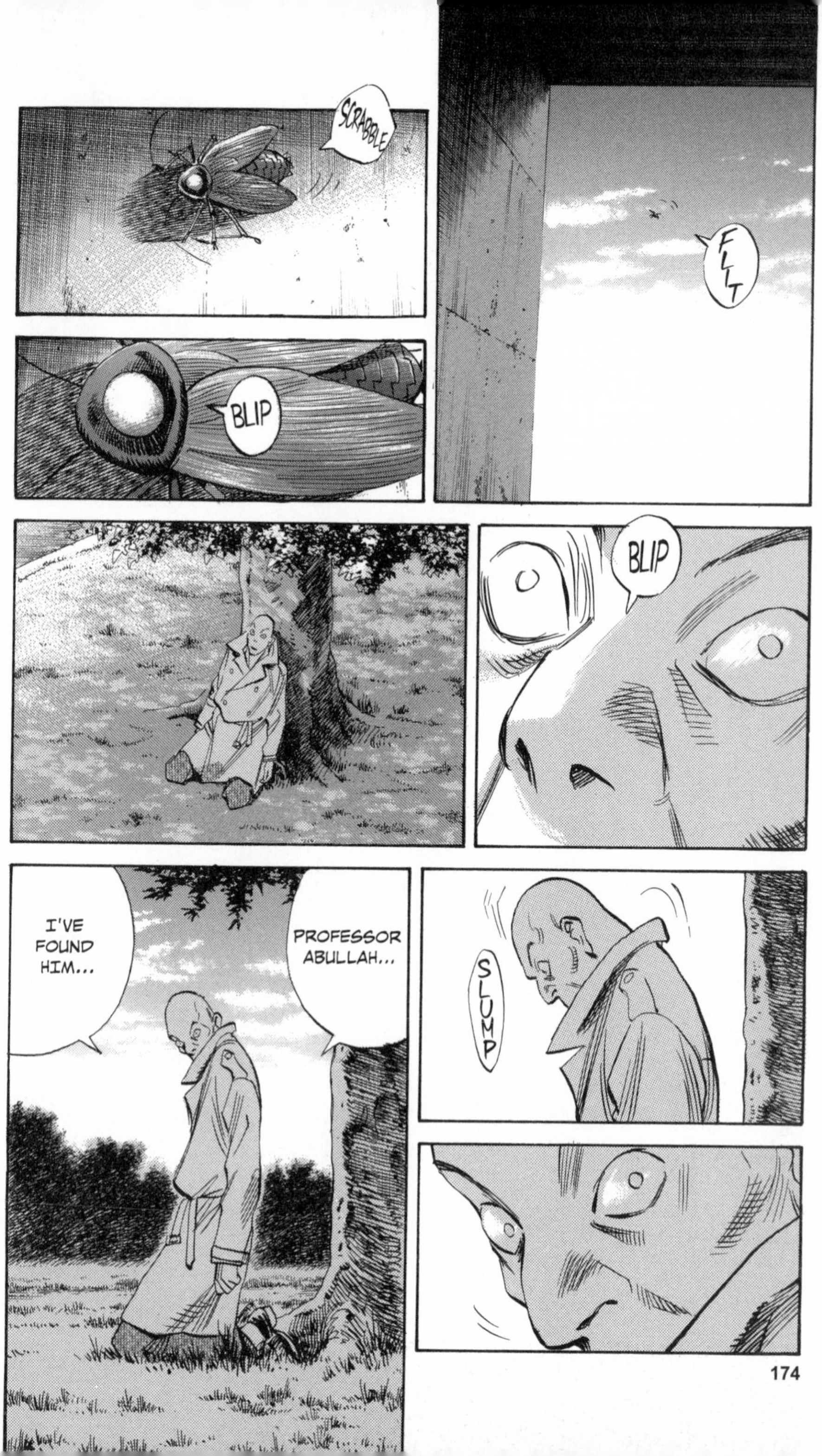
FLIT
SCRABBLE
BLIP
BLIP
SLUMP
PROFESSOR ABULLAH...
I'VE FOUND HIM...

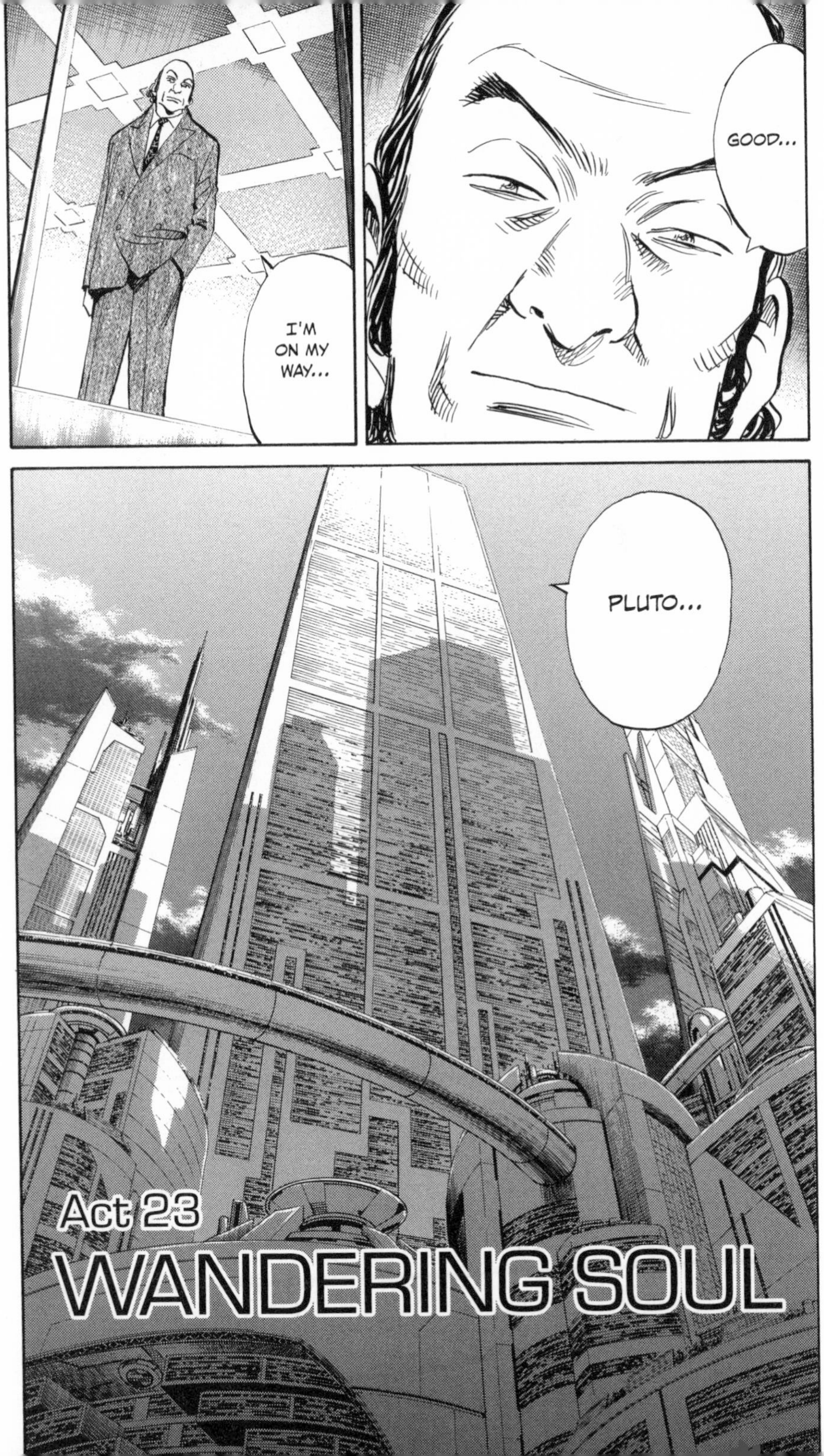
GOOD...
I'M ON MY WAY...
PLUTO...
Act 23
WANDERING SOUL

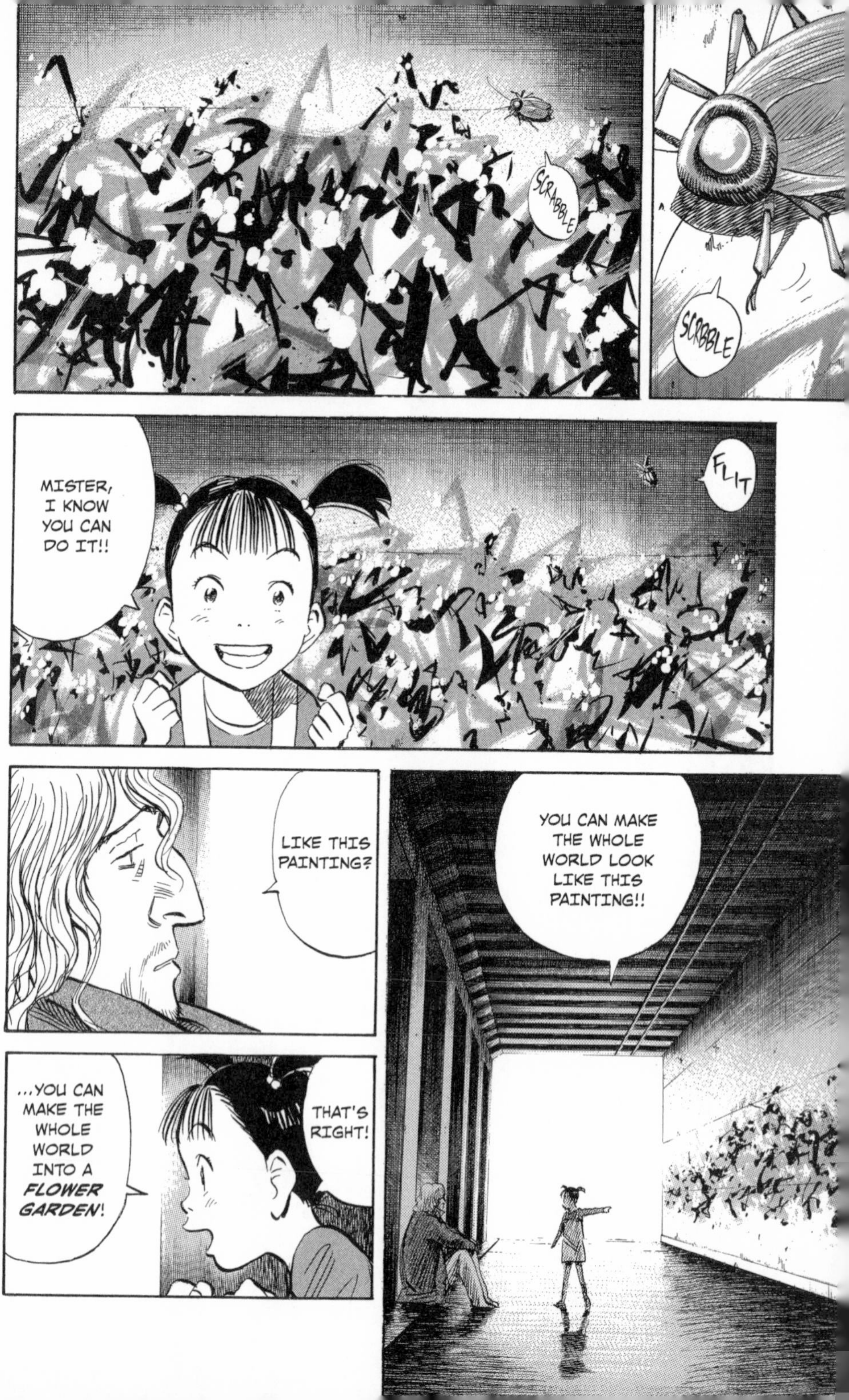
SCRBBLE
SCRABBLE
FLIT
MISTER, I KNOW YOU CAN DO IT!!
YOU CAN MAKE THE WHOLE WORLD LOOK LIKE THIS PAINTING!!
LIKE THIS PAINTING?
THAT'S RIGHT!
...YOU CAN MAKE THE WHOLE WORLD INTO A *FLOWER GARDEN*!

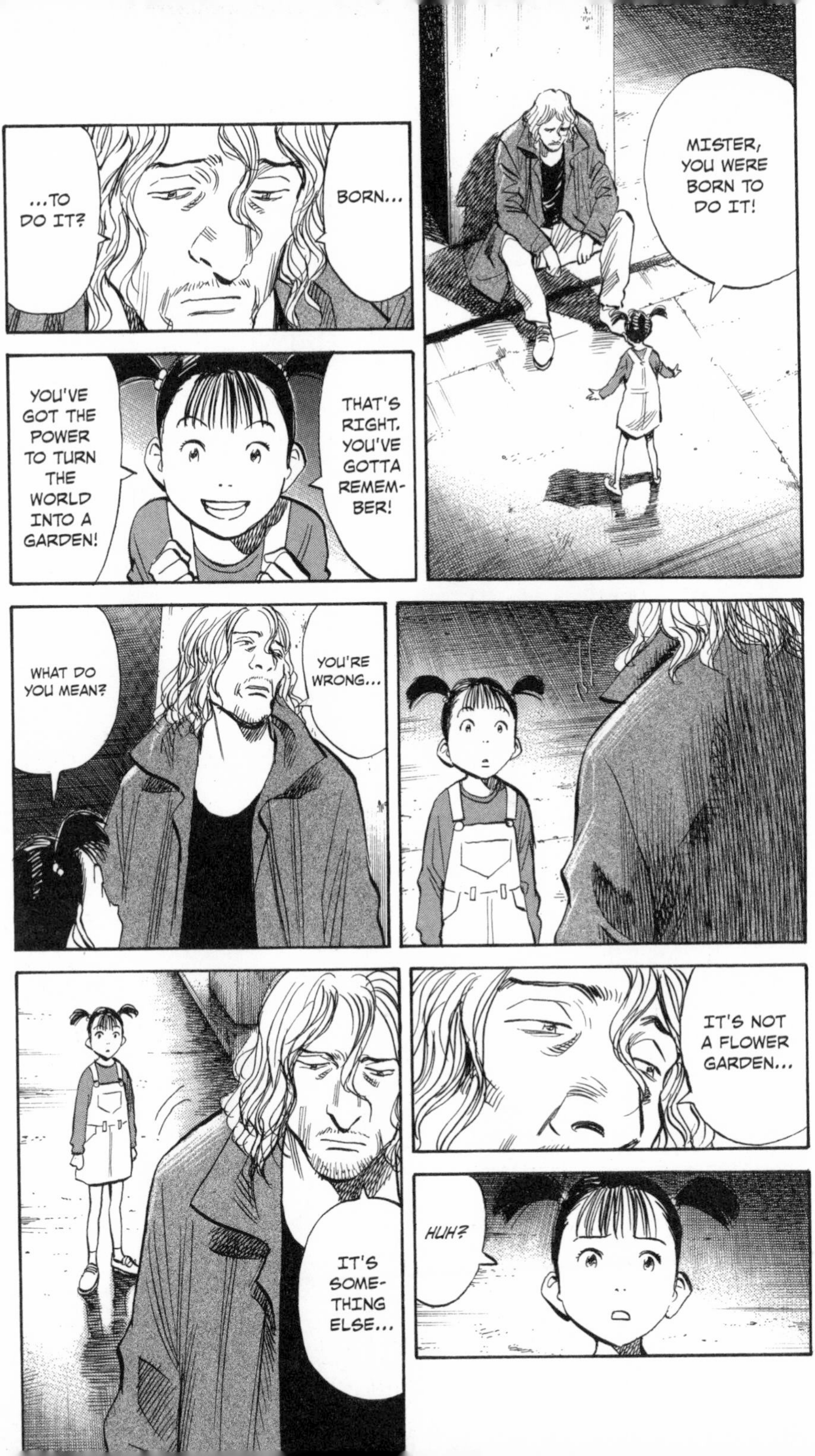
MISTER, YOU WERE BORN TO DO IT!
BORN...
...TO DO IT?
THAT'S RIGHT. YOU'VE GOTTA REMEMBER!
YOU'VE GOT THE POWER TO TURN THE WORLD INTO A GARDEN!
YOU'RE WRONG...
WHAT DO YOU MEAN?
IT'S NOT A FLOWER GARDEN...
HUH?
IT'S SOMETHING ELSE...

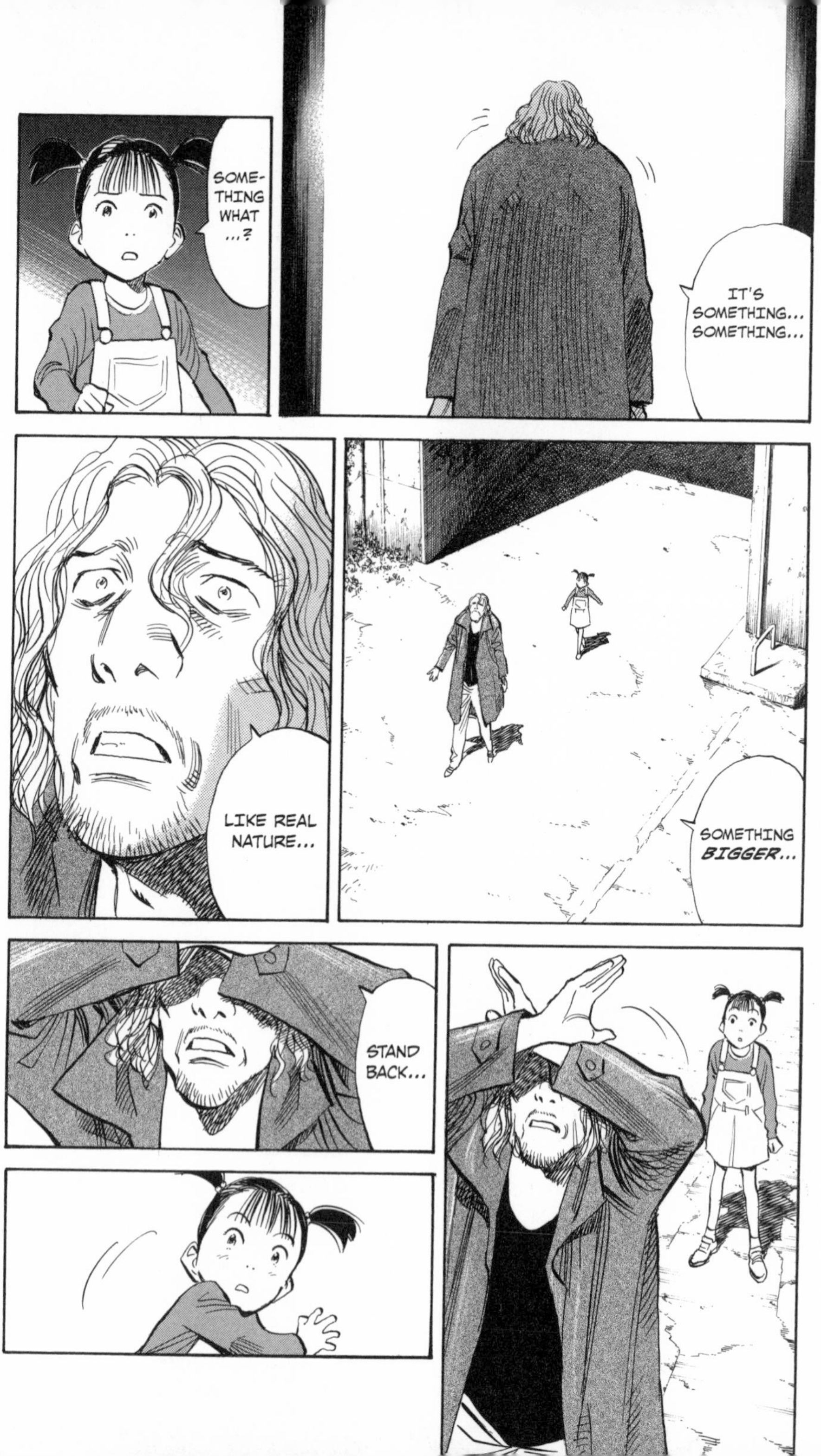
IT'S SOMETHING... SOMETHING...
SOME-THING WHAT ...?
SOMETHING BIGGER...
LIKE REAL NATURE...
STAND BACK...

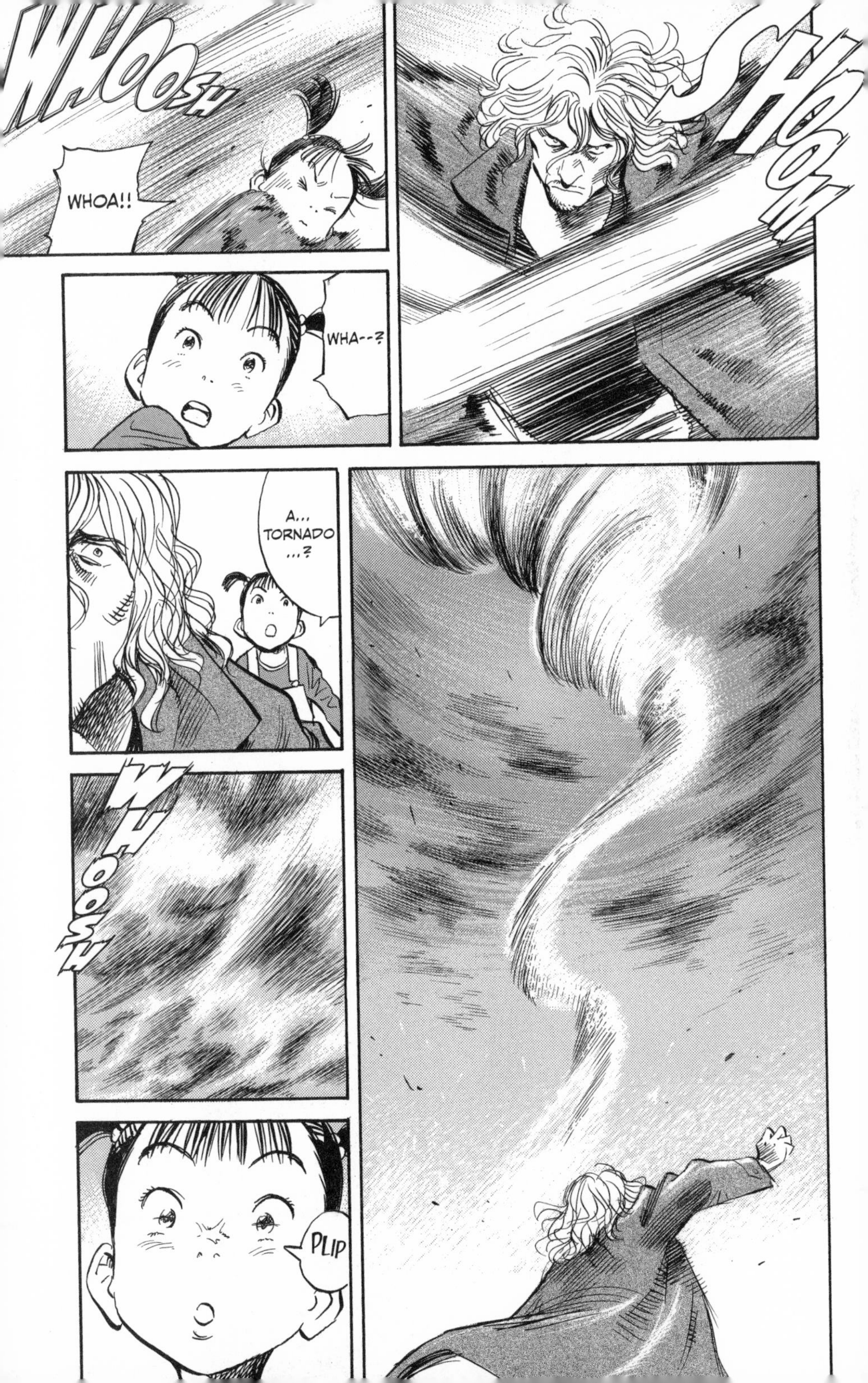
SHOOM
WHOOSH
WHOA!!
WHA--?
A... TORNADO ...?
WHOOOSH
PLIP

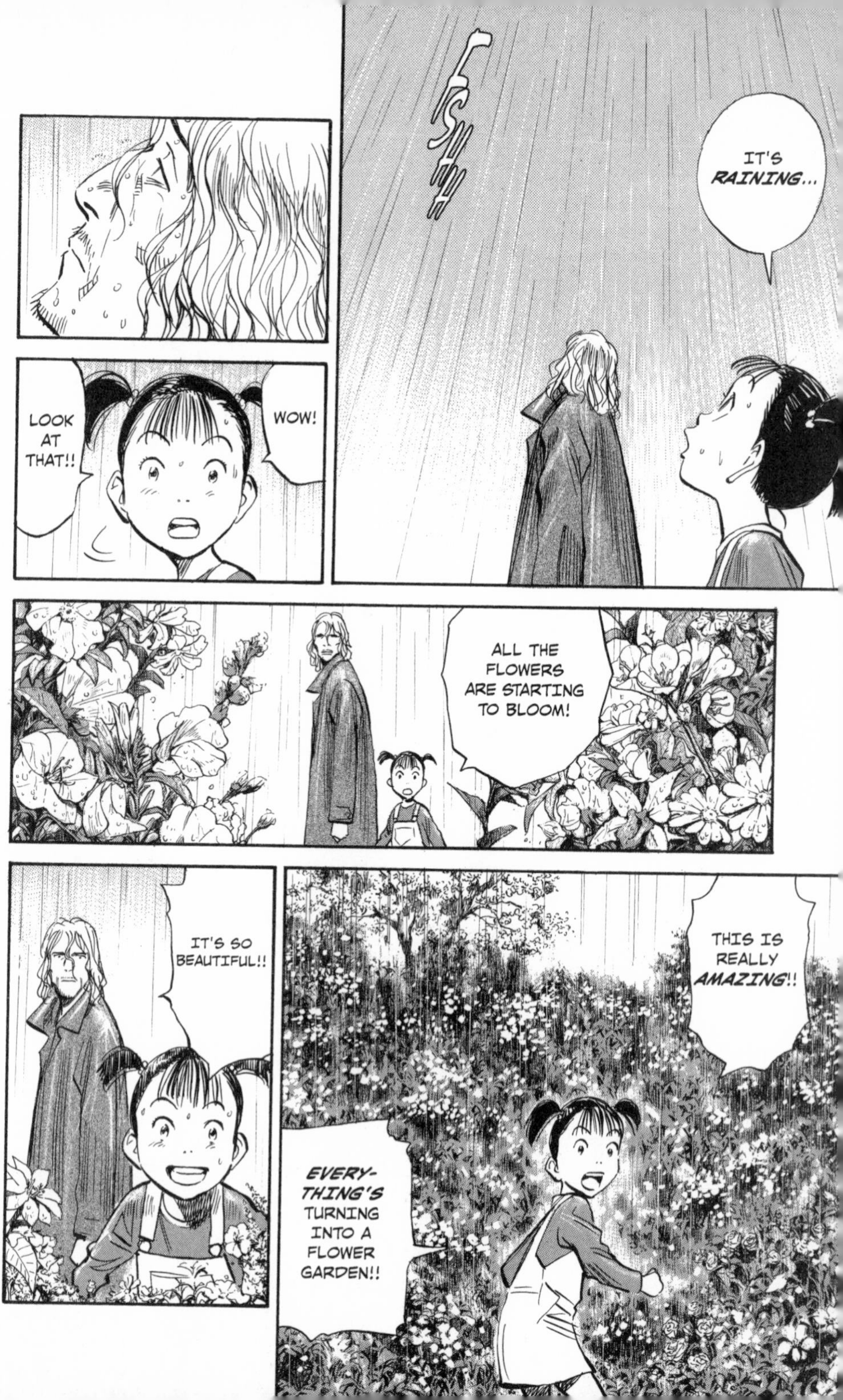
FSHH
IT'S RAINING...
WOW!
LOOK AT THAT!!
ALL THE FLOWERS ARE STARTING TO BLOOM!
THIS IS REALLY AMAZING!!
EVERYTHING'S TURNING INTO A FLOWER GARDEN!!
IT'S SO BEAUTIFUL!!

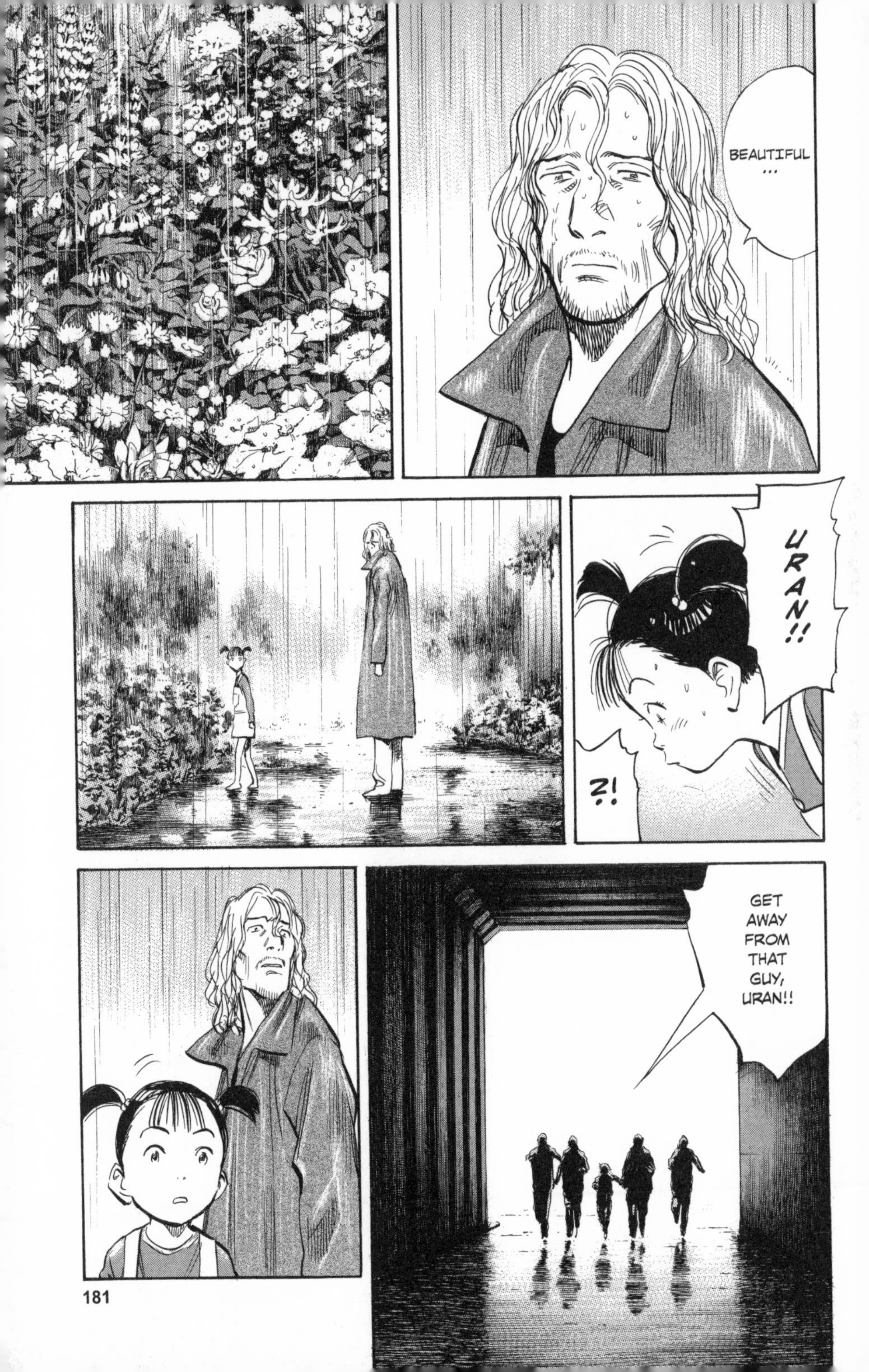
BEAUTIFUL ...
URAN!!
?!
GET AWAY FROM THAT GUY, URAN!!

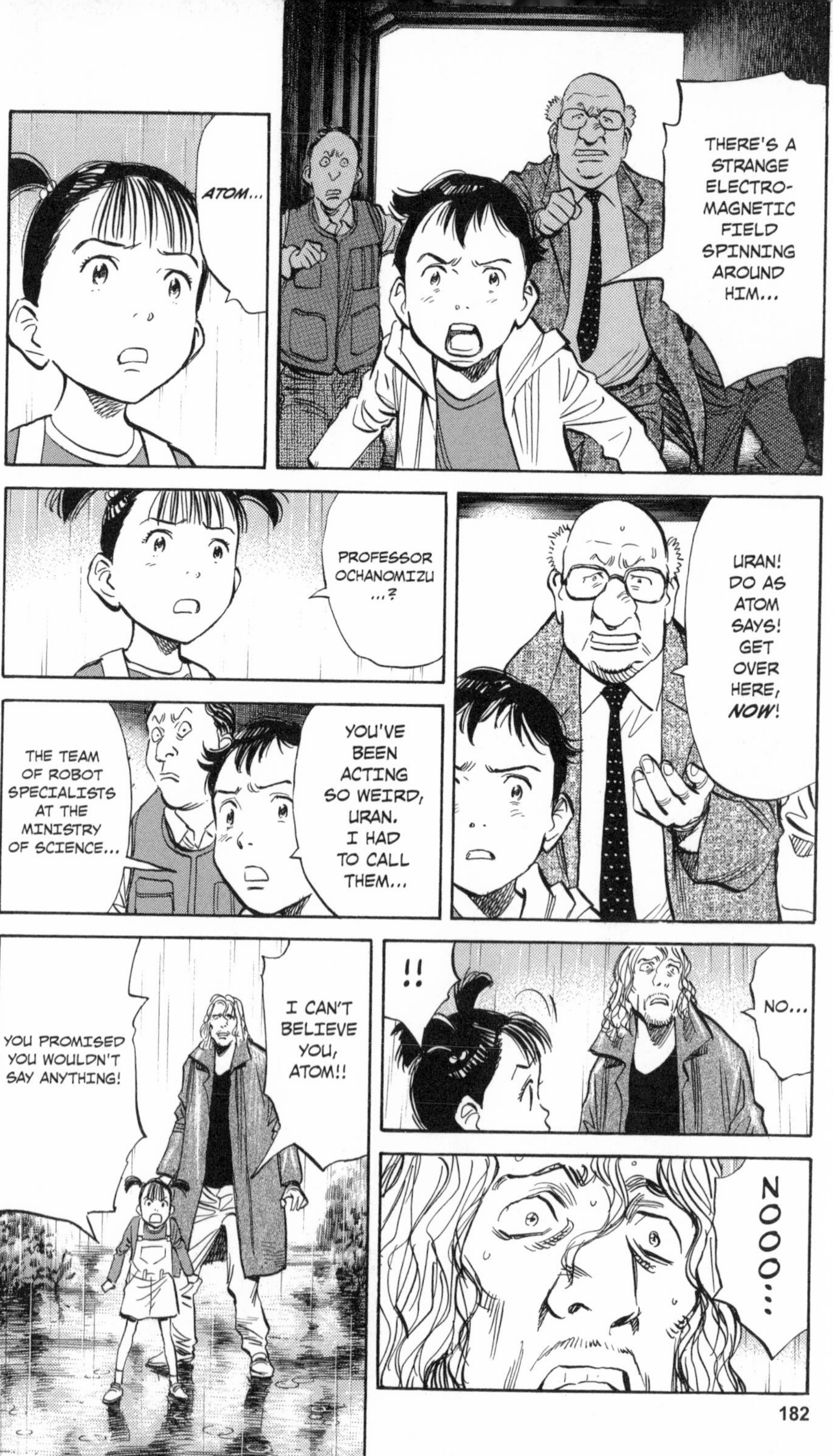
THERE'S A STRANGE ELECTRO-MAGNETIC FIELD SPINNING AROUND HIM...
ATOM...
URAN! DO AS ATOM SAYS! GET OVER HERE, *NOW*!
PROFESSOR OCHANOMIZU ...?
YOU'VE BEEN ACTING SO WEIRD, URAN. I HAD TO CALL THEM...
THE TEAM OF ROBOT SPECIALISTS AT THE MINISTRY OF SCIENCE...
!!
NO...
NOOO...
I CAN'T BELIEVE YOU, ATOM!!
YOU PROMISED YOU WOULDN'T SAY ANYTHING!

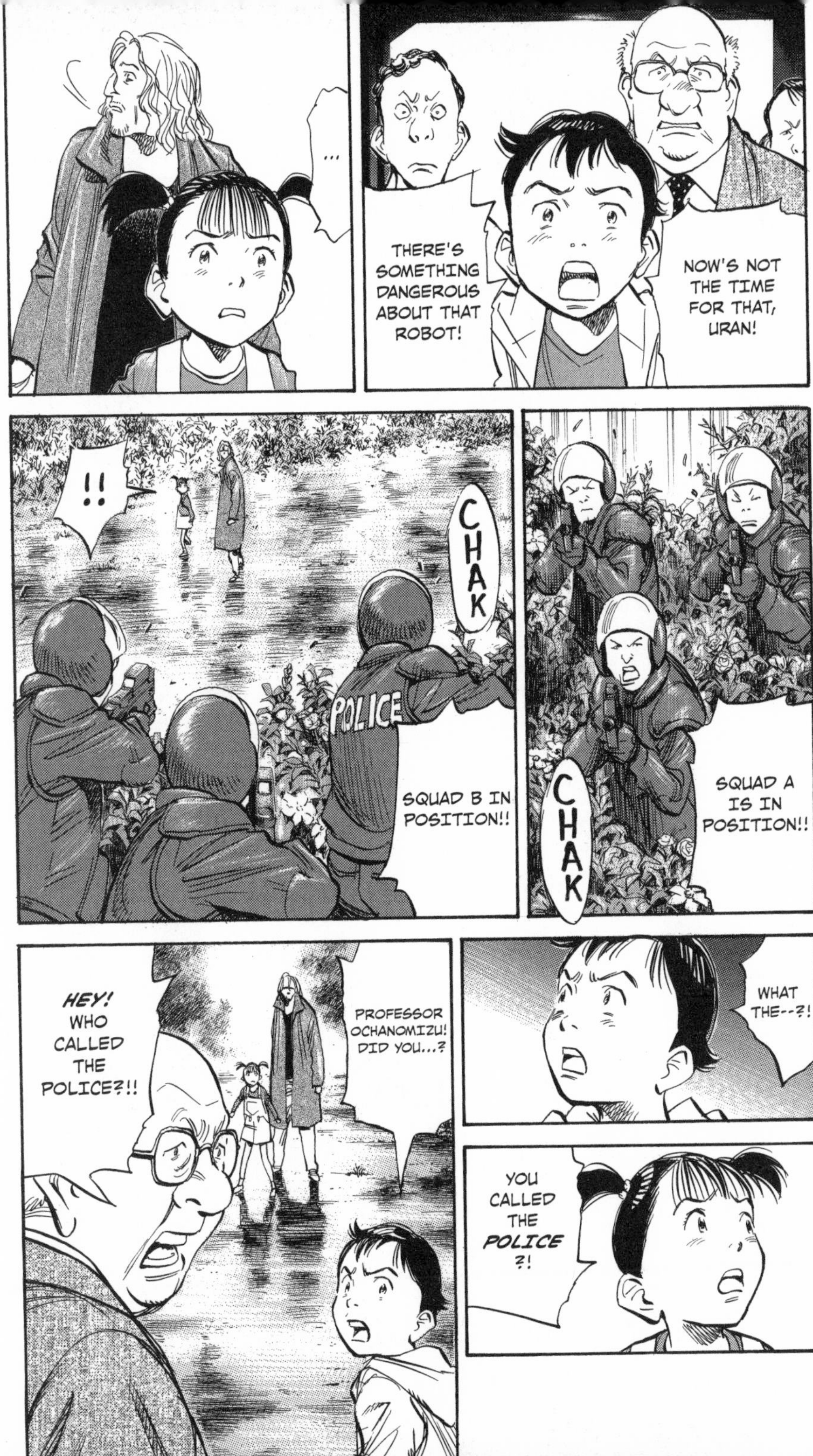
NOW'S NOT THE TIME FOR THAT, URAN!
THERE'S SOMETHING DANGEROUS ABOUT THAT ROBOT!
...
SQUAD A IS IN POSITION!!
CHAK
CHAK
SQUAD B IN POSITION!!
!!
WHAT THE--?!
YOU CALLED THE POLICE?!
PROFESSOR OCHANOMIZU! DID YOU...?
HEY! WHO CALLED THE POLICE?!!

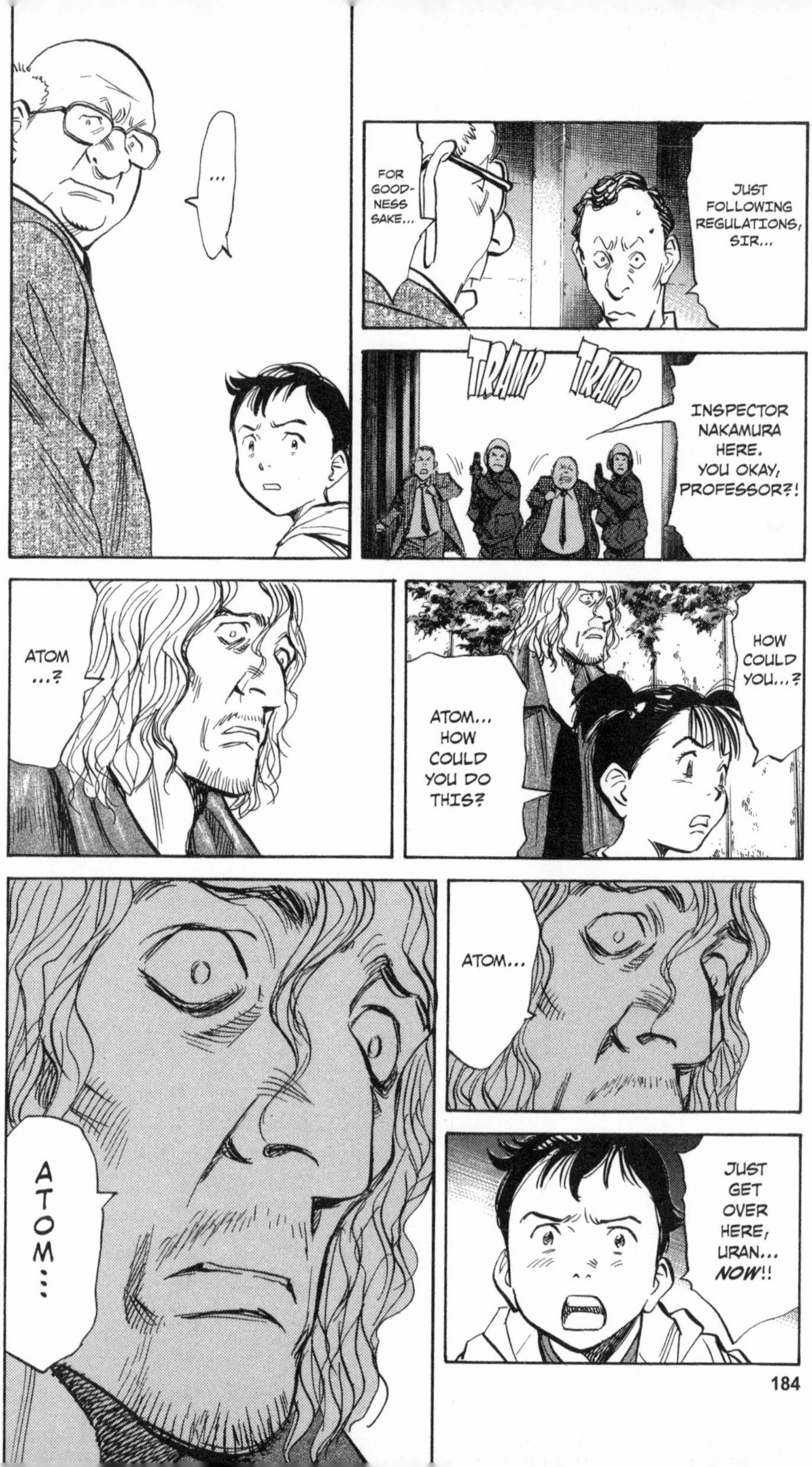
JUST FOLLOWING REGULATIONS, SIR...
FOR GOODNESS SAKE...
TRAMP TRAMP
INSPECTOR NAKAMURA HERE. YOU OKAY, PROFESSOR?!
...
HOW COULD YOU...?
ATOM... HOW COULD YOU DO THIS?
ATOM...?
ATOM...
JUST GET OVER HERE, URAN... NOW!!
ATOM...

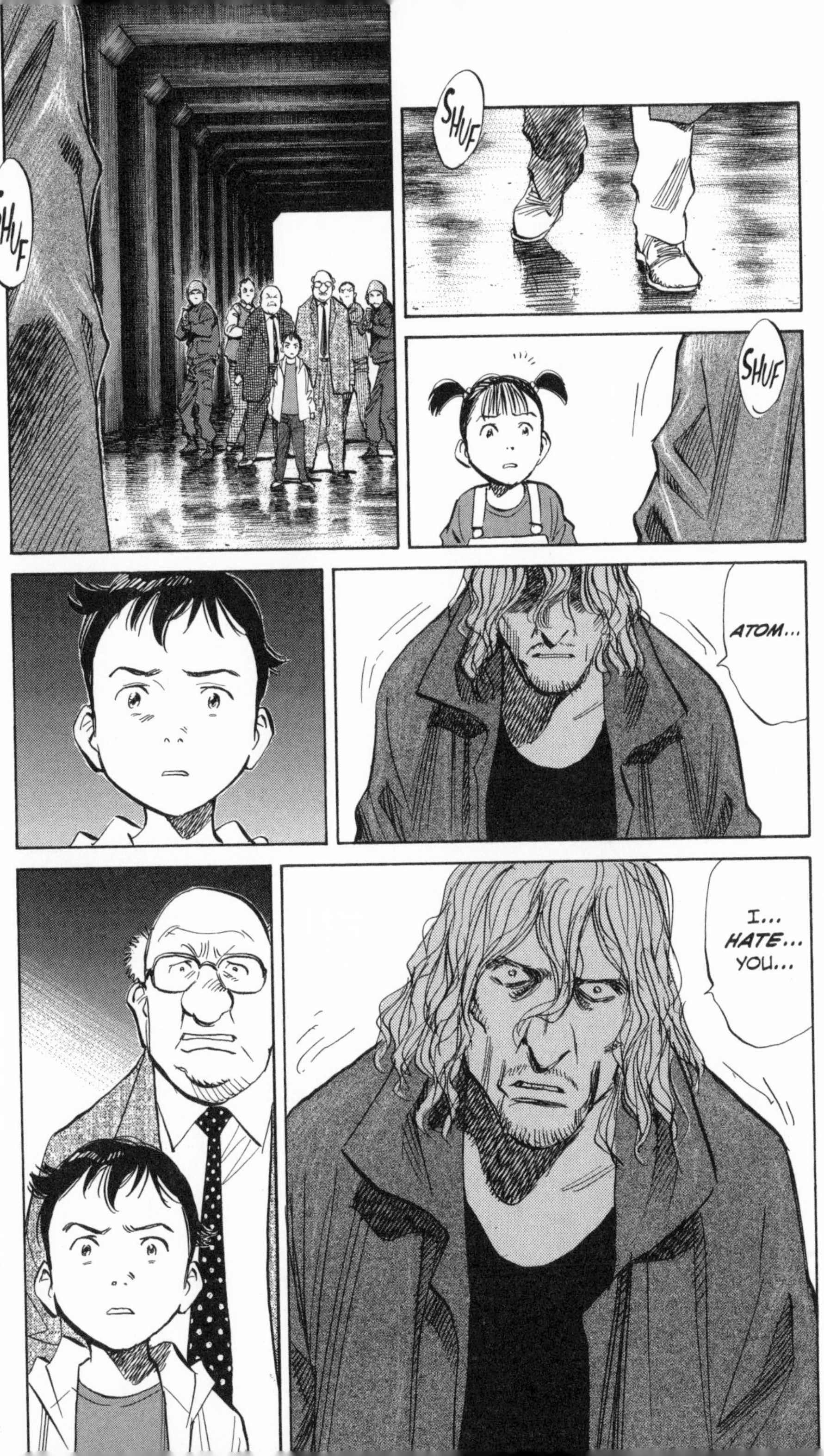
SHUF
SHUF
SHUF
ATOM...
I... HATE... YOU...

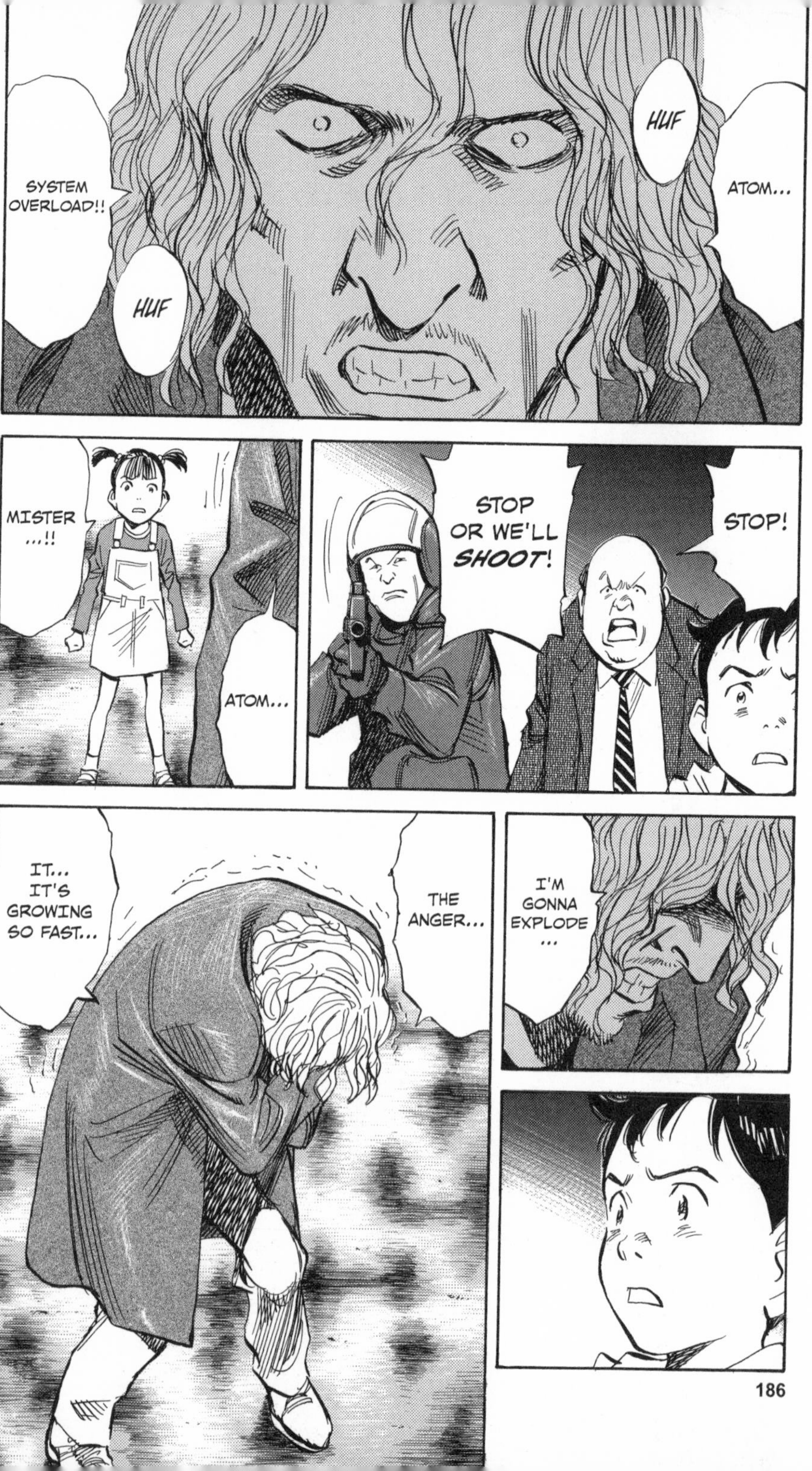
ATOM...
HUF
SYSTEM OVERLOAD!!
HUF
STOP!
STOP OR WE'LL *SHOOT*!
MISTER ...!!
ATOM...
I'M GONNA EXPLODE ...
THE ANGER...
IT... IT'S GROWING SO FAST...

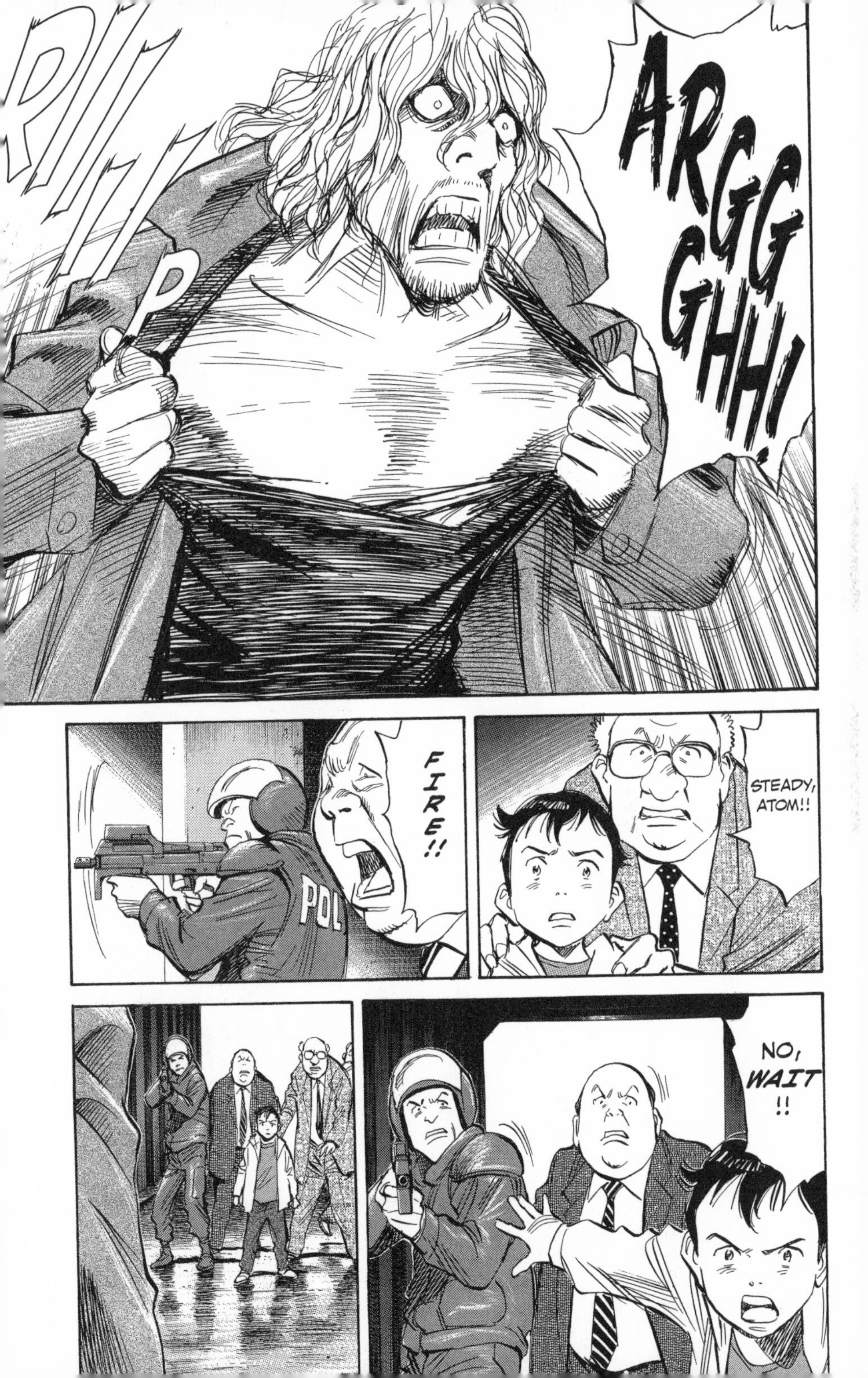
ARGGGHH!
RIIIP
STEADY, ATOM!!
FIRE!!
POL
NO, WAIT!!

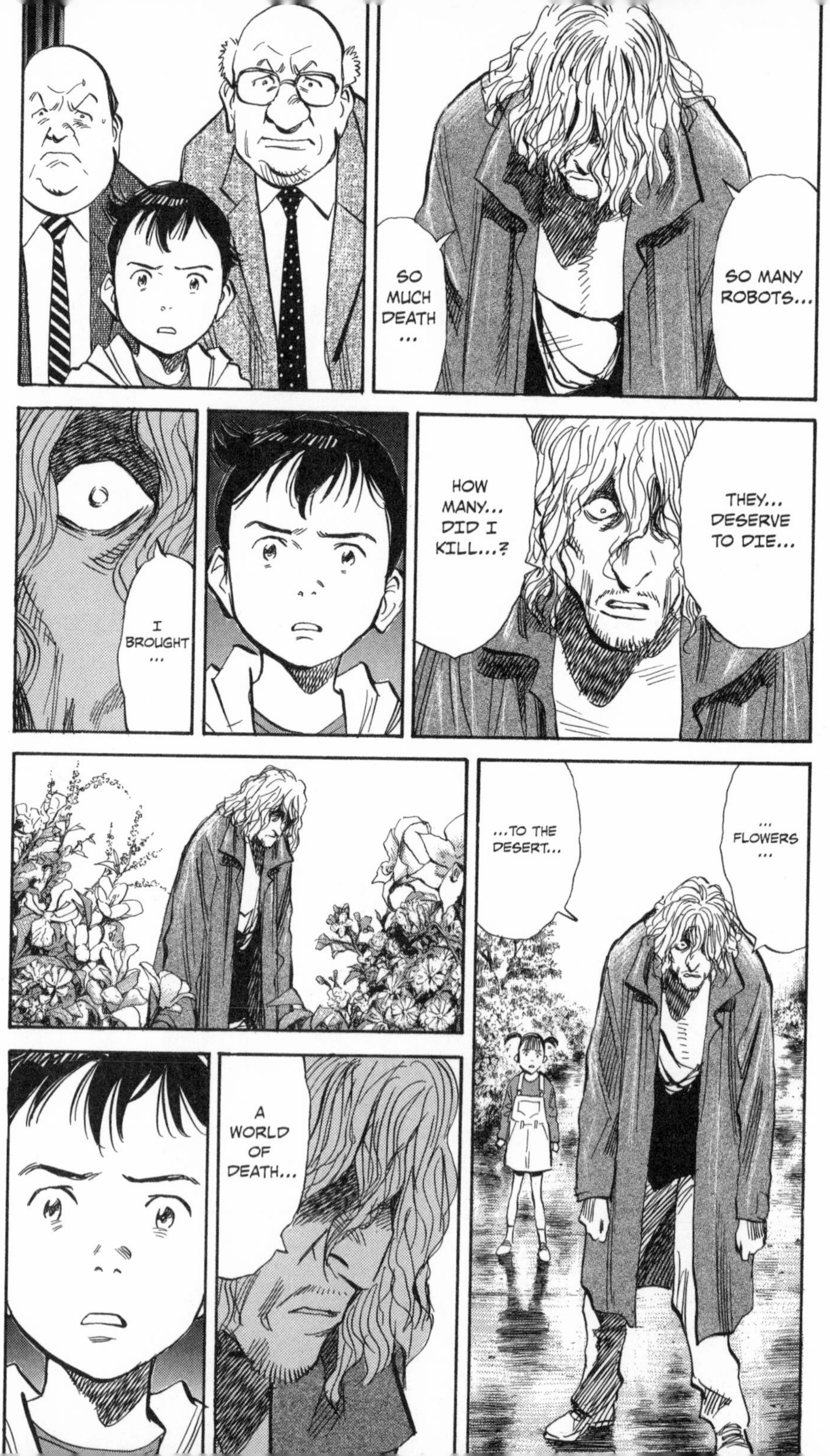
SO MANY ROBOTS...
SO MUCH DEATH ...
THEY... DESERVE TO DIE...
HOW MANY... DID I KILL...?
I BROUGHT ...
... FLOWERS ...
...TO THE DESERT...
A WORLD OF DEATH...

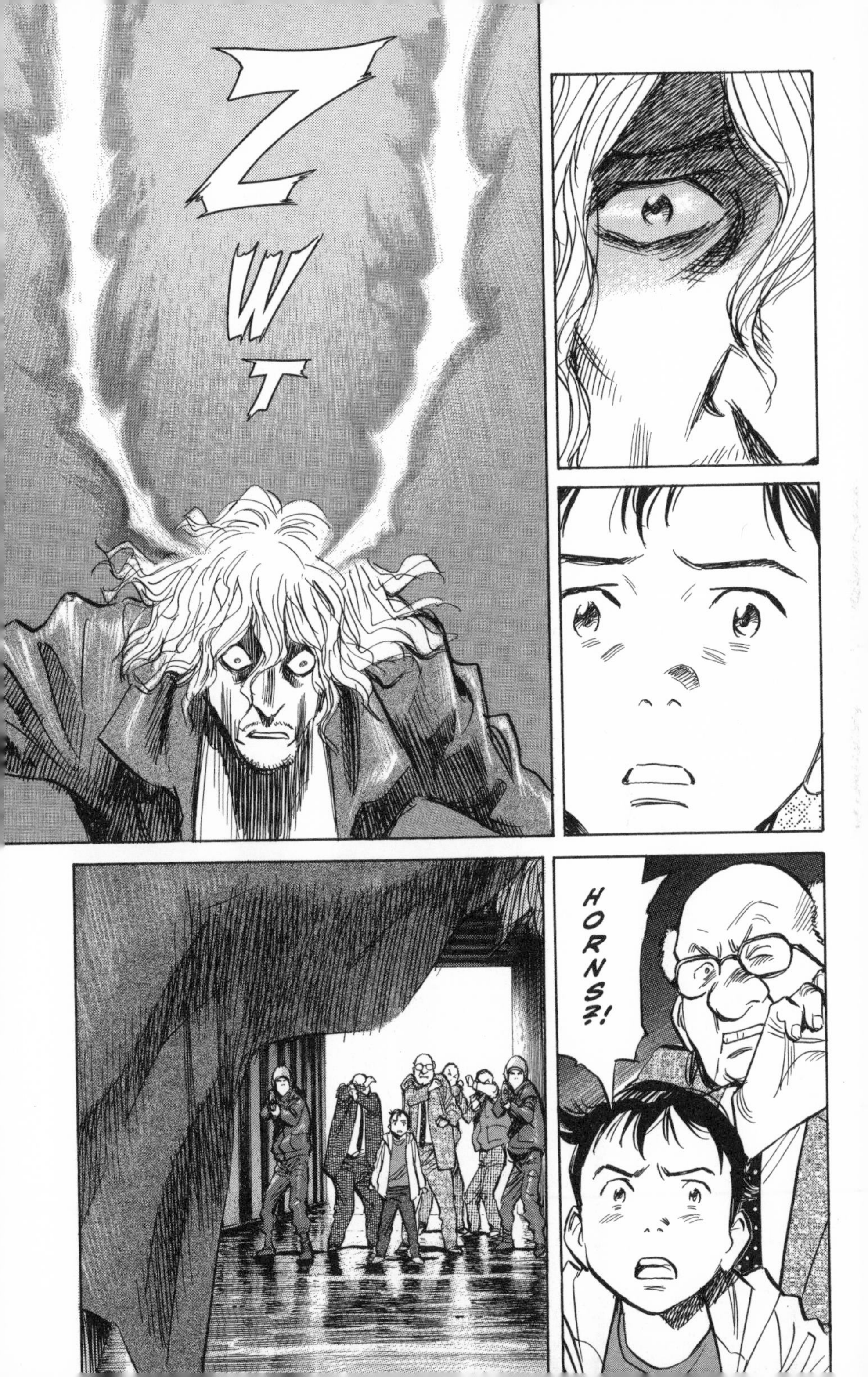
ZWT
HORNS?!

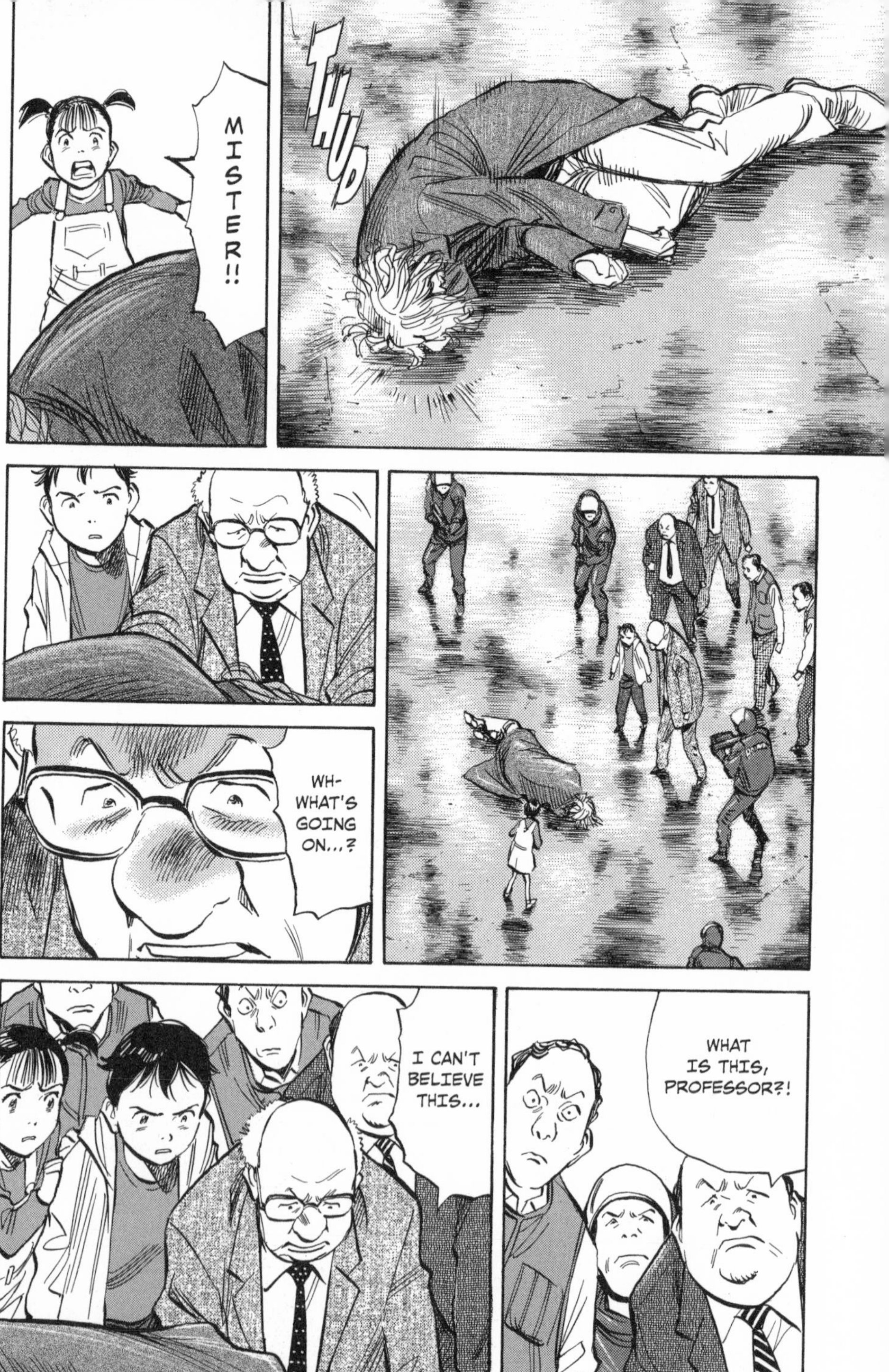
THUD
MISTER!!
WH-WHAT'S GOING ON...?
WHAT IS THIS, PROFESSOR?!
I CAN'T BELIEVE THIS...

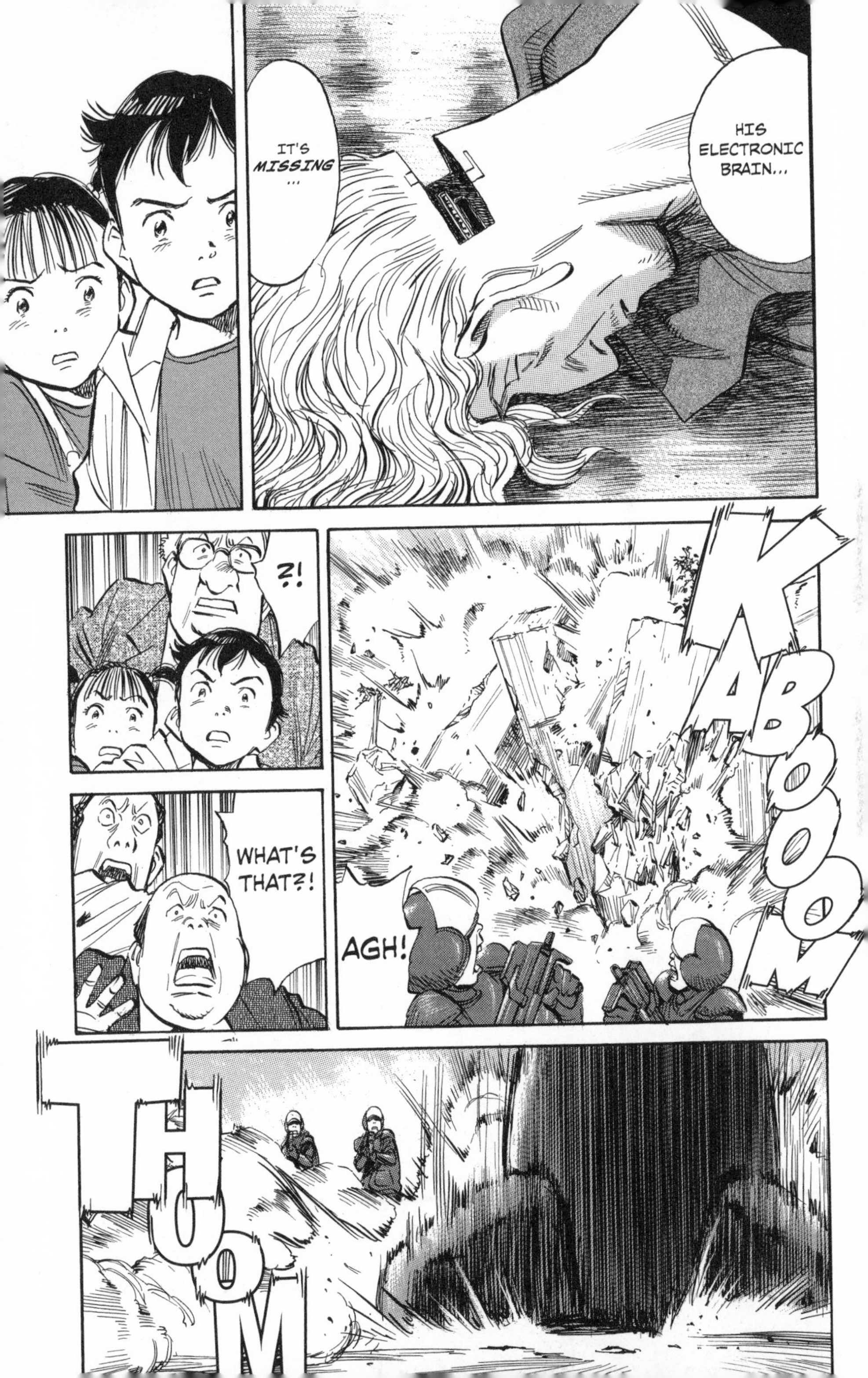
HIS ELECTRONIC BRAIN...
IT'S MISSING...
KABOOOM
AGH!
?!
WHAT'S THAT?!
THOOM

THAT IS MY BODY.
PSHOOOM!
HUH?
WHAT THE--?!
I AM A CONSTRUCTION ROBOT, WORKING AT THE REDEVELOPMENT SITE.
HUH?
UPON COMPLETING MY 100 HOUR SHIFT...
I DISCOVERED MY OFF-WORK HOURS BODY WAS MISSING.
Y-YOU MEAN THAT THIS BODY...
...IS YOURS?!

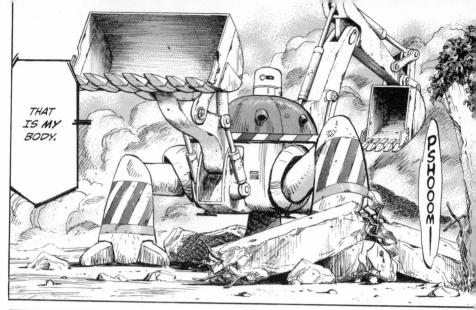

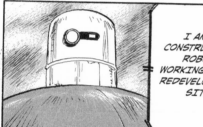

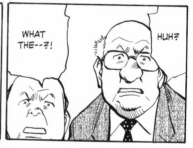

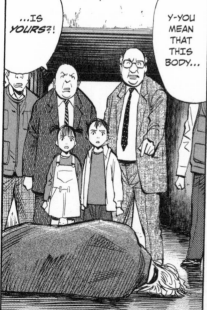

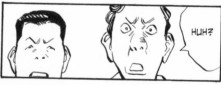

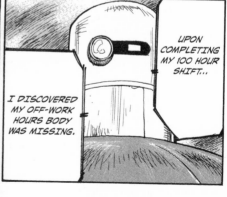

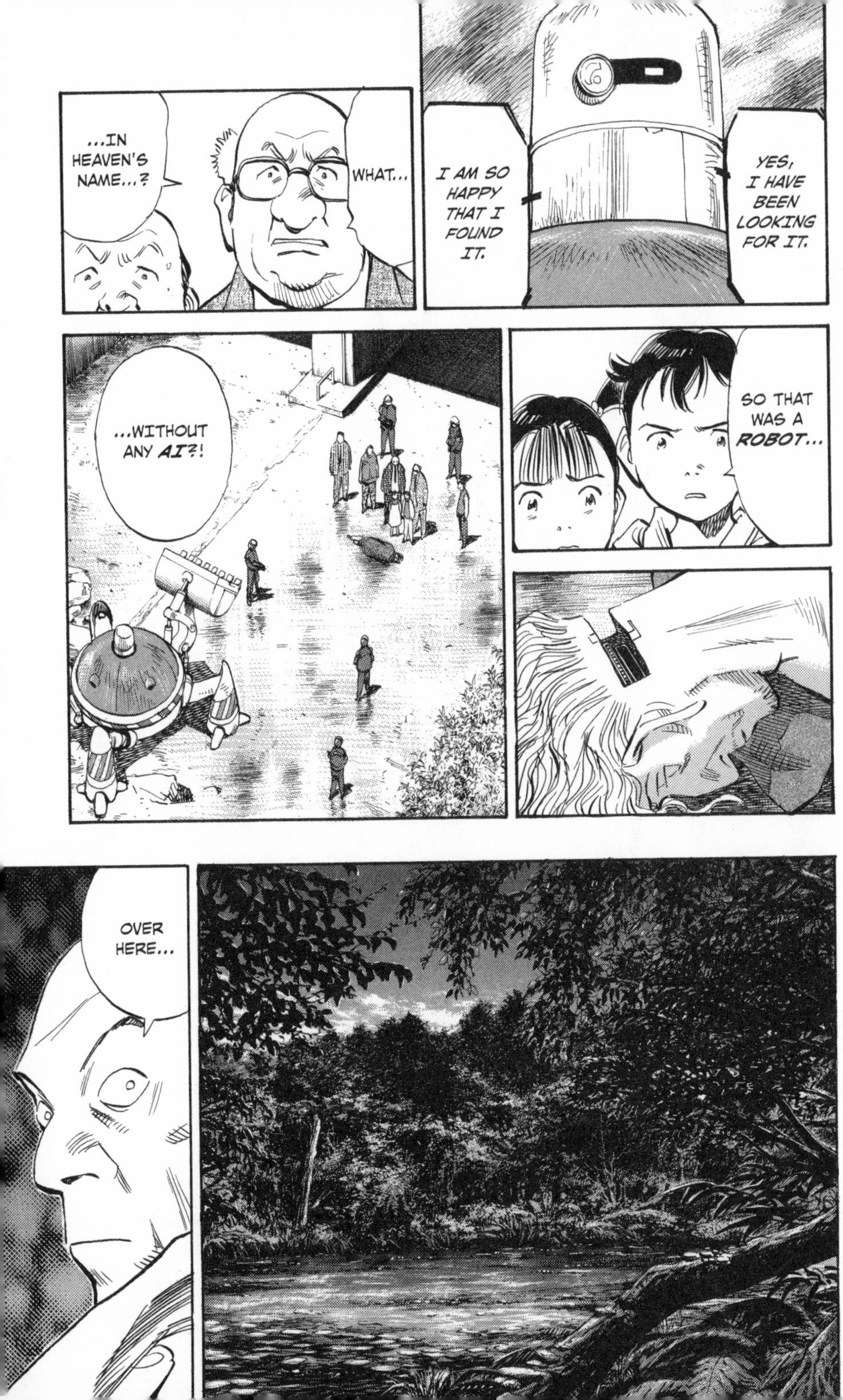
YES, I HAVE BEEN LOOKING FOR IT.
I AM SO HAPPY THAT I FOUND IT.
WHAT...
...IN HEAVEN'S NAME...?
SO THAT WAS A ROBOT...
...WITHOUT ANY AI?!
OVER HERE...

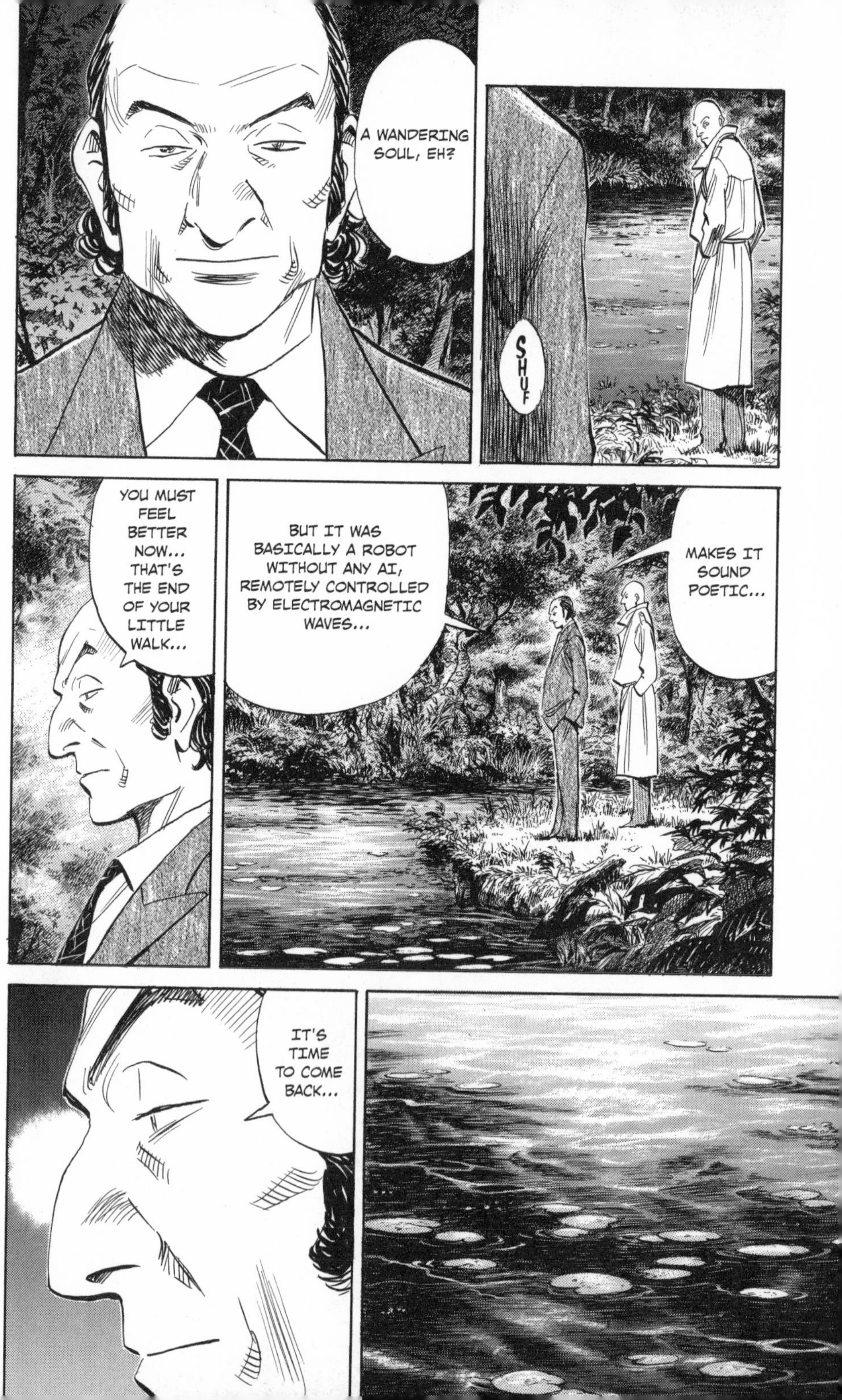
SHUF
A WANDERING SOUL, EH?
MAKES IT SOUND POETIC...
BUT IT WAS BASICALLY A ROBOT WITHOUT ANY AI, REMOTELY CONTROLLED BY ELECTROMAGNETIC WAVES...
YOU MUST FEEL BETTER NOW... THAT'S THE END OF YOUR LITTLE WALK...
IT'S TIME TO COME BACK...

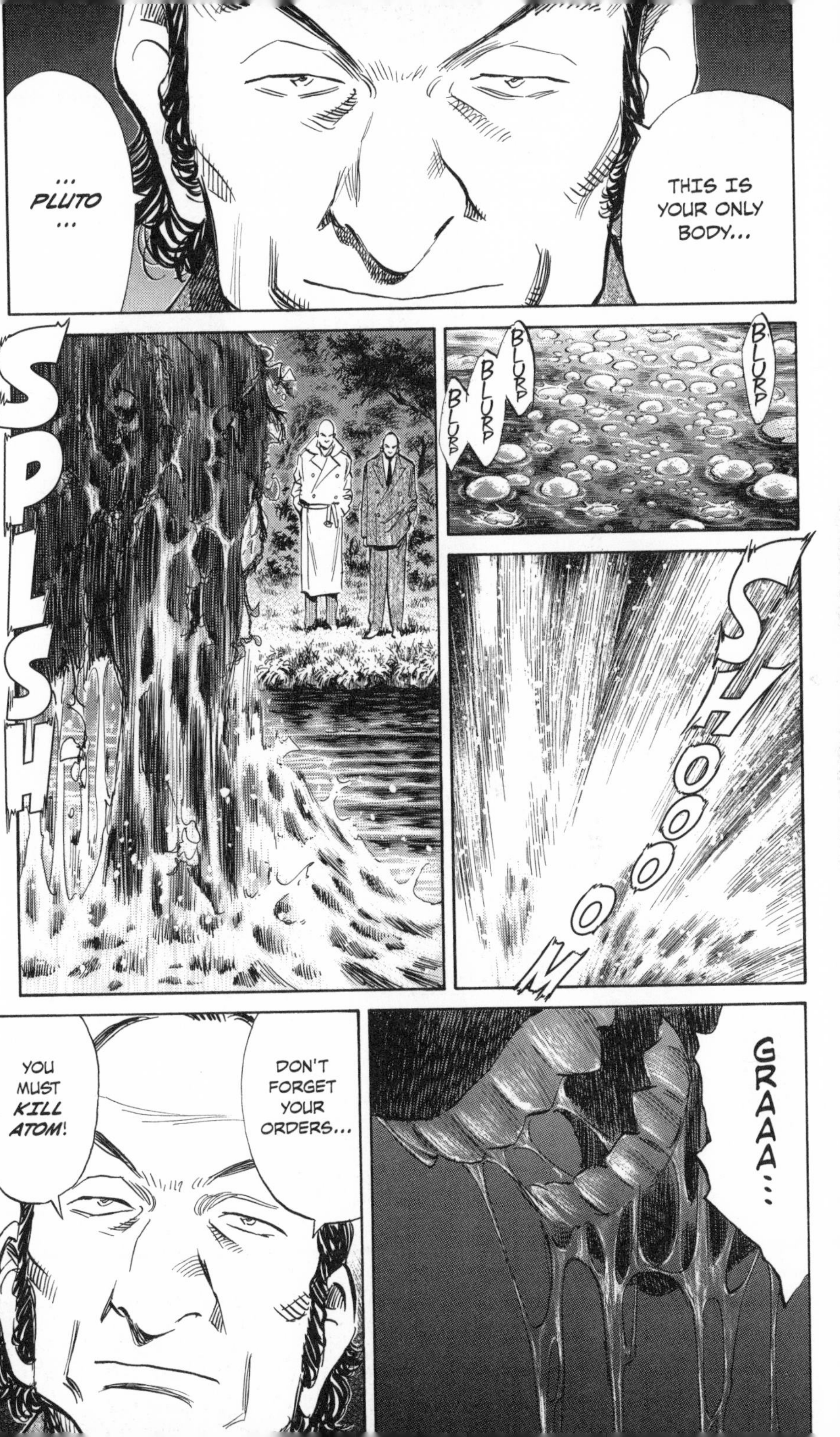
THIS IS YOUR ONLY BODY...
...PLUTO...
BLURP
BLURP
BLURP
BLURP
SHOOOOOM
SPLSH
GRAAA...
DON'T FORGET YOUR ORDERS...
YOU MUST KILL ATOM!

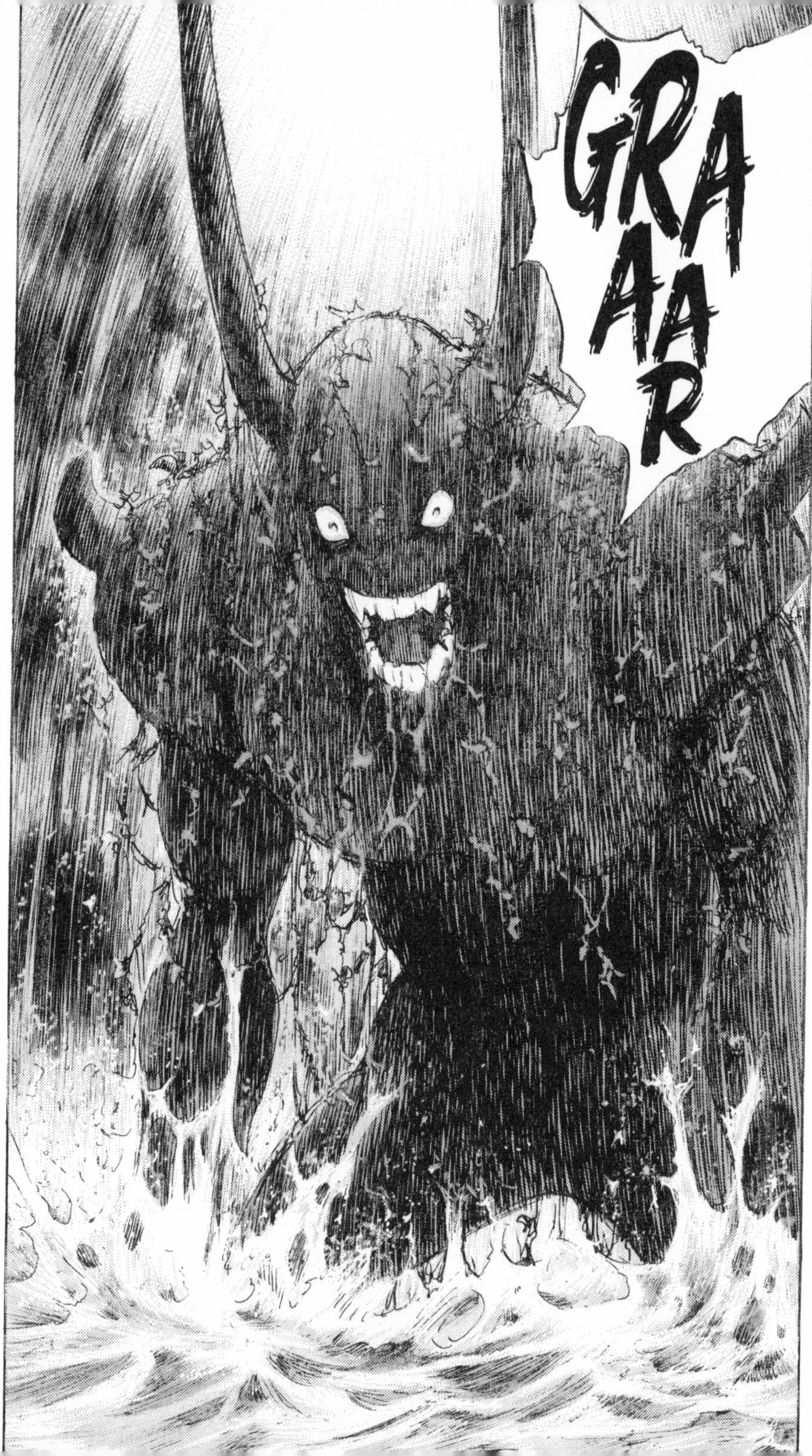
GRAAAR

The late Osamu Tezuka, a manga artist for whom I have the utmost respect, created the series *Astro Boy*. This timeless classic has been read by countless numbers of fans from when it was first created in the fifties to now. As a child, "The Greatest Robot on Earth" story arc from *Astro Boy* was the first manga I ever read that really moved me and inspired me to become a manga artist. With *Pluto* I've attempted to infuse that story with a fresh new spirit. I hope you enjoy it.

NAOKI URASAWA

Manga wouldn't exist without Osamu Tezuka. He is the Leonardo da Vinci, the Goethe, the Dostoevsky of the manga world. Naoki Urasawa and I have always felt that his achievements and work must not be allowed to fade away. Tezuka wrote that Atom, the main character of his most representative work *Astro Boy*, was born in 2003. This was the same year that we re-made "The Greatest Robot on Earth" story arc from the *Astro Boy* series. Who was Osamu Tezuka and what was his message? For those of you readers who are interested in *Pluto*, I highly recommend you read it alongside Tezuka's original work.

TAKASHI NAGASAKI

POSTSCRIPT
WHY IS PLUTO INTERESTING?
Fusanosuke Natsume, Manga Columnist

NOV 2 2 2010

Naoki Urasawa is great! Enough said...

But seriously, this is supposed to be a commentary on the incomparable *Pluto*, so even if I wanted to, there's no way I could just leave it at that.

So why is *Pluto* so interesting? Sure, thrilling events unfold, and we're drawn into the story by the author's superb skill and direction, but if that's all there is to it, we really wouldn't need any commentary. The real questions are "Why Urasawa?" and "Why *Pluto*?"

I'm sure those who have read the first volume of *Pluto* will recall that Atom, the hero of Osamu Tezuka's story, doesn't make an appearance until the very end of that volume. In fact, the plot seems to revolve around the everyday life of a robot policeman named Gesicht who looks like a plain, middle-aged man. Readers find themselves pulled along, wondering what sort of story this will become, with Atom only making his appearance at the very last moment. And even then, we are surprised to find that Atom looks just like a normal little boy.

The series moves on to the next volume, and readers start to wonder, "Wow, is this Urasawa's version of Atom? What kind of powers will he have? What kind of role will he play?" And again, Atom's sister Uran appears at the last minute at the end of volume two. One could simply be impressed with the novel manner in which Urasawa introduces these famous characters, but there is actually much more going on here. Urasawa cleverly sets up the reader to be his accomplice.

As originally conceived, *Pluto* was supposed to be a remake of the 1964 *Astro Boy* story arc "The Greatest Robot on Earth" as interpreted by Naoki Urasawa. At the time, Urasawa was already famous for *Monster* and *20th Century Boys*. Word of the project generated the predictable expectations and anticipation that any homage to Tezuka's classic manga would. Urasawa's goal was not only to draw in readers who were unfamiliar with Tezuka but to wow old Tezuka fans and real manga aficionados. That's why there are provocative references to characters from Tezuka works other than *Astro Boy* and hints of other episodes. But at the same time, the story adheres to Urasawa's distinct worldview and perspective on human nature.

I am amazed by Urasawa's use of characters and episodes that are so very Tezuka-like but that are at the same time infused with his own distinctive sensibility. These characters include Superintendent Tawashi (known as Detective Tawashi in Tezuka's original) and Inspector Nakamura (Detective Nakamura in the original story, who was later promoted). Homage sequences include the patrol car designed to look like a dog; the scene where Uran has an encounter with wild animals (this refers to the Red Cat episode, although Uran didn't originally play a role in it); or the one about the obsolete robot maid (probably referencing the "Future" volume of Tezuka's *Phoenix*). I'm sure, however, that there are many readers who are completely unaware of these references, who simply enjoy the story on its own level.

In other words, readers of different ages with different levels of manga literacy can all enjoy reading *Pluto*. Urasawa has created a multi-layered cocktail—with one layer a high level collage of homage to Tezuka, and another that is comprised of Urasawa's own themes, for example the idea that human-style emotions and personalities may be determined by external forces.

Another interesting factor about *Pluto* is Urasawa's artwork and direction. Until he entered university, his drawing style showed the influence of Shinji Nagashima or Tezuka's works from the seventies. Urasawa's drawing exercises from his school days are amazingly similar to what Tezuka was doing in the seventies in terms of drawing style, direction